THE GREAT
NEW ORLEANS
KIDNAPPING CASE

" The polite, but consequential negro policeman."

Black policeman. From Edward King, *The Great South: A Record of Journeys in Louisiana, Texas, The Indian Territory, Missouri, Arkansas, Mississippi, Alabama, Georgia, Florida, South Carolina, North Carolina, Kentucky, Tennessee, Virginia, West Virginia, and Maryland* (Hartford, CT: American Publishing Company, 1875), pg. 57.

THE GREAT NEW ORLEANS KIDNAPPING CASE

Race, Law, and Justice in the Reconstruction Era

Michael A. Ross

OXFORD
UNIVERSITY PRESS

OXFORD

UNIVERSITY PRESS

Oxford University Press is a department of the
University of Oxford. It furthers the University's objective
of excellence in research, scholarship, and education
by publishing worldwide.

Oxford   New York

Auckland   Cape Town   Dar es Salaam   Hong Kong   Karachi
Kuala Lumpur   Madrid   Melbourne   Mexico City   Nairobi
New Delhi   Shanghai   Taipei   Toronto

With offices in

Argentina   Austria   Brazil   Chile   Czech Republic   France   Greece
Guatemala   Hungary   Italy   Japan   Poland   Portugal   Singapore
South Korea   Switzerland   Thailand   Turkey   Ukraine   Vietnam

Oxford is a registered trade mark of Oxford University Press
in the UK and certain other countries.

Published in the United States of America by
Oxford University Press
198 Madison Avenue, New York, NY 10016

Library of Congress Cataloging-in-Publication Data
Ross, Michael A. (Michael Anthony)
The great New Orleans kidnapping case : race, law, and justice
in the reconstruction era / Michael A. Ross.
      pages   cm
Includes bibliographical references and index.
ISBN 978-0-19-977880-5 (alk. paper)
1. Kidnapping—Louisiana—New Orleans—Case studies.
2. Trials (Kidnapping)—Louisiana—New Orleans.
3. New Orleans (La.)—Race relations.
4. New Orleans (La.)—History—19th century.   I. Title.
      HV6602.N49R67   2014
   364.15'4092—dc23   2014004846

1 3 5 7 9 8 6 4 2

Printed in the United States of America
on acid-free paper

For Ashley

CONTENTS

—❀—

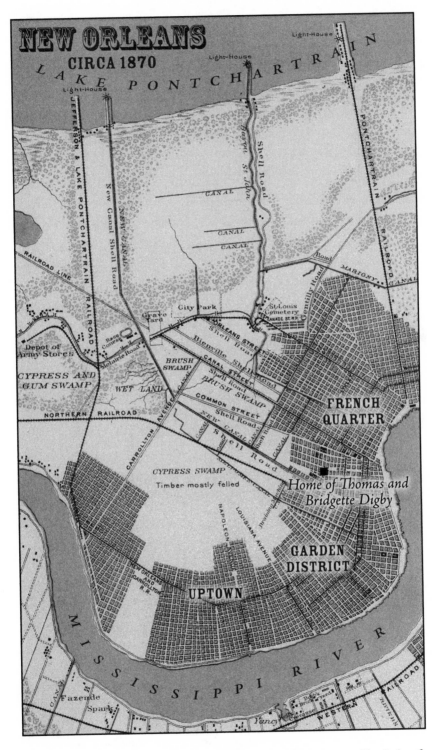

New Orleans circa 1870. Adapted from *Approaches to New Orleans*, Prepared by Order of Maj. Gen. N.B. Banks, February 14, 1863.

THE GREAT
NEW ORLEANS
KIDNAPPING CASE

INTRODUCTION

Mention courtroom dramas that took place in the past in the American South and certain images come to mind. A courthouse with Greek revival columns and domed clock sits in the middle of a town square, a statue of a Confederate soldier standing guard. Inside, the courtroom is hot. The spectators, segregated by race, sit in crowded rows, cooling themselves with hand fans. An all-white jury of men dressed in khakis and sweat-spotted white shirts watch the proceedings from the jury box or the courtroom's front rows, while the white sheriff and his deputies pass jokes amongst themselves. Seated at the defendant's table is a man accused of committing a terrible crime against someone of the opposite race. If he is white, he is in a suit and looks unperturbed, confident he will be acquitted by a jury of his peers. If he is black, he is in farmers' bib overalls, staring downward glumly, equally certain of a grim result. Recreated in innumerable plays, movies, and books, it is a scene that occurred all too often in real courtrooms in Decatur, Jackson, Sumner, Meridian, and the rest of the Jim Crow South. Those stock characters, along with the appalling photographs of lynchings and vigilante acts, symbolize for many racial injustice in the South before the Civil Rights Movement.[1]

The most famous of these trials, real and fictional, took place in the twentieth century. Harper Lee's *To Kill a Mockingbird* was set in Depression-era Alabama.

The real-life trials of the Scottsboro Boys and the murderers of Emmett Till and Medgar Evers occurred in the 1930s, 1950s, and 1960s. Yet the outcome of each seems so intertwined with the past that they can serve as allegories for the injustice African Americans had suffered in the South since the days of slavery and the Civil War. The tragic fates of Tom Robinson and Haywood Patterson, and the shameful exonerations of J. W. Milam and Byron de la Beckwith, stand in for more than a century of lesser-known verdicts poisoned by prejudice. Even though the past is complicated by instances in which African Americans, including slaves, received justice from white judges and juries, the conventional accounts retain their illustrative power. Because the law and legal procedures favored whites, justice for blacks was the exception, not the rule.[2]

The subject of this book, the Great New Orleans Kidnapping Case of 1870, shares some similarities with the Southern courtroom dramas that are etched in the American memory. Five years after the Civil War, the state of Louisiana charged two black women with kidnapping Mollie Digby, the young daughter of an Irish immigrant family in New Orleans. The white-controlled press used Mollie's disappearance to create a moral panic, claiming she had been kidnapped for use as a Voodoo sacrifice. Because all black people were now free, newspaper editors warned readers to expect ever more horrific crimes committed by black individuals unless the perpetrators were found and incarcerated. When prosecutors eventually charged two women of color with the crime, many white Louisianans assumed they were guilty well before their trial began. White editors labeled the defendants "the child stealers" and, even in high summer, standing-room-only crowds flocked to a sweltering New Orleans courtroom to witness the proceedings.[3]

But there end the parallels between the Great New Orleans Kidnapping Case and the kangaroo-court trials of the Jim Crow era. Had the Digby case occurred in the early twentieth-century South, the result would have been foreordained. Black defendants charged with committing sensational crimes against whites had little hope for acquittal. Yet in 1870 in New Orleans no one could be sure of the outcome of the trial of "the child stealers." The evidence against the defendants was mixed. Some facts suggested guilt, others innocence. But because 1870 was the height of Radical Reconstruction in Louisiana, the state government that prosecuted the defendants was not dominated by white supremacists bent on keeping African Americans in line. The governor was a young, idealistic Union army veteran. Blacks and whites served together in the Louisiana legislature, on the New Orleans police force, and on juries. Louisiana's new constitution guaranteed black citizens due process of law, as well as equal access to restaurants, theaters, and public accommodations.[4]

Complicating matters further was the fact that the accused in the Digby case were Afro-Creoles, members of the prosperous mixed-race class that had flourished in New Orleans under Spanish, French, and even American rule. Many Afro-Creoles—a group that included doctors, lawyers, newspaper editors, poets, cotton factors, and merchants—were then serving in the Reconstruction government. They were part of a New Orleans culture that accepted and sometimes embraced relationships between wealthy, white, Francophone men and "mulatto" or mixed-race women. Although the Anglo-Americans who arrived in the city after the United States purchased Louisiana in 1803 found racial "amalgamation" appalling, they were unable to completely eradicate the ties between white and black Creoles.[5]

Reconstruction placed new pressures on the city's Creole community. After Appomattox, ex-Confederates, fleeing war-ravaged areas of the South, migrated to New Orleans, bringing with them their more rigid racial mores. At the same time, thousands of former slaves, exercising their newfound freedom, moved to the city as well. Racist whites warned their French-speaking white neighbors to abandon their old behaviors, to distance themselves from their mixed-race friends and relatives, to side with the forces of total white supremacy, or risk living in an "Africanized" society. Their vitriol increased when African Americans, backed by Northern bayonets, gained the right to vote, hold office, and serve on juries. The opponents of Reconstruction demanded racial solidarity. For the "white man's government" to be restored, the city's "old ways" had to disappear. Everyone of African ancestry—even the wealthiest, lightest-skinned Afro-Creoles with family ties to elite whites—had to be consigned to a subordinate class. Because the defendants in the Great New Orleans Kidnapping Case were Afro-Creoles accused of a crime against a white person, the tension between New Orleans's racial history and the goals of reactionary white supremacists surfaced repeatedly in the newspaper coverage and trial testimony. It almost certainly shaped the jury's deliberations. But unlike the trials of the Jim Crow era, the outcome, thanks both to the city's history and the changes wrought by Reconstruction, was in doubt even as the jury's foreman stood in a jammed courtroom to announce the verdict.[6]

The Great New Orleans Kidnapping Case is a work of micro-history. It follows poet William Blake's injunction to "see a world in a grain of sand." It mines a single historical moment for insights into both the history of New Orleans and the Reconstruction era. Focusing in detail on a once famous but now largely forgotten episode—the 1870 kidnapping of Mollie Digby and the investigation and trial that followed—it does more than recreate an intriguing whodunit and courtroom drama. It uses a close, ground-level view of the Digby case to illuminate Reconstruction's larger possibilities and limits. It finds embedded in the story of a sensational trial moments of contingency that help explain both how Reconstruction might have succeeded and why it failed.[7]

Ever since Reconstruction ended in 1877, many have questioned whether the North's effort to bring a new social, economic, and political order to the old Confederacy had any real chance for success. Some say the Radical Republicans' attempt to revolutionize the South was a fool's errand, that by giving black men the right to vote and by integrating state governments they pushed too far, too fast, and thereby spurred the violence and racial animosity that followed. Others believe Reconstruction was one of those rare moments in American history when real change in race relations was possible. All agree that New Orleans was important to the story. If the Republicans were ever going to build a biracial society in the South, their best shot was in the Crescent City. New Orleans's population included thousands of moderate white businessmen who had opposed secession and rebellion until shots were fired and who might once again be convinced to put economic progress ahead of racial animosity. It also included the Afro-Creoles—a class of educated, cosmopolitan mixed-race men and women that could provide the politicians and public officials to impress moderate whites that biracial government could work. Recognizing this threat, white supremacist Democrats in New Orleans aggressively obstructed Republican rule in the courts and the streets. The Great New Orleans Kidnapping

Case quickly became intertwined with these momentous events as both Republicans and white reactionaries tried to exploit the event for their own purposes. It became a story filled with small moments that had larger implications and one that turned an unlikely group of previously little-known individuals—a working-class Irish family who lived in the "back of town," a cigar maker turned detective, and two beautiful, stylish, and publicity-shy defendants—into significant actors in the unfolding drama of Reconstruction.[8]

Chapter One

A KIDNAPPING IN THE BACK
OF TOWN

Until their daughter was kidnapped, little distinguished Thomas and Bridgette Digby from other Irish immigrants living in New Orleans. They were just two of the thousands of "famine Irish" who arrived in the city in the 1840s and 1850s to escape the desperate circumstances in their native country. They lived in a flood-prone corner of New Orleans known as the "back of town," a working-class neighborhood near the cypress swamps where housing was cheap. Thomas drove a hackney cab, and Bridgette took in laundry and sewing while caring for their three children. They worked long days, aspired to something more for their family, knelt in the pews of St. Joseph's Church, and lived largely anonymous lives. In June 1870, however, the Digbys became victims of a terrible crime that would make their names known to newspaper readers as far away as Philadelphia and New York.[1]

The Digbys' ordeal began late in the afternoon of Thursday, June 9, a day when the close heat of the subtropical New Orleans summer had already arrived. While Bridgette finished her household chores, prepared dinner, and waited for Thomas to return to their home on Howard Street, their two children played outside under the supervision of Rosa Gorman, a seventeen-year-old next-door neighbor whom Bridgette sometimes paid to babysit. At the end of each workday, quiet Howard Street turned into a bustling block, as the Digbys' neighbors walked home from their jobs as laborers, stevedores, wheelwrights, draymen, and clerks. Holding the Digbys' baby daughter, Mollie, in her arms, Rosa Gorman greeted passersby while she kept an eye on ten-year-old Georgie Digby, who was playing with his friends on the wooden sidewalk.

Soon two African-American women with whom Rosa had chatted several times before stopped to coo at seventeen-month-old Mollie. No one found this unusual, despite the racial tension that plagued the city after the Civil War. In the back of town, Irish and German immigrants lived side by side with both former slaves and people of African descent who had been free before the war. Women and men, black and white, often paused to lavish attention on Mollie because of her blue eyes and bright blond hair. One of the two women who did so that after-noon, Rosa later told police, was of mixed race, quite attractive, and wore a stylish white dress with spots and a white seaside hat trimmed with blue ribbon. She was, Rosa said, "about twenty-five years of age, very tall and thin, with a pretty face and straight features almost like a white woman's." Her name, Rosa thought, might have been Martha Gaines. The woman's friend, Rosa reported, was "a low, heavy set negress," dressed plainly in calico and a reddish bonnet, who did not talk much.[2]

Rosa and the women spoke amiably until Rosa noticed flames and smoke billowing from a storefront two blocks away. Seligman's Photographic Studio was on fire. Soon a fire engine, its bell clanging and horses at full gallop, raced past, followed by a crowd running toward the conflagration. Caught up in the excitement, Rosa announced that she too wanted to watch the fire company battle the blaze. "Hold Molly," Rosa said to Georgie Digby, "while I see where the fire is." Before she could hand Mollie to her brother, however, the mu-latto woman interjected, "No bubby, I will take the baby," extending her arms. Accepting what she thought was a kind offer, Rosa passed Mollie to the woman. Leaving Georgie in her care as well, Rosa joined the throng headed down the block toward the burning studio.[3]

After Rosa left, the shorter woman asked Georgie if he knew where Miss Mary Cooks, a neighborhood seamstress, lived and, if so, to lead them there. When Georgie said he did, the woman took him by the hand as her companion cradled Mollie in her arms, and together they walked a block and a half to the house where Georgie thought Miss Cooks lived. But once there, the short woman shook her head and said, "Oh no bubby, this is not the place," and they led Georgie farther away from home. When they reached the public market on the corner of Dryades and Lafayette streets, the woman in the seaside hat handed a "two-bit bill" to Georgie and sent him to a fruit stand to "get some bananas for his sister." Georgie did as he was told, but when he returned with the fruit both his sister and the women were gone. Georgie ran up and down the block searching for them, but they had vanished. He then hurried home to tell his mother what had happened. Bridgette was in the kitchen when her son brought the news that his sister was missing. She immediately rushed out to the sidewalk, looked up and down the block, and shouted her daughter's name. She called to a neighbor to find her husband and alert the police. She then turned, looked down at her terrified son, ripped the bananas he was still clutching out of his hands, and threw them into the street.[4]

Although Mollie's disappearance created a stir in the Digbys' neighborhood, it did not immediately warrant unusual notice in New Orleans as a whole. Hundreds of children went missing in the city every year. Most were later found and returned to their parents. In a metropolis plagued by crime and violence, moreover, Mollie's disappearance was just one of many unsavory events that day. On that same Thursday, a boy stabbed his friend in the head in a dispute over a ball game. A jewel thief robbed a posh Garden District home. Two toughs fought a gory knife battle on St. Claude Avenue. A drowned child was found floating in the Mississippi River. A prostitute in the Tremé neighborhood stole $30 from a customer. Someone poisoned two family dogs. And two women in a saloon bloodied one another with broken ale bottles as they fought over a lover. Because crime was so common, most incidents received little attention. If a crime occurred in a poor district, on the docks, or in one of the infamous concert saloons, or if its victim was an immigrant or black person, it seldom warranted more than a sentence or two in the "City Intelligence" columns of the dailies.[5]

The kidnapping of Mollie Digby would be different. Editors soon recognized sensational potential in the story. Although, as one noted, "it was several days before the public made up its mind that the child was really stolen," interest in the case grew as readers learned that Mollie was abducted by a "fashionable, tall, mulatto woman, probably for the purpose of receiving a ransom."[6] Here was a storyline to strike fear into parents throughout the city. For elite white families in Garden District mansions and French Quarter townhouses who relied on African American nannies to care for their children, the idea of a seemingly respectable light-skinned woman abducting a white baby for ransom was terrifying. "Every mother who has a bright eyed, sunny haired child," the *New Orleans Times* observed, "feels a terrible anxiety in this mystery." The story gained additional traction when Mollie's father, a hackney driver, cobbled together a $500 reward for the return of his child. No questions would be asked, he claimed. "Fathers! Mothers! Friends! Every human being with a heart in his bosom," the reward notice read, "help us find our darling child—our only little daughter."[7]

The tense racial and political atmosphere in New Orleans also increased interest in the crime. The passions caused by the Civil War had not cooled as summer arrived in 1870. It was the height of Radical Reconstruction, when the Republican-controlled national government attempted to bring a new social, economic, and political order to the defeated South. From Virginia to Texas, officials backed by federal troops registered black men to vote, and Congress required states to draft new constitutions that protected the civil rights of African Americans. In New Orleans, many whites seethed as the new order emerged. Although the city still had a white majority, tens of thousands of former slaves—freed by the Thirteenth Amendment—had poured from plantations into its working-class neighborhoods. After the passage of the Fourteenth and Fifteenth Amendments, black residents voted, served on juries, held government jobs, and ran for office. Louisiana's new state constitution mandated that licensed businesses must welcome the "patronage of all persons without distinction or discrimination on account of race or color." All over town black men and women tested the boundaries of their new civil rights by demanding service in bars, restaurants, coffeehouses, and other public places that had previously welcomed whites only. The state legislature, which included black elected officials, announced plans to integrate the city's schools.[8]

For many whites, particularly those who had supported the Confederacy, it was all too much to bear. Because New Orleans had been spared the destruction suffered by other Southern locales during the war, many former Confederate leaders settled in the Crescent City after Appomattox. Confederate generals John Bell Hood, Jubal Early, Simon Bolivar Buckner, and Joe Wheeler became prominent citizens and actively kept the spirit of the "Lost Cause" alive.[9] Embittered ex-Confederates joined secret paramilitary organizations devoted to overthrowing the Republican regime, such as the Knights of the White Camellia and, later, the Crescent City White League. The Louisiana Legion, a menacing white militia pledged to "keeping the negroe straight," drilled in the city's streets. John Campbell, a former United States Supreme Court justice who resigned to join the Confederacy, spoke for many of his fellow white New Orleanians when he wrote, "We have Africans in place all about us, they are jurors, post office clerks, custom house officers & day by day they barter away their obligations and duties. The Southern communities will be a desolation until there is a thorough change of affairs in all the departments of government....Discontent, dissatisfaction, murmurings, complaints, even insurrection, would be better than the insensibility that seems to prevail."[10]

Black residents of New Orleans were as determined to exercise and protect their new rights as ex-Confederates were to deny them. They knew that the federal troops, stationed downriver from the city at Jackson Barracks, would not be around forever. Soon they might have to protect themselves. Some formed their own self-defense associations. Many others enlisted in the newly organized biracial state militia.[11] In a city where everyone, black and white, lived on a crowded sliver of high ground along the river, incidents of daily city life took on new significance. Riding the streetcars, shopping for groceries, even walking on sidewalks could be fraught with racial friction. In this hothouse atmosphere, the Digby case struck a nerve and came to symbolize whites' racial fears. A brazen kidnapping of a white baby by a woman of color was another disturbing sign that the antebellum social order had been overturned. "No popular event or public calamity," the *Picayune* later claimed, "ever engaged more fully the feelings and sympathies of the masses."[12]

New Orleans newspaper editors used the Digby kidnapping and other crimes allegedly committed by black residents to foment a moral panic among the city's white inhabitants. Although the elite whites who had once run

Louisiana's government had been driven from the state legislature, they still controlled most of the state's newspapers and used their editorial columns to incite fear and discontent. They exaggerated charges of Republican corruption, maligned any act by the biracial legislature no matter how beneficial, and seized on sensationalized crimes and incidents that had racial dimensions.[13]

Because Louisiana's Reconstruction governor, Henry Clay Warmoth, had integrated the New Orleans police, many whites predicted that black police-men would wink at fellow African Americans who committed crimes against white people. Opponents of Reconstruction saw their worst fears confirmed by the Digby case. One angry editorial after another argued that the kidnap-ping proved that a force made up of "all shades of race and color" was incapable of solving heinous crimes. "Can it be possible that with our immense police force nothing can be done in this matter?" a typical editorial asked. "Must we make the humiliating confession to the world that our children may be snatched from our very thresholds in the bright light of day, and we be left hopeless of recovering them?" In any other city, the *Picayune* claimed, "detectives would long since have found the child or discovered what became of her." Editors called the investigation "the sorriest spectacle of incompetency ever witnessed." It proved that the city's police were "either incompetent, corrupt, depraved—or worse."[14]

As days and weeks went by without good news, the press circulated a rumor from the Digbys' neighborhood that Mollie had been abducted for use as a human sacrifice in a Voodoo ritual. Since colonial times, Voodoo practitioners in New Orleans had celebrated the feast day of John the Baptist each June 23 with ceremonies near Lake Pontchartrain on a night known as St. John's Eve. Even though large crowds of curious white onlookers often turned out to watch these observances, many whites now feared a sinister connection between the Digby abduction and the St. John's Eve rituals. "The impenetrable secrecy in which this cruel deed is involved," an editor noted, "has excited a general sus-picion that the child was stolen for sacrifice on St. John's Eve." Another paper exclaimed, "the rumor that Molly Digby has been sacrificed at a voudou orgy is so horrible that it must be either confirmed or dispelled."[15]

The rumor tapped into white New Orleanians' longstanding fear of Voodoo priests and priestesses. Before the Civil War, government officials worried that

Voodoo leaders such as Marie Laveau and her daughter, Marie the Second, could incite slave revolts. Their presence destabilized the racial status quo that had bolstered slave society. The fact that some white people also believed that the Laveau women possessed magical powers had made them even more of a threat. New Orleanians of both races bore witness to the Laveaus' ability to use charms and incantations to curse cruel slaveholders, freeze policemen in their tracks, and fix the outcomes of court proceedings. Convinced of the women's omnipotent powers, some whites secretly called Marie the First to their bedsides during yellow fever outbreaks or visited the Laveaus' house on St. Ann Street seeking homeopathic remedies. Such widespread confidence in the Laveaus' abilities fed the fears of police, politicians, and editors who accused Voodoo practitioners of cannibalism, devil worship, and other figments of fevered white imaginations.[16]

During Reconstruction, Voodoo men and women in New Orleans took advantage of the freedom to practice their religion openly. Although Voodoo practitioners considered themselves to be Catholics, many frightened white residents saw the postwar Voodoo renaissance as yet another example of impending social chaos. White reactionaries, vowing to fight the "Africanization" of the city, used sensationalized accounts of Voodoo ceremonies to malign black culture and to portray black people as unfit to vote or govern. White editors demanded that Voodoo priests and priestesses "be closely observed by the police to prevent the intolerable excesses to which their ignorance and fanaticism lead." For many of the city's white residents, the Digby rumors confirmed those fears. During Reconstruction, one commentator warned, black people had "passed so much out of, and beyond the influence of white civilization" that "Voudouism" was flourishing. "It is horrible to think," he added, "that the little child of Mr. Digby has been sacrificed to this savage superstition."[17]

To many white readers, allegations that Mollie Digby had been sacrificed in a Voodoo ritual did not seem farfetched. Few whites understood Voodoo, and newspapers regularly highlighted those practices most jarring to white sensibilities. When police officers and passersby stumbled upon Voodoo "altars" on doorsteps, street corners, or medians, reporters described the altars' contents with macabre fascination. "Officer E. Planchard reports having found on the neutral ground on St. Bernard Street, near Clairborne, a calf's head swimming in a bowl of whiskey, illuminated with candles, the eyes of the head were studded with tacks," a typical newspaper account read. "Next to the bowl were some napkins and a pitcher with a red candle in it, one silver dollar, three silver picayunes and three nickels. There was also a black chicken, legs broken, laying alive on the napkins, and the whole outlay surrounded with black and white crape." Whites charged that Voodoo priests and priestesses used these displays and other sinister icons and *gris-gris* to pervert democracy by intimidating credulous black citizens on Election Day.[18]

After the Digby kidnapping, the press published lurid and allegedly factual accounts of Voodoo women sacrificing white children like Mollie. One reporter, claiming to have interviewed "a professed Voudou priestess," said that white children "of such an age as to imply innocent blood" were offered as "a horrible allusion to the crucifixion of the Savior." Such ceremonies, he continued, included an intricate ritual in which a naked priestess circled "a large iron cauldron containing a snake" while performing "a wild and fiendish dance." The priestess then pulled the snake from the cauldron and draped it around the shoulders of her followers. After each celebrant had "submitted to this loathsome touch," the human sacrifice followed, "the innocent blood of the child being sprinkled upon the cauldron, upon the snake, and upon all the worshippers."[19]

As editors pushed readers from concern to hysteria, many New Orleanians became certain that Mollie had indeed been sacrificed by religious fiends. "The singular and mysterious disappearance of very young children every few years," a newspaper in neighboring Mobile reported, "has led to a firm conviction in the minds of many that they were sacrificed on Voudou altars." The abduction of the Digby baby so close to St. John's Eve fit the pattern. In New Orleans, the editor concluded, "thousands believe such was the purpose of its abduction, since neither Mr. Digby nor his friends have any knowledge of any specific reason why his child was taken."[20]

As coverage of the Digby abduction became more sensational, prominent white women from the most famous New Orleans families adopted the Digby case as their own. In late June and early July wealthy women of New Orleans would usually be preparing to leave town for cooler climes. Just as many theaters and restaurants closed for the season each summer, elite families put linen covers on furniture, packed white dresses, suits, and Panama hats into trunks, and set off by rail and steamboat for the coast, the North, or Europe. But in 1870, Matilde Ogden, Armantine Allain, Louisa Huger, and wives of dozens of the city's other richest financiers, merchants, and cotton factors took time to march to police headquarters to demand resolution of the Digby case. They also went *en masse* into the back of town—a neighborhood they ordinarily avoided—bringing food and other gifts to the Digbys' modest house. Surprised and touched by their concern, Thomas Digby issued a statement in the newspapers thanking "the ladies of New Orleans for the unexpected kindness and sympathy they...extended to his wife and himself."[21]

By intertwining themes of motherhood, crime, and race, the Digby case provided an opportunity for the city's elite women to enter the public debate over Reconstruction and to express publicly their anger at Governor Warmoth, his biracial police force, and the emerging racial order in Louisiana. Raised in a culture that required them to behave as traditional ladies, most elite women left public commentary on politics, business, and civic affairs to men. But in early July, sixty-one prominent women presented a petition to Warmoth urging him to do something so "that the painful feeling of the community in regard to this lawless outrage may be allayed by the early restoration of the child to those who love it."[22] The press applauded the "petition...made to the Governor by our ladies" and demanded that Warmoth offer a state reward for Mollie's return.[23]

Warmoth, wanting desperately to prove the competence of his government to the city's elite, responded by becoming personally involved in the Digby investigation. Shortly after receiving the women's petition, he offered a state reward of $1,000 in the Digby case—$500 for recovery of the child and $500 for the arrest and conviction of the abductors. He also ordered New Orleans's chief of police to put the city's entire police force "on watch" for the baby and kidnappers, and to send handbills describing the crime, the perpetrators, and the reward to postmasters and police authorities in Mississippi, Alabama, Tennessee, and the rest of Louisiana.[24]

Warmoth knew that many white Louisianans questioned his qualifications and abilities. He had just turned twenty-eight years old that May and was one of the youngest governors in United States history. A Union army veteran from

Illinois, Warmoth compensated for his inexperience (his critics dubbed him "the boy governor") with a combination of idealism, cunning, and exuberance. Although most of the state's white population opposed him as a Republican "carpetbagger" elected with black votes, Warmoth believed that he could win over many former Confederates by offering a bold plan for reconstructing New Orleans and Louisiana that would have made the prominent Kentucky Whig Henry Clay, for whom he was named, proud. Like other centrists in his party, Warmoth hoped that with Republican guidance, the South could be rebuilt in the North's economic image and might soon be crisscrossed with railroads and filled with mills, factories, and prosperous free laborers. His ambitious agenda included building public schools, roads, and canals. He wanted to dredge the river, repair the levees, and enhance water quality and sanitation. By so doing, he thought he could win the political affections of the state's white businessmen and overcome their objections to biracial rule.[25]

As part of his plan to improve the state, Warmoth modernized and professionalized the New Orleans police force, which had been poorly paid, notoriously corrupt, and often staffed by illiterate thugs as violent as the criminals they pursued. Warmoth put the city's police under state rather than local control, renamed the force the Metropolitan Police, and required police recruits to pass literacy tests and background checks. Before they hit the streets, recruits also underwent medical screenings to ensure they could handle the rigors of the job. Instructors from New York and Boston trained new officers in the latest policing techniques. Members of the force received new uniforms, badges, waterproof capes, and Winchester repeating rifles. A special police board punished or fired officers spotted loafing on the job or those who failed to make arrests. To attract career professionals, policemen were offered pensions, and the families of officers killed or injured on the job received annuities.[26]

The Metropolitan Police added other innovations as well. Some police units patrolled the city on horseback, those on foot worked in pairs rather than alone, and police boats plied the Mississippi River along the wharves. Police engineers expanded the network of telegraph call boxes that linked neighborhoods to precinct houses. Each beat cop now carried a key to these cast-iron boxes, which contained cranks that could be turned to alert the precinct to send an emergency patrol wagon. To integrate them into the larger community, the Metropolitans also took on social service roles—transporting accident victims to hospitals, finding lost children (in 1870 they returned more than 150 children to their families), and housing the homeless at night. Warmoth also expanded the ranks to almost seven hundred men, a force size that would not be surpassed until the twentieth century.[27]

Despite these improvements, Warmoth's police faced daunting challenges in a city where crime and violence were endemic. Although the graceful townhouses of French-speaking Creoles and the impressive government buildings built by the Spanish gave it an air of sophistication and stability, New Orleans was from its inception a rough port on the edge of swamps and wilderness. The Mississippi River, the city's lifeblood, brought barges and flatboats filled with cotton, flour, cereals, and cured meats, but it also brought countless vagabonds, thieves, con men, pimps, prostitutes, high-stakes gamblers, filibusters plotting foreign adventures, drunkards, and rough frontiersmen. Fracases erupted regularly in the brothels, saloons, dance halls, and gambling pits where men watched dogs, roosters, and rats fight to the death. Tens of thousands of hard-drinking Irish and German immigrants also crowded into the city's barrooms. Over half of the city's population was foreign born. As the newcomers fought for jobs, housing, and power, the city's political contests became brawling and bloody affairs.[28]

Even the wealthy were prone to violence. French-speaking planters, armed with revolvers and sword canes, clashed with parvenus from Tennessee and South Carolina. Their hair-trigger sensitivity to perceived slights rendered New Orleans the "dueling capital of the South." Accounts of duels on the levee, in the parks, and under the fabled "Dueling Oaks" regularly appeared in the city's papers. Travelers to New Orleans noted that even refined gentlemen carried revolvers, multiple-barrel "duckfoot" and "pepperbox" pistols, "slungshots," and bowie knives. To observers it seemed as though everyone was armed. For decades New Orleans was one of the most dangerous places in America.[29] Little changed after the Civil War as criminals flocked to the city from war-ravaged regions of the South. Warmoth's administration found "mountains of crime to contend with" in a city "crowded with men of the very worst character" who believed "the city's police force was so corrupt and inept that illegal deeds would go unpunished."[30] Warmoth hoped his modernized force could control the violence, change the city's image, and win over law-abiding citizens. He recognized that the Digby case provided a critical test. He knew that many white New Orleanians viewed the integrated Metropolitan Police as an occupying army, even though only 11 percent of the officers were Northern-born and only 28 percent were African Americans. White conservatives simply could not stand the thought of armed black policemen patrolling the streets with full authority to arrest whites. But if the Metropolitans could solve the Digby abduction, a high-profile, racially explosive case, their success might be an important step in building public confidence in the integrated force.[31]

The investigation would also be a chance for Warmoth's new, handpicked police chief, thirty-one-year-old Algernon Sidney Badger, to prove himself. Badger, who had been on the job for only a month, had been serving as the city's harbormaster when the previous police chief, George Cain, resigned in anger over the lack of cooperation he received from the white citizenry. Originally from Massachusetts, Badger was a tall, powerfully built Union veteran, with a bushy mustache and square jaw, famous for his courage under fire. He knew well the challenges he faced; he had seen firsthand the ferocious animosity many white Southerners held for Northerners. In April 1861, an angry, gun-wielding mob had attacked Badger's 6th Massachusetts Infantry as the men changed trains in Baltimore en route to Washington in response to President Lincoln's first call for volunteers. Four of Badger's comrades died in the melee. As a civilian in New Orleans after the war, he had witnessed ex-Confederates shooting unarmed black men and their white allies during the 1866 New Orleans Riot.[32]

Badger recognized, though, that not all white Southerners had been enthusiastic rebels. Throughout the South, tens of thousands of unionists opposed secession and resisted conscription into the Confederate army. In 1862, when his Massachusetts regiment arrived in New Orleans after the city fell into Federal hands, Badger helped recruit New Orleans unionists to enlist in the Northern ranks. In a city where many German and Irish immigrants, businessmen with Northern backgrounds, and Whiggish Southern-born whites had opposed secession, more than five thousand white men eventually joined Union regiments. During the Mobile campaign, Badger led the 1st Louisiana Cavalry

U.S.A—an outfit made up mostly of New Orleans horsemen—in several bat-tlefield cavalry charges and a daring mission behind enemy lines to bring pro-visions to a convent of nuns in Bay St. Louis. As police chief, Badger would recruit many of these same men into the Metropolitans' ranks.[33]

While serving briefly as the New Orleans harbormaster after the war, Badger had demonstrated an ability to win over some ex-Confederates with his sound judgment, decency, and fair dealing. When he married the widow of a Crescent City merchant, several prominent former secessionists attended the ceremony. At a time when the conservative press routinely charged Northern officials with corruption, no one impugned Badger's honesty. And despite the fact that he had no experience with police work, even some conservative news-papers welcomed his selection as the new police chief. "His appointment," the *Daily Picayune* noted, "is favorably commented upon, and he will enter upon the discharge of his duties with the confidence...of the people." Warmoth could hardly have made a better choice than Badger to win the grudging respect of the white citizens of New Orleans. Even the Republican Party's future in New Orleans seemed to hinge on his performance. As the party's newspaper said of Badger when he assumed the post in May 1870, "Much is expected of him, and we sincerely hope he will not disappoint his friends."[34]

Strategically, Badger assigned John Baptiste Jourdain, his most skilled Afri-can American detective, to the Digby investigation. If a black detective found the Digby baby or her abductors, it might help dispel white fears that black policemen would not solve or punish crimes committed by blacks against whites. Jourdain was literate, a moderate man who would represent the Metro-politan Police well in the field, in the press, and, if the investigation succeeded, in the courtroom.

Detective Jourdain joined regular officers in seizing mulatto women throug-hout the city who fit the description of the kidnappers and bringing them to precinct houses for questioning. They also took black women named Martha into custody whether or not they resembled the "Martha" Rosa Gorman had described. Because Mollie Digby had a bald spot caused by a boil on the back of her head, officers stopped black nursemaids who had white children in their care and checked the babies for this identifying mark. Responding to the rumors that Mollie had been captured for use as a human sacrifice, the police also arrested more than a dozen "prominent Voudous," even when it was clear they had no connection to the crime. "Their influence over the negro population is such," the New Orleans *Times* said of the Voodoo detainees, "that with proper appliances the truth may be brought out."[35]

The massive citywide search by the police failed to impress white critics of the force. "This starting out of seven or eight hundred policemen may seem an exhibition of acumen by some, but we fail to perceive it," the *Times* remarked. Was it efficient to check every white baby in the city for boils when detectives could instead be scrutinizing the Digbys' day-to-day life for clues?, some wondered. Did Thomas Digby have enemies? Had any of his acquaintances behaved unusually? Rather than investigating "every person in any way connected with the Digbys," hostile observers charged, Warmoth's detectives displayed a "woeful lack of systematic effort" and deductive acumen.[36]

Many African Americans viewed the arrest and interrogation of black women with ambivalence. On the one hand, they wanted the integrated Metropolitan Police to succeed and felt the force was being unfairly criticized by the white press. On the other hand, they thought officers were unjustly harassing black women. In late June, the John Brown Pioneer Radical Republican Club, a leading black political organization from the Digbys' Third Ward neighborhood, issued a public proclamation about the case. The club's members were staunch supporters of Radical Reconstruction who had campaigned to remove the words "white" and "colored" from the state's laws and who funded lawsuits against inns, hotels, restaurants, and other businesses that denied club members equal service. They felt torn as black policemen aggressively interrogated many of their neighbors. In their proclamation they asked whether the police had convincing evidence "that the child of Mr. and Mrs. Thomas Digby was kidnapped by a colored woman" and wondered whether the Digby case was being used "to create prejudice and distrust against the colored people as a class." At the same time, they asserted that the Metropolitans were "as efficient a police corps as can be found in any city" and were "making use of all means in human power to bring the guilty to justice." The conservative press quickly picked up on this apparent contradiction and lampooned the "Sable John Brown Club" for "its praise of the police who, it complains, have been guilty of unjustly arresting thirty colored women."[37]

White editors also continued their attacks on Warmoth's police, particularly after five weeks passed and Mollie Digby had not been found. Some even began to suggest that the citizens should organize and solve the crime themselves. "The subject has gained so much notoriety," a typical editorial suggested, "that it would not surprise us if a formation similar to a vigilance committee was created among citizens in different wards, for the determined and express purpose of doing police duty, not only to hunt the baby, but to ferret out the culprit." Vigilance committees had a long and unsavory history in the nineteenth-century United States, where such "organizations" often amounted to mobs ransacking the homes and businesses of African Americans, immigrants, or other unpopular groups. In violence-prone New Orleans, the mere mention of agitated whites forming a vigilance committee alarmed black citizens.[38]

Public anger only increased when it was learned that Bridgette Digby had become so distraught by her daughter's disappearance that her family committed her to the Louisiana Retreat, an asylum run by the Catholic Sisters of Charity for poor women suffering from monomania, melancholy, and other mental distress. "The mother has become insane," newspapers reported, "brooding over the thought that her darling babe has been immolated on the altar of Voudouism." Editors asked readers to imagine themselves in the Digbys' situation. "Let any parent bring home the case to themselves; what would be their feelings to know that their precious darling was last seen in the hands of a negro woman, supposed to belong to the infernal creed?"[39]

Other rumors began to swirl about Mollie Digby's fate. Some speculated that she had been abducted by a band of Gypsies who had recently pitched tents on Metairie Ridge on the outskirts of town where they sold "conjure charms" to former slaves and poor whites. "From time immemorial this class of wanderers has been noted for kidnapping and child stealing," the *Times* claimed. "If a colored woman committed the crime, she may have been an accomplice of theirs." The Gypsies had recently decamped and were last seen traveling toward Baton Rouge. Editors urged the police to hunt them down. Another rumor alleged that Mollie's father, Thomas, had recently brawled with a Spanish passenger in his cab, that "Martha" was the Spaniard's girlfriend, that the abduction was an act of revenge, and that the couple and the stolen child were aboard a steamer headed for Havana. Badger speculated publicly that Mollie had been abducted by a woman who hoped to extort money from an ex-lover and to "palm the child off on him as the fruit of their illicit intercourse."[40]

With each passing day, criticism of the Metropolitan Police detectives grew increasingly harsh. Newspapers charged that Warmoth's detectives strolled around "with their hands in their pockets" or pursued "ridiculous rumors, imparted by scared negroes." The officers seemed incapable of thorough detective work. The *Times* alleged that their seeming inability "to work intelligently, systemically, and practically to discover the authors of this giant crime…shows they are not possessed of sufficient intelligence to do so."[41]

As the frustration and publicity surrounding the case swelled, so did the reward money. In addition to the $1,000 offered by the governor and the $500 reward posted by Thomas Digby, two businessmen and the editor of the *Republican* newspaper offered their own rewards for the return of the child. Anyone who found Mollie Digby and her kidnappers would now receive $2,500 (about $40,000 in 2014), a considerable sum, particularly in the city's sluggish postwar economy. Although some editors feared such lavish reward offers would inspire copycat crimes, most viewed the rewards as a reflection of the community's fevered concern about the baby's fate and a lack of faith that the Metropolitan Police could solve the crime on their own.[42]

Other business leaders offered their services free of charge to the Digbys and the investigation. The Southern Express Company carried Thomas Digby's letters and papers at no cost, and the Western Union Telegraph Company "sent his dispatches on the same liberal terms." When the city marshal in Canton, Mississippi, telegraphed in mid-July that he "had arrested a woman, with a child in her possession, whose appearance corresponds with the description given in the advertisement," the Jackson Railroad Company gave Thomas free passage to Canton to see if Mollie had indeed been found. When he arrived there, however, he "was sadly disappointed," as the child was not his daughter.[43]

With a large reward waiting to be claimed, interest in the investigation spread outside the Gulf region. For weeks, newspapers from Mobile to Opelousas had been covering the case. Then in late July, the Associated Press sent out the story on the telegraph wire. On July 21, the *New York Times* reported that New Orleans was "in a state of sympathetic excitement over the loss of a child belonging to a Mr. Digby, who was spirited away by a mulatto woman." Noting the size of the reward being offered, the *Times* added that "the whole police force of the city is on watch." Soon papers in Chicago, Cincinnati, Memphis, Nashville, Richmond, and other major cities picked up the story. The abduction of Mollie Digby became national news.[44]

Leads poured in from across the state and the Gulf South. From upriver came word that the crew of the steamboat *Wild Wagoner* had spotted a mulatto woman on board carrying a white baby and "answering perfectly the description of the abductress." When members of the crew interrogated her, she at first said the baby was hers, but then "confessed that its parents were dead, and that she had taken it to raise." Although the crew doubted her story, they waited too long to detain her. The woman disappeared from the boat when it stopped at Baton Rouge. Police there telegraphed Chief Badger, who sent a special officer to interview the passengers, dockworkers, and steamboat employees. By the time the detective arrived, however, the trail had gone cold and he "failed to obtain a single clue." Every day Badger received dozens of new letters and telegrams from people who had seen a black woman with a white baby fitting Mollie's description on boats or trains headed north, or hidden in rural cabins, or walking on country roads or wooded paths. Badger sent his black detectives to Port Hudson, Alexandria, the sugar parishes, and Mississippi to pursue the most promising leads, all to no avail. Despite the massive manhunt, it seemed that Mollie Digby might never be found.[45]

Chapter Two

DETECTIVE JOHN BAPTISTE JOURDAIN AND HIS WORLD

The Digby case unfolded at a time when Americans had become fascinated with true crime stories. Newspaper editors who had once emphasized business and political news discovered that accounts of sensational crimes sold papers. Although the Digby abduction was not as lurid as the bloody homicides that garnered most national headlines, the rumors of Voodoo, the large reward, and the Louisiana subtropical setting made the tale exotic, while the crime itself touched Victorian sensibilities. The investigation, with its false leads and scenes of domestic anguish, was unfolding like the popular serialized mystery novels of the day. Many Americans in 1870 were in the midst of reading Charles Dickens's serial cliffhanger *The Mystery of Edwin Drood*, published in six monthly installments, when the kidnapping occurred.[1]

Chief Badger's decision to assign John Baptiste Jourdain, his top black detective, to the case added to its public interest. In 1870, police detective squads were just coming into their own, particularly in the South. Until the mid-1840s, American urban police forces did not employ detectives; before then, the role of policemen, night watchmen, and town constables was to prevent crimes, not to solve them. Cities usually depended on common citizens to identify criminals. Even with the rise of professional policing in the 1830s, officers focused their energies on prevention and made most arrests based on evidence that witnesses had voluntarily brought forth. After Boston introduced the first detective squad in 1846, other American cities, including New Orleans, followed suit, and detectives quickly became the most glamorous figures in law enforcement. Stories, both real and fictional, of whip-smart sleuths deciphering clues, using disguise, spotting telltale signs, and outsmarting wily criminals captured the American imagination. True crime tabloids like the *National Police Gazette*, as well as the short stories of Edgar Allan Poe, helped propel the national obsession with detective work.[2]

Jourdain's race added complexity to the story. Until Reconstruction, all police detectives in the United States had been white. Even in 1870, police departments in the North still had not hired black patrolmen, let alone detectives. The Boston force would not add a black officer until 1878; in New York City, the ranks remained all-white until 1911. But in the South, five cities employed black officers. Reconstruction, it seemed, had brought real change; only a few years earlier, the idea of a black man serving on a Southern police force in any capacity would have been unthinkable. Now Jourdain, a black detective, was assigned to a major case in the South's largest metropolis, following leads, interrogating white and black witnesses, and using his deductive skills to solve a sensational crime. The Digby investigation was the first case to make national news that featured a black sleuth.[3]

Detective Jourdain was forty years old and relatively new to the police force when he was thrust into the national spotlight. He was tall, grey-eyed, delicately featured, and dapper. The press described him as "intelligent and well-educated." In an era obsessed with skin color and the traits many believed came with it, a federal official described Jourdain as "slightly colored." He displayed, one reporter wrote, "little... exhibition of African lineage." Jourdain came from "a wealthy colored family, but slightly tinctured with Ethiopian blood," the *Daily Picayune* added. Official antebellum documents identified Jourdain, like many other men and women of mixed race, as "mulatto," while persons with darker complexions were labeled "black" or "negro." In casual conversation, many New Orleanians called all light-skinned persons of color "quadroons," even though that term was a legal designation for a person who had a single grandparent of African ancestry.[4]

Born in New Orleans in June 1830, Jourdain was the son of a free woman of color who had once been enslaved and a white Creole descendant of one of Louisiana's founding families. Relationships like his parents' were common in New Orleans, where wealthy, white Francophone men often had children with "mulatto" partners. Unlike the Americans who had settled in New Orleans after the United States acquired Louisiana in 1803 who opposed racial "amalgamation," Jourdain's parents were part of a French and Spanish colonial culture that tolerated interracial relationships. In part because there were many more white men than white women in early New Orleans, white men regularly established relationships with women of color. In some cases, these couples lived apart, with the Creole men providing their mistresses with allowances and houses or apartments. Others formed long-term unions, some cohabitating for a lifetime. If children followed, white Creoles regularly "stood up" for their mixed-race offspring by attending their baptisms and giving them enough money to ensure their education and community standing. Often the children took their father's name. Jourdain's father, J. B. V. Jourdain, had nine children with two mixed-race women: four with John's mother, Marie Smith; and, after Marie's death, five with Aimee Gilbert.[5]

Jourdain's father was one of those white Creoles who lived openly with his mixed-race partners. Unwilling to bend to the Americans' racial mores, J. B. V. and Marie (and later Aimee) raised their children together in a house near the French Quarter, and they legally documented J. B. V.'s ties to his mixed-race sons and daughters. J. B. V. and Marie had John baptized in 1831 at St. Louis Cathedral, with Pierre Fabre, a wealthy white Creole who also had children with a free woman of color, serving as godparent and co-signing the baptismal certificate.[6] By formally acknowledging paternity, John's father assured his son legal protections in a system increasingly shaped by Americans' rigid racial views. The Americans called interracial relationships like that of Jourdain's parents "abominations" and "illicit connexions," and the Louisiana Civil Code of 1825 explicitly denied mixed-race children the right to inherit property from their white father unless the father acknowledged paternity in legal documents. Mixed-race sons and daughters had few claims that could survive a challenge by a "legitimate" white heir. But if, like J. B. V., the father "had been so lost as to shame as to make an authentic act of his degradation" by baptizing his mixed-race offspring, the children could inherit paternal property. While he was alive, J. B. V., who never married a white woman, gave his son both money and real estate. On the eve of the Civil War, John Jourdain was worth more than $10,000, earned a substantial living from rents, and worked as a skilled cigar-maker.[7] In public, Jourdain spoke proudly of his father. "I am a colored man, but my father is a white man and a gentleman," he told a congressional commit-tee shortly after the Civil War.[8]

As a Creole of color (or Afro-Creole), Detective Jourdain belonged to a class of mixed-race men and women unique to the Gulf Coast. Although the term *creole* had different meanings in different societies, in colonial Louisiana anyone born in the colony was called a Creole. Over time, Louisianans, black and white, who identified with French culture and language and feared being overwhelmed by the American parvenus who arrived in New Orleans after the Louisiana Purchase, self-identified as Creoles. Afro-Creoles of Jourdain's class considered themselves to be cosmopolitan gentlemen and ladies. Bilingual and mannerly, they looked to Paris for aesthetic inspiration. Many elite Afro-Creole men wore stylish silk pants, leather slippers, and fine jackets. They dined with silver utensils, filled their homes with books and mahogany furniture, attended the opera, published their own newspaper, studied classical literature, formed exclusive Masonic lodges, and drew inspiration from the egalitarian ideals of the French Revolu-tion. Their ranks included writers, poets, painters, sculptors, and composers, as well as doctors, merchants, and skilled artisans. Although they constituted only 7 percent of the South's free black population in 1860, Louisiana's Afro-Creoles held almost 60 percent of all the real estate owned by the region's free black people.[9]

Even under the slave regime, Creoles of color took great pride in the Fran-cophone identity they shared with white Creoles. Both white and black Creoles practiced Gallic Catholicism, read French-language periodicals, and relished wine, food served with rich sauces, and French colonial architecture. White Creoles patronized black Creole butchers, grocers, tailors, carpenters, masons, and mechanics. They attended plays, cockfights, and circuses together, albeit on a segregated basis. In New Orleans, on Grand Opera nights, Tuesdays and

Thursdays, a portion of the gallery at the *Theatre d'Orleans* was occupied by *gens de couleur libre*. And the city's Francophone Masonic lodges accepted members across race lines. Both white and black Creoles felt culturally besieged by the arrival of tens of thousands of Americans after 1803 and subsequent waves of German and Irish immigrants. They disdained the rough Kentucky flatboatmen, nouveau riche South Carolina planters, impecunious Irish, and blunt Northern merchants filling the city's newer neighborhoods. There were limits to this affinity amongst Creoles, of course. White Creoles expected Creoles of color to know their place in the racial hierarchy. Breaches of etiquette, improper remarks, or untoward gestures could cause confrontations. But the relationship between white and black Creoles was usually one of good will and mutual respect. On the eve of the Civil War, Jourdain strengthened his Creole ties by marrying Josephine Celina Planchard, a free woman of color whose parents were both black Creoles.[10]

Despite their privileged stature compared to most African Americans in the Deep South, Jourdain and other Afro-Creoles could not fully escape the legal and social constraints free black people endured in a slave society. When the United States acquired Louisiana from France, the Americans by treaty guaranteed the citizenship rights of the French and Spanish populations who lived there—including the rights that free persons of color had held under Spanish and French rule. Free black people would, as a result, continue to have the right to buy and sell property, to make contracts, to sue and be sued, to testify in civil and criminal trials, and to own firearms. They could even have white people arrested for assaults, batteries, frauds, and other crimes. On the other hand, the new American regime also made it a crime for "free people of colour… to insult or strike white people" or to "presume to conceive themselves equal to white." Afro-Creoles who refused to defer to whites or who failed to "speak or answer them but with respect" faced fines or imprisonment.[11]

Afro-Creoles could neither vote nor sit on juries; nor, despite paying taxes, could they send their children to the public schools. Instead, they organized their own private schools, and some even sent their children to school in France. In 1850, one thousand free children of color in Orleans Parish attended private Catholic schools. As the national debate over slavery intensified in the decades preceding the Civil War, however, and slaveholding whites grew fearful that black Creoles were promoting abolitionism (despite the fact that many Creoles of color themselves owned slaves), the Louisiana legislature passed new acts restricting the mobility of free persons of color. They were required to register with a parish judge and to carry papers that proved their free status. Any free black person caught writing or using language that whites felt could incite slave rebellions or escapes faced three to five years' hard labor in the state penitentiary.[12]

In the 1850s, when the anti-immigrant American Party nicknamed the "Know-Nothings" won municipal elections in New Orleans, "Know-Nothing" mayors filled the ranks of the police force with violent thugs who harassed both Irish immigrants and black residents. Police arrested black men, including respected Afro-Creoles, on flimsy charges and raided black churches where the clergy allegedly preached anti-slavery sermons. New city ordinances banned free persons of color from cabarets, coffeehouses, and saloons and eventually required all religious meetings to be led by white people. Other laws segregated public transportation, hospitals, and cemeteries. Some American editors demanded the expulsion of all free black people from the state. But in a city where Creoles of color provided needed services and had blood ties to wealthy whites, police still treated Afro-Creoles more leniently than freed slaves, black sailors, prostitutes, suspected abolitionists, and free blacks born out of state.[13]

Even as their legal status deteriorated along with that of other free persons of color, Jourdain and his brothers Victor and Edouard fiercely guarded their family's honor. In 1856, police arrested Victor Jourdain for clubbing a white man named J. J. Krauss with a "loaded" lead-filled cane, a weapon favored by Parisian gentlemen. Victor felt Krauss had disgraced their sister Victorine by reneging on a promise of marriage. Because interracial marriage was illegal under Louisiana law, Krauss had pledged to travel with Victorine to Paris to marry her there. When Krauss instead simply cohabitated with Victorine in New Orleans "without any antecedent formality," Victor fumed. A bloody fight ensued when Victor attacked Krauss wielding his weighted cane. Police arrested Victor and sent him before the city's First District Court, but somehow he escaped serious punishment. Although no trial record exists, he was a free man shortly thereafter, and, in a city where affairs of honor were common, he seems to have been penalized lightly, if at all, for defending his sister's reputation.[14]

The Civil War created a major dilemma for John Jourdain and other Afro-Creoles. When Louisiana seceded from the Union in 1861 after the election of Abraham Lincoln, some Afro-Creoles, particularly those who owned slaves themselves, saw the war as an opportunity to impress elite whites with their loyalty. Many even hoped to fight for the Confederacy. New Orleans's free men of color were proud of their place in the martial lore of Louisiana; they had fought for Spain against the British in the American Revolution and with Andrew Jackson at the Battle of New Orleans during the War of 1812. Although Jefferson Davis and other national rebel leaders seemed unlikely to welcome black soldiers, Louisiana's Confederate state government organized an Afro-Creole militia, the Louisiana Native Guards, and more than one thousand free persons of color volunteered. If the South won its independence, Afro-Creoles' fealty to the cause might safeguard their rights in a new nation committed to the perpetuation of race-based slavery. Other Afro-Creoles, including Jourdain, recognized that fighting to defend the Confederacy was folly and that black men's best hope for gaining equal rights was a Union victory. While some elite Creoles of color felt little solidarity with enslaved African Americans, they knew the sting of racial prejudice all too well. And most Confederate leaders were inveterate white supremacists. Jourdain believed siding with the Confederacy was treason, and he refused to join the Native Guards even as men he respected signed up. "I am not a rebel," Jourdain announced, "and never will be."[15]

Jourdain's political instincts proved correct. The Confederate leadership in Richmond treated the Louisiana Native Guards with contempt; the militia never received arms or orders from Confederate generals who had no intention of using black troops. New Orleans, moreover, did not remain in the Confederacy for long. The city fell quickly, captured by Union troops in April 1862. At that point, most Creoles of color pledged allegiance to the Union, and many offered to fight for the North. Even some members of the Louisiana Native Guard who had initially sided with the Confederates switched sides and offered their services to Lincoln's army. Although Union General Benjamin Butler was initially hesitant to enlist free black men, particularly men of such uncertain loyalties, necessity warmed him to the idea when a Confederate attack to reclaim the city seemed imminent. Afro-Creole leaders impressed Butler with their sophistication. In a famous letter to Secretary of War Edwin Stanton, he noted that "in color, nay, also in conduct, they had much more the appearance of white gentlemen than some of those who have favored me with their presence claiming to be the 'chivalry' of the South."[16]

Jourdain was elated when Butler issued a general order inviting free black men from Louisiana to enlist in the Union Army. In his call for volunteers, Butler appealed to Afro-Creoles' proud heritage and their forebears' bravery fighting with Jackson at the Battle of New Orleans. Most important, he announced that his black regiments would be "paid, equipped, armed, and rationed as are other volunteer troops of the United States." Here was a chance for Afro-Creoles to be treated as equals and to prove their worth on the battlefield. Butler even declared that black men could be commissioned as officers, a role Afro-Creoles coveted. Rather than serve side by side with the escaped slaves whom Butler had also enlisted, Creoles would lead as officers of the line. Men of Jourdain's class flocked to the recruiting stations Butler opened in the city. Jourdain, who helped raise a company of Creole men from the Tremé and French Quarter, received a commission as a 1st Lieutenant, and he and his men were mustered into the Union army on July 4, 1863. Word of Robert E. Lee's defeat at Gettysburg the day before and the Confederate surrender of Vicksburg that afternoon must have added to the jubilant mood.[17]

Shortly before Jourdain's service began, however, a new general replaced Butler as commander of Union forces along the Gulf Coast. Like Butler, Nathaniel Banks enlisted black soldiers, but he viewed them as a necessary evil. As governor of Massachusetts, Banks had opposed enrolling black men in his state's militia. As a Union general, he needed the manpower black troops provided but detested the idea of black commissioned officers. He sympathized with white soldiers and officers who resented taking orders from, or even saluting, black superiors. Calling Jourdain and other black officers "a source of constant embarrassment and annoyance," Banks decided his army would no longer grant commissions to black men, and he drove from the ranks the black officers commissioned under Butler. He subjected some to disqualifying efficiency examinations and pressured others to leave voluntarily. He ordered Jourdain and dozens of other black officers to report to his headquarters where he told them "to tender their resignations to save their dignity." They could reenlist or be drafted as privates. Jourdain and other proud Afro-Creole officers complained to no avail that it would be humiliating and bad for morale "for a commissioned officer to be put in the ranks...to shoulder the musket as a private." Jourdain quit. "I was captain of company K, third regiment Louisiana Native Guards," Jourdain later told a congressional hearing. "But, on account of prejudice there was against colored officers, I resigned." "My service was not, indeed, for very long," he added. Mustered out on August 19, he had been in the Union army for less than two months.[18]

Too proud to serve as a common foot soldier, Jourdain spent the remainder of the war as a civilian in New Orleans, waiting to see if a Union victory might lead to full citizenship for men of his class. When President Lincoln announced preliminary plans in December 1863 for organizing a new loyal state government in Louisiana, Jourdain was disappointed because the proposal did not include voting rights for Afro-Creoles. In January, he joined a movement to convince Lincoln to change his mind. After a mass meeting at Economy Hall, he and one thousand other Afro-Creoles signed a petition asking Lincoln to extend the franchise to "all the citizens of Louisiana of African descent, born free before the rebellion." They sent two Afro-Creole leaders, E. Arnold Bertonneau and Jean Baptiste Roudanez, to Washington to meet with the president, and there, Republican Senator Charles Sumner persuaded Bertonneau and Roudanez to transform their petition into an appeal for universal suffrage that asked for voting rights for former free men of color *and* former slaves. When they met with the president, Bertonneau and Roudanez impressed Lincoln, who subsequently penned a private letter to the provisional governor of Louisiana Michael Hahn suggesting that he consider asking his state's constitutional convention to give voting rights to "some of the colored people... as, for instance, the very intelligent, and especially those who have fought gallantly in our ranks." Hahn, however, failed to act on the president's suggestion.[19]

When the war ended, national events dashed Jourdain's hopes for immediate change. After Robert E. Lee's surrender and Lincoln's assassination in

April 1865, President Andrew Johnson issued a sweeping amnesty proclamation and wholesale pardons that let all but a handful of former rebel leaders return to political life. Whites-only elections allowed unrepentant ex-Confederates to regain control of Southern state legislatures and municipal governments. In New Orleans, Confederate mayor John T. Monroe returned to office and once again filled the police force with violent white supremacists, many of whom had served in the Confederate Army.[20]

Slavery was gone, but a new caste system emerged. Across the South, ex-Confederates serving in state legislatures, and in parish, county, and city governments, passed laws known as the Black Codes that were designed to maintain white control of land, labor, and politics. In rural areas, the Black Codes required black citizens to sign labor contracts with employers each January and to honor those contracts or face severe criminal penalties. If black workers could not provide written proof of employment for the coming year, they could be fined for vagrancy and sentenced to involuntary plantation labor. In Louisiana, once a black person signed a labor contract he or she could be jailed for "bad work," "leaving home without permission," or "impudence, swearing, or indecent language to or in the presence of the employer, his family, or agent." Other laws restricted when and where black people could hold meetings or gather in groups after sundown. Penalties for crimes became increasingly draconian. Some Southern states made the theft of a mule or a horse a capital offense.[21]

Jourdain abhorred the Black Codes. Rather than signaling a new day for freedom, the Black Codes eliminated rights Creoles of color had enjoyed before the war. Jourdain spoke out against ordinances he believed to be affronts to male dignity, like those enacted in several Louisiana parishes that denied black men the right to carry a gun. While white men Jourdain regarded as "thugs" and "white trash" could roam the roads "loaded down with weapons," black men—even Creole gentlemen—could not. "If I were to carry a weapon, I should stand a good chance of being arrested—it is unlawful," Jourdain objected. The "ordinances do not prevent [former rebels] from carrying arms; they are overloaded with them; but a loyal man cannot have arms, even at his own house. It was customary, even in the slavery times, for a man to have a gun to go hunting with, but they are not even allowed that."[22]

In New Orleans and across the South, white policemen, sheriffs, juries, and judges enforced the Black Codes and all other laws. Some lawmen still wore their Confederate uniforms as they patrolled rural roads. Officers who zealously enforced the Black Codes often looked the other way when ex-rebels committed violent crimes against black citizens and white unionists. In New Orleans, Sheriff Harry T. Hays, formerly a general in Lee's army, allowed his police officers to harass, beat, and even kill black residents with impunity.[23]

In July 1866, New Orleans policemen led a mob that attacked a biracial state constitutional convention whose delegates were considering the possibility of black suffrage. As Jourdain looked on, policemen surrounded the convention hall, distributed revolvers to the angry white crowd, kicked down the building's doors, and murdered dozens of the delegates inside. In what Union General Philip Sheridan later labeled "an absolute massacre," the mob killed thirty-four black men and three whites.[24]

Jourdain had rushed to the hall as the mob formed because he feared that his brother Edouard, a convention delegate, was inside. He watched aghast as white men he recognized fired guns into the hall's windows and dragged blood- ied delegates into the street. Some of the marauders were former Confederate officers. Others, Jourdain remembered, were "thugs" from "the low class of citi- zens" who had been part of antebellum Know-Nothing gangs. But the mob also included white men he had previously thought to be temperate and reasonable. A few saw Jourdain in the crowd and urged him to "go away." Risking his own life, Jourdain pushed through the throng to reach a police lieutenant he knew. Jourdain implored him, "For God's sake, stop your men from killing these men so." The lieutenant pulled away, but Jourdain blocked his path. "For God's sake, stop these men from this," Jourdain shouted. When the lieutenant growled back, "I'll set fire to the building and burn them all," Jourdain realized that his acquaintance had "turned over to the other side." Jourdain would have fled but for the possibility his brother was in harm's way. "If I had not thought that, I should not have remained...I had to stay there, for I thought he would be brought out dead." Then he saw A. P. Dostie, a white unionist and proponent of black suffrage, pulled from the hall by police, his face covered with blood. The crowd closed in. Someone shouted "Kill the son of a bitch," and Dostie fell as a bullet severed his spine. The mob threw bricks and rocks at Dostie's head as policemen dragged his limp body down the street. Fearing for his own life, Jourdain ran toward Canal Street, where he paid a policemen he knew $5 dollars to find out whether his brother "was dead or alive, or what had become of him." The officer returned later with word Edouard was not in the hall.[25]

When Jourdain reached his Tremé home, his brother was there alive. But the riot was not over. The mob spilled into Jourdain's neighborhood. Policemen and thugs ran through the streets attacking black people who had had nothing to do with the convention. Jourdain saw an officer shoot an old man selling watermelons on Claiborne Avenue. He watched another kill a black carpenter who was working nearby—the officer seized the carpenter's hatchet, told the man to run, and then chased him down, plunging the hatchet into his back. "They passed right in front of my door," Jourdain later testified. "I saw him strike this colored man with the hatchet." After the riot, Jourdain confronted the patrolman about his murderous acts. "He said it was not his fault; it was instructions he had received from his officers," Jourdain reported. "He said a man was bound to obey his officers.... I told him I was very mad against him for doing it; but he said it was not his fault, and I told him when he wished to kill people I hoped he would not do it before my door."[26]

Five months later, when a congressional committee traveled from Washington to investigate what became known as the New Orleans Riot, Jourdain braved death threats to testify before its members. In addition to recounting the gruesome murders he had witnessed, Jourdain conveyed his disgust for the white men he had once respected who revealed their true selves during the riot. "It requires a man to live here with them to know them," Jourdain declared. "They will laugh and smile at you, and at the same time they will put a knife in your back. They will ask you to drink with them... at the same time they will murder you." He was not speaking metaphorically. He had seen prominent white men kill his friends, and now he feared for his own life. As he told the committee, "I have heard them say they will pay me because of this testimony.... Many have advised me to leave the city."[27]

Jourdain's testimony proved to be worth the risk. The accounts that he and other witnesses gave of the riot profoundly influenced public opinion in the

North. The ghoulish details, reprinted in Northern newspapers, confirmed for many Northerners that white Southerners were unrepentant, that President Johnson's lenient Reconstruction policies had utterly failed, and that a much more forceful strategy was necessary. Although Congress had already acted to protect the rights of African Americans by passing the Fourteenth Amendment in 1866, Southern legislatures had refused to ratify it. The accounts of the New Orleans Riot pushed Republicans to act. Three months after Jourdain's testimony, Congress overrode Johnson's vetoes to pass the Reconstruction Acts of 1867, which, among other things, gave African-American men in the South the right to vote. Pursuant to the act, Union military commanders, backed by federal troops, dismantled Johnson's state governments, appointed registrars to enroll black voters, and organized state constitutional conventions charged with reshaping the South's legal, political, and social order. The Louisiana constitutional convention of 1868 was the first major elective body in Southern history with a black majority, and it produced a constitution that seemed to promise a new, racially progressive Louisiana. The document included a bill of rights—the state's first—that voided the Black Codes, protected free speech, and guaranteed equal protection of the laws and "public rights" that included equal access to public transportation and accommodations. Black men could sit on juries, and judges and other public officials had to swear an oath to accept and protect "the civil and political equality of all men." Jourdain seized the moment, joining the Republican Party, serving on the party's Central Executive Committee, and becoming an officer in his neighborhood's "Sixth Ward Republican Club." He became a proud "Radical," marching in torch-lit Republican parades and campaigning for "perfect equality under law," integrated schools, an eight-hour workday, and "the complete, ultimate triumph of Republican principles and policy in Louisiana and the South."[28]

Radical Reconstruction also gave Jourdain another opportunity to prove his worth by volunteering—this time for Governor Warmoth's Metropolitan Police. Jourdain was elated when Warmoth—the first governor elected under Louisiana's new constitution—put out the call for qualified black men to join the New Orleans force, and both he and his brother Victor answered. Jourdain knew that black policemen could be transformative for the city. Throughout his life, he had felt the ill effects of living under a poorly trained and racist police department. The savagery of the New Orleans Riot confirmed what he already knew: an all-white police force would never fully protect black people's lives, liberty, or property.[29]

Warmoth's commitment to creating a modern, professional, and integrated police department played to the strengths of Creoles of color like Jourdain. While rough and illiterate men had previously dominated the police ranks, Warmoth wanted educated, healthy, honest, and diligent officers who would lead by example and uphold Victorian ideals of manly self-restraint. New regulations prohibited officers from using "coarse, profane, or insolent language" and required them to "set an example of sobriety, discretion, skill, industry, and promptness." Rules required officers to pay their debts on time, to "be quiet, civil and orderly," and to "maintain decorum and command of temper." These skills were second nature for Creoles of color like Jourdain who had long relied on their manners and erudition to distinguish themselves from slaves and poor whites. Jourdain could now use those skills to further his career and to demonstrate that black men deserved full equality. But maintaining decorum when faced with whites' violent hostility would not be easy. Whites who abhorred the idea of black policemen insulted, threatened, and attacked black officers whenever they could. Police Chief Badger feared for the lives of his black patrolmen and on one occasion ordered them to take off their uniforms and hide until a white mob dispersed. The conservative press depicted black policemen as incompetents and publicized even their slightest misstep. But Jourdain was undaunted, and, unlike the Union army, the Metropolitan Police would give him a legitimate chance to prove how smart and skilled he was.[30]

For Jourdain and other Creoles of color, Radical Reconstruction provided a singular opportunity to prove that they numbered amongst society's "best men." Given the right to vote, hold office, and serve on juries, Creoles of color seized the moment. Confident that black men of their class could govern as well as (or better than) white men, Afro-Creoles ran for office, accepted patronage posts, or, like Jourdain, joined the integrated police force. During Reconstruction, almost all of the black elected officials from New Orleans and 80 percent of the black officers on the Metropolitan Police came from the mixed-race

Creole community. Afro-Creoles took on these roles knowing that their success or failure could affect the status of all black people in Louisiana. If they failed, they would confirm the prejudices of ex-Confederate reactionaries bent on restoring white supremacy. If they succeeded, they might convince moderate whites to join a biracial coalition committed to economic prosperity and democratic rule. Nowhere was success more crucial than in law enforcement. The Republican government had to prove that it could ensure the safety of persons and property. Jourdain immediately helped the cause by leading several successful investigations that received notice in the newspapers, including a larceny case that led to the arrest of two black women. But the public pressure to solve the Digby case would be far greater than anything Jourdain had experienced. The conservative press had turned the Digby kidnapping into a crime that could not go unsolved. "We may say to the police of New Orleans," the *Picayune* warned, "that unless this child be found, they will suffer a burning disgrace—a lasting shame."[31]

With so much at stake, Jourdain's performance in the Digby case would be weighted with political and social significance. If he could find Mollie Digby or her kidnappers, he might also buoy the spirits of those Northern newspaper readers who hoped Reconstruction would succeed. In New Orleans and along the Gulf Coast, Democratic editors had used the Digby story to criticize Warmoth's Metropolitan Police. In the North, readers of Republican papers like the *New York Times*—readers who had grown weary of reports from the South of Ku Klux Klan violence, Republican infighting, alleged corruption, and voter fraud—might find solace in a successful resolution of the Digby investigation. A true crime story from New Orleans featuring a dashing young Republican governor, his Massachusetts-born police chief, and an expert black detective could cheer Northerners who hoped that Southern whites' resistance to Reconstruction might fade as Republican officials demonstrated their competence. With the national press reporting regularly on the mystery and with so much riding on the success of black police officers, the Digby kidnapping would become the most important case of Jourdain's career.[32]

Chapter Three

A TRACE OF THE MISSING CHILD?

A s almost a month passed without results and public frustration mounted, some New Orleans editors called for Police Chief Badger to hire French detectives. Because there was "still no trace of the missing child," the *Daily Picayune* demanded that Warmoth send "to Paris for some of their sharp officers, who...could take up the case even at this late date, and work it to a successful termination." Real-life detective François Eugène Vidocq and fictitious sleuths created by Edgar Allan Poe and Émile Gaboriau had made Parisian criminologists famous. Using deductive reasoning, cunning, and disguise, French detectives, real and fictional, set the standard for detective work. Unhappy with the efforts of their own force, some Francophone New Orleanians hoped Badger would look abroad for help.[1]

Rather than relying on outsiders, Detective Jourdain hoped to use French techniques to solve the case himself. In mid-July, Jourdain received a tip that a former slave named Rosa Lee who lived in the back of town had told friends that she knew Martha, the rumored abductor of Mollie Digby. Because policemen were "invariably met with silence and suspicion" in black neighborhoods, Jourdain hoped he could dress in workman's clothes and trick Lee into divulging what she knew about the case. As a light-skinned Creole of color, Jourdain would need to play his role well by adopting the dialect and mannerisms of a freedman.

To lend authenticity to his disguise, Jourdain brought along gray-haired Detective Jordan Noble who, at age seventy-two, was the oldest man on the force and one of the few former slaves in the ranks of the Metropolitan Police.

Detective Noble was famous in the city and perhaps an odd choice for an undercover assignment. Born into slavery in Georgia, Noble had earned his freedom after serving as Andrew Jackson's drummer boy at the Battle of New Orleans during the War of 1812. He later accompanied Louisiana troops in the Everglades during the Seminole War, and he served as drummer for the elite New Orleans-based Washington Artillery during the Mexican War. In the 1850s, Noble regularly marched with his drum in patriotic parades alongside white veterans who nicknamed him "Old Jordan." When the Civil War began, he helped organize one of the regiments that volunteered to fight with the Confederacy, but he later switched sides and served in the Union ranks. Like Jourdain, Noble seized the opportunity to join the Metropolitan Police as a detective, and, despite Noble's celebrity, Jourdain believed that he and Noble, like the famous French detectives, could be "masters of disguise."[2]

Dressed in grubby work clothes, the two detectives made their way to the back of town, where they found Rosa Lee just outside of her house. They told her that they were Martha's friends and that they were looking for her. For a time their ruse seemed to work. Unaware of their true identities, Lee "talked very freely to them, saying that she knew Martha, but that she was now in trouble." "How was she now in trouble?" Jourdain asked. "She took Mr. Digby's child about a month ago," Lee responded, "and she has to keep close." Before more information could be elicited, a friend of Lee's walked up and whispered to her that the men were disguised officers. "Her whole manner instantly changed," Jourdain noted, "and she tried to deny what she had previously said." They then arrested Lee and took her to the station house, where she was held for three days. After a lengthy interrogation, Jourdain determined that Lee was simply a braggart who had fabricated her story in order to draw attention to herself. She did not even know a woman named Martha, and she never expected that anyone would report her to the police.[3]

Pursuing all possible leads, Jourdain even convinced Thomas Digby to join him at the City Hotel for a consultation with Madame Ferris, a famed clairvoyant who was in New Orleans for a July performance. Although Chief Badger placed little faith in the power of psychics, Jourdain and many New Orleanians believed in them. Mediums like Ferris were the central figures in a mid–nineteenth-century movement known as Spiritualism, which grew out of the evangelical tumult that convulsed America before the Civil War. Rather than rely on ministers, priests, and other church authorities for insights into the afterlife, Spiritualists believed clairvoyants could make direct contact with deceased family members and historical luminaries.[4]

Even after most traditional churches rejected Spiritualism, hundreds of thousands of Americans participated in séances and magnetic circles with male and female mediums who claimed to communicate directly with the dead. As one of the few antebellum religions that encouraged women to speak publicly (albeit in a hypnotic state), Spiritualism attracted female adherents frustrated by the subordinate roles that more traditional faiths assigned to women. Many prominent national leaders, businessmen, and authors found Spiritualists' claims convincing. Abolitionist William Lloyd Garrison was a believer, as was poet Henry Wadsworth Longfellow. During the Civil War, Mary Todd Lincoln invited mediums to the presidential mansion to conduct séances for senators and cabinet members.[5]

Although Spiritualism was largely a Northern phenomenon frowned upon by Southern Baptists and Methodists, it flourished in Catholic New Orleans— particularly among white and black Creole families. New Orleans had long fostered a reputation as a haunted city, and its newspapers regularly reported ghostly sightings, but Spiritualism took this fascination with the spirit world to new heights. In the 1850s, New Orleans had a flourishing "Magnetic Society," which published its own journal, *Le Spiritualiste*, and elite Creole families hosted séances and spirit circles in their French Quarter townhomes. White people who criticized adherents of Voodoo for their purportedly heathenish practices nevertheless offered their own credulous accounts of communications from dead relatives, Catholic saints, and other spirit guides. By the eve of the Civil War, New Orleans had an estimated 20,000 Spiritualist believers. The movement was still alive in the city in 1870 when Detective Jourdain and Thomas Digby turned to Madame Ferris for help. Henry Louis

Rey, a Creole of color who had served with Jourdain in the Union Army and whose brother Octave was a Metropolitan police captain, held elaborate séances in his home that year, where he and his guests communicated in French with Jesus, Jefferson, Robespierre, Lincoln, Haitian revolutionaries, and deceased local figures like A. P. Dostie, whose murder Jourdain had witnessed in the 1866 New Orleans Riot.[6]

To be sure, séances and magnetic circles were often conscious frauds where practitioners perpetrated rappings, table tilting, and spirit materializations using tricks and mechanical devices. Thomas Digby had already been duped twice, once by a fraudulent "spiritual medium" and again by a fortune teller he had employed. In the latter instance, the *Republican* recounted, "a half demented old fellow undertook, for compensation of twenty-five dollars, to inform the bereaved father exactly where his little one was and her condition. He manipulated shells and cards, but of course furnished no particle of information, when a hard fist persuaded him to deliver up the money."[7]

Some skeptics mocked the police for turning to a medium. The editor of the *Commercial Bulletin*, having caught wind of Jourdain's mission, needled the "over-credulous" police for employing an "astrologer, clairvoyant, and table-rapper." "If she proves to be a prophet," the paper joked, "it is hoped she will next gratify the curiosity of the worshippers of Dickens by solving the 'Mystery of Edwin Drood.'" Others applauded Jourdain for pursuing all possibilities. Madame Ferris, a correspondent to the New Orleans *Times* maintained, had "done so many extraordinary things" that she could "certainly find the child." "Let it be tried," he urged.[8]

The séance with Madame Ferris initially went well. While Detective Jourdain and Thomas Digby looked on, Ferris went into a deep trance from which she emerged with startling information: Mollie Digby was being held captive in a nearby neighborhood. Boarding a streetcar, the trio made their way to the house that Ferris claimed to have seen in her trance. There they found three children, one of whom Madame Ferris identified as the abducted child. It quickly became clear, however, that the medium was badly mistaken. "The bereaved father was not relieved," the *Republican* reported, "for it was not his offspring." "Jourdain," the reporter noted wryly, "made the affair rather amusing by his discovery that the babe was masculine in nature." Publicly embarrassed, Ferris left the city with the crime unsolved.[9]

After six weeks had passed without any credible leads, it seemed unlikely that the Digby baby would ever be found. Then on July 23, Governor Warmoth received a dramatic but cryptic telegram from John F. Torrence, the mayor of Cincinnati, Ohio. "I have information of the whereabouts of Thomas Digby's child," the message read. "Will you guarantee the reward if the child is recovered? The party who has the information wants to know. The child was stolen in New Orleans." Warmoth, eager to see the case solved, promptly telegraphed back confirming that the reward would be paid upon delivery of Mollie Digby. New Orleans papers cheered the news as a major breakthrough. Some papers claimed that Mollie was already on board a train home from Cincinnati.[10]

After four days with no word from Mayor Torrence and no sign of Mollie Digby at the Basin Street depot, Governor Warmoth telegraphed Torrence again, this time demanding that he divulge at once what he knew of Mollie Digby's whereabouts. Torrence finally wired back on July 29 to say that the information would arrive shortly by regular mail. Whoever was the source of the information, it seemed, was so focused on the reward that he or she did not trust the telegraph operators to convey the information securely. Speculation increased that Mollie had been abducted for ransom and that Mayor Torrence might even be in on the scheme. Didn't the mayor recognize the distress his tardiness was causing the Digby family? wondered the editor of the *Bee*. Declaring that "this tardy manner of communicating intelligence" reflected "barbarous inhumanity," the *Picayune* charged that "the speculative individual who purports to have information of the child, seems utterly regardless of everything save securing the reward!"[11]

When a letter from Cincinnati's police chief, James Ruffin, finally reached Warmoth on August 4, it did contain promising details about the crime. A Cincinnati resident named Phil Graw had told Ruffin's officers that he knew Mollie Digby's whereabouts. After Mayor Torrence assured Graw that he would receive the reward money if his information proved accurate, Graw divulged that Mollie was still in New Orleans, that she had been kidnapped for ransom, that her female abductors had been hired by a "colored man" named Joseph Jackson who had an ongoing dispute with Thomas Digby, and that her abductors were moving her from house to house in a poor section of the city in order to keep her concealed. If the Metropolitans moved quickly, they could find the child in a "dirty," one-story frame shack at 4646 Swamp Street. Warmoth turned the letter over to Chief Badger, who sent Detective Jourdain and other special officers to investigate.[12]

Hope that the Digby baby might soon be found dissipated quickly when officers realized there was no Swamp Street in New Orleans. A Marais Street, which means "marsh" or "swamp" in French, bordered swamps in the lower part of the city, but there was no 4646 Marais Street. There was also no sign of a Joseph Jackson, the "colored man" who had been named as the culprit in the letter from Chief Ruffin. After two days knocking on the doors of every house in the vicinity of Marais Street turned up no sign of Mollie Digby, Chief Badger telegraphed Ruffin asking him to press Phil Graw as to the source of his information. A day later, an embarrassed Ruffin telegraphed back that the information had come from Graw's mother—a Spiritualist clairvoyant.[13]

Graw, a Cincinnati paper reported, had spotted the poster advertising the Digby reward in that city's Third Street Police Station. "Lend me that bill," Graw had said to the officer on duty, "I want to show it to my mother. I can lay my hand on that child." He ran the poster home and then returned, excited and out of breath, demanding that an officer come with him to his Sycamore Street house. A Lieutenant Evans followed Graw to his home and there found a middle-aged woman who confidently assured him she could ascertain where Mollie Digby was being held. She instructed the lieutenant to place a plain gold ring on the index finger of his right hand. After he wore the ring for a moment, she removed it, wiped it carefully with a handkerchief, "and through it peered into a glass of Ohio River water." The woman's eyes were "as piercing as lightning" as she stared into the murky liquid. Then she spoke:

I see the child as you shall see it. Poor child, imprisoned, ragged, neglected, sobbing its tender young life away. There—in a low, dirty room, is a small, frame building—the number is almost obscured, over the door; but the eye of the spirit world can see it and decipher it—it is forty-six forty six!...There the scene changes—the water moves. On the corner of that building yonder I see the name of the street. It is—it is—it's Swamp Street.[14]

The lieutenant, the *Commercial* added wryly, "trembled in the presence of this awful influence from a world beyond his ken; and with his knees knocking together and nerves unstrung, he staggered down stairs and out into the open air once more."[15]

In New Orleans, the press ridiculed Mayor Torrence for basing his initial telegram to Governor Warmoth on the word of a "fortune teller." The *Picayune* chastised the mayor for sending on "the ravings of a lunatic." Chief Badger, having been hoodwinked twice by Spiritualist claims, telegraphed Cincinnati's police chief suggesting he give Lieutenant Evans "a dose of salts." The *Picayune* thought "an application of boot leather would have been more to the point."[16]

It was now August, almost two months since Mollie Digby disappeared, and the police seemed no closer to finding her. The child, newspapers claimed, had "effectually disappeared as if it had sunk into the bowels of the earth." With the reward money unclaimed, leads continued to come in, but many New Orleanians felt certain Mollie was gone for good. "All thought the child finally lost," one editor lamented. For Governor Warmoth, Chief Badger, his officers, and the Digbys, the investigation seemed headed for a dispiriting conclusion.[17] Nevertheless, Badger remained unwavering in his commitment to the case. He sent detectives to remote corners of the state to pursue even the vaguest leads. Officers traveled to Gibson's Landing in Concordia Parish on word that two black women were seen carrying a white child along the Mississippi River bank through the willows, and to Bayou Sara where furtive women had also been seen. In both cases the alleged kidnappers were gone by the time Badger's men arrived.[18]

On Sunday, August 7, a police department official named William George received a tip that Mollie Digby was alive and being held in a house in uptown New Orleans. Rather than immediately giving the information to Chief Badger, George, with an eye toward collecting the reward, first tried to follow the lead himself. A thirty-seven-year-old Danish immigrant, George was hated by many whites in New Orleans both because of his politics and the patronage position he occupied. Although he had arrived in the city before the war, he resisted pressure to volunteer for the Confederacy and instead fought for the Union as a captain in the 1st Louisiana Infantry U.S.A. After Appomattox, he joined the Republican Party, and Governor Warmoth rewarded his loyalty with a seat on the Board of Commissioners, the panel that oversaw police affairs. Serving as the board's vice president, George had helped cleanse the force of ex-Confederates. He targeted for removal any officer who had participated in the slaughter of "unarmed martyrs" during the 1866 New Orleans Riot or who was "opposed to Reconstruction and equal rights for all men." George's critics, claiming that he fired first-rate policemen unfairly, called his conduct "dictatorial, domineering, and insolent" and accused him of "petty malignity without parallel." Because Democrats viewed seats on the Board of Commissioners as corrupt positions for party hacks, George's decision to set out on his own to find Mollie Digby supplied ammunition to critics who charged that Republican appointees showed more interest in lining their own wallets than in serving the public. The controversial department regulation that allowed police officials and patrolmen to claim rewards as long as they donated 10 percent of the prize to the "Metropolitan Police Fund" only made matters worse.[19]

According to Captain George's source, a white baby who fit Mollie's description had been seen in the care of mulatto women in Jefferson City, an upriver neighborhood that had only recently been incorporated into Orleans Parish. It was still a largely rural hamlet where cows and pigs roamed the dirt roads, although along the Mississippi it was home to some of the city's most noxious slaughterhouses. Most of the fine homes that would later line uptown streets had not yet been built. When George rode in the mid-afternoon to the address at the northwest corner of Bellecastle and Camp streets where the child had been seen, he expected to find a shotgun shack or bargeboard cottage at the address. He arrived instead at an attractive, vine-covered Italianate house on a large lot surrounded by an iron fence that looked "like the residence of some well-to-do retired family." It did not appear to be a kidnapper's lair. When he called from the locked gate for someone to come out, a mulatto woman emerged.[20]

Standing on the sidewalk outside the gate, Commissioner George asked the woman if a white baby was on the premises. When she said no, George quickly realized the mistake he had made by pursuing the investigation on his own. Intuition told him this might be the right place. Like the descriptions of the kidnapper, the woman was attractive, well dressed, and of mixed race. And his source had seen a white baby there. But under Louisiana law, he needed a warrant to search the house, and to get one he would have go to a judge and swear under oath that he had probable cause for a search. Without a warrant, he could go no farther than the gate, and the woman was now aware she was under suspicion. If Mollie Digby was inside, the kidnappers could spirit her away before George could alert Chief Badger and his men. Mounting his horse, George hurried back downtown to find the police chief. If Badger's men moved promptly and found the Digby baby at that house, George, having provided the information, might still be able to claim the reward for himself.[21]

When George found Badger at the Seventh Street Police Precinct, the chief acted quickly. Although he must have been annoyed that George had not come to him first, Badger would pursue this report with the same vigor as all of the others. Night had already fallen, and George's unofficial visit to the house at Bellecastle and Camp that afternoon meant the suspects might already be flee-ing. Badger summoned Detective Jourdain to the precinct house from his home near the French Quarter, as well as another black detective named J. J. Pierson. It was Sunday evening, both men had been off duty, and Pierson, having been told by a patrolman to come quickly, arrived at the precinct in his civilian clothes rather than his uniform. Badger instructed Jourdain and Pierson to ride to Jefferson City to pursue Commissioner George's lead without delay, and he sent a corporal from the Seventh Precinct with them to show the way.

By the time the three men arrived at Bellecastle and Camp, it was almost nine o'clock. At the locked front gate where George had stood earlier that day, Detective Jourdain shouted angrily for someone to come out from the house, that they were there to find the "stolen child." After a few minutes, a light-skinned African-American boy appeared and asked the detectives what they wanted. "We want to see the lady of the house," Detective Pierson responded forcefully. The boy went back inside, saying he would get his mother and the gate key. For a time no one came back out. The detectives grew increasingly agitated, but they had not secured a warrant either and could not simply break down the gate. After ten minutes had passed, the same attractive mulatto woman who had spoken with Commissioner George came out. The detectives, speaking loudly, demanded that she give them the Digbys' "stolen child." The woman, who identified herself as Ellen Follin, once again denied that any white child was there. But this time, she calmly unlocked the gate and invited the detectives to search the premises. With that, the detectives barged inside. Grabbing lanterns, they ran from room to room "hallooing and screaming" at the frightened people they found there. "Where is the stolen child?" they shouted.

Although the detectives saw no sign of Mollie Digby, much about the house and its occupants seemed peculiar. Follin's home was filled with paintings and handsome rosewood furniture, but the residents—three mulatto children, an elderly black woman, and a white woman who appeared to be in her twenties and in an advanced state of pregnancy—were an unusual group to find living together amidst fine furnishings. In addition, the adolescent boy who had first come to the gate was now gone. When the detectives demanded to know where he had gone, Follin responded that he was her son, that his name was George Blass, and that "he had gone out and was in the habit of going out and coming in late." Detective Jourdain, suspecting a lie, asked her to call her son's name. When she refused, the detectives searched the house, opening closets, looking under beds, checking the garden and small cornfield out back, all without success. Each of the residents denied knowing anything about a "stolen child." Follin did acknowledge that another white woman—in addition to the one now there—had been staying at the house earlier in the week and had a child with black hair and blue eyes "that was just able to creep." Perhaps someone, she suggested, had mistaken that baby for the stolen child the detectives sought.[22]

Before leaving the house empty-handed, Detective Jourdain threatened Follin, telling her he thought that she was lying, that the Digby baby had been there, and that unless she produced her the next day he "would make an affidavit and have the whole house arrested." Follin responded coolly, "Very well, sir, as you please. I assure you, however, I know nothing of the child you are looking for." Offering a carrot with the stick, Jourdain reminded her about the sizeable reward being offered for Mollie Digby's return. With that, the detectives headed back to the precinct house to inform Chief Badger and Commissioner George of the strange and suspicious occupants of the house at Bellecastle and Camp streets. By the time they arrived, however, both Badger and George had gone home, and Jourdain decided that they could wait until the morning to file a report.[23]

While Chief Badger's detectives pursued this new in-town lead, an extensive manhunt was under way for Mollie Digby 160 miles northwest of New Orleans, in central Louisiana. On August 2, a reporter named Brady from the New Orleans *Republican* received a tip that Mollie's kidnappers were hiding her in the former slave quarters of the Compton plantation, near Bayou Boeuf and the town of Cheneyville. The reporter, who, like Commissioner George, may have hoped to claim the reward for himself, asked Governor Warmoth to deputize him so that he could go to Cheneyville to recover the child and arrest the kidnappers. Perhaps because Brady worked for the one newspaper in New Orleans that supported his government, Warmoth agreed and furnished the journalist with papers authorizing him to search for, and arrest, suspects. Brady, joined by two friends, boarded a boat, steamed up the Mississippi to the Red River, and disembarked near Cheneyville on August 8. There he notified a local judge of his mission, secured horses, and headed with his companions for the sprawling Compton estate where his sources told him the Digby baby was being held.[24]

When Brady's party reached the Compton place, they proceeded directly to the former slave quarters, where many of the freedmen and freedwomen still lived. On the eve of the Civil War, the Compton plantation, with almost four hundred slaves, had been one of the largest in Rapides Parish. After the war, many of those laborers stayed on to plant, harvest, and process the sugar cane for pay. Unlike the cotton South, which shifted during Reconstruction to sharecropping and tenant farming that allowed black families to move to cabins on their own rented plot of land, Louisiana's sugar cane production still relied on gang labor. In the state's sugar parishes, many former slaves continued to live in the quarters and toil in teams in the sweltering fields. Even though the former slaves received wages, the Compton estate still had the look and feel of the Old South.[25]

Because Brady's party reached the quarters in the afternoon when almost all of the residents were still working, the only person in sight was a young black girl, about eleven years old. To their surprise, the child seemed to know precisely why they were there. The visitors had not yet uttered a word when she asked, "Where is that little white girl?" "What do you know about a white child?" the startled reporter replied. Two women, she said, had been there with a white baby several times and had that morning left for a secret spot on the plantation, saying that someone was after them. That, she said, was all she knew. Elated by his good fortune and convinced he was close to capturing the kidnappers, Brady headed for the plantation's "big house" to alert the Comptons that fugitives were hiding an abducted child on the grounds. The reporter "imagined how happy he would make the bereaved parents in a few days."[26]

Toche Compton, the plantation's owner, agreed to aid the investigation. Louisiana planters strived to keep their work force, now free, under tight control, and Compton must have been alarmed when emissaries from New Orleans arrived to tell him that black kidnappers were hiding on his land. Springing into action, Compton summoned some of his most trusted black employees and offered them cash rewards if they could find out where the kidnappers were concealed. He and his men also paid their own visit to the old slave quarters to interrogate the girl who had reportedly seen the women with the stolen baby. The frightened girl initially denied knowing anything, but after close questioning claimed "that the lady had given her some money and promised her a new dress" to keep quiet.[27]

By Tuesday morning, word of the search for the kidnapped baby had spread. The Comptons' neighbors had followed the story—and news of the mounting rewards—in the newspapers, and they "flocked in from all points" to assist. When the initial search of the Compton estate failed to turn up the kidnappers, the dragnet expanded to include the surrounding plantations, roads, and piney woods. "Before night," Brady reported, "the whole section of the country was aroused into action." "It was indeed refreshing," he observed, "to find so much humanity and sympathy, and they were all cognizant of the fact that Mr. Digby's infant had been stolen. One idea pervaded the community, and that was to arrest the perpetrators of a horrible crime."[28]

For three days and nights, search parties fanned out across the parish, questioning field hands and any black people walking on public roads. For African

Americans along the Red River, it must have been a harrowing week. At a time when terrorist organizations such as the Knights of the White Camellia were prowling the countryside, parties of white men on horseback with torches could not have been a welcome sight, even if in this case they were aiding a search authorized by the Republican governor.[29]

On Friday, August 12, a traveler arrived claiming that he had seen two black women with a white baby driving in an old wagon on the road to Alexandria. A half-dozen riders rode off to overtake them. Reports also circulated that clothing belonging to Mollie Digby had been found in a cane field. Certain they were "only three hours" behind the culprits, additional rescuers began "saddling horses to proceed with the search." Before those posses returned, however, a New Orleans newspaper that had taken three days to reach Cheneyville by boat arrived with dramatic news. Back in the city, Mollie Digby had been found.[30]

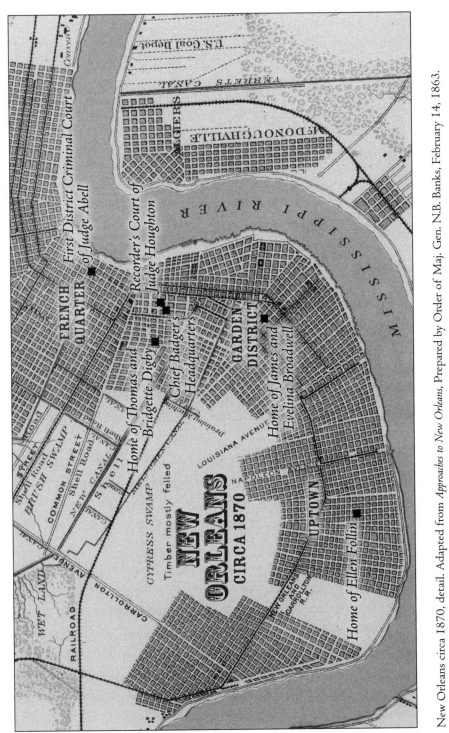

New Orleans circa 1870, detail. Adapted from *Approaches to New Orleans*, Prepared by Order of Maj. Gen. N.B. Banks, February 14, 1863.

Chapter Four

A KNOCK AT THE DIGBYS' DOOR

A ugust was always a difficult month in New Orleans. Relentless heat and humidity made afternoons unbearable. Laborers on the docks and levees risked sunstroke and heat exhaustion. At night, residents slept fitfully under netting as swarms of mosquitoes poured through open windows and into their homes. Foul smells rose from the city's gutters and sewers. Antoine's and other fine restaurants simply closed from July until fall. The city's baseball clubs stopped playing, and most theaters shut down. Late summer threats of hurricanes and yellow fever loomed ahead. Longtime residents remembered all too well the destruction wrought by the August hurricanes of 1856 and 1860 and the terrible yellow fever epidemic of 1853 that killed more than 10,000 New Orleanians.[1]

Although many who could escape the city in August did so, dutiful businessmen, judges, lawyers, and almost all of the working class stayed on the job. Newspapers called these unfortunate souls "can't get aways." Editors urged city-bound readers to move slowly, wear light-colored, loose-fitting cotton clothing, and avoid heavy meals. Those with access to ice rubbed chunks of it on their wrists and ankles. Some solace could be found in the summer plums, black grapes, pears, cantaloupes, tomatoes, new potatoes, and snap beans that arrived from outlying parishes for sale in the public markets. And itinerant

Italian vendors pushed carts through the streets, shouting out their wares in thick accents, "ice cream, ice cream." But these small seasonal joys could not overcome the discomforts and dangers of August. Even rolling afternoon thunderstorms brought a mixed blessing, providing momentary relief from the heat and the dust but turning the city's unpaved streets into muddy rivers.[2]

August 1870 was particularly excruciating for Thomas and Bridgette Digby. Early in the month, Thomas brought Bridgette back from the asylum, but she remained psychologically fragile. With large rewards for their daughter still posted, leads continued to surface, but most yielded nothing. Thomas worried that each time Bridgette's hopes were raised, then dashed, she moved closer to another emotional collapse. Thomas therefore left Bridgette behind whenever he accompanied Detective Jourdain or went on his own to places where Mollie had reportedly been seen. "Remembering how often she had been bitterly disappointed," he told a reporter, he "insisted on her remaining at home."[3]

Thomas had also begun to bridle at newspaper coverage that portrayed him as someone in need of charity. In the mid-nineteenth century, men were expected to be independent, strong patriarchs who shielded their wives and children from the rough-and-tumble world. Although Mollie's kidnapping had led Thomas to accept help from wealthy matrons, black police officers, upperclass businessmen, the Sisters of Charity, and a "carpetbagger" governor eight years his junior, Thomas refused to be viewed as a piteous or dependent person. He told reporters that during his family's ordeal "he never received one cent of money from man, woman, or child." Although he offered his sincere thanks to the "kind ladies whose sympathies made their dark hour lighter," to the Western Union Company for allowing him to send free telegraph messages, and to the Jackson Railroad for free trips "whenever he started on any scent of his child," he wanted it known that the kindness he received "had never taken...a pecuniary shape."[4]

Despite newspaper accounts noting that the Digbys "[did] not move in the higher circles of society," Thomas had good reason to be proud of the life he and Bridgette had built in New Orleans. Although the wealthy might view the Digbys as poor because they lived in the working-class back of town, Thomas owned his own house, his cab, and a team of horses. He had posted a $500 reward for the return of his daughter. Despite the daunting challenges Irish immigrants to Louisiana faced, he had achieved financial autonomy. Eighteen years earlier he had fled Ireland, leaving behind a country where most Catholics lived on rented plots in thatch-roofed mud huts with dirt floors and more than one million people had starved to death after fungus turned the potato crops to black slime. In late fall 1851, he had sailed to Liverpool and there purchased passage on the *Loodianah*, a cargo ship that carried cotton from the American South to English textile mills and then filled its empty hull with steerage passengers for the return trip. After eight weeks and 5,000 miles at sea in crowded, lice-infested quarters, eighteen-year-old Thomas had disembarked in New Orleans, a rough, dangerous city where anti-immigrant gangs roamed the streets and the best jobs were held by the native-born.[5]

In New Orleans, Thomas entered a labor market where the Irish took the dirty jobs natives did not want or those considered too dangerous to be performed by costly slaves. His countrymen dug latrines, drained fields and swamps, stoked steamboat boilers, manned screw-jack gangs, and cleaned slop and offal from the streets. Almost 20,000 Irishmen died from accidents and yellow fever while digging the city's New Basin Canal. A lucky few found work as policemen, then a low-skill job that required little education. But when the anti-immigrant Know-Nothing Party took control of City Hall in the 1850s, they fired most of the Irish officers. Irishwomen, for their part, competed with free black women for work as domestic servants, chambermaids, bakers, and cooks. Some sold homemade goods in public markets. Others toiled as laundresses and seamstresses. Eventually Irishmen fought their way onto the docks, replacing free black men as longshoremen and stevedores. The Irish then took over the lucrative draying business—driving the carts and wagons that hauled goods from the docks to warehouses and stores. Visitors to the city in the 1850s noted that thousands of Irish drays filled the streets. Irishmen, including Thomas Digby, soon moved into the hack and cab business, carrying passengers around the city for fares and tips. Economic conditions for many of the city's Irish slowly improved. Most still lived in the poor neighborhoods near the docks or back swamps, and hard-drinking, hard-fighting Irish still filled the city's jails, but men like Digby increasingly became part of a "labor aristocracy."

They owned the tools of their trade. Their wives no longer had to work outside the home. They bought houses that had windows, chimneys, wooden floors, and separate living quarters, all of which were luxuries back home. They had tables, chairs, and beds. Most of all, they were fiercely proud of being "tenants no more." Although Thomas Digby appreciated the help and kind deeds his family had received, he wanted it known that he was not a charity case.[6]

On Tuesday morning, August 9, the Digbys were still asleep on what would be one of the hottest days of the summer. At dawn, the humid air had already reached a temperature of 83 degrees. Thomas and Bridgette, having slept fitfully, were in bed as the city came to life outside. Butcher and milk carts rumbled by, lamplighters extinguished gas lights, and newsboys on the corners hawked the morning papers. In the distance, the first factory bells and whistles "summoned workmen to their toils," and the air began to fill with the roar of carts, wagons, and streetcars.[7]

Shortly after 6 a.m., a knock on their front door roused the Digbys from bed. Bridgette dressed first and went to see who was there. Outside on the porch, a stout, well-dressed, elderly white man with grey sideburns greeted her with dramatic news. "Is Mr. Digby in?" the gentleman asked. "I think I have your child." Without offering his name, the man stepped inside and announced that he "had accidentally come into possession of a child the previous night" whom he "had every reason to believe was hers." At first Bridgette was taken aback. But when her visitor, who appeared to be a respectable person, calmly reiterated that he was almost certain he had her child, Bridgette became "greatly elated." The man then asked if she would be willing to come with him to his house in the Fourth District to claim the baby. Before Bridgette could respond, Thomas emerged from the adjoining room in his nightclothes and said, "I will go." Fearing another false alarm, Thomas told Bridgette she should wait at home while he went to see if the child was really Mollie.[8]

Like Bridgette, Thomas was impressed by how certain the man seemed that he had their daughter. Perhaps Mollie really had been found. As he dressed, Thomas reminded the visitor that if the baby was indeed Mollie, the visitor was "a very lucky man," because "the person who returns his child will get $3000 or $4000, probably $5000, more, indeed, than was advertised in the papers." The gentleman replied, "I didn't come here to see about rewards, but to restore the child. The reward is an after consideration." He added that he would tell Thomas how "he came by the child" at the proper time. Digby responded, "I don't want to know anything about it." Digby's advertisement had said no questions would be asked, and he intended to honor that pledge.[9]

Although the Digbys did not recognize him, the gentlemen in their house had once been a celebrated figure in New Orleans. He was James Madison Broadwell, who before the Civil War had captained some of the city's most famous Mississippi River steamboats. Broadwell had been a man of some renown in a society that revered the captains of the grandest boats and where thousands still gathered on the levees to watch steamboats race (as they had in July 1870 when the *Robert E. Lee* battled the *Natchez*). In his long career he captained the *Amaranth, Atlantic, Eclipse, Southern Belle,* and *Sultana.* He had once made headlines by transporting Mexican War volunteers from Ohio to New Orleans without charge. He was so esteemed that advertisements for painkillers, cholera remedies, and other nostrums featured his endorsements. Of all the ships Broadwell once piloted, he was proudest of his time at the helm of the *Eclipse,* one of the longest, fastest, most luxurious steamboats ever to operate on the Mississippi. Crewed by 120 men, with smokestacks that reached 100 feet, and enormous engines powered by sixteen massive boilers, the *Eclipse* was known as "the boat of the age." Its passengers stayed in plush staterooms, sipped wine from Swiss glassware, and ate sumptuous meals from French china using pearl-handled cutlery. In the boat's ornate saloon, guests danced to quadrille bands under stained glass skylights, gothic arches, and ceilings decorated with frescoes. Most of all, the *Eclipse* was swift. In 1853, it set the record for the fastest run ever from New Orleans to Louisville, completing the 1,455-mile trip in four days, nine hours, and thirty-one minutes. Despite the fact that a collision with another ship had destroyed the fabled boat in 1860, Broadwell referred to himself as "the captain of the *Eclipse*" long into his retirement. As he stood in the Digbys' home on the morning of August 10, however, Captain Broadwell preferred to remain anonymous.[10]

Once Thomas dressed, he and Broadwell set off for the Fourth District accompanied by the Digbys' white bulldog, which Thomas said was "Molly's dog." Taking the Baronne Street and Jackson Avenue streetcars, with the dog in Thomas's lap, the pair rode uptown to where the warehouses and crowded streets of the business district gave way to stately residences with manicured grounds. Broadwell lived on Chestnut Street, between Joseph and St. Andrew, in an affluent neighborhood favored by cotton factors, sugar brokers, commission merchants, attorneys, retirees, and other members of the upper middle class. Although Thomas did not yet know Broadwell's name, the captain's two-story Greek revival house confirmed Digby's impression that he was a man of some wealth. The house may not have been as grand as the massive mansions being built in the nearby Garden District and along St. Charles Avenue, but Thomas thought Broadwell's home "an elegant one."[11]

As they entered the yard, Thomas spotted a white woman on the latticed side gallery "walking up and down... with a child in her arms." It was Broadwell's wife, Evelina, and when she saw her husband arrive with Thomas Digby, she came to them with the child and, extending her arms, offered the toddler to Thomas. The child was crying and had two boils on her face. Thomas recoiled. "Is that my Molly?" he asked in disbelief. Although she had blond hair and blue eyes, Thomas did not recognize her. "Do you not know your child?" Mrs. Broadwell asked. "No," Thomas replied. Finally agreeing to take the child in his arms, Thomas examined her closely but was still unsure the girl was Mollie. Evelina, perplexed that a father would not recognize his nineteen-month-old child after only two months' absence, suggested that he should take the baby to his wife to let her determine if this was indeed their daughter. At first, Thomas declined. "I don't want to take it, for fear it isn't my child," he stammered. But after Evelina insisted, Thomas agreed to take the child to his wife, saying that if it was not Mollie he would return her promptly.[12]

Before Thomas left, Captain Broadwell proposed they show the child to the dog. Thomas had said it was "Molly's dog;" perhaps her pet might recognize her. Thomas agreed the idea was worth a try, but when he knelt down with the girl, "the dog looked around but displayed no unusual emotion or any sort of demonstrations." So Thomas set off for home with the child in the hope that Bridgette might be able to identify her.[13]

Unlike Thomas, Bridgette immediately claimed the child as hers. When Thomas walked through his front door holding the baby, Bridgette ran to him and declared that her beloved daughter had been found. "I would know it anywhere," she exclaimed. "A mother cannot be deceived." Bridgette would later claim that the year-and-a-half-old child also instantly recognized her, crying "Mammy! Mammy!" Outside, where neighbors had gathered, Thomas announced that his daughter had been returned. A cheer went up. Some in the crowd hurried off to tell others the news, and word of Mollie's return spread through the back of town "with the quickness of wind." Within minutes, men, women, and children began flocking to the Digbys' house from all directions. A newspaper reporter who arrived at the scene noted that "the narrow streets were literally crowded with an eager mass of human beings....White and black, young and old, appeared equally delighted." When Bridgette brought the child outside for the crowd to see, "the wildest excitement prevailed." People clapped, shook hands, and embraced. Bridgette stood on the banquette (as Orleanians called the raised sidewalks common in the city), shedding joyful tears and holding "the little one tenderly in her arms...her whole countenance radiant with unspeakable happiness."[14]

At their home on Chestnut Street, James and Evelina Broadwell waited anxiously to learn if the baby was indeed Mollie. At 9 a.m., Captain Broadwell, unable to wait any longer, set out once again for the Digbys' house. When he reached Howard Avenue forty minutes later, he found "a large crowd running in and out" of the Digbys' residence. He asked a man standing on the edge of the throng what had happened, to which the man replied, "The lost child has been restored." Broadwell pushed in further and saw Thomas Digby holding the child, "singing and dancing" and "very jubilant." To his relief, Broadwell also heard a man in the crowd shout at Thomas, "Where did you find Molly?" "Uptown somewhere," Digby responded, "I don't know." Mollie was returned to her parents, and Digby, it seemed, was going to protect Broadwell's anonymity. Satisfied that all was well, Broadwell went downtown to run errands before returning home to tell his wife the good news.[15]

Shortly after Broadwell departed, however, police officers arrived at the Digbys' house. Chief Badger had heard Mollie was home and he was eager to speak with her parents. The officers asked Thomas and Bridgette to accompany them to police headquarters in a carriage that Badger had sent. The Digbys complied, and, with Bridgette cradling Mollie in her arms, they boarded the carriage and headed for Badger's Carondolet Street office as the crowd cheered once more. When they arrived, the police chief, Detective Jourdain, Commissioner William George, another detective named Leonard Malone, and a reporter from the *Picayune* were waiting for them. It quickly became evident that Badger did not intend to honor the pledge Thomas had made in his reward advertisement that "no questions would be asked." After a long, costly investigation that had garnered national publicity, the chief was determined to bring the kidnappers to justice. He insisted that Thomas tell him all he knew about the couple that had returned Mollie.[16]

At Badger's request, Thomas Digby reluctantly recounted the events of that morning, the arrival of the stranger at his door, the trip to Chestnut Street, and the joyous reunion at home. Digby also claimed that in all the excitement he had neglected to ask the stranger his name, despite the fact that the men had spent almost two hours together. All he had needed to know was that his Mollie was back at home, safe and sound. Rather than accuse Digby of lying, Badger insisted that he lead them to the house on Chestnut Street so that the chief could ascertain "particulars from the gentleman and lady, whoever they might be." Faced with a resolute chief of police, Thomas capitulated and agreed to escort Badger and his men to the house he had visited earlier that day. It was early afternoon as the Digbys, Chief Badger, Detectives Jourdain and Malone, and the other assembled men pushed through the crowd that had gathered outside police headquarters and boarded carriages bound for Chestnut Street.[17]

When Badger and his men reached the Broadwells' house, they found no one home. Evelina, worried when her husband did not return promptly, had set out on her own for the Digbys' house and had yet to return. James was also still out. Rather than return to headquarters, Badger announced that they would simply wait on the banquette for someone to arrive. As he, his men, and the Digbys lingered in front of the Broadwells' home, curious neighbors came out to see what was happening. When they realized that Thomas and Bridgette Digby, along with their now-famous daughter Mollie, were waiting there, they quickly spread the word. Soon Chestnut Street was "thronged with ladies, all eager for a view of the much-talked-of infant." Even as the mid-afternoon temperature neared

90 degrees, the crowd grew larger and more animated. Men, women, children, and servants all wanted "to catch a peep at the 'lost child'" who lay asleep in her "mother's arms, quite overcome by the heat and bustle."[18]

When Evelina Broadwell returned home an hour later, she was startled to find a large crowd of neighbors, strangers, and policemen gathered outside her house. On her trip to the Digbys', she had gleaned from neighborhood boys that Bridgette Digby had identified the infant as her own and that the jubilant parents had gone out "to give the child a ride." She did not realize that the "ride" had been to police headquarters to meet with Chief Badger or that the police would be waiting for her when she returned home. She asked a bystander "what was the matter, and was told that it was the lost child, which had been found." When she then unlocked her front gate, Chief Badger, his men, and Thomas Digby followed her into the yard. Evelina turned and asked Thomas Digby calmly, "Are you the father of the child?" Thomas said yes, his wife had instantly recognized Mollie. "I am so glad you have your baby," Evelina replied. Badger asked Evelina if she and her husband were the ones had who returned the child. She acknowledged that they were. Well, Badger said, "we want to investigate the matter."[19]

Evelina invited the men into the house. Bridgette Digby remained outside with Mollie and the growing crowd. Once inside, Badger's demeanor became stern. He insisted that Evelina divulge everything she knew "about the matter." Evelina refused, saying they should wait for her husband to return. Badger replied that they could not, and would not, wait. When Evelina mentioned that Digby's reward advertisement had said "no questions would be asked," Badger growled "that a crime has been committed against the State, and that Mr. Digby can only speak for himself and could not possibly interfere with the course of justice." "You must tell," Badger threatened; "if you don't tell you have to stand the consequences." Would she "prefer appearing before a court?"[20]

Badger's browbeating worked. Rather than waiting for James to return, Evelina told Badger and the other men in the room how Mollie had come into their possession the previous day (August 8). Late in the afternoon, she said, the son of a black woman whom they had known for many years had come to their door. He asked that the Broadwells come immediately to his mother's house, for she had something urgent to tell them. Evelina asked the boy if his mother had fallen ill. He replied that she had not, but that the matter was very important. The Broadwells agreed to go and sent the boy home to tell his mother that "they would be up" as soon as James, who had been cutting trees in the yard, washed up and put on fresh clothes. Around 7 p.m., the Broadwells had made their way by streetcar to the home of their friend, the boy's mother, who lived in the Sixth District in the uptown neighborhood that had until recently been called Jefferson City.

When they reached their friend's house, Evelina continued, they learned that she had in her care a white child who had been left at her gate "some days before" by a veiled white woman she did not know. Their friend suspected the baby might be Mollie Digby, and she asked the Broadwells what they thought she should do. She was afraid that she might be accused of kidnapping the child. Evelina examined the girl but was not convinced it was Mollie. The child did have blond hair and blue eyes, but she seemed to be a bit younger than Mollie, who would by then have been nineteen months old. Published descriptions of Mollie had also said that she had a boil on the back of her head that could be used as an identifying mark, but this child instead had two boils on her face. Evelina thought it unlikely it was "the lost child," but said that if it was, their friend should take her to her parents. "It would be a God-send for the father to have the child returned," James had chimed in. But their friend replied that she could not be the one to return the child. "I am colored," she said. "They will say I stole the child if I take it there." Would the Broadwells, she wondered, be willing to take the baby to the Digbys? Evelina was reluctant. She feared that they too "might get into difficulty by taking the child home." James, however, was more amenable. He thought there "was no danger, as the paper said there were no questions to be asked." If the child were indeed Mollie Digby, he argued, they would be doing the family a great service. There was also, of course, the possibility that they could claim the reward. Evelina acquiesced, and that night they brought the child to their Chestnut Street house. There James re-read the description of Mollie in the reward advertisement and "became satisfied that it was the lost child." The baby spent the night with the Broadwells, and at first light James went to the Digbys' house with the news that Mollie might have been found.[21]

Along with Chief Badger, Commissioner George listened intently to Evelina's story. Only two days earlier, George had been in Jefferson City, searching for Mollie at the house at the corner of Bellecastle and Camp. As he listened, he wondered whether Broadwell's "colored" friend might be the same woman he and then Detective Jourdain had interrogated Sunday afternoon. When Evelina finished her story, Badger insisted that Evelina name the woman and reveal where she lived. Evelina replied that she did not want to answer those questions, as she was "confident the woman was innocent of any connection with the affair criminally" and she "would not like to have her brought into trouble." Her friend, Evelina said, "though colored, was perfectly reliable and not capable of stealing a child." Commissioner George interjected, "Is the woman named Ellen and does she live at the corner of Bellecastle and Camp?" Evelina was stunned. "Yes, that is the woman," she sputtered, "but I beg that you will not trouble her, as she knows nothing of the abduction. I have known her a long time, and know her to be above anything of the kind." Ignoring her pleas, Badger abruptly stood up, ended the interrogation, and announced that they would head uptown immediately to the house that George and Jourdain had visited just two days earlier.[22]

As the men exited the Broadwells' yard and passed through the crowd outside, Thomas Digby said something loudly about a "thief." The crowd grew agitated. Evelina heard someone shout "that the house ought to be torn down and the inmates hung." Recognizing that there might be trouble, Badger left two officers behind on Chestnut Street. Evelina Broadwell locked her door, cowered inside, and waited for her husband to return.[23]

POYDRAS MARKET.—Drawn by John Durkin.

Public Market. New Orleans had public markets like this one throughout the city. The kidnappers sent Georgie Digby to the Dryades Street Market to buy bananas. Louisiana Image File, Louisiana Research Collection (hereinafter LaRC), Tulane University.

Citizens of all classes frequented the public markets. Louisiana Image File, LaRC, Tulane University.

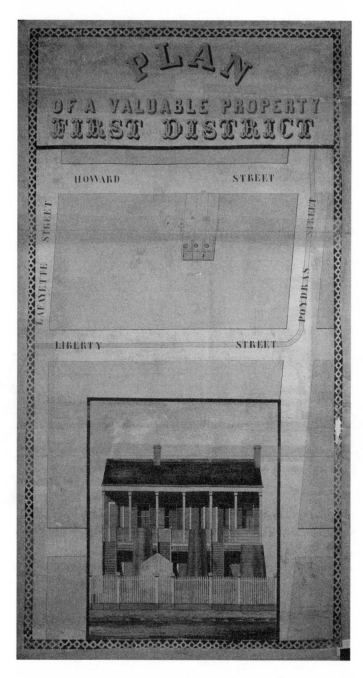

The Digbys' neighbors, the Gormans, occupied this house on Howard Street in 1870. Rosa Gorman was in charge of Mollie and Georgie Digby on the afternoon of the kidnapping. The cylindrical wooden containers in front of the house in the drawing are cisterns used to collect rain water for drinking. Plan Book 87, Folio 21, Courtesy New Orleans Notarial Archives.

The Digbys' Howard Street neighborhood was demolished in the mid-twentieth century. The New Orleans Superdome and surrounding buildings stand on the site. The street on the right in this photo (today's La Salle Street) was the Digbys' block in 1870. Photo: Harold Baquet.

A CREOLE FAMILY AT THE OPERA.

AT THE OPERA. — LOGES GRILLÉES.

THE NEGRO GALLERY.

Creole families at the New Orleans French Opera House. Louisiana Image File, LaRC, Tulane University.

Creoles strolling after a matinee. Louisiana Image File, LaRC, Tulane University.

Depiction of a Voodoo ceremony. E.W. Kemble, "Voodoo Dance" from *Century Illustrated Monthly Magazine*, November 1885 to 1886 (New York: The Century Co.), Vol. XXXI, New Series, Vol. IX, p. 807.

Democratic periodicals regularly printed cartoons mocking the biracial Reconstruction legislatures in the South. This cartoon depicts a debauched Louisiana legislature run by African Americans and poor "scalawag" Southern whites. Louisiana Image File, LaRC, Tulane University.

Governor Henry Clay Warmoth, Governor of Louisiana, 1868–1872. Library of Congress, LC-DIG-cwpbh-03725.

A. S. BADGER,

CHIEF OF POLICE.

Metropolitan Police Chief Algernon Sidney Badger. From Edwin L. Jewell, *Jewell's Crescent City Illustrated* (1874), pg. 33. Library of Congress.

ON THE LEVEE AT NEW ORLEANS.

A black policeman patrolling the levee during Reconstruction. Louisiana Image File, LaRC, Tulane University.

"A blind beggar hears the rustling of her gown, and stretches out his trembling hand for alms."

The woman depicted here is wearing a veil of the type that was fashionable at the time. From Edward King, *The Great South: A Record of Journeys in Louisiana, Texas, The Indian Territory, Missouri, Arkansas, Mississippi, Alabama, Georgia, Florida, South Carolina, North Carolina, Kentucky, Tennessee, Virginia, West Virginia, and Maryland* (Hartford, CT: American Publishing Company, 1875), pg. 19.

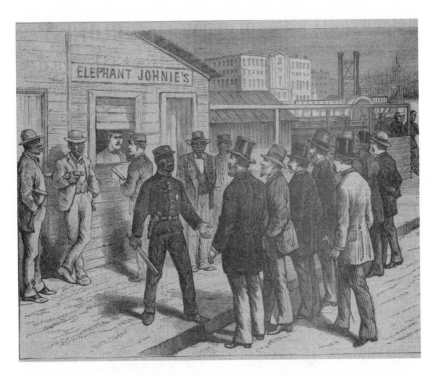

A black police officer addressing a crowd. Louisiana Image File, LaRC, Tulane University.

A midnight race between the steamboats *Eclipse* (right) and *Natchez* in 1854. James Broadwell was captain of the *Eclipse*. Artist, Frances F. Palmer. Printmakers: Currier & Ives.

"The negro nurses stroll on the sidewalks, chattering in quaint French to the little children."

African-American nannies escorting white children were a common sight in New Orleans. From Edward King, *The Great South: A Record of Journeys in Louisiana, Texas, The Indian Territory, Missouri, Arkansas, Mississippi, Alabama, Georgia, Florida, South Carolina, North Carolina, Kentucky, Tennessee, Virginia, West Virginia, and Maryland* (Hartford, CT: American Publishing Company, 1875), pg. 30.

Chapter Five

THE ARREST OF THE ALLEGED ACCESSORIES

One of the men hurrying uptown with Chief of Police Badger was Detective Leonard Malone, the most experienced detective on the force. Until then, Malone's role in the Digby case had been limited; he had helped search homes in the Marais Street neighborhood based on the faulty information provided by the Cincinnati psychic, but that was all. Governor Warmoth and Chief Badger had hoped that Detective Jourdain would get credit for solving the Digby case, but with the crime seemingly close to being solved, Badger brought in a white veteran. Malone was known for his dogged interrogations and uncanny ability to remember names, faces, and the details of crimes. A burly Irishman with a bushy mustache and a lingering brogue, Malone, like the Digbys, had immigrated to New Orleans with the great wave of "famine Irish" in 1846 and had served on the police force ever since. His twenty-four years of police work were remarkable at a time when mayors regularly purged the police ranks to make room for their political supporters. One police chief after another had kept Malone on duty because of his reputation as a master investigator and his encyclopedic knowledge of the career criminals who populated the city's saloons, coffeehouses, bordellos, and back alleys. New officers, unfamiliar with the complexities of the New Orleans underworld, found Malone's guidance indispensable. He had even kept his job in the 1850s when "Know-Nothing" Mayor John T. Monroe fired most immigrant officers and in 1865 when Monroe returned to power and once again purged the Irish.[1]

Malone regarded police work as "a calling." During the Civil War, he put politics and sectional interests aside and served under both the Confederate and Union regimes. He so impressed Union General Benjamin Butler that Butler made him a precinct chief despite his previous affiliation with the Confederate administration. Known for being scrupulously honest and conscientious, Malone refused to take bribes or plant evidence. Over the years, he collared a rogues' gallery of infamous bank robbers, con men, jewel thieves, and murderers, including the notorious Creole burglars Pierre Bertin and Jean Capdeville. It was said that Malone "never relaxed his search for a criminal once he was put on his tail." With the Digby investigation reaching a crescendo, Badger hoped Malone could help close what had been a long and frustrating case.[2]

When Chief Badger and his men reached the house at Bellecastle and Camp, they moved forcefully. Ellen Follin was home when they arrived, and although she feigned surprise that the chief of police was at her door, she certainly must have known why he was there. Detectives Jourdain and J. J. Pierson and Commissioner George had been at her house on Sunday, looking for the very child she had given to the Broadwells on Monday evening. Now the detectives fanned out through her house, rounding up everyone inside and then separating them for questioning. Detective Jourdain and Chief Badger interrogated Ellen Follin in one room, while Detective Malone questioned Follin's son, George Blass, her other children, her elderly mother, and the pregnant white woman—Minnie Green—in another.

Detective Jourdain was fuming because he believed Follin had lied to him two days earlier. "Why the devil," he now asked her, "did you not tell me Sunday night that you had the child?" "You asked me for a stolen child," Follin objected. "I had no stolen child in my possession." "Did you give a child to Captain Broadwell last evening?" Jourdain fired back. "Yes, I did give a child to Captain Broadwell," Follin allowed, explaining that she had not known for certain on Sunday that the toddler was "a stolen child." The little girl, Follin continued, had been at her house for about a week. On the previous Wednesday, August 3, Follin had been standing at her front gate at noontime, waiting for her son to return from Magazine Street with groceries. As she waited, a white woman, "dissipated in appearance" and wearing a veil, walked up with the toddler in her arms. The woman, Follin claimed, "asked me to let her leave the child there until she came back—at the same time pointing in the direction of the grocery." Although the request was odd and the veiled woman spoke in a "hurried and agitated manner," Follin nevertheless agreed to watch the child. But when the woman did not come back, Follin was left wondering what to do. When her son returned, she "directed him to bring the child on the gallery out of the sun." For the past week, Follin had waited for the woman to reappear, growing more apprehensive each day that she did not.[3]

Detective Jourdain, unassuaged, asked Follin, "why didn't you tell us that a strange child was in your house?" Follin made no reply, but the answer must have been evident to all involved. Even if Follin's story were true, by Sunday night she knew as a result of Commissioner George's visit that the child might be Mollie Digby, so she feared that she would be accused of the kidnapping. That was what she told the Broadwells on Monday when she insisted that they be the ones to return Mollie to her parents. If Follin's story of the "veiled woman" was untrue, then it was likely that she was either the abductor or an accomplice to the crime.[4]

While Jourdain and Badger questioned Follin, Detective Malone gleaned incriminating information from Follin's son, George Blass. Malone questioned the young man about his role in the events of Sunday evening when he had initially met Detectives Jourdain and Pierson at the front gate but then mysteriously disappeared. His mother had claimed at the time that "he had gone out." Blass confessed that he had not left but instead had hidden with Mollie in his arms behind the large cistern in the backyard. He explained that because the child had been "cross and crying," he had taken her out back and, when he heard the detectives shouting inside, he hid with her so that she would not be frightened. When the detectives had searched the house and the Follins' small cornfield, they had failed to look behind the cistern. Blass had waited until they were gone to reemerge.[5]

Blass also told Malone that Mollie had been at the house for nearly three weeks, rather than one week as Ellen Follin had claimed. Other residents of the house initially contradicted Follin's account as well. Mary, Follin's aged mother, reportedly told Malone the child had been there for a month. When Malone and Chief Badger questioned Minnie Green, the pregnant white woman living with the Follins, she indicated that the child was already there when she arrived at the house on July 22. Green said that throughout her stay she had heard "the newspaper accounts of the 'lost child' read in the house...but it never occurred to her that the little girl in the house was the child in question."[6]

Malone was also able to ferret out why Minnie Green, a white woman from a wealthy Alabama family, was living with a black family in New Orleans. Elite white women in the South normally limited their interaction with black men and women to working relationships. Although they might have cordial relations with black seamstresses, cooks, or domestics, respectable white women did not visit, socialize, sit together in public, or eat together in private with black women who were not their employees. Minnie Green, Malone learned, was living with the Follins because of her pregnancy. Follin, it appeared, operated what was known as a "lying-in hospital"—a place where women from society families who became pregnant out of wedlock could go during their pregnancies "to conceal their shame." Green told Detective Malone her family owned a plantation on the Alabama River, about eighty miles above Mobile. She was married, but her husband "[had] not been with her for more than a year." Given that Green was "largely *enceinte*" and "very near her accouchement" (as the newspapers termed her pregnancy), it was clear Green's husband was not the father.[7]

Although Green might normally have been unwilling to board with a black family, the stigma of carrying a bastard child at home in Alabama was greater. It was a time, after all, when even using the word "pregnant" was considered salacious, and many happily married women stayed indoors during their "confinement" rather than display the changes in their figures. Adulterous women, or those pregnant out of wedlock, violated even greater taboos. Follin's New Orleans home, tucked away in a sleepy neighborhood, was far enough from Alabama that no one would learn of Green's predicament. Although Follin was black, her house had the material trappings of respectability. Follin's residence, the newspapers noted, was "handsomely furnished" with fine armoires, rosewood tables, china, and other appointments that indicated that the owner "does not want for money."[8]

For Ellen Follin, running a lying-in hospital (a "House of Secret Obstetrics," one newspaper called it) was a resourceful, if risky, occupation. Employment opportunities for black women in Reconstruction New Orleans remained limited, even for the most educated and refined individuals. While African American men could serve as policemen, legislators, militiamen, and government clerks, most black women still labored as laundresses, housekeepers, cooks, maids, street vendors, or nannies. Others went door to door selling fruits, pies, fabrics, and dry goods. For many Creoles of color like Follin, who saw themselves as a separate class from former slaves and common workers, those jobs would not do. As thousands of former slaves moved into New Orleans, Afro-Creoles clung ever more tightly to the Catholic liturgical traditions, skilled trades, and other social practices that had historically distinguished them from other African Americans. Creole women who viewed domesticity as a marker of feminine virtue and privileged social status considered jobs that entailed working outside the home and under close white supervision (such as laboring as a cook, maid, or laundress) to be demeaning.[9]

Few Creole women, however, could afford to stay home without earning income. This was particularly true for women like Ellen Follin, a thirty-nine-year-old widow with three children. She was not poor by any means; she owned her well-appointed house and five undeveloped lots in her neighborhood. But she also needed a reliable livelihood. Some Afro-Creole women found work outside the home as teachers, music instructors, hairdressers, or other favored occupations. Many more managed to work from home as skilled seamstresses. A few had the capital necessary to establish boardinghouses. Before the war, boardinghouses run by free women of color were known for clean rooms, immaculate sheets, hot coffee, fresh water, and sweet-smelling towels. After her husband died in 1867, Follin created her own economic niche. Perhaps lacking the capital or desire to open a full-scale boardinghouse, Follin instead began renting one or two rooms in her home to wealthy white Gulf Coast women in difficult circumstances. By operating a lying-in hospital, she could use her refined demeanor and discerning taste for economic gain. Her elegant home provided a comfortable—if not entirely respectable—environment for a unique clientele. In a world where her race, gender, and cultural preferences constrained her economic possibilities, Follin found a vocation that allowed her to retain the status that accompanied domesticity.[10]

Her operation did entail significant risk. If the details of her covert hospital became public, her cherished veneer of respectability would be torn away. She might even be subject to criminal charges. Though not explicitly illegal, Follin's activities fell into a legal grey area. Under Louisiana law, if a woman had a baby and tried "either by herself, or [with] the aid and assistance of others," to conceal the birth, the mother "together with all…such persons" aiding and assisting her faced, if convicted, between five and fourteen years in jail. Although usually reserved for cases of alleged infanticide, the concealment law threatened to entangle Follin if any of her clients found themselves accused of that crime. Proving Follin's complicity in a scheme to conceal a birth would be difficult, of course. However unlikely it seemed, she could claim that Minnie Green and the other women who had stayed at her home were simply boarders. Or Follin might be serving as a midwife, even though by the mid-nineteenth century wealthy women usually relied on male doctors who came to their bedsides with medical instruments.[11]

Follin's *modus operandi* became clearer still when Minnie Green disclosed to Detective Malone that Follin had a younger sister named Louisa Follin Murray who conducted a similar business in Mobile. When women from New Orleans needed the privacy of a lying-in hospital, Follin would escort them to her sister's house in Mobile, and when women from Alabama found themselves in a similar situation, Murray would guide them to Follin's house. The sisters could not advertise, of course. Pregnant women would have learned of Follin and Murray in hushed, closed-door conversations. But grapevine knowledge of their services must have been widespread, since Green's family's plantation was hours north of Murray's house in Mobile. Green had spent a month at Murray's abode before Murray escorted her to New Orleans in order for Green, a reporter for the *Bee* surmised, "to be more secure against discovery, and to get rid of proof of her indiscretion remote from her friends and acquaintances."[12]

The facts Minnie Green divulged to Malone turned Ellen Follin's sister, Louisa Murray, into the main suspect in the Digby case. Murray, like Follin, was a beautiful and cultured Creole of color, but she was also at least ten years younger than her sister. Rosa Gorman, the young woman who was watching the Digby children on the afternoon of the abduction, had described the kidnapper as an attractive, fashionable mulatto woman "about twenty five years of age." Follin, who might otherwise have been the primary suspect, was thirty-nine.[13] Green also told Malone that when she had first arrived at Louisa Murray's house in Mobile on June 15, Murray had just returned from a week-long trip to New Orleans. If that was true, it placed Murray in New Orleans on June 9, the day the kidnapping occurred. Green also said that when she and Murray arrived at Ellen Follin's house on July 22, the white baby was already there and Murray appeared to know the child. She called her "Camellia." "Being a stranger," Green added, she had "asked no questions."[14]

Suspicions about Louisa Murray increased when Chief Badger spotted an envelope hidden in a bundle of clothes in Follin's bedroom. Before Badger could seize it, Follin grabbed the envelope and refused to let him see it until Badger "took hold of it and drew it from her hand." The envelope contained money and a cryptic August 7 letter from Murray that mentioned two boats—the *Mary* and the *Frances*—that traveled between Mobile and New Orleans. "The Mary has laid up," the letter read, "so you must send to the Frances the trip after this, and I will send you something." Although Badger could not decipher the letter's meaning, its oblique language reinforced his belief that the sisters were involved in a nefarious scheme. He returned the money to Follin but kept the letter as evidence.[15]

Based on Green's information and the mysterious note, Chief Badger reasoned that Murray "was a party to the abduction and probably the planner of it." He trusted Green's account over Follin's, the press reported, because Green was white and—despite her circumstances—"a woman of culture and refinement" whose "manners and conversation betray[ed] superior intelligence, cultivation of mind, and the habit of mixing in refined society." Accordingly, there was "no reason to doubt the entire truth of what she sa[id] in regard to a matter in which she ha[d] no motive for prevarication."[16]

Badger decided to pursue Murray and meanwhile to charge Ellen Follin and her seventeen-year-old son George Blass as "accessories to the kidnapping of Mr. Digby's daughter." Following procedure, he sent Detective Malone to the Recorder's Court to secure an arrest warrant. While they awaited Malone's return, Badger warned Follin that she was in serious trouble, that everyone in her house told contradictory stories, and that "perhaps they were all equally guilty in concealing the child." He warned that he "[might] to lock up the whole household to get to the bottom of it." But Follin stuck to her story of the veiled woman. When Malone returned an hour later with a warrant in hand, Badger and his men took Follin and her son into custody. In what must have been a humiliating moment for her, curious neighbors looked on as officers loaded the two into a police wagon and carted them off to the Sixth District station.[17]

While the detectives escorted the prisoners to jail, Badger returned to his Carondolet Street headquarters. He found Captain Broadwell waiting for him. Broadwell was fuming. He told Badger that his actions were "unwarrantable and unjustifiable." How dare he interrogate and threaten his wife? How dare he bring "a mob" to his street and intrude upon "a lady alone in the house?" Badger had acted dishonorably. The reward advertisements had said no questions would be asked. Had he been present, Broadwell declared, things would have been different. And, he continued, the arrest of Ellen Follin was "an outrage." Follin was "entirely innocent," and he "would infinitely prefer taking her place in jail than have her remain there."[18]

The chief tried to calm Broadwell. At a time when men in New Orleans still on occasion resorted to duels to resolve "affairs of honor," Broadwell's charge that Badger had violated his home and threatened his wife could have been a precursor to violence. Badger apologized for the crowd that had formed outside Broadwell's house and for questioning Evelina without her husband present. But, he added, the "circumstances were unavoidable." A crime had been committed against the state, and he was determined to move swiftly to bring the perpetrators to justice. Broadwell was not mollified. He stormed out still "greatly incensed," vowing to hire a lawyer to defend Follin and her son, and cursing Badger for trying "to make capital of the affair."[19]

Next, Broadwell burst into the offices of the New Orleans *Times* to protest an item in that day's afternoon edition. The article announcing the recovery of the Digby baby also hinted that Broadwell might be part of the kidnapping plot. Broadwell told the paper's editor, Edward Hancock, that the piece was "derogatory to his character," and "if it was not corrected in the morning issue, [he] would take means to have it corrected." Unfortunately for Broadwell, the *Times* article would be only the first of many speculating about his connection to Ellen Follin and the abduction of Mollie Digby. The next day the *Bee* and the *Commercial Bulletin* also questioned "the relations that appear to have existed" between Broadwell, his wife, and the accused.[20]

Before returning home, Broadwell took the streetcars back uptown to the Sixth District station to try to have Follin and her son released on bond. There he was told he could not see the prisoners; they were being moved in the morning to the First District precinct house on Lafayette Square, as that was the precinct for the Digbys' neighborhood where the kidnapping occurred. Follin and her son would be arraigned at the First District Recorder's Court the next day. If Broadwell wanted to try to bail them out, he could do so then and there.[21]

With two alleged accomplices in custody and the primary suspect identified, the day's evening papers urged the police and the courts to administer swift justice. "This sort of crime," the *Picayune* declared, "if permitted to pass unwhipped of justice, will be incentive to the wicked, stimulated by the hope of reward....The terrible anguish which the Digby family have felt for months now may be the experience to others to-morrow." "If only little Molly Digby could speak," the *Picayune's* editor concluded melodramatically, "what a story she might tell. What an insight it might give of the effect of evil passions, of the fearful depravity of men's and women's hearts."[22]

Chapter Six

THE WOMAN IN THE SEASIDE HAT

I t had been a long day for Chief Badger. Surrounded for hours by crowds
and reporters, he had been threatened and had issued threats of his own.
But before he could rest, he had to take the steps necessary to apprehend
his prime suspect, Ellen Follin's sister, Louisa Murray. He wanted to move
quickly before word reached Mobile that Follin was in custody. But seizing a
suspect in another state was complicated. The arresting officer would need both
a judge-issued warrant and a formal rendition request written from Governor
Warmoth to the governor of Alabama. It was early evening and time was short
if Badger wanted his officer on the overnight boat to Mobile. He also needed
to decide whom to send on the mission. If Murray had somehow learned she
was now implicated in the Digby kidnapping, she might already have fled or
gone into hiding. There could be some sleuthing to do. Badger decided to send
Detective Jourdain.

Time was of the essence. Chief Badger called Jourdain to his office, and
together they rode to the Baronne Street home of Judge Gardner P. Houghton
to secure a warrant, and then on to Governor Warmoth's house on Coliseum
Square. Both men were home and quickly prepared the required documents.
Warmoth surely must have been pleased that the Digby case seemed close
to being solved. Armed with the warrant and the rendition papers, Jourdain

rushed off to the docks on Lake Pontchartrain to catch the overnight mail boat to Mobile where he intended to arrest Mollie Digby's alleged abductor and bring her back to New Orleans.[1]

Detective Jourdain's mission was another striking example of how Reconstruction had upended the South's legal and political order. For most of the nation's history, African Americans had only been on the wrong end of renditions—pursued as alleged fugitives. During the antebellum period renditions of white and black fugitives regularly became national *causes célèbres* as they intertwined with the roiling debates over slavery. Article 4 of the United States Constitution stipulated that fugitive criminals and runaway slaves who fled from one state to another did not find safety by crossing state lines. Instead, fugitives had to "be delivered up" to state officials or the slave catchers who came to apprehend them. But because the Constitution did not define what "delivered up" meant (who would be required to do the delivering up? Governors? Sheriffs? Federal officers? Private citizens?), a long national debate began. Congress tried to resolve this ambiguity by passing an "An Act respecting Fugitives from Justice, and persons escaping from the Service of their Masters." Known to most Americans as the "Fugitive Slave Act of 1793," the law required slave owners and slave catchers who captured alleged fugitive slaves to bring their captives before a local magistrate or federal judge before returning home. The judge would determine if the alleged runaway was indeed a former slave rather than a free person of color abducted by mistake. In cases involving fugitive criminals rather than slaves, the act obligated state governors to participate in the "delivering up." When a governor received a written rendition request from a fellow governor, along with a warrant, indictment, or affidavit charging a fugitive with a crime, he was required to order the arrest and return of the accused even if he doubted the charges were true or just.[2]

Rendition cases fueled sectional animosities. Many Northern states obstructed the renditions of fugitive slaves by passing personal liberty laws requiring trial by jury and other protections for the alleged runaway slaves and by prohibiting their states' officials from aiding slave catchers. When Congress passed a new Fugitive Slave Act in 1850 that increased the role of federal marshals and magistrates in the process, it only created more friction. Abolitionist mobs attacked federal officers enforcing the law, and state judges countermanded federal slave commissioners' decrees. Northern governors enraged the South with their delaying tactics. Iowa's Samuel Kirkwood famously obstructed the rendition to Virginia of Barclay Coppock, one of John Brown's raiders who had avoided capture at Harper's Ferry and fled to his home state. When Virginia's governor sent Kirkwood a rendition request, he delayed acting on it long enough for abolitionists to secrete Coppock out of the state and on to Canada. Southern governors could also be obstructionist, refusing rendition of slave catchers accused of kidnapping free black people from the North. Few on either side of these debates could have imagined that in the not-too-distant future a Louisiana governor would send a black detective on a rendition mission to a neighboring Deep South state. The irony could not have been lost on Jourdain as he headed to Mobile bearing rendition documents addressed to Alabama's chief executive.[3]

As the mail boat steamed across the warm waters of Lake Pontchartrain and out into the Gulf of Mexico, Detective Jourdain devised "a little plan." Although he knew that Alabama Governor William Hugh Smith, a centrist Republican who shared Warmoth's political views, would cooperate fully, he worried the process might take several days. The governor was in Montgomery, over 150 miles from Murray's home in Mobile. Jourdain decided that upon his arrival the next morning he would find Murray first and worry about the paperwork later. Doing so would allow him to put his detective skills to use. He hoped to use deception to trick his suspect into saying something incriminating, and only then seek formal approval from Governor Smith for her extradition.[4]

Jourdain decided to go to Murray's house dressed as a gentleman rather than in his blue-flannel police uniform. Earlier in the investigation, Jourdain and Detective Noble had had some success disguising themselves as workmen in order to glean information from black citizens who might not talk to the police. Now, dressed in a fine suit, he would tell Murray he was a friend of Ellen Follin's and that Ellen had sent him to Mobile to alert Murray that she was in trouble as a result of the Digby child. This deception might lead Murray to implicate herself. She might even admit to having taken Mollie to Follin's house (and in the process discredit Ellen's and George's story of the veiled woman).

Jourdain's plan to pose as Follin's gentleman friend was a ruse for which he was perfectly suited. Follin and Murray were, like Jourdain, educated Afro-Creoles. He possessed the refined manners and light skin that Murray would expect of a member of their class and a friend of her sister's.[5]

Although small in number, Murray and other Afro-Creoles in Mobile shared a common culture with their New Orleans counterparts. The city of Mobile, like New Orleans, had a French and Spanish heritage, and in both places a class of educated, mixed-raced, French-speaking Creoles emerged. As in Louisiana, Alabama's antebellum government had granted free Creoles of color rights that most black people did not enjoy. They could own property, travel freely at night, and testify in court. Although Alabama law made it unlawful to educate slaves, the state allowed black Creoles to attend private schools, including schools created especially for them by the Catholic Diocese. As in New Orleans, Mobile's Afro-Creoles formed their own benevolent societies and lodges. They had their own fire company. Some owned slaves, and some also attempted, unsuccessfully, to volunteer to fight for the Confederacy. After the war, many of Mobile's black political leaders came from this elite group.[6]

Ellen Follin and Louisa Follin Murray were members of this class. The sisters were probably descendants of Auguste Firmin Follin, a white French refugee from Saint Domingue who, along with thousands of other émigrés, fled the Haitian Revolution and settled in the American South in the early nineteenth century. Born in Alabama in 1831 and 1842, respectively, Follin and Murray grew up there as free women, received formal educations, and learned genteel manners and taste. In 1856, Follin moved to New Orleans with her mother. Louisa remained in Mobile and eventually took the surname Murray, perhaps from the man who fathered her daughter, Emmetta (although by the time of the Digby case no man lived in her household). Both women were property holders. Follin owned the house at Bellecastle and Camp Streets as well as other land in New Orleans. Louisa owned a large house in Mobile on Sengstak Street, in a neighborhood where many Afro-Creoles resided. The sisters clung to the traditions of their class, customs that had protected Creoles of color from some of the worst effects of slavery and racism both before and after the war.[7]

Detective Jourdain planned to use the traditions of the Afro-Creole community against Murray. Jourdain believed that because he too was a Creole, he could gain Louisa's trust and entrap her. When his boat arrived in Mobile at dawn on the morning of August 11, he went first to the office of William Turner, Mobile's chief of police, and asked for help detaining "a quadroon" woman named Murray who was a suspect in the abduction of Mollie Digby. Chief Turner, a Republican and a Union Army veteran, had worked briefly in New Orleans after the war as a law partner of Governor Warmoth. Eager to help, he ordered one of his officers to escort Jourdain to Murray's neighborhood and then stay out of sight while Jourdain attempted his deception. Jourdain and the officer rode to Murray's house at the southeast corner of Chestnut and Sengstak Streets, where Jourdain put his plan into action.[8]

When Louisa Murray answered her door, Detective Jourdain, dressed in his civilian finery, told her his tale—that he had been sent by her sister Ellen with troubling news from New Orleans. Murray, tall and elegant, gave him a concerned and quizzical look. By her response, Jourdain could tell she had not yet learned of her sister's arrest. The trap was set. Jourdain told her that Ellen was in trouble because of the child Murray had left with her. "That I left with her?" Murray responded incredulously. "I do not understand you." "Your sister says you left a white child at her house last week," Jourdain lied. "Oh no, sir. I was at my sister's house several weeks ago when a veiled woman came to the gate and asked permission to leave a child for a short time." Still purporting to be a friend of her sister's, Jourdain pressed Murray on this point. He was confused. "You were present then when the child was left at your sister's?" "Yes, it was only a short time before I left," she replied. "You never saw it before?" he added. "Never," she responded. That was curious, he said, because Minnie Green, the young lady Murray had escorted to her sister's from Mobile, said the child was there when they arrived and that Murray "seemed to know it well enough to call it Camellia." "I called it Camellia because it was white [like the blossoms], and I knew no other name," Murray countered. "I am very fond of children and always address them by pet names." "But your little niece, Ellen's daughter, says you brought the child to her mother's," Jourdain rejoined. For a moment Murray flinched. Jourdain saw a "transient flash" of fear in her eyes. But then, in an instant, she regained her composure. "The child is mistaken," she said.[9] By that point, Murray must have suspected that Jourdain was a foe rather than a friend. Like New Orleans, Mobile had also integrated its police force during Reconstruction, and the new black appointees included a number of Creoles of color. Murray may have surmised that Jourdain was actually an officer of the law. Rather than panic or become defensive, however, she calmly parried his questions with the skills, he remembered later, of a "sharp and active business-woman."[10] Realizing that his deception had exhausted its usefulness, Jourdain informed Murray he was not a friend of her sister's, but a police detective with a warrant for her arrest. Murray seemed unfazed by this revelation. She displayed, Jourdain later reflected, "no surprise or agitation." When he asked if she would peacefully go to New Orleans with him, Murray replied calmly, "I will go wherever you wish," adding that had she known her sister was in trouble she would have gone to New Orleans earlier. Murray's stoicism impressed Jourdain. Though he suspected Murray and her sister were lying about how Mollie Digby came to Follin's house, her demeanor convinced him that she was someone he could trust to voluntarily accompany him back to New Orleans without his having to use force.[11]

When he took Louisa Murray to Chief Turner's office, Jourdain "did not request him to lock her up." He told Turner that although he had rendition papers from Governor Warmoth, he did not believe he needed them because "she had made no objection to going with me to New Orleans." Turner remarked that normally he would have to submit the request to Governor Smith in Montgomery, a process that could take time, but if Murray agreed to go willingly, he would have no objection to Jourdain's taking her to New Orleans that evening. Turner asked Murray directly if she was willing to forgo the formal rendition process, to which she replied, "Certainly, sir: I have already told the gentlemen so." She did not, she said, want to "interpose any delay." All she asked was that she be allowed to go home "to pack her trunk." Jourdain and Turner agreed. Jourdain telegraphed Chief Badger that he had Murray in custody and would return on the next boat, and then he accompanied Murray back to her house. "She came with me willingly, and gave me no trouble," Jourdain said later. "She inspired me with confidence and I put no restraint on her. While we remained in Mobile she came and went as she pleased." His confidence was not misplaced. When she finished packing, Murray, wearing a fine white dress, accompanied Jourdain on the overnight packet to New Orleans. In the morning, Chief Badger, Detective Malone, and a crowd of reporters and onlookers would be waiting when Jourdain and his prisoner arrived.[12]

On August 10, while Jourdain was in Mobile apprehending Louisa Murray, New Orleans residents awoke to morning papers filled with accounts of the interrogation and arrest of Ellen Follin. Reconstruction-era editors recognized that sensational crime stories sold papers, and the Digby case seemed to get better by the hour. Reporters from all five major New Orleans newspapers combed the city looking for new facts and revelations. One resourceful reporter from the *Picayune* even gained access to Follin and her son George Blass in their cells in the Seventh Precinct house, where the alleged kidnappers had been moved the previous evening. Despite the fact that prisoner interviews violated police protocol, the reporter, perhaps through bribery, convinced Ellen's and George's guards to let him speak with the pair.[13]

An attorney would almost certainly have advised the prisoners not to talk to the press. But neither Ellen or George had met with a lawyer, even though under Louisiana law anyone accused of a crime punishable at hard labor had the right to counsel. Both agreed to the interview despite the fact that the *Picayune*, like other Democratic papers, was no friend of New Orleans's black citizens. The paper's editors opposed Radical Reconstruction and black civil rights, and had portrayed the abduction of Mollie Digby as a sign of growing racial chaos. The reporter already knew from other sources that Ellen and George had told conflicting stories about when Mollie Digby arrived at their house at Bellecastle and Camp Streets, and he hoped to trip them up once again.[14]

The reporter quickly found, however, that Ellen Follin would not be easy to manipulate. She was, he acknowledged, an impressive woman, an Afro-Creole who possessed the manners, taste, and intelligence that had long earned her class the grudging respect of elite white New Orleanians. "Mrs. Follin," he wrote of their meeting, "was very neatly, indeed quite elegantly attired, and gave evidence of possessing a very bright mind." She was "cautious and reserved and apparently frank" as she calmly maintained her innocence, recounting her story about the veiled woman leaving the baby on August 3. Her son George, who struck the reporter as "a bright, intelligent lad," now offered the same story as his mother. George, the reporter noted, had previously told Detective Malone "that the child had been in the house more than three weeks." This change in George's account was, the reporter commented, "to say the least quite suspicious."[15]

The reporter also outdid his journalistic rivals by traveling uptown to interview Follin's other two children and her aged mother, and the pregnant boarder Minnie Green. "Leaving the prisoners," he wrote, "[I] went up to the house of Ellen Follin, corner of Camp and Bellecastle streets, and proceeded to interrogate the inmates." No one had advised anyone in the house that speaking with the press might be a mistake. Minnie Green told the reporter what she had told Detective Malone, that she had come to New Orleans with Louisa Murray on July 22 "and found the little child in question there then." Murray, she reported, had called the child both Camellia and Charley "in a tone and manner which indicated she knew all about her." Follin's fourteen-year-old son, Thomas, offered that "the child had been there some time, but couldn't say how long." Her eight-year-old daughter, Mary, told the reporter she "[missed] Charley, and wants her to play with." And Follin's mother claimed that the child had been there "at least three weeks," but "she asked no questions as there were frequently children about the house, and it was none of her business." Noting that some of these statements contradicted Follin's claim that the Digby baby had been at her house for only a week, the reporter concluded that the evidence pointed to Follin's guilt and to the guilt of whoever "instigated her to the commission of an act." "It only remains for the police to work up the case," he wrote.[16]

The next morning, August 10, Follin learned that Captain Broadwell was a man of his word—he had hired one of the city's most acclaimed citizens as counsel for her and her son. When they were brought to the Recorder's Court for arraignment, Theodore Gallier Hunt was there to represent them. Hunt, a tall, dapper, sixty-five-year-old man with wavy grey hair and thick sideburns, was a lion of the New Orleans bar known for his courtroom bravado and ornate speeches. Prideful, even pompous at times, Hunt had a résumé to match his ego. Over his long career, he had served as the New Orleans District

Attorney, a criminal court judge, a U.S. congressman, and an officer in the U.S. army during the Mexican War and the Confederate army during the rebellion.[17]

Some readers outside New Orleans who were following the Digby story might have been surprised to find an ex-Confederate of Hunt's stature defending an Afro-Creole woman in a racially charged case, but others would have remembered him from his prewar days in Congress when he was a moderate Southern voice amidst the secessionist din. Born in South Carolina, Hunt was an antebellum unionist. He and his three brothers moved to New Orleans in 1833 after John C. Calhoun and the states' rights "nullifiers" took control of South Carolina's politics. In Louisiana in the 1840s and 1850s, Hunt defended slavery but denounced Southern ideologues who advocated secession. As a congressman in 1854, he gave a famous speech on the House floor during the tumultuous debates over the Kansas-Nebraska Act in which he opposed repealing the Missouri Compromise. As he was one of the few Southerners to speak against the repeal, Hunt's speech "electrified" the audience. Like many New Orleans businessmen, Hunt feared that secessionist firebrands underestimated the damage disunion would do to the South's economy. During the election of 1860, Hunt backed John Bell, the presidential candidate of the Constitutional Union Party who sought compromise between the North and South. It was only after Fort Sumter, when the fighting began in 1861, that Hunt supported the Confederacy rather than oppose his friends, family, business associates, and adopted home state. Despite being fifty-six years old, he joined the Confederate army.[18]

During the war, Hunt fought as a colonel under Robert E. Lee in the bloody Peninsula campaign. His combat career was relatively brief, however, because of his knack for irritating his superiors, who allowed him to resign after serving only fifteen months. Confederate General Lafayette McLaws described Hunt as "an old gentleman of independent manner and an open talker" who had "a considerable opinion of his influence and of his ability both as a soldier and a member of society." In 1864, Henry Allen, the Confederate governor of Louisiana, appointed Hunt adjutant general, an administrative post he held until the end of the war. After Appomattox, Hunt swore renewed allegiance to the Union, received a pardon from President Andrew Johnson, and resumed his legal career in New Orleans.[19]

Readers who remembered Hunt's unionism may have seen his participation in the Digby case as a sign that white Southern moderates were willing to
accept Louisiana's new legal order. The state's 1868 constitution guaranteed all
citizens, white and black alike, the right to counsel, and Hunt's representation
of Follin and her son demonstrated that black citizens could now obtain the
best defense they or their friends could afford. Having a former Confederate
general and proponent of slavery represent two black defendants accused of
being accomplices to a notorious kidnapping lent legitimacy to a new system
that promised due process for all.

Governor Warmoth would have viewed Hunt's participation less optimis-
tically. While Hunt had opposed secession and pledged renewed loyalty to the
Union soon after Appomattox, he was also a fierce critic of Radical Reconstruction. Hunt had hoped that the state governments that President Johnson
organized in the summer of 1865—the governments that enacted the Black
Codes—would survive. Hunt's brother Randell had been elected to the U.S.
Senate by Louisiana's postwar legislature, but congressional Republicans who
viewed Johnson's governments as illegitimate refused to let him take his seat.
When Congress replaced the Black Codes legislatures—first with military rule,
then with Warmoth and the "carpetbaggers"—Hunt and his brothers fought
back, joining the litigation that obstructed Warmoth's economic development
campaign. As Warmoth sought to use the Digby case to prove that his police
force and district attorneys could solve and successfully prosecute crimes committed by blacks against whites, Hunt once again stood in the way.[20]

To Ellen Follin, Hunt would have been a familiar and comforting face. Although the newspapers did not report it, Hunt had previously provided Follin
with legal services. He had long been Captain Broadwell's family attorney, and
in an 1867 inheritance matter Broadwell had Hunt appointed as attorney for
Follin and her children. And although the press played up the significance of
Hunt's defending Follin, his role was to some extent unremarkable. Before the
war, white lawyers regularly provided legal services for Afro-Creole businessmen and their families. They drew up wills and contracts, litigated commercial
disputes, and even defended them against criminal charges. Many Afro-Creoles
had the means to pay lawyers' fees, while in other instances elite whites with

whom Afro-Creoles shared commercial, social, and kinship ties picked up the tab. It was only Reconstruction's heated atmosphere that gave Hunt's efforts on behalf of Follin larger political significance.[21]

In the Recorder's Court, Hunt entered a plea of "not guilty" for his clients after Judge Houghton read the charges against them. The Louisiana criminal code, Houghton reminded the accused, made it a crime to "forcibly seize and carry" a person from "one part of this state to another" or to "imprison or secrete any person without authority of law." A kidnapping conviction could mean five years at hard labor in the state penitentiary, a penalty that applied equally to the kidnapper and to "all persons aiding, advising, or abetting" the kidnapper.[22]

When Hunt asked that the prisoners be freed on bail, Judge Houghton seemed reluctant. Houghton regarded "the offense imputed to the prisoners as a very grave one." But Hunt knew that Louisiana's constitution guaranteed the right to bail except in capital cases, and the state had not charged Follin or her son with a capital offense. No matter how grave Houghton thought their alleged crime, Hunt insisted, the judge had to allow them bail. Houghton conceded, but added that he "thought it his duty to weigh all the circumstances well before fixing the amount of bail." Hunt knew what was coming. Houghton, in a courtroom full of reporters, was going to grandstand by setting the bail high. Hunt, armed with the knowledge that Louisiana's bill of rights, like the federal Bill of Rights, prohibited "excessive" bail, warned Houghton that he would immediately appeal an unfavorable decision. Any effort to set exorbitant bail, Hunt admonished the judge, would "only cause delay and vexation." Houghton adjourned the court until the afternoon, saying he would announce his decision then.[23]

The legal sparring between Hunt and Judge Houghton highlighted the ironies surrounding the case. Forty-five-year-old Houghton, a Warmoth appointee, had moved to New Orleans from Massachusetts on the eve of the Civil War. Although Houghton and Hunt had both been unionists, Houghton had resisted the post-secession social pressure to join the Confederate army. New Orleans fell into Union hands in April 1862, just before the Confederacy began forcibly conscripting men like Houghton into the Southern ranks. Houghton's refusal to enlist did not reflect a fear of fighting; he wanted to fight on the right side. In the fall of

1863, nine days after Lincoln issued his Preliminary Emancipation Proclamation, Houghton enlisted in the Union army's First Louisiana Cavalry, U.S.A. For the next year and a half, he and the regiment's other pro-Union New Orleanians fought rebels and helped free slaves across the Gulf South. In the Digby case, however, Houghton's role had changed. He was determined to demonstrate that Republican judges would be tough on black citizens accused of crimes. It was Hunt, the venerable ex-Confederate and defender of slavery, who was seeking fair treatment for the two black defendants. For readers who knew nothing of Hunt's previous ties to Broadwell and Follin, it would seem that the politics of Reconstruction had turned the world upside down.[24]

When the court reconvened later that day, Judge Houghton announced that bail would be fixed at $5,000 for Ellen Follin and $1,000 for George Blass. The amounts were astronomical at a time when bail was usually set at less than $200. When determining bail, judges weighed the seriousness of the crime, the defendant's finances, ties to the community, and risk of flight. Yet even for major crimes, and even when committed by itinerants with few or no local connections, bail over $1,000 was extremely rare. Even the wealthiest New Orleanians would have been hard pressed to raise $5,000 bail at a moment's notice. Judges did accept pledges of personal property in lieu of the actual bail money, but all of Ellen Follin's property combined was worth less than $3,000. Before Hunt could protest the judge's decision, a white man named Henry C. Dawes who had been watching the proceedings stepped forward and offered to serve as a surety in the case. Dawes, an engineer, lived on stately St. Charles Avenue, a mile away from Follin, and pledged his property as collateral for the bail. He told Judge Houghton he owned $10,000 in real estate, free from encumbrance. Originally from Massachusetts, Dawes had lived in the city since 1836, but whether he knew the defendants or was simply a sympathetic spectator was unclear. Captain Broadwell chimed in that he, too, was willing to be bondsman. Houghton replied that he "did not doubt it, but that Mr. Dawes was sufficient" and he was "compelled to accept him." Ordering the release of the accused, Houghton set August 21 for a preliminary hearing in the case. After signing the bonds, Follin and her son, escorted by Broadwell, Hunt, and Dawes, left the courtroom and headed home.[25]

The next morning, August 12, the mail boat carrying Louisa Murray and Detective Jourdain arrived at the landing on Lake Pontchartrain, where the pair disembarked and boarded the railroad that ran from the lakefront into the city. Outside Chief Badger's Carondolet Street headquarters a crowd had already gathered, eager to glimpse the alleged abductress from Mobile. As Jourdain and Murray arrived shortly before 8 a.m., reporters noted with surprise that Murray, the prime suspect in the Digby abduction, was not constrained in any way. Instead, the crowd watched as a striking woman wearing a silk dress and a white hat ornamented with flowers stepped lithely from the cab and walked up the steps into Badger's office.[26]

Although New Orleans newspapers usually used crude stereotypes and slurs to refer to African Americans, the reporters who saw Murray that day wrote breathlessly of her beauty and fashionable taste. She was "a remarkable woman," the *Commercial Bulletin* reported, "such a woman as would attract the attention of those casually passing her on the street. She is tall and has a good and graceful figure, and is stately in her movements. She is a bright mulatress, and so stylish as to present a marked contrast in her air and bearing to other women of her type." There was nothing, another journalist wrote, "gaudy or showy about her appearance but a display of excellent taste." Editors who had hoped the alleged abductor would be, as initially rumored, a strange Voodoo priestess that they could use an example of a black population run amok, now reported that Chief Badger had in custody a woman of "engaging and dignified appearance."[27]

The flattering descriptions of Murray's beauty, manners, and taste would be repeated again and again. Murray's attractive appearance, as well of that of her sister, Ellen Follin, became a central theme in accounts of the Digby Case—a theme that reflected both the lingering respect many white New Orleanians had for Afro-Creoles and their shock that women of that class might be kidnappers. Even though many Afro-Creoles had made themselves odious by fighting for the Union or serving in the Reconstruction government, whites still tended to consider Afro-Creoles superior to former slaves. They were educated men and women whose scrupulous manners and dress reflected a commitment to the values of respectability many upper- and middle-class whites held dear. They could be reasoned with. They could be held to their word. Ties formed by generations of economic alliances, backdoor intimacies, and cultural affinities had frayed during the war and in the hothouse racial atmosphere of Reconstruction, but they had not unraveled entirely. To be sure, some whites viewed educated and well-dressed blacks simply as uppity members of a degraded class. Former Confederates who moved to New Orleans from war-ravaged regions of the South and working-class whites who resented aspiring black people often treated Afro-Creoles with contempt. But the respect many longtime white residents still held for Afro-Creoles made Murray's and Follin's alleged roles in the Digby abduction particularly jarring.[28]

The reporters' focus on Murray's and Follin's gentility also mirrored coverage of sensationalized nineteenth-century crimes in other cities where the police accused seemingly respectable people of heinous acts. As America transformed into an industrialized society, elite city dwellers and aspirants to bourgeois respectability increasingly relied on dress, etiquette, and manners to distinguish themselves from the hoi polloi on crowded streets. Americans made etiquette manuals and magazines like *Godey's Lady's Book* bestsellers, and men and women studied periodicals and guidebooks to determine which linens, sofas, watches, glassware, and cutlery items could signal their superiority to the urban masses. Yet as factories mass-produced luxury items that allowed the appearance of gentility to be purchased, fear increased that swindlers, confidence men, and conniving women might use the trappings of respectability to dupe the unsuspecting. Because clothes, manners, and taste allowed urban dwellers to decide whom they could trust in a city crowded with strangers, people who misused such attributes for ill-gotten gain were particularly destabilizing and dangerous. Middle- and upper-class citizens knew to steer clear of rough neighborhoods and rogues in coarse clothing. Well-groomed criminals in suits or fine dresses were a more insidious threat. In his 1870s guidebook *Criminals of America*, detective Philip Farley warned readers of pickpockets who "dress well, put on a quiet, unassuming demeanor, and slip modestly into a crowd" and of villains like the beautiful and educated blackmailer Helen Graham "who might have... shone in the most brilliant circles of refined society" if not for her criminal soul.[29]

Similar fears surfaced in the press coverage of the Digby case but with an added dimension because the deceptively refined women in question were black. If they were guilty, their deception was cause for a different concern—that their polished looks and manners might lead a fine family to invite them into their parlors and drawing rooms as servants. Louisa Murray, one newspaper remarked, was an "engaging and dignified" woman whose "manners are those of an intelligent waiting maid accustomed to the society of elegant and refined ladies, whom she imitates in dress and conversation." If women like Follin and Murray could be kidnappers, to whom could white parents entrust their children and homes? In a city already destabilized by war and Reconstruction, the Digby trial made readers grapple with the unsettling idea that polite respectability could be counterfeited by friends, acquaintances, *and* trusted employees.[30]

In addition to her looks and dignified bearing, newspapers also noted Murray's poise even during heated questioning by the police. When Detective Jourdain ushered Murray into Chief Badger's office, the chief and Detective Leonard Malone were waiting. For the next hour, Malone, Badger's most skilled interrogator, used trick questions, threats, and cold logic to induce Murray to implicate herself. But Murray remained calm and answered Malone's questions adroitly, just as she had when Jourdain arrived at her door in Mobile. She did admit that she could not be sure whether she was in New Orleans on June 9, the day the kidnapping occurred. She had been in the city in June, but she could not recall the exact dates. From the other details of her story she could not be shaken. She denied that Mollie Digby was at Follin's house when she arrived there on July 22 from Mobile with Minnie Green, or that she had taken Mollie by the hand and called her "Camellia." The child, she said, had been left at Follin's house by a veiled white woman while she was there. Despite Detective Malone's best efforts, Murray retained her composure.[31]

By midmorning, when it had become clear that further questioning would be pointless, Chief Badger took Murray in his private carriage to the Digbys' house on Howard Avenue. Badger hoped that either ten-year-old Georgie Digby or Mollie's babysitter Rosa Gorman could identify Murray as the abductress. As Badger's carriage turned onto the Digbys' block, dozens of curious neighbors followed on foot. Thomas Digby was waiting at the top of his steps, and he invited Badger and his prisoner into his house.

Thomas and Bridgette Digby remained calm as Murray sat in a rocking chair in their front room. Here, in their house, was the alleged abductress, a woman the police believed had caused the Digbys illimitable anguish. Murray was, moreover, a Creole of color, and Irish immigrants and Afro-Creoles had sparred ever since the first waves of famine Irish arrived. Elite Creoles, white and black, found the Irish vulgar, dirty, and wedded to a backward version of Catholicism. Creoles of color resented the fact that until 1868 rough Irish immigrants could vote and hold office while they could not. The Irish found the Creoles similarly distasteful. The fact that Creoles did not close businesses, theaters, or gaming houses on the Sabbath shocked them. And they resented the haughty Creoles of color who held skilled jobs they coveted. Despite the prejudice Irish faced in both the Old and New Worlds, most displayed little empathy for black people and their travails. Many Irish in the 1850s joined organizations like the Working Men's National League that denounced nativism and slavery but also advocated colonizing black people out of Louisiana. Perhaps because Thomas had worked closely with Detective Jourdain during the investigation, he did not reveal any racial animus toward Murray and instead remained collected as he asked her about her possible role in his daughter's abduction. "Contrary to the general expectation," the press noted, "there was little or no upbraiding."[32]

During the conversation, Thomas went into the bedroom and came back with Mollie in his arms. He asked, "Madame, do you know this child?" To which Louisa Murray responded, "Yes, I saw it at my sister's house." "How long ago?" Digby asked. "Three weeks ago next Tuesday," Murray answered, sticking with her story even though her discussions with Jourdain, Badger, and Malone had alerted her to the discrepancy between her own account and her sister's. "Are you aware that your sister says she did not have it in her house until a week ago last Tuesday; how do you account for that?" Digby inquired. "I do not know anything about that; there is some mistake," Murray replied.[33]

After Digby finished questioning Louisa Murray, Badger sent Kuntz Stollberger, his carriage driver, to pick up Rosa Gorman at the confectionery store on the corner of Canal and Rampart Streets where she worked. Because it was Gorman who had handed Mollie Digby to the kidnapper on June 9, Badger knew that her identification of Murray would be essential to the case. When

Badger's driver reached the shop, Gorman strenuously objected to going with him. In June, Bridgette Digby had scolded her for leaving Mollie in the care of strangers. Gorman now said she had been "put to too much trouble already on account of the child." Although Stollberger eventually convinced her that she had no choice but to come along, nearly an hour passed before he returned to Howard Avenue with Gorman in the carriage. During that time, the crowd had grown and now filled the entire street outside the Digbys' house.[34]

When the carriage finally arrived, Chief Badger asked Louisa Murray to step out onto the banquette. Police officers cleared a path through the throng so that Rosa Gorman could reach Murray. Georgie Digby was also now on the sidewalk, at his parents' side. Badger, whose case against Murray might be won or lost at this moment, asked both Rosa Gorman and Georgie Digby if the woman standing before them was the same person who had left with Mollie Digby in her arms on June 9. At first, Georgie "seemed confused, and apparently uncertain." Gorman too seemed unsure, saying that Murray might be the woman, but that she could not be certain because the woman in whose care she had left Mollie was wearing a seaside hat. Then Stollberger, Badger's driver, "in a moment of inspiration," took a seaside hat from a young black woman who was standing in the crowd "and directed Louisa Murray to put it on."[35]

Louisa stepped back inside the house, removed the more fashionable hat that she was wearing, and placed the seaside hat on her head. As she came back outside she joked to Chief Badger that, given the crowd and the costume change, "she would do very well to go into the theater after awhile." Once she returned to the banquette wearing the new hat, Georgie instantly exclaimed to his father, "That's the lady, pa, that's her." Badger asked him again, and Georgie said, yes, Murray was the woman who had taken Mollie in her arms, and her black friend had given him twenty-five cents to buy bananas. But Rosa Gorman was still unsure. Although she was somewhat "more assured" that Murray was the woman, she could not say so for certain. One reporter claimed that Murray, who had seemed very calm became greatly agitated upon being identified, appeared to tremble, and then muttered, "I'm pretty well shown up." But another said Murray "stood the test so well…that all who saw her conceded that, guilty or innocent, she was a woman of iron nerves."[36]

Only the *Republican* reported that two other black women stepped forward out of the crowd to announce that they too had been outside the Digbys' house on June 9 and had seen the person who walked off with Mollie. One of the women was known in the neighborhood as Sukey and the other as Aunt Jane. Both said Louisa Murray was not the woman they had seen. The kidnapper, they claimed, was "more stoutly built." Badger did not want to hear it. There was a long tradition in New Orleans of the police not taking black witnesses seriously, and throughout the South most black people had, until Reconstruction, been barred from testifying in courtrooms in cases that involved white people. It quickly became obvious that both the police and the press would simply ignore Sukey's and Aunt Jane's exculpatory statements. Badger was convinced he had the kidnapper in his custody. He loaded Murray into his carriage once more, and the crowd jeered her as they drove off. Once back at the First District Station, Badger locked Murray into a cell on an upper floor.[37]

Badger did take seriously, however, the claims of August Singler, a young, scruffy white man who appeared at the station house later that afternoon claiming that he too had witnessed the June abduction and could now, if given the chance, identify the kidnapper. Singler, in his early twenties, was a family friend of the Digbys who worked during theater season as a bill poster, pasting advertisements for plays and operas on walls and fences. It was Singler whom Bridgette Digby had sent to get her husband on June 9 when she learned that Mollie had been taken. Singler now told Badger that he had been standing on the corner of Poydras and Howard streets that evening, when the fire broke out two blocks away at Seligman's Photography Studio. Before he headed for the fire, a crying child had caught his attention. It was Mollie Digby in the arms of a "mulatress." Little Georgie Digby and another black woman were there too. The woman holding Mollie was trying to quiet the child by giving her a piece of candy. He then heard the woman ask Georgie to show them where a certain dressmaker lived down the street, to which Georgie had replied, "I don't want to go, I don't want to go." But then the trio walked off, and Singler moved on to the fire. Later, when he returned, he found Bridgette Digby in hysterics, and at her command he ran as fast as he could to Thomas Digby's cab stand to inform him that his daughter was missing.[38]

Badger accepted Singler's story, apparently without asking him why he had waited so long to give his eyewitness account to the police, particularly given his friendship with the Digbys and the large rewards being offered for useful information. Instead, he brought Singler to Murray's cell to make a positive identification of the suspect. Before they entered, Badger asked if Singler wanted to see Murray in a seaside hat. Singler said it was not necessary, that he remembered "the woman's face he saw petting the child, and would know it again under any hat." Her face, he claimed, was "vividly impressed" upon his memory. Badger asked Murray to come out of her windowless cell and sit under a gas light. Singler immediately declared that she was the woman he had seen that day. He said he "could not be mistaken; there was no possibility of mistake; she was the woman." Pleased, Badger thanked Singler for coming forward.[39]

Badger's investigation was going well. The day had begun with his best black detective arriving from Mobile with the prime suspect. By early afternoon one key witness had positively identified the suspect as the perpetrator of the crime, and another was almost certain Murray was the right person. Then, in the late afternoon, a third witness appeared who also positively identified Louisa Murray as the kidnapper. After a tense summer in which Badger and his detectives had been criticized relentlessly, it appeared the Digby case had been solved. The *Republican* newspaper applauded Detective Jourdain for his "indefatigable and most intelligent pursuit of any clue." Even the Democratic press acknowledged as "commendable" the "celerity and skill manifested…by the arrest of this woman."[40]

With Murray in custody, Thomas Digby also took the opportunity to praise those who had secured Mollie's return. Digby told reporters he was "the happiest man in the world" and that he wished to "thank the community for all of their support." He was particularly grateful to those who "assisted him during the trying hours when he hunted for his child, to the ladies who took such a great interest in his sad case, to the Superintendent of the Jackson Railroad, the Southern Express, the press, Governor Warmoth, and the police."[41]

The *Louisiana State Register*, the official statewide newspaper of Louisiana's Republican Party, used Murray's arrest to scold Democratic papers for their sensational coverage of the case and for their repeated criticism of Badger's police force. Chiding Democratic editors for "having gone into hysterics" over the salacious rumors that Mollie had been abducted by Voodoo priestesses, the *Register* noted that its reporters "never credited the exaggerated stories of the baby being offered as a sacrifice to the voudous." The *Register* claimed to have believed "from the first that [the baby] had been taken for adoption, or to be palmed upon some unfortunate parent as a long lost child" and that "the event never acquired that horrible character which others have painted it with." With Mollie now returned safely to her parents and Louisa Murray arrested, the editors who had used wild tales of Voodoo blood rites to slander the police looked silly. The police force, the *Register* added, "used great caution and perseverance, not withstanding the abuse which has been heaped upon it. And we believe the facts will justify us in declaring that it was owing to the vigilance of the policemen that the child was surrendered."[42]

For Louisa Murray, the day could not have been worse. She had voluntarily traveled with Detective Jourdain from Mobile to New Orleans, certain that she could convince the authorities of her innocence. The detective had seemed to be a reasonable and fair man, but when she arrived she was turned over to Chief Badger and Detective Malone. Neither was Afro-Creole like Jourdain, and both seemed set on pinning the crime on her, even if she was innocent as she claimed. She had remained calm, answered questions forthrightly, and cooperated, but it had done no good. When three white people identified her as the kidnapper, she knew her troubles were just beginning.

At the end of the day, police officers took Murray to the Recorder's Court, where she was formally charged with kidnapping Mollie Digby. When her sister and nephew had appeared in the same court the previous day, they were aided by Captain Broadwell and Theodore Hunt, but she had no such benefactors. Murray scanned the faces in the courtroom and asked several times if anybody there had been sent to represent her. When she realized she "was destitute of friends," a reporter noted, "she was much depressed." After Murray pled "not guilty," Judge Houghton set her bail at $5,000, as he had for Follin. This time, however, no one stepped forward to secure her bail. Houghton therefore ordered that Murray be confined in the city's notorious parish prison, where, in the absence of bail, she would remain until the preliminary hearing nine days later.[43]

Apparently abandoned by her New Orleans family and charged with a terrible crime, Murray swooned. After having held up so well, she fainted twice en route to the prison and had to be revived by her guards.[44]

The press hoped the police would pressure Murray to confess to the crime and expose her co-conspirators. Who, editors wanted to know, had put Murray up to the kidnapping and why? Rumors had circulated that Captain Broadwell or some other wealthy citizen had paid her to take the child as part of some larger plot. Murray had acknowledged during her interrogation that she was acquainted with both Broadwell and his wife, although she did not implicate them in the crime. "Perhaps Louisa Murray may not have the same reason for keeping silence that her sister has," the *Picayune* posited. "The dread of punishment may unseal her lips; and then the public will learn who are the parties who prompted her and her associates to the commission of this great wickedness." The police had to find all the culprits, even if the trail led to citizens of "high social position."[45]

In the days following Murray's arrest and imprisonment, the Digby case once again became national news. Newspapers across the country had been following developments in the story since mid-July, when the Associated Press put the news of Governor Warmoth's reward offer and the frenzied search for Mollie Digby on the wire. "For weeks and months the people all over the land wherever newspapers are read...have been in sympathy with the parents of the lost or stolen child in New Orleans," a Memphis paper proclaimed. "The interest taken was almost as great in Memphis, St. Louis, and Cincinnati, as in the Crescent City." Editors North and South ran lengthy, detailed accounts of the events of August, beginning with Captain Broadwell's appearance at the Digbys' door. Readers learned of the interrogation of Broadwell's wife, Evelina, the arrest of Ellen Follin and her son, and Detective Jourdain's trip to Mobile to apprehend Louisa Murray.

Readers in Chicago, New York, and other cities woke to headlines announcing that Mollie Digby had been found alive and her kidnappers arrested. The *New York Times* heralded the "Discovery of the Digby Child at New Orleans." The *Chicago Tribune* proclaimed that "The New Orleans Mystery" had been unraveled. "Found at Last," the *Cincinnati Enquirer* added, "The Lost Child of

New Orleans at Home Again." In Richmond, where the *Dispatch*'s front page normally featured only local items, the account of Mollie's return filled two full columns under the headlines "Recovery of Little Molly Digby—She Is Found in a Handsome Residence in New Orleans—The Lost Baby Recognizes Its Mother—Mysteries Yet to Solve."[46]

Chapter Seven

THE RECORDER'S COURT

For many white New Orleanians it was not enough that Mollie Digby had been returned to her parents; a strong message had to be sent to potential criminals. While conceding that Ellen Follin and Louisa Murray deserved "a fair and impartial trial," most of the city's editors wanted the sisters convicted and made to pay for their crimes. From the public's point of view, the *Republican* argued, "the great matter is not so much the finding of the lost child, as the punishment of its abductors: for the finding of the child effects the happiness of a single family, while...punishment of the criminals is the only safeguard for the peace of thousands of families who would never feel safe in the sacred surroundings of home, were not this crime pursued to the uttermost." The *Picayune* urged that the accused be "prosecuted with strength and severity," or "the same offense may be repeated." In Louisiana, kidnappers and their accomplices could be jailed at hard labor for up to twelve years, but some citizens expressed concern that twelve years was "inadequate" and thought a life sentence seemed more suitable.[1]

A conviction might also help convince white Louisianans that the Reconstruction government's judicial system dispensed punishments equally to both races. Many Democrats viewed the courts established during Radical Reconstruction as illegitimate because black men served on juries and most, but not all, of the judges were Republicans. The *Commercial Bulletin* spoke for many when it claimed that the courts were so filled with "miserable and contemptible petti-fogging carpetbaggers" that it made the "practice of law and the administration of justice as broad a farce and as complete a burlesque as ever was seen upon a theatrical stage."[2]

Democrats criticized the judicial system even though the district attorney for Orleans Parish, Charles Henry Luzenberg, was a former secessionist leader, Confederate veteran, and member of the Democratic Party. White voters had elected Luzenberg to a four-year term in 1866 before Radical Reconstruction began, and, as a conciliatory gesture, Warmoth and the Republicans had let him keep his position after 1868 when they could have used the loyalty provisions in Louisiana's new state constitution and the Fourteenth Amendment to force him from office. Conservative whites seemed unimpressed, and allowing Luzenberg to stay on meant Democrats—either Luzenberg himself or the lawyers he employed—prosecuted most criminal cases in New Orleans. Warmoth's biracial police had to rely on ex-Confederates to prosecute the offenders they apprehended, and all too often Luzenberg had failed to mount rigorous cases against white defendants who were accused of politically or racially motivated violence. The Digby case would be different. With the Democratic press demanding that Murray and Follin be punished, Luzenberg and his lawyers could be counted on to vigorously seek a conviction.[3]

Whatever the outcome, the Democratic press was ready to exploit the verdict for maximum political effect. If Luzenberg's prosecutors secured a guilty verdict, Democrats could hail the efforts of the district attorney's office and paint Follin and Murray as examples of a black population that was out of control. But if the state somehow failed to put the sisters behind bars, they could blame the result on shoddy police work. Editors were already laying the groundwork by suggesting that Badger's detectives had left too many key questions unanswered. Chief Badger and his men, the *New Orleans Times* maintained, owed "it to the community to make every circumstance connected with this crime as clear as the noon day sun or to frankly own their incompetence and resign."[4]

For Murray and Follin, of course, the legal proceedings would be a matter of grave importance. Murray, in particular, understood what was at stake, as she had been languishing since her arraignment in the infamous Orleans Parish Prison. Urban prisons in 1870 were unpleasant everywhere in America, but the Orleans Parish Prison and the state's penitentiary were notoriously foul. Built in 1834 on former swampland, the parish prison was a hulking, dank, rat-infested structure that had been bypassed by the prison and sanitary reform movements. Its inmates were crowded, often five at a time, into ten-by-twelve-foot cells that had no beds or blankets. They slept on the floor and shared a single slop bucket. British journalist William Howard Russell, who toured the facility in 1862, called it a "dreadful place" that filled him with "sickness and loathing." Conditions deteriorated further after the Civil War when the city moved psychiatric patients under municipal care into the building as well. The prison, said a physician, became a "disgrace to civilization and humanity," with "cells whose heat, filth, and noisome smells in the morning cannot be described."[5]

For almost two weeks, the elegant and refined Louisa Murray sat in a cell in the women's section of prison, side by side with thieves, prostitutes, and beggars, in surroundings made worse by a deadly August heat wave. During her incarceration, she received a visit from her sister's lawyer, Theodore Hunt, but he came bearing bad news. They had yet to find someone willing to post the $5,000 bond required for her release. Unless a benefactor could be found, she would remain in jail. During those long days and nights, she must have wondered whether, if convicted, she could survive twelve years in the parish prison or the similarly decrepit Louisiana State Penitentiary in Baton Rouge. A lengthy prison term at hard labor might be fatal.[6]

Had Murray and her sister faced trial four years earlier during Presidential Reconstruction, their chances of being acquitted would have been slim. In the past, the laws and judicial system of Louisiana had been stacked against black litigants. Before the war, free black people accused of serious crimes received jury trials, but the juries were always all-white. Although white juries did sometimes acquit black defendants in criminal cases, black defendants faced laws and racial predispositions that tilted the legal system against them.[7] Even after emancipation and Confederate surrender, black people faced discriminatory laws and legal procedures. When President Andrew Johnson allowed ex-Confederates to regain control of the South's state legislatures after

Appomattox, they enacted the Black Codes that prohibited black testimony against white defendants, making crimes against African Americans difficult to prove. Because whites worried that freed slaves would commit crimes and refuse to work, they cracked down hard. All-white juries readily convicted black defendants while allowing offenses against black people to go unpunished. In Texas, almost five hundred white men were put on trial for the murder of black men and women in 1865 and 1866, but not one was convicted. Black Southerners understandably had little confidence in the judicial system. It was only after Congress overrode Johnson's vetoes and brought Presidential Reconstruction to an end in 1867 that African Americans began to receive a modicum of justice in postwar Southern courts. For Murray and Follin, the legal changes wrought by Radical Reconstruction came at a propitious time.[8]

On August 20, the day of the preliminary hearing, a crowd gathered early on the corner of St. Charles Avenue and Lafayette Street, hoping to find seats in Judge Houghton's courtroom. "The community feels an interest in this investigation which perhaps is unexampled in the history of crime in New Orleans," one Saturday morning paper announced. Although the hearing was only a preliminary one, state prosecutors took the unprecedented step of issuing subpoenas to eighteen witnesses, including Thomas, Bridgette, and Georgie Digby; Rosa Gorman; Chief Badger; Detectives Malone and Jourdain; and James and Evelina Broadwell. Many commentators expected prosecutors to present evidence that would unravel some of the mysteries surrounding the kidnapping. New Orleanians, black and white, wanted answers. "The interest felt in the case is not confined to any class" the *Picayune* reported. "Every description of people manifest the same concern and appear to be influenced by identical feeling."[9]

The Digby case presented a dilemma for Judge Houghton, the former Union cavalry officer appointed to the Recorder's Court by the Republican-controlled city council. Houghton knew that Warmoth and Badger wanted swift justice and favorable publicity for the courts and the city's biracial police force. He also understood that the prosecutors wanted to use the proceedings to satisfy the public's thirst for immediate answers. Why else would the state want to put eighteen witnesses on the stand in a preliminary hearing? Houghton's problem, however, was that he was judge of the Recorder's Court, a tribunal with limited jurisdiction. The role of his court was simply to sift through the many cases on the city's criminal docket and decide which ones deserved to be sent on to a grand jury for an indictment and the 1st District Criminal Court for a full trial.

In a city deluged with petty crime, the Recorder was a committing magistrate—a judge with the power to issue fines for small, nonviolent offenses, to dismiss cases for which the police offered little or no evidence to support their charges, and to clear cases from the docket by sending petty offenders to the city's workhouse. Although the Recorder gave more care to cases involving capital punishment or long prison sentences, Houghton's only task was to ascertain, as speedily as possible, whether there was "probable cause for sending before a jury for trial parties who may have been offenders against the law." Only accusations deemed "wholly groundless" could be dismissed. If the police and prosecutors offered even minimal evidence of guilt, Houghton was duty bound to send the case forward. Most Recorder's Court hearings lasted less than an hour.[10]

Houghton understood, however, that if he followed the normal procedure and quickly passed the case on to a grand jury and the district court, the press, the public, and the governor might not get the answers they wanted for months. The path from Recorder's Court to grand jury to trial could be lengthy. Moreover, the case offered Houghton a moment in the local and national spotlight. At age forty-five, he may have been frustrated by his role as judge of a low-level court meting out justice to pickpockets, drunks, vagrants, prostitutes, and petty swindlers. Until the Digby case, Houghton's courtroom was best known for its unwashed clientele, low ceilings, tiny windows, and an odor "worse than that of rum, tobacco, and musk well-mingled." Whatever his motives, Houghton approved the prosecution's request to put multiple witnesses on the stand, even though that much testimony might take days rather than hours and backlog his court for months. His decision promised to turn the preliminary hearing into something akin to a trial, and, as a result, the press and the public clamored to be admitted to the proceedings. Reporters who had covered the Recorder's Court and knew its malodorous flaws warned potential spectators that the hearing "will be densely crowded and the air in the courthouse during the long hours of proceedings anything but fragrant."[11]

In an effort to make room and to offset the hygienic limitations of his usual clientele, Houghton decided to allow only well-dressed, respectable citizens to attend the hearing. At 9 a.m. on the 20th, having made quick work of the handful of other cases scheduled for that morning, he ordered the court officers, who were reinforced by police, to empty the courtroom of the "mixed crowd" that had claimed seats during the early proceedings. Grateful reporters and "upstanding" onlookers applauded. "The crowd of loafers were compelled to take sidewalk positions," the *Republican* cheered, "and for the first time in the history of the Recorder's Court it became possible for ladies and the decent portion of the public to obtain seats." But even with restricted admission, the courtroom quickly filled to capacity as spectators crowded together on the narrow benches and stood along the walls.[12]

Murray and Follin must have been mortified when they realized that the proceedings had become a public spectacle. Until their arrest, both women had led very private existences. Now, intimate details of their lives would be unveiled in a crowded courtroom and in newspaper accounts. They must have found little solace in the fact that public trials were designed to protect the accused from arbitrary and unjust convictions. English common law, the U.S. Constitution's Sixth Amendment, and most state constitutions required public trials as a means of allowing the public to monitor whether defendants were "fairly dealt with and not unjustly condemned." The presence of interested spectators also ensured that judges, lawyers, and jurors remained "keenly alive to a sense of their responsibility and to the importance of their functions." A judge could exclude people attracted by "prurient curiosity," but they could not shut their courtroom off completely. Yet, for Murray and Follin, two women whose dress and manners projected a desire for respectability, the protection of a public trial may have seemed more like a punishment.[13]

Once the spectators had taken their seats, court officers shepherded the prosecution's witnesses to reserved benches in the front of the court. The roomed buzzed with conversation as the key players in the Digby drama filed in. James and Evelina Broadwell entered first, followed by an unwilling Rosa Gorman, the Digbys' babysitter, forced by subpoena to participate. Detectives Jourdain and Malone took seats beside Chief Badger. Finally, Thomas and

Bridgette Digby arrived with their son, Georgie, their friend August Singler, and the now-famous Mollie. The Digbys had also brought along Jack, Mollie's white bulldog. Of the eighteen witnesses subpoenaed by prosecutors, only Minnie Green, Ellen Follin's pregnant boarder, was missing.

Heads turned as Ellen Follin and her son George Blass entered the court room. As they had done ever since their arrest, reporters once again took note of Follin's fashionable attire, composure, and striking beauty. She wore a spotted dark grenadine dress with a white waist, which they described as staid but stylish. A thick brown veil almost entirely hid her face. Looking "calm and unexcited," she ignored the gawking gallery and took a seat next to her son and her lawyers, Theodore Hunt and A. A. Atocha, a new addition to the defense. As she waited for the hearing to begin, she fanned herself and consulted quietly with the two men.[14]

The jailer then brought Louisa Murray into the courtroom. Unlike Follin, who was free on bail and allowed to sit on a bench near the spectators, Murray had not found a bondsman and therefore suffered the indignity of being locked in the dock—the raised platform enclosed by iron rails designed to hold prisoners who might use a hearing or a trial as an opportunity to escape.[15] Murray was wearing "a dress of brown checked summer silk and a very light brown and rather fleecy veil." According to one reporter, she was "a handsome quadroon" with "small features, thin drawn up lips," and "a wealth of glossy hair" knotted in a chignon. The two sisters were "strikingly alike," the *Picayune* found. "Both are tall beyond the average woman, and slenderly formed. They are...mulatresses, but are by no means deficient in good looks. They dress with exceeding care and evince in their apparel a great deal of taste." Thus far they had both demonstrated the poise and dignity expected of members of a genteel class. "They have borne their trying situation with a nerve and address which would do credit to the courage of men," a reporter proclaimed.[16]

At 10:15, Judge Houghton took his seat, and the court crier announced the case. "A thrill of expectation passed through the audience as the clerk called out the names of Louisa Murray, Ellen Follin and George Blass," the *Picayune* reported. Some commentators noted that Blass's surname was different from his mother's and speculated about as to what that might imply. The two sisters revealed no emotion as the clerk then read aloud the police affidavits accusing Murray of the kidnapping and Follin and her son of having been being accomplices in the crime.[17]

Theodore Hunt, the old lion of the bar who was now defending both sisters, introduced Atocha, the young lawyer who would be assisting him. Called "A. A." in the press, Alec Alexander Hypolité Atocha, a thirty-six-year-old white Creole, was well known in New Orleans thanks to the controversial post he held during the Civil War. After Northern forces occupied the city in 1862, Union General Nathaniel Banks appointed Atocha judge of the military court that handled civil and criminal cases while the city's civilian courts were closed due to the war. As provost judge (as the post was called), Atocha, a New Orleans native who had opposed secession, earned the enmity of many white residents for punishing Confederate sympathizers, flag desecrators, and blockade runners, and for handing out sentences that many locals felt were unduly harsh. His supporters, however, considered Atocha a stern but fair jurist who was as hard on unruly Union soldiers as he was on rebels and common criminals. When a Union private stole a watch from a captured Confederate officer, Atocha sentenced him to six months in prison. Another Northern soldier spent thirty days in jail for drawing his bayonet in a New Orleans barroom after being refused service. Although many whites viewed Atocha as a traitor to the South, President Lincoln considered native Louisianans like Atocha who had remained loyal to the Union essential to his plans for reconstructing the state.[18]

Both during and after the war, Atocha was also a prominent leader in Louisiana's Republican Party. He gave impassioned speeches at torch-lit rallies, held political meetings and celebrations in his Garden District home, and headed the Louisiana delegation to the Republican national convention in 1864 that nominated Lincoln for a second term. He helped found and lead the Crescent City Republican Club, an organization composed of Southern men who had converted to the Republican Party. He did so knowing the risks that being a Republican leader in the South entailed. Several close friends died at the hands of the mob during the 1866 New Orleans Riot. Later that year he was moments from fighting a duel with a political foe when the police intervened.[19]

Atocha might even have run for governor during Reconstruction had a debilitating disease not undermined his stamina. Soon after the war, he began to suffer from bouts of fever, back pain, and vomiting caused by chronic nephritis, a kidney affliction then known as Bright's Disease, which was made worse by the bloodletting and laxatives doctors prescribed as cures. Because the symptoms came and went, Atocha could not predict when he might be bedridden for days or weeks at a time. Rather than seek high office, Atocha therefore became a criminal defense attorney who accepted clients when he was feeling well enough to take them on.[20]

As a lawyer, Atocha gravitated to sensational cases—his clients included accused bigamists, counterfeiters, and murderers. In March 1870, he won a celebrated acquittal in the "Boston Club Homicide" trial of a prominent New Orleans banker who was accused of murdering a fellow member of the city's most prestigious club. Fresh from his victory in that high-profile case, Atocha volunteered to join Follin and Murray's defense. It is not clear how, or if, Atocha was paid for his services, but the case promised maximum publicity for the lawyers involved. Theodore Hunt welcomed Atocha's assistance but made clear to the court that he, not Atocha, would be the principal defense attorney in the proceedings.[21]

To lead the prosecution, District Attorney Luzenberg tapped the services of David M. C. Hughes, a former Confederate officer who returned from his summer cottage on the north shore of Lake Pontchartrain to participate. Hughes was a New Orleans native who, unlike Atocha, had favored secession and fought enthusiastically for the Confederacy. He had gained fame for a daring escape he made as a prisoner of war. Captured at Port Hudson, Louisiana, in May 1863 during the fighting there, Hughes was taken back to Union-occupied New Orleans and loaded onto the steamer *Maple Leaf* with other captives bound for federal prisons in Virginia and Delaware. On June 10, as the *Maple Leaf* neared the Virginia coast, Hughes and the other prisoners overpowered their guards, forced the crew below decks, and steered the ship to Confederate-held territory, where they escaped in lifeboats. Hughes now benefitted from Governor Warmoth's decision to retain Luzenberg in his post. A Republican district attorney would probably not have chosen a lawyer with a celebrated Confederate past to prosecute the Digby case in the Recorder's Court.[22]

Hughes would be assisted in the prosecution by another ex-Confederate, a young lawyer named Alexander Dalsheimer. Known for his fiery courtroom demeanor, the twenty-eight-year-old Dalsheimer was from a Jewish family that had prospered in Louisiana. His father, Leopold, a French immigrant, and his uncle, Nathan Dalsheimer, owned dry goods and clothing stores in New Orleans, Baton Rouge, and Natchez. The Dalsheimers were pillars of a small but thriving Jewish community that had adopted many of the customs and political views of their Catholic and Protestant neighbors. Before the war, Alexander's father owned slaves and embraced secession. Like most of the city's other prominent Jews, he supported the Confederacy. U.S. Senator Judah P. Benjamin, a Jewish New Orleanian who resigned from the Senate when Louisiana seceded, served in Jefferson Davis's cabinet. Hundreds of Jews from New Orleans joined the Confederate army. Many, including the handful allowed into the elite Washington Artillery, earned decorations for valor at Shiloh, Antietam, Gettysburg, and other battles.[23]

Dalsheimer's military career had been undistinguished. He entered the Confederate army as a private and was discharged at the same rank. Taken prisoner at the Battle of Corinth in October 1862, he regained his freedom by signing a parole agreement in which he promised never to fight again for the South. Dragooned back into service by a Confederate army desperate for manpower, Dalsheimer was in uniform again in time to surrender when Vicksburg fell in 1863. Paroled once more, he returned to New Orleans, married the well-known poet Alice Solomon, and studied law. Perhaps to compensate for his lack of martial glory, he cultivated a reputation for aggressive courtroom behavior. He often shouted at witnesses and fellow attorneys, roaring like an enraged lion.[24]

To open the hearing, Judge Houghton asked if the defense planned to call any witnesses. Unlike in a grand jury proceeding, defense counsel had the right under Louisiana law to present witnesses in a preliminary examination. To Houghton's surprise, however, Theodore Hunt announced that no defense witnesses would be summoned. He and Atocha were simply "anxious to hear what the state had to prove." Even without defense witnesses, he suggested, the state's case would be shown to be without merit and dismissed.[25] Prosecutor

Hughes, in a voice loud enough to be heard out on the sidewalk, exclaimed that by refusing to call defense witnesses Hunt was ignoring the "voice of the people." Public excitement about this case was so intense that the people deserved to hear all the evidence now, including witnesses for the defense. Under normal circumstances, Hughes's task would have been easy. In a preliminary examination all the prosecution had to do was to satisfy the judge that there were grounds for sending the case on to a grand jury. The fact that Mollie Digby was found at Ellen Follin's house itself might have been sufficient to satisfy that requirement. But Hughes felt the pressure from the press and the public for immediate answers and wanted the defense to cooperate with his plan to turn the preliminary examination into a major courtroom event. Hunt was not swayed, however. No defense witnesses would be presented. The lawyers took their seats.[26]

Judge Houghton then called the names of the scheduled witnesses, and all responded except one, Follin's pregnant boarder, Minnie Green. "Where is Mrs. Green?" Houghton asked. "She is sick," answered Follin's son, George Blass. Hughes jumped to his feet. Green, he said, was essential to the state's case. She was the one who had told police the Digby baby was at Follin's house when she arrived in mid-July. Louisa Murray and Follin both claimed the baby was left at the house in August, after Green's arrival. Hughes moved that the court issue an attachment for Green and send officers to bring her in. "This is a case of great public importance," Hughes intoned, "one that has unusually aroused public sympathy. Sickness must, therefore, be very severe to excuse non-attendance." Everyone in the room must have suspected, of course, that Green's "sickness" was her pregnancy, which Hughes did not feel was sufficient cause for Green not to appear. Hunt countered for the defense that he had a certificate from a local doctor documenting that Green was too ill to attend. Hughes replied that he would not accept a physician's note unless he saw the doctor sign it himself. Hunt handed the note to Judge Houghton, who examined it and announced that he knew the doctor involved and recognized his handwriting. Houghton proposed an unusual solution: when it came time for Green's appearance, they would go to Follin's house to take her testimony rather than requiring an ill woman to travel to court. Hughes grudgingly accepted the judge's plan.[27]

Judge Houghton then questioned Hughes about his intention to call George Blass as a witness, reminding him that a defendant could not be compelled to testify against himself. Hughes, an experienced lawyer, of course knew the rule and announced that the state had decided not to prosecute Blass further. Hughes would instead use him as a witness against his mother and aunt. George's account of the events at Follin's house contradicted his mother's story in key details and would help the state's case even if George proved uncooperative. The judge dismissed George from further prosecution and asked him to take a seat with the other witnesses. George complied, but did not look relieved, as he would now be compelled to testify as a witness for the prosecution.[28] Houghton then instructed court officers to take George Blass, Detective Jourdain, the Broadwells, Thomas Digby, and the other witnesses out of the room and separate them so as to "prevent collusion of testimony."

By the time Houghton called the prosecution's first witness, Chief Algernon Badger, to the stand, it was already past noon. Outside the temperature had reached ninety degrees, and in the courtroom spectators fanned themselves in the humid air. Badger took the oath as administered in Louisiana—Christians swore on the New Testament, Jewish witnesses on the Old. With his mustache, square jaw, and pressed uniform, Chief Badger looked imposing and professional. Hughes asked him to provide an overview of his involvement in the case. Badger obliged, recounting the events of June 9, explaining that he had learned of the kidnapping from Thomas Digby only a short time after it occurred, he immediately went to the scene, and from that moment on had aggressively followed every lead. Contrary to press reports, he and his detectives had taken the case seriously from the outset and had not needed public pressure to goad them into action. The investigation, he acknowledged, had been long and difficult, but the big break came on Sunday, August 7, when Police Commissioner William George received the tip that Mollie Digby had been seen at Ellen Follin's house at the corner of Bellecastle and Camp. He had sent Detectives Jourdain and Pierson to the premises, a visit, he said, that frightened Follin and spurred her to return Mollie Digby to her parents via Captain Broadwell.[29]

He and his men, Badger continued, had pieced together the rest of the puzzle on Tuesday, August 9, when Thomas Digby led them to Evelina Broadwell, who

in turn implicated Follin. His questioning of Follin and her family that afternoon convinced him that he had found the culprits. Follin had offered an unlikely story that six days earlier, on Wednesday, August 3, a veiled white woman
"dissipated in appearance" had simply abandoned the child at her house. Upon
"close questioning" she had also given conflicting accounts of when she turned
Mollie over to the Broadwells. First she said it was on August 6, the day before
Badger's detectives initially came to her house, then she admitted it was actually on the 8th, the day after the police visit. When he learned that the other
residents of the house had all told different stories as to when and how Mollie
Digby had arrived there, he had become certain that Follin was lying.[30]

Chief Badger now added a new detail to the story. He testified that Ellen
Follin's eight-year-old daughter, Mary, had told him that her Aunt Louisa, not
a veiled white woman, had brought the baby to the house. That information,
Badger asserted, had led him to send Detective Jourdain to Mobile to apprehend Louisa Murray. In his earlier statements to the press, he had made no such
claim. If he could demonstrate its truth, it would be a damning piece of evidence. Unfortunately for prosecutors, unless they put Follin's daughter on the
stand, Badger's claim might in a formal trial be excluded by the judge as hearsay.
Mary would have to testify and be cross-examined, and she was not one of the
eighteen witnesses the prosecutors had subpoenaed thus far.

Once Murray was in custody, Badger continued, she too told a story that
conflicted with Follin's. Although she echoed her sister's claim that a veiled
woman had brought Mollie Digby to Follin's house, Murray said the woman
did so on Tuesday, July 26 or Wednesday, July 27, a full week before Follin said
the child arrived. Combined with the fact that several witnesses later identified
Murray as the kidnapper, the sisters' contradictory and convoluted stories had
convinced Badger of their guilt.[31]

As Badger testified, "the breathless silence of intense excitement" gripped
the crowded courtroom. Badger had not suggested a motive for the kidnapping,
but he had presented compelling details that pointed to the defendants' guilt.
Spectators watched Follin and Murray, observing their every move and gesture,
and searching for reactions that might reveal their guilt or innocence. During
most of Badger's testimony, the sisters did not flinch. When Badger disclosed

the revelation made by Follin's daughter, however, Murray "smiled disdainfully," eyed the chief "fiercely, and muttered to herself."[32]

On cross-examination, Hunt demonstrated his formidable skills as a defense attorney. He seized on the fact that Badger's version of the events of August 9 had changed. In previous discussions with the press, the chief had attached great significance to the "coded" letter sent by Murray to Follin, which he had confiscated. He had implied that the letter, not statements made by Follin's daughter, had led him to Murray and exposed the conspiracy. In his testimony, however, he did not even mention the allegedly incriminating note. Hunt homed in: Why had he kept the letter as evidence? What did he think it meant? Where was the letter now? In response, Badger testified that while he was at Follin's house on the 9th she "took something out of a bundle of old clothes and crumpled it up in her hand. It was a letter and contained money." When Follin "crumpled up the letter," he became suspicious and "took hold of the letter and drew it from her hand." The note, written in pencil, was from Murray in Mobile and included the strange message about the packet ships *Mary* and *Frances*. Badger now claimed that when he was unable to decipher its meaning, he returned the letter and the money to her, but then "when he learned from the children that Aunt Louisa had brought the child to the house," he kept it as evidence. Hunt asked Badger if he had the letter with him. Badger said that he did. Hunt then asked that it be "produced into evidence," even if "it pertained to nothing in the world."[33]

Hunt had thought quickly. He obviously did not believe Badger's claim that Follin's daughter had implicated Louisa Murray. If it were true, the child would surely be there as a witness. Badger now apparently had doubts whether the letter he had confiscated from Follin had any bearing on the case; otherwise, he would have mentioned it in his testimony. Although Badger had initially suspected that the coded letter referred to Mollie Digby, the note's veiled language might instead have been used to protect the identity of one of the sisters' pregnant clients. Thanks to the press coverage, everyone in the courtroom now knew that the sisters operated covert lying-in hospitals.

During his cross-examination of Badger, Hunt also suggested that from the moment the detectives first came to her door, Ellen Follin had been subjected to inappropriate shouts, intimidation, and threats. After her arrest, the police had interrogated her relentlessly and violated protocol by allowing journalists to question her in her cell. The combined effect of those tactics explained her contradictory statements. She was understandably flustered. Badger admitted that he had threatened to arrest her whole family, that at times Follin "exhibited considerable agitation," and that some of her statements were "not entirely voluntarily made." But pressuring suspects, even ladies, Badger countered, was the nature of police work, and within that context he was "not aware of any improper influences being brought to bear on these women to get them to answer questions."[34]

Prosecutor Hughes next called Thomas Digby to the stand and asked him to describe the day he learned his child was missing. Digby, speaking with his thick Irish accent, recalled where he was in the early evening of June 9. "I was on St. Charles Street with my carriage and team of horses when a young man by the name of August Singler came and informed me that my child was stole." Leaving his post, he had rushed home with Singler at his side, and "there was a crowd at the door when I got there." "I was informed that two colored women stole the child," Digby continued. "I went to the water closet to search it, kinder doubtin' the child was stole, and was satisfied at the time the child wasn't there. I got into the cab and immediately went to Captain Badger." To his credit, Badger had stopped what he was doing and returned with Digby to Howard Avenue. Badger had interviewed neighbors and accompanied Digby's son, Georgie, to the corner of Dryades and Lafayette, "where the two colored ladies sat when they gave him two bits to go after some bananas." For the next two months, Thomas had done little else but search for Mollie. "I have been traveling sixty-one days and sixty-one nights to find my child," he testified.[35]

Digby also described the morning Captain Broadwell arrived at his door. Broadwell, he said, was beaming when he told Mrs. Digby that he "thought he had her little girl." Although at the time he did not yet know Broadwell's name, Digby could tell he was a gentlemen. In an era when adding the title "mister" connoted respect, Digby, a carriage driver, said "I was thankful to him for calling me Mr. Digby." Digby then recounted how he and Broadwell had traveled by streetcar to the captain's house on Chestnut Street, where he and Mollie were reunited.[36]

Hunt's cross-examination of Digby was surprisingly aggressive. The defense attorney seemed either not to care about or not to recognize the sympathy for Digby in the courtroom and the city. Digby had said and done all the right things since his daughter's disappearance and had become, in the eyes of many interested observers, a tragic protagonist. Hunt, who had once been a member of the anti-immigrant Know-Nothing Party and perhaps still held some animosity for the Irish, hammered Digby. Why had he not recognized Mollie when he first saw her at the Broadwells' house? Raising the extraordinary possibility that the child was not really Mollie at all, Hunt wanted to understand how a father could not know his daughter. "I recognized my child at once," Digby answered. Hunt knew differently.

"Did you not doubt at first that it was your child?" Hunt asked again.

"The child, when Mrs. Broadwell gave it to me, flung her arms around my neck and kissed me."

"But before that?"

"I did not see the child until I took it out of Mrs. Broadwell's arms," Digby now claimed. "I told Mrs. Broadwell who asked me what I would do with the child if it was not mine, that I would bring it back—but said Madam, I don't think we will trouble you again." Digby's story had changed, and Hunt could prove it. He would raise the issue again when James and Evelina Broadwell took the stand.[37]

Hunt turned next to the issue of the reward advertisement Digby had placed in the New Orleans newspapers. "Did you not, Mr. Digby," Hunt asked, "promise to make no inquiries in case your child was restored to you?" Hughes objected instantly: "Do not answer the question. It has nothing to do with this case. This is an offense against the community, and the State prosecutes it." Hunt addressed Judge Houghton: "The question is what credit should be attached to Mr. Digby's veracity? After he had solemnly advertised and promised that no questions should be asked, he takes an angry crowd around [the Broadwells'] house, and then prosecuted the very parties who returned him his child, trusting to his word given in his card." "Digby is only a witness, and is not the prosecutor," Hughes countered. "He had no right to promise anything, and his promises amount to nothing, and his [advertisements] in the papers were worthless." Hughes returned to one of his favorite Latin phrases, reminding Judge Houghton that the prosecution reflected the *vox populi*—the will of the people. Houghton sustained Hughes's objection. "I will not press it," Hunt said, conceding. Hunt asked Digby a final question: "Did you not on your second visit to Captain Broadwell's say to the crowd outside that the house ought to be burned down?" "No, I did not," Digby replied.[38]

Before Digby left the stand, junior prosecutor Dalsheimer, on redirect, asked him to clarify one point. Although Digby had just testified that he recognized Mollie instantly upon taking her into his arms, Dalsheimer wanted to make sure it was clear that Mollie's appearance at the time was different from what it had been on the day of the kidnapping. "What condition was the child in when you saw her?" Dalsheimer asked. Digby responded that she had "been badly cared for" and "was covered in boils all over her face." With that, Digby was dismissed, and he took a seat in the audience.[39]

Perhaps the most crucial moment in Digby's testimony was his recollection that it was August Singler who had come to his cab stand on June 9 to inform him that his child had been taken. Singler had become the prosecution's most important witness, for he had positively identified Louisa Murray and claimed to have witnessed the abduction. But he had also taken more than two months to make his claims to the police, and he had admitted that he had said nothing about witnessing the crime to the Digbys at the time. If Singler had witnessed the kidnapping, was it plausible that he would not have announced that fact to Thomas Digby on June 9 as the two men searched the Digbys' house and yard for the child? Why Hunt did not raise this issue while cross-examining Digby is unclear. Had he simply missed the importance of Digby's revelation?

Dalsheimer next called Leonard Malone, the city's most venerable detective, and asked him to describe his role in the investigation. Malone's account of the events differed little from Chief Badger's. He described the interrogation of the residents of Ellen Follin's house and the questioning of Louisa Murray, and said he had heard both sisters give contradictory statements as to the date Mollie Digby was allegedly left by the veiled woman at Follin's house. Although Murray had told him that she "did not take the child by the hand and call it familiarly 'Camellia,'" she had admitted that she might have been in New

Orleans on the day Mollie was abducted. Dalsheimer also asked Malone to describe his interactions with Captain Broadwell during the investigation. Had Broadwell done anything to draw Malone's suspicions? "Mr. Broadwell seemed to be greatly excited," Malone replied. Before he could say more, junior defense counsel Atocha objected to the line of questioning. It was immaterial, he told Judge Houghton. "We have nothing to do with Broadwell." To this, Dalsheimer, hinting at possible prosecution theories about motives for the crime, responded, "you may have more than you think." Houghton, however, upheld the objection. Dalsheimer turned his witness over to the defense.[40]

On cross-examination, Hunt attempted another risky gambit. Despite the fact that Detective Malone was known for his probity, Hunt challenged his motives and veracity rather than his facts. "Do you ever read the newspapers?" Hunt asked. "Yes, sir," Malone responded. "Did you ever," Hunt continued, "read the Governor's proclamation offering a reward for the conviction of the abductress, and do you expect to get it?" Before Malone could answer, prose-cutor Hughes objected, saying that Malone's "character is beyond approach and above injury." His reputation "cannot be attacked by the idea that he would be the recipient of the reward. It is only a reward to induce the officers to use more zeal, but it can never be supposed that an old officer, well known, would come here to perjure himself on account of a reward."[41]

Judge Houghton ruled that Malone must answer the question; Louisiana criminal procedure required judges to give wide latitude to counsel's efforts on cross-examination to expose the motives and prejudices of witnesses. Malone answered by saying that he knew of the posted reward but did not deserve it. "If I was the man who received the child, I should claim the reward, but I am not even the man who caused the arrest."[42]

Despite Malone's skillful response, Hunt had struck a nerve. Ever since Governor Warmoth had announced the $5,000 reward for the return of Mollie Digby, critics had questioned whether members of Badger's police force should be eligible to claim it. Some detractors considered the Metropolitans so "depraved and corrupt" that they might even collude with the kidnappers to claim the money. "That there are men, and many of them, on the police who, for profit, would combine with criminals, even in the commission of such dreadful crimes, there can be little doubt," the *Commercial Bulletin* had charged in July. "If they find that kidnapping can be made profitable by getting rewards, there are men among them who would not hesitate to protect child stealers and share the rewards."[43]

Later in the summer criticism had increased when William George, the police board member who received the tip that led to Follin's house, demanded that Warmoth pay him the reward. "It strikes us Police Commissioner George should rest satisfied with his official salary and his share of the very handsome monthly bonus paid to the Board by the gambling fraternity," the *Times* had editorialized. Some commentators had proposed that Warmoth turn the reward money over to a committee of respectable citizens who would then "invest said rewards in the best city stocks for the benefit of the found child." By accusing Malone of impropriety, Hunt sent a warning. If he could accuse the city's most celebrated detective of committing perjury or trumping up evidence simply to collect the reward, no one on the force was above suspicion.[44]

As Malone finished on the stand, it was already late afternoon. Judge Houghton, looking at the list of witnesses yet to testify, realized the enormity of the task he had undertaken. He announced that the case would adjourn until Monday morning at 11 a.m. "If we do not work faster than we have today," he warned, "we will not get through."[45]

Before Houghton left the bench, Theodore Hunt made a request of the court. He asked the judge, "in the name of humanity," to reduce the bail for both Louisa Murray and Ellen Follin from $5,000 to $2,500. Because of the excessive bail and "the excited state of public opinion," no one had been willing to post bond for Murray who, as a result, had been forced to endure the brutal conditions of the parish prison. Hunt also announced that Henry C. Dawes, the white steamboat engineer who had posted Follin's bail, wanted to withdraw as surety "owing to the pressure of public opinion." Although originally from the North, Dawes had lived in New Orleans for decades, and he now suffered the same fate as other Southern whites who seemed to side with blacks during Reconstruction. Called "scalawags" by their critics, they faced intense pressure from those who hoped to restore white supremacy. For Dawes, the insults, threats, and social ostracism had proved to be too much, and he wanted to end his role in the Digby case. Under Louisiana law, sureties like Dawes could "at any time before final judgment release themselves from all liability and have the bond cancelled." If Dawes backed out, Follin would join Murray in jail. Hunt believed that he could raise bail money for both defendants by taking out a mortgage on Follin's property, but doing so might take time.[46]

When prosecutor Dalsheimer interrupted to insist that the bail not be reduced, both Hunt and Atocha tried to outshout him. "It [is] a matter for the court to decide and about which [Dalsheimer] should have nothing to say," they declared. But silencing Dalsheimer was nearly impossible, and he bellowed on that "as far as the interests of humanity are concerned, those interests are on the side of the state. Humanity sympathized with the bereaved parents of the stolen child." If the court had set bail at $5,000 before any evidence was heard, Dalsheimer wondered, why would it reduce it after hearing numerous facts that implicated the accused? The public would not stand for it. Hunt retorted, "the court has nothing to do with popular sentiment; it is a court of justice. One of these women is a stranger to the city, the other, although wealthy, is under the ban of public sentiment."[47]

Judge Houghton sided with Dalsheimer and declined to reduce the amount of bail. But he added that because Dawes had not appeared in person to renounce his bond, he was still responsible for Follin's appearance and would be until the end of the trial. So until Dawes came to court, Follin could go home. Murray would be returned to jail. At that moment, a man named William Green stood in the audience and offered to serve as Louisa Murray's surety. Although he had not played any role in the case thus far, Green, who lived a block away from Follin on Camp Street, told the court that he would pay Murray's bond. Green was a successful black businessman who, despite being barely literate, had opened a coffee stand in the public market on Magazine Street and then a successful oyster saloon nearby. Green announced that he held property valued at $16,000 and was willing to pledge a house he owned at the corner of First and Annunciation Streets as security for Murray's appearance in court. After Judge Houghton received assurances from others in the room that Green did indeed own real estate, he accepted Green as Murray's bondsman. Court adjourned, and Murray was able to leave with her sister. Outside, curiosity seekers still

lingering on the sidewalk watched Murray, Follin, and their relatives and supporters board streetcars to go home.[48]

Saturday and Sunday night were both intensely hot. Even in the rural Sixth
District where Follin lived, "away from the brick walls and stone pavements"
of the city, the temperature lingered around ninety degrees after sunset. "Lying
in bed under a mosquito bar," the *Picayune* complained, "was like taking a steam
bath." But for Louisa Murray, who had been sleeping on the floor of a crowded
cell in the parish prison, a bath, a bed, and an open window in her sister's house
must have felt glorious.[49]

Chapter Eight

A HIGHLY UNUSUAL PROCEEDING

A s the proceedings in the Recorder's Court headed into their second day, it seemed that everyone in New Orleans, rich and poor, black and white alike, was discussing the case. What was supposed to be a routine preliminary hearing had mushroomed into a courtroom spectacle, and in churches, public markets, and coffeehouses, the testimony dominated conversation. "It is talked of in the street, the saloon, in the family circle, everywhere indeed," the *Picayune* reported. "Each person has his or her own theory of the case... and speculates upon the probability of its turning out this or that way." Women seemed particularly riveted. "It is not surprising that it interests women," one editor opined. "It is a crime that more nearly touches them than men. It appeals to their affections, and has in it all a woman's love for her offspring." Everyone hoped the remaining witnesses would provide answers to the many mysteries surrounding the crime. "As to the guilt or innocence of the accused the judgment of the community is not made up," claimed the editor. "They may be guilty or they may be innocent. This fact the present inquiry is designed to determine."[1]

Crowds hoping to view the proceedings arrived at the courtroom early on Monday morning, August 22. Judge Houghton stationed police in the corridors with instructions to admit only those of "position and standing in the community" who "might be relied on to make no demonstration in favor or against the accused." Officers turned away all but the best-known or best-dressed citizens, a policy that resulted in an incongruous scene. Because Houghton had also put several petty cases on the docket for that morning, the refined spectators who claimed seats as soon as the doors opened watched the judge issue cursory justice to reeking drunks, barroom brawlers, and other rough characters. Those cases were "gone through hurriedly, and the woebegone wretches, fresh from their debaucheries, were fined and dismissed, scarcely attracting a glance from the audience."[2]

At 11 a.m., as Houghton prepared to resume testimony in the Digby case, he learned that Louisa Murray and Ellen Follin had yet to arrive. "Whisperings ran through the room," a reporter noted, "and the faces of the audience were directed eagerly to the door." Some spectators wondered if the defendants had fled. Theodore Hunt, who had arrived on time, spoke up for his clients, asking the judge for patience and pointing out that watches and clocks varied and that the women "lived far up town." He was certain, he said, "they would be in court shortly." Houghton, irritated, declared a recess until 11:30.[3]

During the recess, Follin and Murray appeared, accompanied by Hunt's co-counsel, A. A. Atocha. Although elegantly dressed, Follin looked somewhat "careworn." Murray, however, seemed "bright and cheerful." Having secured bail, she no longer had to stand in the prisoner's dock, and she conversed freely with her counsel. Her eyes roved inquiringly around the room, "observing the sentiment that surrounded her." Her confident demeanor once again made an impression. "There is a look and action about this woman," the *Picayune* declared, "which shows she is not to be daunted by circumstances."[4]

At 11:30, Judge Houghton returned to the bench. The clerk called the names of the accused, officers led the witnesses out of the room, and the second day of testimony began. The star witness that day was Detective John Baptiste Jourdain. For Governor Warmoth and Chief Badger, Jourdain's testimony was important. Their best Afro-Creole detective, he had helped solve a case that had garnered national headlines. He would now testify in a courtroom filled with reporters and the elite white citizens Warmoth most hoped to impress. If his testimony proved him to be an intelligent, fair, skilled, and reasonable officer of the state, it would be an important symbolic victory for the Republican regime. Quiet excitement permeated the room as the grey-eyed detective was sworn in.[5]

Prompted by prosecutor Hughes, Jourdain described his two visits to Ellen Follin's house, first with Detective Pierson on August 7 and then with Chief Badger and Detective Malone on the 9th. He acknowledged that on his second visit he was angry that Follin had lied to him two nights earlier. He also admitted to upbraiding Follin's son George Blass, shouting "you damn little rascal, why did you not tell me on Sunday night, when I asked you for the child? Where did you have it?" Blass, Jourdain recalled, confessed "that he had taken the child into the garden." When Jourdain then confronted Follin with her son's admission, "she replied that he was crazy, or something to that effect."[6]

Jourdain recounted how the facts led to Louisa Murray and his journey to Mobile, formal rendition request in hand, to find her. He told of his unsuccessful ruse to lure her into admitting her guilt and how Murray resolutely denied having brought Mollie Digby to Follin's house. Murray, Jourdain continued, told him that she had been visiting New Orleans on July 25 when a veiled white woman left the Digby baby at her sister's house and that she had left for her home in Mobile that evening. He further testified that after he returned to New Orleans with Murray in custody he was able to verify a part of her story by examining the records of the steamer that sailed nightly from New Orleans to Mobile. As soon as he heard Murray's version of events, he had recognized the discrepancy between the sisters' accounts. Follin had stated that the veiled white woman left Mollie Digby at her house on August 3; Murray said the date was July 25 and that she had left that evening for Mobile. Jourdain had asked the captain of the Mobile ship if he could see the passenger lists for July, and the "books of the boat" confirmed that Murray "did go to Mobile on the 25th of July, and arrived there on the 26th, the following day." Even if the story of the veiled woman were true, and Jourdain had his doubts, one of the sisters was either lying or badly mistaken about the date.[7]

In his cross-examination, Atocha questioned the tactics Jourdain and his fellow detectives had employed. Because New Orleans had only recently formed a detective squad, what "special officers" (as detectives were sometimes called) could and could not do was still a subject of debate. Atocha seemed bent on demonstrating that in the Digby investigation Badger's men had repeatedly crossed the line into unethical or even illegal behavior. The defense hoped to show that publicity, political pressure, and the lure of the reward had caused Badger and his men to run wild—making threats, shouting at vulnerable women and children, violating prison procedures, entering houses without warrants, and lying about their identities. Any contradictory or incriminating statements made by the innocent defendants could then be explained away as the result of stress caused by overly aggressive police practices.

Atocha asked Detective Jourdain who had authorized him to lie to Louisa Murray in Mobile, both about his identity and about what her sister had said. "Those statements," Jourdain replied, "were invented by me to further a little plan of my own. I desired to entrap Louisa into saying something that would incriminate her. I invented them for the occasion." Prosecutor Hughes, recognizing what Atocha was trying to do, objected. "Officer Jourdain's private plan...has nothing to do with the case," Hughes protested. Louisa Murray was not entrapped. "Detectives choose their own way of working up cases, and those plans do not legitimately constitute a part of the evidence of the case." Judge Houghton agreed, noting that Murray had spoken with Jourdain voluntarily even after he revealed his identity.[8]

Atocha next shifted his focus to Jourdain's actions on the two nights he searched Follin's house and the means he had used to extract information from the women and children in residence there. "At any of your visits to Ellen Follin's were there any threats made?" he asked. "Yes, sir. I made threats," Jourdain answered. "I stated that I believed [the baby] was there, and unless produced the succeeding day, that I would make an affidavit and have the whole house arrested."[9]

"Do you know of any one threatening an old colored woman there—forcing her to tell something?" Atocha continued.

"Yes, sir. I threatened her," Jourdain replied unapologetically.

Prosecutor Hughes, flabbergasted by the testimony of his own witness, blurted at Jourdain, "I protest this. Why do you answer such questions? You are not on trial." Why would Jourdain admit that he had threatened Ellen Follin's mother? Hughes wanted Jourdain to appear as an exemplar of police professionalism, not someone who menaced helpless old women and violated the public's sense of decency by obtaining evidence from the vulnerable through coercion and deception. "I am replying for myself. I will tell the truth," Jourdain responded. Judge Houghton instructed Hughes to sit down. The court would "permit this sort of examination to facilitate the trial."[10]

"What was your language to her?" Atocha resumed.

"I made those threats that I would arrest the whole house," Jourdain replied. "I wanted the child turned up; I was bluffing of course.... [I said] well this whole house will be pulled."

"Were the people frightened at your bluffing?" Atocha asked. "Yes," Jourdain responded, "the whole house was scared."

"It seems so," prosecutor Hughes interjected. "The child turned up the next day!" As laughter filled the courtroom, Atocha objected to Judge Houghton. The prosecution was playing to the crowd, he complained. "I am getting a little tired of the constant interruptions of counsel opposite—at the constant attempt at wit....We only ask fair justice. Let us conduct the case in a proper and legal way."

"I have no objection to answering any question put by the counselor for the defense," Jourdain intervened. "I thought I succeeded in scaring them," he said in response to Atocha's query into whether the residents of Follin's house were frightened. "I acted so as to scare them."[11]

"Has all your testimony here today been made freely?" Atocha asked as a final question.

"Certainly," Jourdain responded. "I am not at all uneasy about what I have said or done."

Prosecutor Dalsheimer, exasperated with Jourdain, asked to reexamine him. Although Louisiana law had once included a rule that a lawyer could not discredit their own witness, it had long since been abandoned, and Dalsheimer now challenged Jourdain. "Why didn't you tell me all this about the threats on the direct examination?" Dalsheimer asked the detective.

"Because you didn't ask me," Jourdain retorted.

"Whenever a witness goes on the stand, he takes a solemn obligation to tell the whole truth," Dalsheimer admonished.

After Jourdain growled back, "I have done so, sir," Dalsheimer stalked back to his seat.[12]

His testimony completed, Jourdain left the stand, having in some respects done an excellent job. He had shown that he was a thorough and quick-witted detective who verified facts and pursued leads aggressively even when the suspects were fellow Afro-Creoles. His efforts had caused Ellen Follin to surrender the Digby baby to the Broadwells, and his detective work had proved that at least one of the defendants was lying about the date Mollie Digby first appeared at Follin's house. For Governor Warmoth and Chief Badger's purposes, however, Jourdain's testimony was not all it should have been. Warmoth hoped to convince elite white New Orleanians that they had nothing to fear from biracial government and that Afro-Creoles like Jourdain were competent, cooperative, and moderate men willing to follow white leaders. In his testimony, however, Jourdain had demonstrated that he could not be controlled even by the state's lawyers. To be sure, Jourdain was defending police practices that today raise few objections, but in the nineteenth century the bullying and entrapping of women and children played poorly in the press and with judges and juries. The prosecution had expected Jourdain to minimize the role of coercion in his investigation, but instead his unvarnished testimony had so infuriated Dalsheimer that he treated Jourdain as a hostile witness. For whites already uneasy with black leaders asserting political autonomy and black citizens demanding service in white establishments, Jourdain's forceful independence would have seemed part of an unsettling trend.

Jourdain's testimony ended late in the afternoon. In normal circumstances, Judge Houghton might have adjourned until the next morning. But with six witnesses still to testify and the case having already occupied two days, Houghton was determined to press on and hear the much-anticipated testimony of Captain James Broadwell and his wife, Evelina. Rumors had swirled around the Broadwells since the day James appeared at the Digbys' door. Reporters wanted to know how they were connected to Ellen Follin and why the couple had taken such an interest in her defense. Even though they were being called as witnesses for the prosecution, the Broadwells, some observers believed, might yet be implicated in the crime. The courtroom buzzed as the stocky, fiercely proud captain of the *Eclipse* took the stand.

At prosecutor Dalsheimer's request, Broadwell explained that his involvement in the case had begun on August 8 when Ellen Follin's son came to their door to say that his mother needed urgently to see him. Broadwell's wife, Evelina, had asked the boy if Follin was sick. He had said no, but it was important that Broadwell come right away. Once Broadwell, who had been working in his yard, had changed into proper clothes, he and his wife took the streetcar to Follin's house, where she told them "that a child had been left with her some days before...and she wished me to take it to its father, for if it was the stolen child, as she feared it was, she as a colored woman, would be suspected of being the thief and abductor." Over his wife's objections, Broadwell had agreed to do so. "I told [Evelina] there was nothing to fear, as it would be an act of humanity," Broadwell testified, "and [I] expected also some pecuniary benefit. We then took the child and brought it home on the streetcars." The next morning he had gone to see Thomas Digby and asked him to come to the Broadwells' house to identify his daughter.[13]

Broadwell had been very surprised, however, when Digby did not immediately recognize Mollie. "Mr. Digby, when he first saw it, seemed astonished and amazed apparently," Broadwell testified. "He said, is that my Molly? My wife offered him the child. He shrunk back from it." Perhaps the girl was not Mollie Digby at all, Broadwell had wondered. She was "broken out with heat, and had one or two little boils—I think on its nose, or in that neighborhood," but she was not so disfigured as to be unrecognizable. Digby, Broadwell said, "consented to take it into his arms," although "the child did not recognize him as far as I could discover." Digby, Broadwell continued, "then proposed to take it to its mother to have it identified, saying he really did not know if it was his child or not; to which I assented and said certainly. I told him if this was not his child to bring it back." Although Digby's inability to identify the child was perplexing, Broadwell hoped she was indeed Mollie—both for the sake of the family and for his own chance of claiming the reward.[14]

Broadwell was in the midst of recounting the events that followed, including his trip to the Digbys', where Bridgette Digby identified the child as Mollie, as well as his anger at Chief Badger for attracting a crowd to his house and arresting Ellen Follin, when Prosecutor Dalsheimer interrupted and began grilling Broadwell, one of his own witnesses, just as he had Jourdain.[15]

"Why," Dalsheimer asked Broadwell, "were you not afraid that you would be suspected by taking the child of having stolen it?" "I took the child on the consciousness of doing the right thing and the [reward] advertisements of the father," Broadwell answered. Dalsheimer pressed on. "Which had the most influence on your conduct in returning the child, the consciousness of doing a good action or the advertisement of the father?" "Money was a second consideration," Broadwell asserted.

"You say you believed the woman [Ellen Follin] was innocent of the abduction of the child," Dalsheimer noted, changing course. "What induces this belief?"

"My knowledge of the woman's character. I have been her business agent for four years."

At last, evidence of Broadwell's connection to Follin had emerged. Broadwell was Follin's business agent. But what did that mean? And why would Broadwell, once a famous steamboat captain, handle business affairs for a woman who ran a lying-in hospital?

Dalsheimer pressed the point. "What is your knowledge of Ellen Follin?" he asked. "Since the death of her husband I have had charge of her business," Broadwell said.

"Was she married?" Dalsheimer asked.

"I can't say if she was married or not," Broadwell replied. "She passed as such. Mr. Angelo Blass was...who I called her husband," Broadwell replied.

"Was he a white man?" Dalsheimer queried.

"Yes, both in principle and color."

Dalsheimer saw an opening. "If a white man in principle and color, how white was he?"

"As white as you," Broadwell answered.

"How white am I?" parried Dalsheimer.

"I leave that to the court to decide," Broadwell responded, to laughter from the audience.

Atocha stepped in for the defense, objecting to the line of questioning. "This is a quarrel between the counsel and his own witness!" he declared.[16]

Dalsheimer was purposefully dragging the case once again into the complex realm of New Orleans race relations. He hoped to show that Ellen Follin, despite her refined appearance, was a woman of bad character capable of kidnapping a child for ransom or other nefarious purposes. Not only did she run a disreputable business, she had flouted standards of public decency by cohabitating out of wedlock with a white man.

Dalsheimer led Broadwell to explain his close relationship with Ellen Follin and her "husband," Angelo Blass. Blass, an Italian immigrant, had worked as a bartender for Broadwell on the *Eclipse* and other boats, and Broadwell admired him. "He was a thrifty man," Broadwell added. "He accumulated money, and he left his family well off in the world." Broadwell respected Blass's love for Follin, and he referred to her as Blass's wife despite the illegality of interracial marriage. Louisiana law had long prohibited such marriages, yet everyone was aware that Afro-Creole women often cohabitated with white men. Relationships like that between Blass and Follin, based on mutual affection, had been particularly threatening to an antebellum social order built upon the premise that black people and white people were inherently unequal. The couple had defied the law by claiming to be husband and wife, but Blass may also have "passed" as black in an effort to make their relationship legally acceptable. In the 1860 census that listed Blass and Follin living together with their children in the house at Bellecastle and Camp, Blass was identified as a "Mulatto," even though other extant documents describe him as white. During Radical Reconstruction, Louisiana law was changed to allow "all persons of whatever race or color" who had lived together before 1868 as man and wife to have their marriages formally recognized, but Angelo Blass had died the year before.[17]

Broadwell's revelations about Blass and Follin also helped explain why Follin's son George used the name Blass rather than Follin. Like Detective Jourdain, he had adopted his white father's name. Ellen Follin, herself a mulatto, may have hoped that her children could someday pass as fully white and thereby gain the economic and social opportunities that came with whiteness in a society stratified by race. As Oscar Dunn, the black lieutenant governor of Louisiana under Warmoth, wrote of "passing" in New Orleans, "if a black woman has a mulatto child, and that child married a white man, she may have children so bright you cannot say they are colored; so you see it is only a matter of two generations." Many racist whites, however, prided themselves on being able to identify mixed racial characteristics. As the Recorder's Court proceedings began, a reporter for the *Times* noted that George Blass had lighter skin than his mother, "with a face combining in its chief characteristics the peculiarities of an Italian and a Negro."[18]

Prosecutor Dalsheimer hoped to use Follin's relationship with Angelo Blass against her. Louisiana's Reconstruction legislature had in 1868 repealed the antebellum law that prohibited interracial marriage, but most white people regarded that repeal as one of the most abhorrent acts of Warmoth's regime. And because Blass died in 1867, his marriage to Follin had been illegal from start to finish.[19]

Dalsheimer was also intent on getting Broadwell to admit in open court that Follin's current profession ran afoul of social norms. Everyone in the room knew by now that she operated a lying-in hospital. The newspapers had reported that fact repeatedly ever since her arrest. But no one had said it on the record. In his effort to paint Follin as an immoral woman capable of kidnapping, Dalsheimer prodded Broadwell, the man who managed her affairs, to admit that she made a living sheltering wayward women. "What was the nature of your business transactions with Ellen Follin?" Dalsheimer asked. "I collected rents, paid taxes and insurance policies," Broadwell answered. He had been doing so since Angelo Blass's unexpected death three-and-a-half years previously, at the age of forty-nine. When Blass died, he left all of his property to Follin and their four children, but Follin had limited financial and legal expertise. Broadwell had agreed to help her and arranged for Theodore Hunt, who now was defending Follin, to file the documents that formally transferred Blass's property to Follin and her children. "Do you know the amount of her annual taxes?" Dalsheimer asked, luring Broadwell toward a discussion of her main source of income. "I do not," Broadwell responded. "Try and see if you can't remember," Dalsheimer nudged. Hunt objected for the defense, wondering if "this was again an attempt to discredit his own witness." Atocha, Hunt's co-counsel, countered, "Let him go on, we assuredly have no right to complain. But I think it decidedly interesting." "I wish the defense would leave me alone and let me conduct the case as I see fit," Dalsheimer groused before cutting straight to his main point.[20]

"What is Ellen Follin's occupation?" he asked Broadwell directly.

"Ellen Follin's business is minding her own business," Broadwell snapped back.

Dalsheimer turned sarcastic. "What is the stock and trade of Ellen Follin's minding her own business?"

Broadwell exploded. He was not going to let Dalsheimer impugn either his honor or Follin's. "Why don't we settle this question outside," he snarled.

Judge Houghton interceded, urging Broadwell not to "get excited." Broadwell, barely controlling his rage, answered the question. Before Blass's death, Follin "helped Angelo make his money" by bringing ill men home and nursing them back to health. Her current activities were equally commendable. "She is a well-behaved industrious woman, who supports her family by sewing, washing, the products of her garden and her income from rents. She lives in her own house...lives on her money, and pays her taxes." Dalsheimer's voice rose as he expressed his frustration to Judge Houghton. "I have asked proper questions which Captain Broadwell has replied to impertinently. I demand a categorical answer. Captain Broadwell evades my questions, and I mean to make him answer them if the truth is in him."[21]

Hunt then objected once again, this time to Dalsheimer's tone. "I want to know if Mr. Dalsheimer expects to force anything from the witness by roaring like the king of the beasts?"

"I am not the king of the beasts," Dalsheimer replied, this time while smiling. "There are other beasts besides me, greater ones; beasts at this very forum." The audience laughed. But Dalsheimer would not let his previous point go. "Does Ellen Follin ever take boarders or lodgers?" he asked.

"Not to my knowledge," Broadwell claimed.

"Have you been in her house since this prosecution commenced?" Dalsheimer wondered.

"Yes."

"Who did you see in the house besides Ellen Follin?"

Broadwell knew who Dalsheimer was asking about and acknowledged he "saw a white lady who the papers designate as [Minnie] Green."

"Were you not aware she was a lodger?" Dalsheimer asked.

"No I was not," came the reply. Broadwell added that on his previous visits to Follin's house Minnie Green was not there, nor was the Digby baby. The first time he saw the Digby baby at Follin's address was when he and his wife went there on the evening of August 8. At that time Follin told him that the child had been there since the previous Wednesday (August 3), and he believed her.

As his final question Dalsheimer asked Broadwell, "Did you return to Mr. Digby the same child you received from Mrs. Follin?"

"Yes, it was the same child," Broadwell replied disgustedly.[22]

On cross-examination, Hunt asked Broadwell if he thought Follin led an immoral life. Broadwell replied that Ellen Follin and Angelo Blass were his close friends, and he knew them to be upstanding people. Follin's house, he said firmly, "was always decent. She never had a lewd house. Ellen does not lead a lewd life."[23]

Hunt then turned to Judge Houghton and protested the fact that both Ellen Follin and the Broadwells had been subjected to a smear campaign. He noted that even though the Broadwells had done a good deed by returning Mollie Digby to her parents, their "characters have been aspersed and motives questioned since the beginning of these arrests. They have been held up to public obloquy and their connection with the case persistently misrepresented." To prove the point, the defense asked to submit as evidence a letter Evelina Broadwell had recently received in the mail. Judge Houghton perused the note and agreed that it could be read into the record. It read:

New Orleans, August 18, 1870

Mrs. Broadwell—If you wish to know why your husband takes such an interest in the woman, Ellen Follin, I have to inform you that she is his mistress.

A True Friend

P. S. She has a child by him.[24]

Prosecutor Hughes objected immediately. The letter, he argued, "was not signed and carried with it no responsibility." It could not be admitted as evidence of anything, "unless the man who wrote the letter should be brought into court." The defense replied that the letter demonstrated the gross aspersions being cast at the Broadwells by the public, the press, and the prosecution. The letter "was designed to embitter his domestic relations and raise up strife in his family" by accusing Captain Broadwell of "living in public concubinage with this woman."[25]

The courtroom was in an uproar. People had expected something salacious to emerge from Broadwell's testimony, and now it had. Rather than coming from the prosecution, it was introduced by the defense in an effort to demonstrate that the rumor-mongering public was out of control. To restore order, Judge Houghton banged his gavel and called for a five-minute recess.

When the court reconvened, Evelina Broadwell took the stand. Much of her testimony echoed her husband's, although she placed greater emphasis on her initial discomfort with Ellen Follin's request that they return the Digby baby to its parents. Evelina recalled that when Follin asked, "What am I to do with the child?" she had replied that "it ought to be returned to the father, of course," but had then said to her husband, "I don't want to have anything to do with it; we might get into difficulty by taking the child home." However, when her husband "said he thought not, there was no danger, as the papers said no questions would be asked," Evelina had acquiesced.[26]

Evelina also corroborated her husband's recollection that when Digby arrived at their house "he didn't know his child." She had asked Digby directly, "Do you know your child?" and he had said "no." She "insisted on his taking it three times," but he said "I don't want to take it, for fear it isn't my child." Eventually, at her urging, he had agreed to take the baby home to see if his wife recognized her. Digby left and an hour later so did her husband. When her husband did not return, she too went to the Digbys' house. "I wanted to see if it was the child, and some boys showed me the house," she testified. There she learned that Bridgette Digby had identified the baby as her own.[27]

On cross-examination, Hunt asked Evelina if she believed she had been mistreated by the police. In reply, she recalled how frightened she had been to find Chief Badger and an angry crowd at her door the day they returned Mollie to her family. When she approached her house, the scene had seemed ominous "as the crowd in front was becoming large" and "some were engaged in fitting keys to the lock, others trying to force the gate." Four men, including Badger and Thomas Digby, had surrounded her, and she felt she had no choice but to allow them inside, since the situation outside seemed perilous. Badger had then proceeded to browbeat her. He had demanded to know where the Broadwells found the child, and threatened her with prosecution if she did not tell him. Meanwhile, the crowd was shouting threats from the street. Terrified, Evelina had revealed Ellen Follin's name. Badger and his men had immediately left, heading uptown. As they did, Evelina recalled, "Mr. Digby said something about a 'thief' and some one out in the street cried out that the house ought to be torn down and the Broadwells hung." Judge Houghton asked Evelina if she thought "that the Chief brought the crowd there." She replied, "I don't think he gathered up the crowd, but he didn't drive them away.... He could have gone out on the front gallery and told them to go away."[28]

When Evelina Broadwell's testimony concluded at 7 p.m., Judge Houghton insisted that he and the lawyers go to Ellen Follin's house to take the testimony of Minnie Green, whose pregnancy prevented her from appearing in court. The attorneys reluctantly agreed. After a long, hot day in the courtroom, judge, lawyers, and a reporter from the New Orleans *Times* all took carriages uptown, where they set up a candlelit court in Follin's dining room. Minnie Green came downstairs, and Judge Houghton swore her in. He asked her to "make a statement of all she knows of this trial." She began slowly: "My name is Mrs. Minnie Green; I am a married woman, and my husband's name is...." Here she paused, before saying, "Green, of course." Judge Houghton then asked, "are you residing here?" to which Green replied, "For the present I am temporarily residing here."[29]

Prosecutor Dalsheimer, determined yet again to demonstrate for the record that Follin conducted an immoral operation, immediately went to work discrediting his own witness, prodding her to admit that Minnie Green was not even her real name. "Are you known by any other name?" Dalsheimer asked.

"I am not aware that I am known by any other name," she answered.

"Were you ever known by any other name than Minnie Green?" he asked more specifically.

"I do not wish to divulge it" she replied, adding, "I had another name certainly."

Dalsheimer tried again. "Did you ever give a name other than that to any one since you were in the house?" At that point, Atocha spoke up in Green's defense. "The witness for the state is not being examined, but cross-examined!" he charged. "And prosecuted!" Hunt chimed in. Dalsheimer's course was "improper and illegal" and indicative of how the state had acted against defenseless women throughout the Digby investigation. Judge Houghton, increasingly frustrated with the attorneys' bickering, shook his head. The witness, he ruled, must answer the question.

"Yes," Green said. She had once given another name, but she did not now want to say what that name was. Back in May while she was at Louisa Murray's house in Mobile, she told a census taker that her name was Minnie Roset, but that too was likely an alias. Hunt could not resist getting in a dig at Dalsheimer. "You have come here to discredit your own witness and have done it," he said mockingly. Dalsheimer replied that he "simply wished to identify the witness." Judge Houghton urged the attorneys to move on.[30]

Dalsheimer may already have known that Green was not going to be as useful a witness as he had once hoped. According to the police, Green had said that Mollie was already at Ellen Follin's house when Green arrived on July 22. Green had also allegedly told the police that Louisa Murray recognized the child and called her "Camellia." But now, testifying in a makeshift courtroom in Follin's house, she corroborated Follin's story that the child did not appear until August 3. "It was here to my knowledge from the 3rd until the day previous to its being given to its father," Green stated. "I asked no questions concerning the child, being a stranger in the house."[31]

Certain that his witness had turned against him, Dalsheimer interrupted and again demanded to know her real name. "Have you any other name?" he bellowed. "The state has a right to establish the undeniable identity of the witness." Atocha objected for the defense, reminding Dalsheimer that the prosecution had subpoenaed Minnie Green, that she had testified to her name under oath and they therefore "had no right to go into the lady's history. It was a cross-examination they had no right to make."[32]

An exasperated Judge Houghton pronounced the case a "remarkable one." The defense had called no one to the stand, but one witness after another seemed to have become defense witnesses while testifying. "I rule that the witness answer the question," Houghton continued. "Now, madam, answer the question—since you have been in this house have you given another name?"

"If I have, I don't know it," Green replied.

"The witness is being obstinate," Dalsheimer admonished. "Have you not already said under oath that you gave another name?"

"You confused me so much that I have forgotten what I said," Green answered.

Judge Houghton had had enough. "The hearing of this case is adjourned until further notice," he declared. "It is impossible to continue under such circumstances."[33]

When word of Minnie Green's uncooperative testimony reached the public, the press turned on her. "It cannot be disguised that the great kidnapping case changes its aspect with the rapidity of a drama," the *Picayune* editorialized. "Statements are made by persons at one time which they subsequently modify and change until scarcely an original feature is left." The paper reminded readers that Green had previously told Chief Badger that the child in question was at the house on July 22 and that "she remembered the circumstance distinctly" because "it was a white child in a colored family." But since the police released Ellen Follin from jail, "a serious change has come over Miss Green's recollection. The wand of enchantment has descended, and the evidence wears an entirely new and different aspect." Her version of events was like a card trick: "now you see it and now you don't see it."[34]

Late Monday evening, a heavy rain started to fall, accompanied by thunder and lightning. A tropical system the newspapers called an "equinoxial storm" had moved in from the Gulf of Mexico. The downpour continued through the night and all the next day. Many streets, particularly in low-lying neighborhoods like the back-of-town filled with muddy water. Some avenues, the *Republican* quipped, became "navigable for Red River steamboats." The *Picayune* called for "the authorities to be looking well to the levees of the canals at the rear of the city."[35]

Neither the rain nor the flooding deterred the numerous spectators who arrived at the courtroom early Tuesday morning for what promised to be a day of compelling testimony. The *Picayune* observed that "the sloppy, muddy streets, could not prevent the populace crowding to the courtroom, with an appetite undulled by previous revelations, still anxiously watching for more." The prosecution planned to put Rosa Gorman, August Singler, and Georgie Digby—three crucial witnesses—on the stand. Each of them had identified Louisa Murray as the woman who kidnapped Mollie Digby. If all three provided convincing testimony and withstood cross-examination, the state would have a very convincing case. Prosecutors had yet to provide a motive for the crime, but three positive identifications of Murray as the kidnapper might well seal the sisters' fate.[36]

At 11 a.m., as the hearing-turned-quasi-trial was set to resume for a third day, Judge Houghton learned that Ellen Follin and Louisa Murray were once again late. Furious, Houghton announced that "if they do not present themselves shortly, I will be compelled to impose a fine on each." Theodore Hunt, who had spoken up for his tardy clients the previous morning, said resignedly, "I shall offer no objection to anything the court determines upon." But A. A. Atocha told the judge that because of the rain the streetcar tracks were "covered with mud and apparently out of order." After forty-five minutes passed, Houghton issued attachments for Murray and Follin, sent court officers to find them, and adjourned the proceedings until 1 p.m.[37]

When the sisters finally arrived shortly after noon and the court resumed, Atocha tried to appease Judge Houghton, who was ready to fine them for contempt of court. The defendants' "tardiness caused infinite trouble and expense," Houghton lectured. He had dozens of other cases to hear and the defendants had insulted the court by being late two days in a row. "I am aware an offense against the dignity of the court has been committed," Atocha genuflected, "but before the penalty is inflicted I beg the court to listen to the excuse." Murray and Follin, Atocha reported, had left Follin's house on time, but as they were leaving, a man who falsely claimed to have been sent by Atocha appeared. The imposter, intent on delaying the women to cause them trouble with the court, told them Atocha was coming to get them and they should wait at the house. He then "began filling their ears with declarations that had no origin except in his own mind." Eventually the sisters grew suspicious and "started for the cars." The man followed them, "persecuting them with his attentions, and insisting on being heard." He pursued them onto the streetcar, at which point "they were compelled to call a policeman to protect them." As a result, "the car was delayed and the man fled." This type of harassment, Atocha added, was typical of what Murray and Follin were experiencing each day. "This is only one of the persecutions to which these women are subjected," Atocha averred. "Whatever shall be the ultimate result of this case, I for one shall stand by them. If it be not true that they have been persecuted this morning, your honor can ascertain it by telegraphing [the Seventh Precinct]. I beg your honor will not fine them." Prosecutor Dalsheimer tried to interject, but Houghton told him to "stay quiet." The judge would give the defendants one more chance. "The excuse you give is satisfactory," he said. "I will simply remind these parties that they were a half an hour late yesterday."[38]

The bailiff called Rosa Gorman, the Digbys' testy young neighbor, to the stand. Gorman, who had been babysitting Mollie Digby when the child was kidnapped, was a reluctant witness. She had previously complained of having been "put to too much trouble already on account of the child," and she may have still felt the sting of Bridgette Digby's criticism of her for leaving Mollie with strangers. On August 12, she had been dragooned from her job at a Rampart Street candy store by Chief Badger's driver, who had brought her against her will to the Digbys' house, where she had identified Louisa Murray as the kidnapper. Gorman now found herself once again compelled to appear, this time by the prosecution's subpoena. Had she refused, she could have been fined $1,000 and imprisoned in the parish jail for three months or more.[39]

Judge Houghton opened the questioning of Gorman by asking her to tell what she knew about the case. Gorman, no doubt hoping to make her time on the stand as brief as possible, was terse. Pointing at Murray and Follin, Gorman said that on "the evening of the 9th of June, these two colored women came up Howard Street. I am not positively certain it was they, but I think they are the persons."[40]

Prosecutor Dalsheimer knew immediately that he had a disaster on his hands. Having uttered only two sentences, Gorman had already admitted that she could not *positively* identify Louisa Murray as the kidnapper. Further, she had identified Ellen Follin as the woman who accompanied the kidnapper on

June 9. No one else had placed Follin at the scene of the crime. The woman seen with the kidnapper was reportedly short and dark-skinned. Follin, who was being charged only as an accomplice for hiding Mollie Digby at her house, was tall and light-skinned. Trying to control the damage, Dalsheimer asked that he, rather than Judge Houghton, be allowed to ask the preliminary questions. Houghton replied that he wanted to hear the witness make her statements first.[41]

Gorman continued. On the night of the kidnapping, Mollie Digby was playing "on the banquette...and the two colored women were talking to [her]." A fire broke out down the street, and Gorman wanted to see it. One of the colored women offered to watch Mollie, and Gorman accepted the offer. That was all she knew. By the time she returned from the fire, Mollie was gone. Again pointing at Louisa Murray, Gorman declared, "I cannot say it was this one."[42]

When Judge Houghton finally turned Dalsheimer loose, the prosecutor did what he could to turn Gorman's testimony around. Gesturing at the accused, Dalsheimer asked the witness, "Have you ever seen them before?" Gorman replied, "The one with the blue veil [Louisa Murray] looks very familiar to me. The other I never saw before." "Do you remember the occasion on which you saw Louisa Murray?" Dalsheimer queried. "I do not," Gorman replied uncooperatively. She had, at the very least, seen Murray eleven days earlier when she was asked to identify her outside the Digbys' house. "Could you identify the woman who took the child?" Dalsheimer asked. "I thought I once could, but she has gone out of my mind," Gorman answered. "Does Louisa Murray look like her?" Dalsheimer asked. "Objection!" Atocha interrupted. "The prosecution is leading the witness." Dalsheimer rephrased his question. "Who did the woman look like then?" "She looked like Louisa Murray," Gorman conceded.[43]

Dalsheimer pressed on, determined to make Rosa Gorman positively identify Louisa Murray as the kidnapper. "Did you ever see Louisa Murray before this trial?" he asked. "Once I saw her with Captain Badger," Gorman said, now recalling the day she was asked to identify Murray. Atocha seized on her answer, requesting that it "be set down literally" in the record—Gorman had said she had seen Murray "once," not twice. "How was she dressed then?" Dalsheimer resumed. "She was dressed the very same way she is now," said Gorman. "Had she the same kind of hat on?" the prosecutor asked. "No," said Gorman. "She put a seaside on."

"Did you recognize her then?" asked Dalsheimer. "She looked very much like the woman who took the child," Gorman replied. "What remark did you make then relating to her identity?" Dalsheimer asked. "I made no remark but one," Gorman answered. "When she put the seaside on, I said she looked very much like the woman who took the child."[44]

Raising his voice, Dalsheimer tried once more. "Did you or did you not once say that you identified her as the woman?" Atocha objected. The question again was "very leading, and presupposes the answer," but Judge Houghton told Gorman to respond. "I once stated that she was the one," Gorman answered, even though the most she had ever said was that the seaside hat made her "more assured" that Murray was the kidnapper. Dalsheimer, having salvaged something from Gorman's testimony, rested. Even though Gorman had said flatly that she could not positively identify Murray as the abductor, Dalsheimer had made her admit that she once had done so.[45] On cross-examination, Atocha also found Rosa Gorman uncooperative. Delighted by her acknowledgement that she could not confidently identify Murray as the kidnapper, Atocha also wanted her to testify that Chief Badger had violated police procedures on August 12 when he asked Gorman to identify Murray at the Digbys' house. Atocha believed that Badger's driver had told Gorman in advance that they had Mollie's kidnapper in custody and that Gorman *must* identify her. Once she arrived, the police chief, in front of a large crowd, pressured Gorman to implicate Murray. When she seemed uncertain, Badger had used the cheap trick of placing the seaside hat on her head. Unfortunately for Atocha, Gorman was as unwilling to help him as she was to assist Dalsheimer.

"Who brought you to Louisa Murray?" Atocha asked her. "He was a cab driver. I don't know his name," Gorman answered. "Did the cabman who came after you deliver a message to you?" Atocha continued. "He said I was wanted at Mr. Digby's house," Gorman replied. Atocha asked Gorman to identify the cabman, and she pointed to Kuntz Stollberger, Badger's driver, who was in the audience. Prosecutor Hughes acknowledged he was the driver for the chief of police. "Where did he take you?" Atocha asked. "To 181 Howard Street," Gorman responded. As soon as she arrived, Murray was brought outside for her to identify. "When I was face to face with her they asked me if she was the woman who took the child." She told Badger she was not sure, but they then gave Murray the seaside hat to put on. "Who was it who [gave] the seaside hat to Louisa Murray?" Atocha inquired. "I do not remember," Gorman replied.

Atocha asked Gorman "to please look at [Chief] Badger and see if he wasn't the person."

"I can't say. I don't remember."

"Why was it put on her?"

"I can't say," insisted Gorman.

"When the seaside was put on Louisa Murray were you not immediately asked if she didn't look like the woman who stole the child?"

"Yes."

"Did she seem frightened?" Atocha asked as his last question.

"Not apparently—she was smiling," Gorman recalled.[46]

Once excused, Gorman quickly exited the courtroom. She may have believed that her uncooperativeness would keep her from being called as a witness if the case moved on to the district court. Despite her grudging testimony, however, she now was indispensable to the defense. She may not have given Atocha everything he wanted, but her testimony did seem to create reasonable doubt about Louisa Murray's guilt. Gorman had spoken directly to the kidnapper, and she was not sure Murray was the same woman.

The next witness, August Singler, did not share Gorman's uncertainty. When Judge Houghton asked him to describe his connection to the case, Singler said that he was a close friend of the Digbys, that he was standing on Howard Avenue on June 9, and that he had seen Louisa Murray kidnap Mollie. He was certain, he said, that it was Murray he had seen commit the crime. Because he worked posting theater bills and most New Orleans theaters had closed in June for the summer, he was unemployed on June 9 and was passing the time outside the Digbys' house. Like Rosa Gorman, he was drawn by the excitement surrounding the fire at Seligman's Photography Studio. Before he headed that way, however, the Digbys' crying child had caught his attention. He had seen Louisa Murray with Mollie in her arms, accompanied by little Georgie Digby and another black woman. Murray was trying to quiet the child by giving her a piece of candy, but the child "fought at her face." He could also hear Georgie saying, "I don't want to go, I don't want to go." Then Singler heard Murray ask Georgie to show her where a certain dressmaker lived down the street. Georgie, Singler claimed, finally agreed to guide Murray, and the trio walked off. Singler had gone toward the fire.[47]

When the police later apprehended Murray, Chief Badger had brought Singler to Murray's cell. There Badger had asked him if he wanted to see Murray in a seaside hat, but Singler had said it was not necessary. He remembered "the woman's face he saw petting the child, and would know it again under any hat." Murray's face, he testified, was "vividly impressed" on his memory. When Badger had Murray come out from her cell and sit under a gas light, Singler had immediately said it was she; he "could not be mistaken; there was no possibility of mistake; she was the woman."[48]

Prosecutor Dalsheimer was pleased with Singler's testimony. Unlike Gorman, Singler did not equivocate. "Are you sure the woman Louisa Murray now sitting there is the woman?" Dalsheimer asked his witness, pointing at Murray.

"Yes, sir, I am positive she is the woman I saw talking to Georgie Digby the evening of the 9th of June at the corner of Howard and Poydras streets," Singler declared.[49]

Atocha cross-examined Singler for the defense, knowing that it was crucial to discredit him as a witness. If Singler's testimony stood unchallenged, Murray and Follin were in trouble. Atocha, however, believed the young man was lying. If he was a good friend of the Digbys and saw their children being led away against their will, why didn't he intervene? Why had Singler not come forward earlier with a description of the kidnapper? It seemed unlikely that someone who had witnessed the abduction would remain silent for almost two months, particularly with large rewards at stake. Why did he not say something during the hours he spent with Thomas Digby on June 9 looking for Mollie? How could he not have told Digby that he had witnessed the kidnapping?

"How long have you known Thomas Digby?" Atocha asked Singler. "I have lived in the neighborhood for seven years and have known Digby for just over a year," Singler replied. "During that time I have been intimate with him. I have been in and out of his house nearly every day." "Have you ever been in his employ?" Atocha asked. "No, sir," Singler replied. "Have you assisted him in searching for the child?" "Yes, sir."

"While so assisting him have you not had frequent conversations with him about the loss of his child?" Atocha queried.

"Yes, sir."

Atocha changed course momentarily. "How was Louisa Murray dressed that evening you saw her talking to Georgie Digby?" he asked. "She had on a calico dress, spotted, sort of second mourning, and a seaside hat with a blue ribbon," Singler said.

Atocha closed in. How could he have such a precise memory the kidnapping and what the kidnapper was wearing and not have told Thomas Digby. "Did you see Mr. Digby that day?" Atocha asked.

"Yes," Singler replied, "about half-past 8 o'clock" when he informed Thomas that Mollie was gone.

"Didn't you give Mr. Digby a description of the woman you saw talking to his children?"

"I did not."

"Have you conversed with Chief Badger or any of his officers about this case?" Atocha asked.

"Only once. At his office. It was the occasion of my coming there to identify Louisa Murray," Singler responded.

"How did you know she was there?"

"I was informed so."

"Who informed you?"

"Mr. Digby sent word to my house."

Atocha pounced. "How is it that you never had any communication with Mr. Digby about the description of this woman whom you saw talking to his children, and yet he sent for you to identify Louisa Murray?" he asked.

"Because there are more than me who know her," Singler replied cryptically.

"That is not an answer to my question," Atocha fired back. "How is it that you never had any communication with Mr. Digby about the description of this woman whom you saw talking to his children, and yet he sent for you to identify Louisa Murray?"

"I have had conversations with his wife about her, and I presume she told him."

"Why didn't you say that at first?" Atocha wondered.

"I didn't understand you."

"When did you speak to Mrs. Digby about it?"

"A day or two afterward."

"What did you say to her?"

"I don't recollect."

"Did you then or at any time give Mrs. Digby a description of the woman you say you saw?"

"Yes, sir I did."

"Did you ever give it to Mr. Digby?"

"No, sir."

Atocha had backed Singler into a corner. Singler testified that he was in and out of the Digbys' house every day and that he helped Thomas search for his daughter. Was it plausible that he would never mention to Digby that he saw the kidnapping occur? Atocha did not think so. He believed that Singler, perhaps at Thomas Digby's request, invented his story on August 12 after Rosa Gorman and George Digby had trouble positively identifying Murray.

Atocha then challenged Singler's account of the kidnapping itself. "You described the woman to Mrs. Digby just as you saw her, did you not?" continued Atocha. "Yes, sir," Singler replied. "How far were you from her at the time she was talking to the children?" Atocha asked. "About ten feet." "Was the woman's back or face to you?" "Her side face," Singler answered. "I thought you would take middle ground," Atocha said sarcastically. "I asked you purposely, and was satisfied you would answer as you did....How much of her features were visible?" "I saw all her features," Singler said. "While she was talking to the child it said 'Dada' and pointed to me. At this the woman turned squarely around and looked me in the face." Atocha let his incredulity spill out. "A beautiful explanation. The counsel couldn't have done it better." Atocha took his seat. "I have no more questions."[50]

Judge Houghton excused Singler and ordered a short recess. When the court reconvened, ten-year-old Georgie Digby took the stand despite the fact that the prosecution knew that the testimony of children could be problematic.

In a Recorder's Court examination, it was up to the judge to decide if the child's faculties were "sufficiently developed" to understand the obligation to testify truthfully. Before the boy was sworn in, Judge Houghton asked him if he understood the nature of an oath. Georgie said that he knew "if he told the truth he would go to Heaven, but if he lied he would go to the devil." Satisfied with that reply, Houghton had the bailiff administer the oath.[51]

The judge then asked Georgie to describe the afternoon his sister disappeared. Georgie said that he was playing with other children in the street when Rosa Gorman left him and his sister with the two "colored" women. One of the women had asked him if he knew where a dressmaker named Mrs. Cook could be found. "I told her, yes," Georgie said. "I showed her where Mrs. Cook, the dressmaker lived and she said 'Oh, no bubby, that's not the place.'" They had walked on until they got to Philippa and Lafayette Streets. There one of the women gave him a two-bit bill to go and get bananas. When he came back, the women and Mollie were gone.[52]

"Would you know the colored woman if you saw her again?" Dalsheimer asked Georgie.

"Yes, sir," he answered.

"Look around and see if you can point her out," Dalsheimer told the boy.

"There she is," Georgie said, pointing to Louisa Murray. "The yellow woman took the child, that last one...she has on a blue veil."

"How was she dressed?" Dalsheimer then asked.

"She had on a white dress." Georgie answered.

"Was it all white?"

"No, sir. It had spots on it."

Dalsheimer knew then that he had another problem. August Singler had testified that Murray was wearing a somber, calico "second mourning" dress. Georgie Digby said she was wearing a white dress. Even if it had spots, no one would confuse a white dress with the somber "second mourning" dresses Victorian women wore during the second year after the death of their husbands.

The discrepancy was also not lost on Atocha, but in his cross-examination, Atocha first raised the fact that Georgie had not always been so certain Murray was the kidnapper. He asked the boy whether he had initially recognized

Murray when police brought her to his house on August 12. "My father asked me if that was the woman and I told him no, this was not the woman," Georgie responded. But once they put a seaside hat on her, he continued, she looked familiar. "Then I said 'yes, that's the woman!'" the boy testified. "I know'd it was the woman as soon as she put the hat on."[53]

Atocha then led Georgie to further undermine Singler's testimony. Because he was sequestered in Houghton's chambers while Singler testified, the boy did not know Singler had claimed that he saw Mollie crying and hitting Murray, that Murray tried to calm her with candy, and that Mollie pointed at Singler and said "dada."

When the woman who kidnapped Mollie was holding her, "did the baby say anything at all?" Atocha asked.

"No sir," George answered.

"Did she slap anybody's face?" Atocha asked.

"No, sir."

Dalsheimer, recognizing the danger, tried to object. Atocha appealed to Judge Houghton, saying, "Fair play is a jewel you know. We have a right to the answer." Houghton agreed.

"Did this woman give Molly any cakes or candy?" Atocha asked the boy.

"No, sir," he answered.

"Do you know Mr. Singler?" Atocha continued.

"Yes, sir."

"Does he often come to your house?"

"Yes, sir."

"Did you see him at the corner where Molly was taken away?"

"No, sir."

"Recollect as well as you can whether you saw Mr. Singler that day," Atocha instructed Georgie.

"No, sir, I didn't," Georgie replied, "Mr. Singler was not there."

Atocha ended then, confident that he had struck a decisive blow. Not only did Georgie's testimony directly contradict Singler's, the boy said he did not see Singler at the scene. If Georgie Digby's testimony was true, Singler had willfully perjured himself, a crime punishable by "no less than five years in prison."

Dalsheimer had put three witnesses on the stand to identify Murray as the kidnapper. Rosa Gorman said she could not do so. Georgie Digby said he could, but only after police costumed Murray in a seaside hat. August Singler, it appeared, had fabricated his story out of whole cloth.[54]

Georgie Digby's testimony ended in the late afternoon, so Judge Houghton adjourned the court until noon the next day. "If it is within the bounds of possibility the case must be concluded tomorrow," he announced before gaveling the day to a close.[55]

Louisa Murray and Ellen Follin headed home in the rain, lifting their dresses as they crossed the muddy avenue to the streetcar. Some members of the press remarked that the sisters were holding up remarkably well. "It cannot be disguised that they are bold, intelligent and shrewd," the Picayune commented. "They have borne their trying situation with a nerve and address which would do credit to the courage of men.... Occasionally, as the witnesses would testify to some point, a fact that bore most heavily upon them, their faces would flash with an emotion of momentary fear and anger. But the feeling was transient, and passed away with the rapidity of thought."[56]

By the next morning, the rain had slowed but not stopped. Many streets in New Orleans remained flooded. Despite the weather, another overflow crowd arrived for what would be the last day of the Digby proceedings in the Recorder's Court. "At an early hour, long before the court convened, people began to come in and pick out favorite seats in the courtroom," the Picayune reported. "Notwithstanding that this examination has already consumed three days, the public interest and excitement appears in no ways abated." A large number of women, in particular, braved the rain, expressing "a determination to see the last of it."[57]

At Judge Houghton's request, prosecutor Dalsheimer and defense lawyer Atocha arrived at court two hours early. Houghton told the men that he wanted to make a quick trip uptown to complete Minnie Green's testimony before the courtroom proceedings began at noon. The judge had been frustrated two nights earlier when their first effort to hear from Green had descended into pointless bickering. Houghton believed that a smaller entourage might create "less occasion for legal wrangling," and he thought Atocha and Dalsheimer would be more cooperative than Theodore Hunt and David Hughes, the two senior attorneys. At 10 a.m., Houghton, Atocha, Dalsheimer, a court clerk, and a reporter for the *Times* traveled by carriage to Ellen Follin's house at Bellecastle and Camp. Minnie Green was there and agreed to testify. She was sworn in and resumed her testimony at Follin's dining room table.[58]

Two nights earlier the examination had stalled when Dalsheimer demanded that Green provide her real name. This time, he simply allowed her to give her version of events. She testified that Mollie Digby was not at Follin's house when she arrived there in July and that she had seen the child for the first time on August 4. Follin, she said, told her then that the girl had been dropped off by a veiled white woman the day before. Three days later, Detectives Jourdain and Pierson had come to the gate, calling for the "stolen child."

"What answer was given to the officers when they asked for a stolen child?" Dalsheimer asked.

"They were told there was no child of such description," Green replied, "They did not ask if there were any other children in the house."

"Was Molly Digby in the house that night?" Dalsheimer asked.

"Oh, certainly. The child had been here a short time," Green replied, adding that since its arrival the child had "slept with the other children and was allowed to roam freely around the house and yard."

"Did Murray or Follin say anything else about the child?" Dalsheimer asked.

"I heard Ellen Follin say she was afraid she would get into trouble about the child, as the woman had not come back to reclaim it," Green answered. "I heard her say that she would send for a friend and have it taken to see if it was a child that those policemen or officers had described. That was on Monday."

Dalsheimer suspected Green may have been forced to confirm Murray's and Follin's story. "Are there any facts connected with this case which you have failed to disclose here through fear that something might happen to you in the future?" he asked. "I desire you be particularly careful about answering this question."

Atocha objected: "Don't attempt to lecture the witness."

"If I have failed I don't know it," Green said. "I have answered the best that I could to your questions."

Dalsheimer tried again. "Is there anything, to your knowledge, that you have not stated?"

"No, sir," She replied.

"Are you afraid to state the whole truth?" Judge Houghton asked Green.

"No, sir; I am not," she responded. "There are no facts that I failed to disclose out of fear."

Dalsheimer went a step further. "Are there any facts connected with this case which you have withheld on account of any anxiety relative to your peculiar situation in the house of Ellen Follin?"

Atocha objected, but Houghton instructed Green to answer. "There are none, as I do not consider my condition as any way peculiar," Green claimed. She was not there to hide, she said; she was there to rest, to be "retired and quiet." Dalsheimer asked additional questions, but Green would not be shaken from her testimony and would not admit that she was at Follin's house for an illicit purpose. Becoming increasingly frustrated, Dalsheimer eventually gave up. "I close the examination most emphatically," he declared.[59]

Atocha's cross-examination of Green gave her an opportunity to clarify when she had first seen the Digby baby and why the police and press were claiming that her story had changed. The newspapers reported that Green had told police that Mollie was already at Follin's house when she arrived there on July 22. In her abbreviated testimony two nights earlier, Green had claimed that Mollie arrived at the house on August 3.

"Was the child in Ellen Follin's house the day you arrived?" Atocha asked Green.

"It was not. I did not see it," she replied.

"From the day that you arrived up to the day you said the child was brought here, did you go about the house and premises freely?" asked Atocha.

"I did," Green answered.

"Did you observe any secrecy or mysteriousness in the actions of the inmates of this house from the 22nd of July up to the time the child was brought here?"

"No, sir."

"Who did you find in the house when you came here the 22nd of July?"

"I saw Mrs. Follin and her children."

"Any strangers?"

"There was a lady here," Green replied. "I was not acquainted with her; I was informed that her name was Mrs. Tracy. She left here on the day the child was brought."

"Didn't Mrs. Tracy have a child?" Atocha asked.

"Yes, sir."

"Did she take that child with her when she left?"

"She did."

"Did you state to any one that when you came here there was a child in the house?" Atocha asked.

"I was asked if, when I came here, there was a child, and I said there was."

"What child did you refer to?"

"The child of Mrs. Tracy," Green said.

To make sure the point was clear, Atocha posed the question again. "The child you spoke of as being here on the 22nd of July when you came, was it Mrs. Tracy's?"

"Yes, sir," Green answered. "It was Mrs. Tracy's child I alluded to."

"Did you ever tell anyone that [the Digby child] was here on the 22nd of July?"

"If I did I am not aware of it, or else I must have been crazy," Green told him.

When Atocha closed his examination, Dalsheimer tried on redirect to once again raise the question of Green's true identity and circumstances. "You say you are a married woman," he began. But Atocha objected, reminding the court that on redirect Dalsheimer was limited to points brought out by his cross-examination. Green's identity was not one of them. Judge Houghton agreed with Atocha, and Dalsheimer gave up in disgust. Houghton then adjourned the proceedings; they were already running late. The men moved quickly to the carriages, hurrying back downtown to the courtroom, where a restless crowd had been waiting for hours.[60]

It was 2 o'clock when the Recorder's Court resumed and the bailiff called Mollie's mother, Bridgette Digby, to the stand. Mrs. Digby's testimony was short, straightforward, and remarkable, given that one month earlier her husband had briefly checked her into a charity asylum. Dalsheimer, treating her gently, asked only a few questions about the day Mollie was abducted and the day she was returned. Bridgette testified that everything she knew about the kidnapping she had heard secondhand from Rosa Gorman, August Singler, and her "little boy." She offered that the descriptions of the abductor they had given her seemed to match "the woman in court." Further, she forcefully stated that the child returned by Captain Broadwell was her daughter, Mollie. "There is no mistake about it," she asserted. "I heard it say 'mama' as soon as it came to the door and I recognized it the moment I laid eyes on it. A mother would know her child anywhere."[61]

Atocha declined to cross-examine Mrs. Digby. Although he could have (and perhaps should have) asked her about August Singler and his claim that he had witnessed the kidnapping, Atocha knew that the poor woman had suffered enough, and he allowed her to leave the stand, her testimony unchallenged.

George Blass testified last. Once a named defendant, Blass was now a subpoenaed prosecution witness, forced to take the stand. It was Blass's disappearance on the night of August 7 that had made Detectives Jourdain and Pierson particularly suspicious. After Blass was sworn in, Judge Houghton asked him to state all he knew about the case. Under Louisiana law, witnesses, like defendants, could not be compelled to answer questions if the answer would furnish evidence to justify a prosecution for a crime. But Blass answered willingly. "The child came to our house on the 3rd day of August and I didn't know any more about it except what I was told," Blass said. "I was told on the 4th of August that a white woman left it at the gate."[62]

Blass then made a statement that caused Atocha, his own counsel, to prematurely jump up to question him. Blass claimed that although the child arrived on the 3rd, "he never saw anything of it until the 7th of August following." Atocha knew this statement was unbelievable. Minnie Green had testified that morning that Mollie had roamed freely around the house and played with the other children. It seemed improbable that Blass, who lived in the house, could have not seen the child for four days. Blass's behavior was suspicious on August 7, and now his testimony was raising doubts. Atocha needed to try to fix the damage, and both Houghton and the prosecutors inexplicably let him interrupt.

"You are the son of Ellen Follin, are you not?" Atocha asked.

"Yes, sir," Blass replied.

"From the time the child came until it left, didn't you live there?" Atocha continued.

"Yes, sir," answered Blass.

"And you didn't see it in the meantime?"

Blass took the hint. "Oh yes, I saw it every day," he said.

"Didn't it eat there, play there and sleep there?"

"Yes, sir."

Dalsheimer jumped back in, realizing that he should not have let Atocha speak out of turn. "You stated a few moments ago that you didn't see [the child] from the time it came until it left," he said to Blass.

"Yes, sir; but I didn't mean it," Blass stammered.

"Were you home when the officers came to search the house?" Dalsheimer asked.

"Yes, sir, at night," Blass answered.

"What did you do when the officers came to your house?" Dalsheimer continued, turning to the issue of Blass's suspicious disappearance that evening.

"They came and tapped at the gate three times," Blass replied. "This frightened us, and Miss Green and myself ran away. We were on the gallery talking at the time."

"Why were you frightened?"

"Because they were hallooing before they got to the house; crying out, 'Holdup! Holdup! Give us Digby's stolen child!'" Blass answered.

"Did you open the gate for them?"

"No, sir. I couldn't find the key and my mother opened it for them," Blass said without explaining how he both "ran away" and answered the gate.

"Where did you go?" Dalsheimer asked.

"In the yard," Blass admitted.

"Who went with you?"

"Miss Green."

"Who else was with you?" Dalsheimer wanted to know.

"The child," Blass replied. "I had it in my arms when the officers came, and I took it with me to the back yard."

"Was Miss Green with you then?"

"No, sir. She stopped in the hall."

Before Dalsheimer could ask another question, Blass announced his opinion that "the officers did not come in like men. They ran hallooing and screaming through the house for Digby's child."

Dalsheimer ignored the declaration. "Could you be seen from the house to where you went with the child?" he continued.

"Yes, sir," Blass answered. "I was [near] the kitchen door; close by it. The trees and shrubbery are not thick in the yard."

"How far were you from the cistern?" Dalsheimer asked, referring to the large cypress barrel in Follin's yard used to collect rain water for drinking.

"I was right by the side of it; it's just at the kitchen door," described Blass.

Dalsheimer did not pursue the obvious question of why, if Blass was hiding by the cistern close to the kitchen door, Jourdain and Pierson did not find him there. Both detectives claimed they had searched both the yard and Follin's small cornfield. As Dalsheimer was the state's prosecutor, he let the point drop without suggesting that the detectives had done a less than thorough job.

"Who told you to take the child out?" Dalsheimer asked as his final question.

"Nobody," Blass replied.[63]

Atocha decided not to cross-examine Blass either. He may have feared that Blass would make another blunder that, once entered in the record, would make his job more difficult if the case went to the criminal court. Or he may simply have recognized everyone's exhaustion after four days of testimony. Either way, Blass was excused.

Atocha then asked that Minnie Green's testimony taken that day be read, and Dalsheimer asked that it be considered as evidence. Theodore Hunt, miffed that he was left behind that morning, objected, but Judge Houghton overruled him. The testimony was read and submitted for the record.

The preliminary examination in the Recorder's Court was almost over. It had been a highly unusual proceeding. Judge Houghton had allowed what should have been a short hearing to expand into something akin to a full criminal trial. It was now his responsibility to weigh the lengthy testimony and determine if the prosecution had presented enough evidence for the case to be sent on to the grand jury and possibly the First District Criminal Court. The hurdle was low. Under Louisiana law, committing magistrates had to send the case on if there was any "positive evidence directly charging the prisoner with the commission of the offense." Questions about the veracity of prosecution witnesses and the accuracy of their testimony were for a jury to contemplate. Houghton could discharge Follin and Murray only if he was certain of their innocence. If he had any doubts, he had to let the case go forward.[64]

Houghton did not take long to make up his mind. Within minutes after Blass left the stand, Houghton declared that he would not attempt to summarize "the voluminous testimony" and would simply announce his decision. He had the defendants brought before the bench. "Louisa Murray having been identified by two witnesses as the person who walked off with the child, I shall send before the First District Court of the Parish of Orleans, on the charge of kidnapping," he decreed. "It also appearing from the evidence of several witnesses that Ellen Follin has had this child in her possession for several days, I shall also send her down as accessory to kidnapping." Some courtroom spectators applauded. Houghton banged his gavel, calling for order. Court officers escorted out a man who shouted "bravo."[65]

Houghton set bail for each defendant at $5,000, the same amount as if they had been accused of manslaughter. Atocha reintroduced the black businessman William Green who was now willing to serve as both sisters' surety. Green stood up, stated that he was worth more than $10,000 above his liabilities, and described the properties he owned. Houghton accepted his pledge, and Green signed the formal documents. Murray and Follin would remain free until their trial.

Houghton's decision to send the case on to the grand jury and criminal court was hardly surprising, given how much emphasis Chief Badger, the Metropolitan Police, and Governor Warmoth had placed on the case. Houghton was a young Republican judge, after all. Nevertheless, Atocha must have been dismayed to hear Houghton assert that "two witnesses had identified Murray," which suggested that Houghton believed August Singler's testimony to be legitimate despite Atocha's seemingly successful efforts to discredit him.

The city's conservative newspapers defended the outcome because Singler, a white man, had identified Louisa Murray as the kidnapper and because Ellen

Follin had hidden Mollie Digby on her premises without notifying the authorities. Both facts were "presumptive of guilt."[66] While Democratic editors praised the hearing's result, they heaped criticism on the Republican judge. Even though the press had initially pressured Judge Houghton to use his court to answer the many questions surrounding the Digby case, editors ridiculed him for allowing the proceedings to take so long. The *Times* called Houghton's performance an "absurd" effort to claim "enlarged powers" for the Recorder's Court. The *Commercial Bulletin* complained that it was "next to impossible that an inquest [could] be conducted with less regard to the rules of evidence, the suggestions of common sense, the proprieties of judicial proceedings, or the law indicating the duty of a committing magistrate." The "wrangling of counsel, the prolixity of the testimony recorded, and the incapacity of the Recorder to confine the investigation to its proper limits" had caused the trial to last four days, "whereas a clearer headed magistrate, would have [had] a far better account of the case completed in seven or eight hours." Only the *Republican*, the pro-Warmoth paper, applauded Houghton's efforts, saying that he deserved a "meed of praise, as few men in his position could have, by any possibility, conducted the case so prudently and correctly."[67]

Democratic editors also lambasted Chief Badger's police. The detectives, they maintained, had been shown to be out-of-control bumblers. They had failed to search for key evidence. "Why wasn't Louisa Murray's house and Ellen Follin's searched for a seaside hat and a spotted calico dress?" a typical editorial asked. The behavior of the black detectives, in particular, had been egregious. Their conduct, the *Times* alleged, was *"outré* in the extreme, to say the least." Why "was not the regular process of law complied with?" Why did they arrive at Follin's house out of uniform and without warrants? And why did they avoid pressing Minnie Green about why her version of events allegedly changed so dramatically? "What inducements were offered? What threats were used?" the *Picayune* asked.[68]

Most galling to conservative newspaper editors was the fact that the prosecutors had failed to offer, or even suggest, a motive for the crime. "There has been a singular omission on the part of the prosecution for the state, in uncovering the real motive for the abduction," the *Times* charged. Despite "the great number of witnesses subpoenaed and the volume of testimony recorded...light was not thrown on the mystery which the public had just reason to suspect."[69]

For Governor Warmoth and Chief Badger, the reaction of the conservative press must have been deeply disappointing. They had hoped the case would demonstrate that their courts and their police were models of skill and efficiency. Their detectives had found Mollie Digby and arrested the alleged culprits, yet the Democratic press had nothing positive to say. Conservative New Orleans refused to give Warmoth's government any credit for a job well done.

In an effort to counter the negative press, Badger's office provided reporters at the *Republican* and the *Times* with a tantalizing new fact. The police revealed that they had pinned down the motive for the crime and promised to prove it if the case moved beyond the grand jury to the criminal district court. As August drew to a close, both newspapers reported that the police believed Murray and Follin were merely "henchmen," while "the true mastermind of the kidnapping plot was Minnie Green."[70]

SKETCHES OF CHARACTER IN NEW ORLEANS.

A depiction of the diverse population of New Orleans. Louisiana Image File, LaRC, Tulane University.

The First Recorder's Court Building. From *Daily Picayune*, April 9, 1891.

Chief Badger and his men raiding a saloon. From Elisha Benjamin Andrews, *The United States in Our Time: A History From Reconstruction to Expansion* (New York: Scribners, 1895), p. 149.

Canal Street in New Orleans during Reconstruction. Louisiana Image File, LaRC, Tulane University.

In this satirical cartoon, Reconstruction in Louisiana under President Grant and the Radical Republicans is depicted as a Greek tragedy. Louisiana Image File, LaRC, Tulane University.

Steamboats at the levee in New Orleans. Louisiana Image File, LaRC, Tulane University.

The infamous Orleans Parish Prison where the police held Louisa Murray. Theodore Lilienthal Photo Courtesy of Gary Van Zante and the Napoleon Museum, Arenenberg, Switzerland.

Although Ellen Follin's house was torn down in the 1920s, these houses from 1870 across the street are built in a similar style and still stand today at the corner of Bellecastle and Camp Streets. Photo: Harold Baquet.

Captain Broadwell's Chestnut Street house was also torn down. This neighboring house still stands and reflects the style of the Broadwells' neighborhood. Photo: Harold Baquet.

Invitation to the Ball of the Twelfth Night Revelers, January 6, 1871. Carnival Collection, Louisiana Research Collection, Tulane University.

A crowd waiting for a Mardi Gras parade. From Edward King, *The Great South: A Record of Journeys in Louisiana, Texas, The Indian Territory, Missouri, Arkansas, Mississippi, Alabama, Georgia, Florida, South Carolina, North Carolina, Kentucky, Tennessee, Virginia, West Virginia, and Maryland* (Hartford, CT: American Publishing Company, 1875), pg. 42.

Detective Jourdain's Family Tomb, St. Louis Cemetery #I, New Orleans. Photo:
Harold Baquet.

Chapter Nine

UNVEILING THE MYSTERY

I n mid-September 1870, as Ellen Follin and Louisa Murray waited to appear before the Orleans Parish grand jury, yellow fever struck the city. With fall approaching, residents thought that they had escaped the summer without an appearance of the dreaded disease. "The season of business" was "at hand" and most summer travelers had already returned from "the seaside, the springs, the mountains, and the lakes." But in the immigrant neighborhood near the French Market, victims began to suffer from chills, fever, and muscle aches. Their noses and gums started bleeding. Soon their skin turned a telltale yellow, they vomited the blood they had swallowed, and their livers failed. Many of the infected died within a week after experiencing the first symptoms of the mosquito-borne illness. By the end of the month, "Yellow Jack" was killing dozens of New Orleanians each day.[1]

New Orleans business leaders who knew from experience that yellow fever caused crippling commercial disruptions cautioned against "unnecessary alarm." In the past, when word of an outbreak traveled beyond the city limits, other ports had quarantined ships from New Orleans, and police had met trains originating from the city to prevent sick passengers from disembarking. In the outlying parishes, panicked residents had even torn up railroad tracks rather than let trains from New Orleans arrive. Epidemics badly damaged the city's reputation and led to a notorious saying: "In New Orleans it requires three persons to start a business—one to die of yellow fever—one to get killed in a duel—and a third to wind up the business of the co-partnership."[2]

When the fever spread uptown to the fine homes of the Garden District and downriver to Jackson Barracks, where eighteen federal soldiers contracted the disease, word went out on the Associated Press wire that yellow fever had again gripped the city. As civic leaders had feared, Galveston and other ports announced that all ships from New Orleans would be quarantined. Interior towns closed their depots to Crescent City trains, and businessmen traveling to New Orleans turned tail and headed home. The fever, one journalist noted, has "revived the evil reputation of our city, and has done incalculable damage to its commercial interests." Because physicians believed yellow fever was caused by foul-smelling gases from swamps, stagnant water, sewage, gutters, garbage, and the "putrescence" from bodies in the city's aboveground tombs, frightened individuals lit barrels of tar to fumigate afflicted homes and neighborhoods. Residents downed lemonade, brandy, wine, citrate of magnesia, mineral water, iron lozenges, and other nostrums that allegedly prevented the disease. A judge ordered Irish laborers digging a railroad bed near Dumaine Avenue to halt their work because turning the soil might have produced the "noxious exhalations." Each day grim-faced officials tacked "mortuary posters" with the names and addresses of fever victims on walls, fences, and lampposts. Some residents complained that the signs, hung at eye level, "[added] to the disorder," much "like a ghost on a highway in the dead of night, inspires more fear."[3] Families of victims draped their doorways in black crepe, and horse-drawn hearses darkened the streets. The very winds, one editor bemoaned, were "heavy with disease and death assails us at every turn."[4]

Nevertheless, determined to carry on business as usual, city officials kept the courts open. The Digby case proceeded to the grand jury. As none of the jurors had contracted yellow fever, they were told to complete their task by determining whether the state had enough evidence against Murray and Follin to justify a trial. Called to duty for a three-month period, the grand jurors had already heard prosecutors present their evidence in numerous criminal cases, in each of which they had had to decide if the state had made a *prima facie* case.

No defense witnesses appeared before grand juries, and no defense attorneys were present. After hearing the state's evidence only, at least twelve of the sixteen grand jurors had to be satisfied that the accused was probably guilty. They did not need to be convinced beyond a "reasonable doubt," but twelve or more of them had to be persuaded that the state was prosecuting the person or persons who had probably committed the crime. If so, they voted to affirm that the prosecutor's indictment constituted a "true bill" and the case moved on for trial.[5]

Accused individuals like Ellen Follin and Louisa Murray benefitted from grand juries, despite the fact that Louisiana Creoles, white and black, had long viewed all juries with suspicion. Grand juries came to America with the English common law. They were meant to thwart malicious government prosecutions; no one could be criminally tried without the consent of a jury of his or her peers. But in Louisiana, long ruled by the Spanish and the French, grand juries arrived late. There were no juries of any sort in legal proceedings in Louisiana during the colonial period. When the Americans came *en masse* after the Louisiana Purchase, they encountered a local citizenry fiercely resistant to English common-law procedures. The French- and Spanish-speaking populations found the common law's adherence to judge-made law and English precedent confusing at best and despotic at worst. They suspected that American judges and lawyers would use common-law courts and precedents to appropriate their property. As hordes of Americans arrived in New Orleans, Creoles also feared the justice American juries might dispense. English-speaking frontiersmen and recently arrived men-on-the-make could not be counted on to reach just verdicts; their decisions would be warped by their cultural and economic allegiances and their desire to supplant the Creoles as the city's power elite. Although President Thomas Jefferson and his territorial governor, William C. C. Claiborne, had hoped to assimilate the *ancienne population* into the American legal system, they eventually compromised with Louisiana's Creoles. Some Roman, Spanish, and French legal principles were allowed to survive in the state's laws of inheritance, property, and contracts.[6]

In criminal cases, however, the Americans insisted that the Creoles embrace trial by jury, *habeas corpus*, and other common-law rights considered essential to liberty. Louisiana's chances for statehood depended upon it. Congress would not confirm a state constitution that failed to follow American criminal-procedure practices. When Louisiana became a state in 1812, its new constitution required that criminal defendants be guaranteed grand juries, trial juries, the right to counsel, and other common-law procedural protections. Although these protections applied to all citizens, Creoles' suspicions about juries and their biases lingered.[7]

For most of Louisiana's history, women, African Americans, common laborers, and other poor people also had reason to fear jury bias. By law, only white men who paid taxes or owned property could serve on juries. Officials were told to select as jurors only those taxpaying or property-holding men "best qualified, from their education and character." To be sure, the great demand for jurors in a crime-ridden city meant that sheriffs often had to include some white workingmen with limited education in the jury pool. But women, African Americans, and the poor still could not expect to be tried by a true jury of their peers.

Reconstruction, however, had brought significant change to Louisiana juries. Women still could not serve, but jury pools for both grand juries and trial juries now included African Americans. In 1868 Republicans rewrote the law so that officials selected jurors from the list of registered voters "without distinction of race or color." In Orleans Parish, the sheriff drew the names of potential grand jurors randomly from a shaken box. Because New Orleans remained a white-majority city, and because most ex-Confederates by 1870 had had their voting rights restored, whites still predominated on most juries. But almost every grand and trial jury, including the grand jury for the Digby case, now had at least one or two African American members. Their presence increased the chances that Murray and Follin's fate would not be determined solely by their race.[8]

For the grand jury proceedings, the Orleans Parish district attorney, Charles Luzenberg, took control of the state's case himself. A dogged prosecutor, the mustachioed forty-three-year-old Luzenberg looked like an agitated bull terrier but was famous for his calm tenacity. Rather than browbeating witnesses and defendants, he methodically dismantled their testimony. Luzenberg signaled his intention to forcefully prosecute the Digby case by making Ellen Follin's son, George Blass, a defendant once more. In July, prosecutor Hughes had dropped the charges against Blass so that the prosecution could compel Blass's testimony in the Recorder's Court. But that decision irked many New Orleanians who believed Blass should be punished for hiding Mollie Digby from the detectives. Luzenberg agreed and believed he had enough evidence to convict all three defendants, even though Blass's testimony in the Recorder's Court could not be used.[9]

Ironically, the unflappable Luzenberg was the son of a famous New Orleans doctor known for his volatile and audacious behavior. Luzenberg's father, Charles Aloysius Luzenberg, was a polarizing figure. Depending on whom one talked to, he was either one of the most innovative physicians in North America or a boorish, self-promoting charlatan. He claimed to have discovered a pathbreaking treatment for smallpox and to have performed surgeries that cured blindness. After penning anonymous articles for New Orleans newspapers trumpeting his alleged medical achievements, he gained international fame when newspapers in the North and Europe reprinted some of his self-promoting stories. Envious colleagues in New Orleans accused him of fraud, alleging that his "cure for blindness" was a common cataract surgery and that his smallpox remedy had been discovered by others years before. Luzenberg's fellow doctors found him "abrupt in speech, uncouth in manners, irritable and petulant in temper, and arrogant and overbearing in his demeanor." Denouncing his conduct as "immoral" and "ungentlemanly," the city's medical society expelled him, and his colleagues at the Medical College of Louisiana removed him from the faculty. The senior Luzenberg responded by challenging his detractors to duels. He was once found practicing his marksmanship on hospital cadavers that he dangled from ropes.[10]

Perhaps to distinguish himself from his temperamental father, District Attorney Luzenberg exuded a "quiet, unostentatious, reserved calm," even, according to his former comrades, on Civil War battlefields. A secessionist before the war, he had helped lead the "Friends of United Southern Action," an organization that favored disunion if Lincoln did not accede to Southern demands that slavery be protected with new constitutional amendments. Despite having been educated at Princeton and Yale, he blamed Northerners for the nation's political woes and viewed opposition to the expansion of slavery as an attack on Southern honor. During the war, he served as a captain in the 13th Louisiana Infantry and was chosen as his regiment's standard-bearer before the bloody Battle of Shiloh. In repeated charges against the entrenched Union position later dubbed "the Hornet's Nest," Luzenberg was seen "coolly and without apparent excitement, holding the colors in the most advanced positions." Severely wounded while leading an assault on Union breastworks at the Battle of Chickamauga, he eventually returned to New Orleans to recuperate and practice law.[11]

During Reconstruction, Luzenberg was a vocal supporter of President Johnson and his lenient Reconstruction policies. In speeches at mass meetings, Luzenberg calmly but firmly denounced Republican "radicalism" and insisted that the policies "of President Johnson be sustained." Elected district attorney in 1866, he refused to resign when Radical Reconstruction began, even though he opposed black suffrage and biracial government. He benefitted when Governor Warmoth and other moderate Republicans insisted on making overtures to ex-Confederates by appointing some of them to patronage positions and allowing Luzenberg and select prosecutors and judges to continue in their positions without challenge. Determined to serve his full term and then run for reelection, Luzenberg stayed on the job even after his wife died in November 1869, leaving him to raise four young sons on his own. When Luzenberg committed to a task, he completed it. And he seemed intent on putting Louisa Murray, Ellen Follin, and George Blass behind bars. On September 16, amid the alarm caused by yellow fever, Luzenberg presented the state's case against the three defendants to the grand jury.[12]

The grand jury Luzenberg addressed was racially integrated. At least four of the grand jurors were black. The rest were white and mostly middle-class. Their ranks included a grocer, a bookkeeper, a blacksmith, a druggist, a dry goods merchant, and three store clerks. To secure an indictment, Luzenberg needed to offer evidence sufficient to convince twelve or more of the sixteen jurors that Murray and her alleged co-conspirators had abducted Mollie Digby and deliberately hidden her.[13]

Because the jurors had access to the unusually lengthy transcripts from the Recorder's Court, much of Luzenberg's work had already been done for him. The Recorder's Court testimony contained eyewitness accounts from August Singler and Georgie Digby that identified Louisa Murray as the kidnapper.

It had been shown beyond a doubt that Mollie Digby had been at Ellen Follin's house and that Follin and George Blass had hidden her from Detective Jourdain. To be sure, key questions had been left unanswered in Judge Houghton's courtroom. But Luzenberg could reasonably argue that there was already enough evidence embedded in the Recorder's Court transcripts to justify sending the case to trial.

Although an indictment seemed likely, the city's newspapers hoped the grand jury would use its power to subpoena witnesses to solve some of the remaining mysteries. In August, Chief Badger's office had leaked to the press the state's theory that Minnie Green was the mastermind of the kidnapping plot. Was there evidence to support this theory? From whom did Police Commissioner William George originally learn of Mollie Digby's whereabouts? The commissioner did not testify in the Recorder's Court; perhaps his source could provide insights into the crime. "The Grand Jury," the *New Orleans Times* urged, "should certainly learn by what remarkable coincidence [Commissioner] George suspected the Digby baby to be in Ellen Follin's house."[14]

Although grand juries met in secret, key details of the proceedings in the Digby case reached reporters. The *Republican* learned that the grand jury had subpoenaed Henry Dawes, the engineer who had been harassed for posting Ellen Follin's bond. The jurors wanted to know his connection to Follin. Might he somehow be linked to the crime? Detectives Jourdain and Malone were also called in to provide additional testimony. And the grand jury subpoenaed Commissioner George, who "it was generally understood…could throw some light on the case if he would." Back in August, it was he who had received the tip that Mollie Digby was at Ellen Follin's house. The grand jurors hoped to learn who had given him that information.[15]

Commissioner George, however, was not a cooperative witness. When the grand jurors asked him "where he first obtained information that the child was secreted in Ellen Follin's house," he refused to answer. He said "he pledged his word to the informant not to reveal his name, and thought it a matter of no moment to the jury." When the jury insisted that he reveal his source, George requested a day's time so that he could ask his informant's permission to disclose his identity. The jury instead demanded an immediate answer, and, under

Louisiana law, they had the power to send him to prison if he refused. George asked if he could have at least two hours, but to no avail. The grand jury's foreman reported George's recalcitrance to criminal court Judge Edmund Abell, who called George to his chambers and told him he must answer the question. Even a police commissioner was not above the law. George had to either reveal his informant's name or be jailed until he did so. Abell told George flatly "that a crime had been charged, and the inquiry of the Grand Jury…must be answered."[16]

Faced with imprisonment, George capitulated. He told the grand jury that he had received the tip from a mixed-race customhouse attendant and low-level Republican Party official named David Wilson, who lived on Camp Street in Ellen Follin's neighborhood. Wilson had seen a child matching Mollie Digby's description in Follin's yard, and, perhaps in hope of claiming the reward, reported her presence to Commissioner George. The grand jury dispatched a bailiff to bring Wilson in, but hours later when an indignant Wilson arrived he denied having "given an iota of information to Mr. George, or anyone else." The jurors seemed "unable to arrive at a conclusion about which of the two to credit," and the conflicting testimony "[left] the matter about where it began."[17]

The grand jurors expressed to Luzenberg their frustration that the state had still failed to offer a possible motive for the kidnapping. Where was the evidence to support the theory that Minnie Green, Ellen Follin's pregnant boarder, had orchestrated the abduction? Although Chief Badger had not provided details when he leaked the theory, newspapers had circulated two conjectures about Green's possible role. One was that she was in the midst of divorce proceedings with her husband in Alabama. The estranged couple, the theory went, had had a child two years earlier. That child, unbeknownst to the husband, had died after he and his wife separated. In the meantime, she had become pregnant with another man's baby, was in a precarious financial position, and wanted her husband to pay alimony. To obtain such payments she needed to claim that their daughter, who would have been nineteen months old in June 1870, was still alive. So, reporters theorized, "it became necessary to procure a female child of about that age in order that additional allowance could be executed for alimony." Minnie Green had then persuaded Louisa Murray to kidnap a child to substitute for her own lost infant. Green's deceased daughter may have even been named "Charley Camellia," which was why Murray and other members of Follin's household had allegedly called Mollie Digby by that name.[18]

The second theory implicating Green was a variation of the first. In that version, outlined in the *Republican* (the newspaper whose editor had direct access to Chief Badger), Green's estranged husband had died, as had the couple's two-year-old girl. Green's father-in-law had planned to leave the girl his estate, which was rumored to be worth fifty thousand dollars. For Green to claim the inheritance, "it would be necessary to produce the husband's living child, and one must be procured to represent it." Murray and Follin "might have undertaken to supply an heiress no matter from what sources." "Since the husband's death," the *Republican*'s account went, Green "'might' possibly have strayed from the path of virtue, the results of which...brought her to the singular position she now occupied." These conjectures, the paper believed, "are made to look reasonable by the conduct of 'Mrs. Green,' she having made two or more statements which do not fully tally."[19]

At least one out-of-town newspaper received these theories with skepticism. The *Mobile Register* asked whether any woman, "however unprincipled," would take the risk of stealing a child simply for money. The *Register* suspected that the real motive "lies, as it were, in Mr. Digby's very neighborhood, and will eventually be traced, if traced at all, from some incident connected either with his own history, or those of his friends and enemies." The *Times*, however, thought that the investigation would now hinge on proving that Minnie Green once had a daughter named "Charley Camellia." It was clear to the *Times* that "the motive was to deceive the law for the purposes of inheritance" and that Green sought to replace her deceased child Charley. If the detectives could "ascertain if there was a 'Charley Camellia' and what became of him or her...they will then hold the thread that unravels the motive and the mystery." The New York *Tribune* saw irony in the fact that a kidnapping plot would be concocted in a lying-in hospital, as that was "the last place in the world where any deficiency of babies might be expected to occasion their abduction from others."[20]

The *Republican* predicted that Louisa Murray would eventually crack, implicate Green, and "reveal all the mysterious facts" rather "than run the risk of a sentence to serve five years in the State penitentiary." But Murray had not buckled yet, and the state's theory remained unsubstantiated. Luzenberg assured the jury that the prosecution would offer a motive at trial but did not want to reveal any details, as the investigation was ongoing. Although proving a motive was not legally essential to gaining a conviction, many observers believed that in the Digby case a motive "must be proved before the prosecution can claim any great strength."[21]

The grand jurors moved reluctantly to their final deliberations. Even without offering a motive, the prosecution was certain that enough evidence implicated the accused to justify sending the case on to the parish's First District Court for a trial. And in the end, at least twelve of the jurors agreed that the state was prosecuting persons who had probably committed the crime. The state had indeed presented a "true bill." If there was a division among the jurors along racial lines, it was not disclosed to the press. Having been formally indicted, Louisa Murray, Ellen Follin, and George Blass all pled not guilty. Judge Abell released them on bond and set the trial date for mid-December 1870 in his First District Criminal Court.[22]

Even as the prosecution moved forward, new leads in the case reached Chief Badger's desk. Because the reward had yet to be paid, fresh information kept turning up. Although Captain Broadwell and Commissioner George had each tried to claim the bounty (Broadwell pledging that "should he obtain the reward [he would] bestow it upon charitable institutions"), Governor Warmoth rebuffed both men. The lure of a $5,000 reward remained.[23] In late September, Badger received a letter from a Mississippi judge who claimed that the "negress" who abducted Mollie Digby on June 9 had been arrested in the town of Summit and made a voluntary confession. Although this news threatened to disrupt the state's case against Murray and Follin, Badger telegraphed Mississippi authorities asking that the woman be held until his detectives could arrive. Though the lead turned out to be yet another dead end based on a false confession, Badger's willingness to pursue it suggested that he still harbored doubts that Murray was their kidnapper.[24]

In October, the yellow fever dissipated as the mosquitoes died. "Yellow Jack" had killed 587 New Orleanians during its short but intense 1870 appearance.

The city's residents now turned their attention for a time from the kidnapping trial and yellow fever to the upcoming November election, which would determine control of the Louisiana legislature. Every night boisterous processions of Democrats and Republicans marched by torchlight through the streets. Democrats urged voters to "drive from office the present set of corrupt and imbecile men" who had filled the police force with "low, ignorant, and brutal negroes" and who forced "the Negro, with his delightful odors into the dress circle of the opera...and into the drawing rooms of the hotels and steamboats." Chief Badger, fearing election-day disorder, asked the federal troops stationed at Jackson Barracks to aid his police force in preventing a recurrence of the mob violence and voter intimidation that had plagued the last round of elections in 1868. On November 7, election day, police and soldiers guarded polling places and patrolled neighborhoods. Troops manned Gatling guns on Canal Street. While reports of election-related violence arrived from Baton Rouge, Donaldsonville, and the state's rural parishes, in New Orleans the balloting proceeded without incident. With many ex-Confederates in Louisiana still boycotting elections, Republicans carried the day, retaining control of both the state legislature and the city government.[25]

Although Republicans held on to the statehouse in Louisiana, election returns from other Southern states that fall were ominous for the party and for the fate of Reconstruction. In North Carolina, Democrats committed to restoring white supremacy recaptured the state legislature. North Carolina, white Southerners crowed, had been "redeemed." It was the third Southern state in which Republicans had lost political control. Virginia and Tennessee had already fallen into the Democrats' hands, and in both of those states a host of laws designed to constrict black people's rights had followed their return to power. Democratic papers in New Orleans cheered the North Carolina results. The *Times* claimed that "the defeat to the carpet-bag hordes" in the "Old North State" foreshadowed "their downfall throughout the South, from the Potomac to the Rio Grande."[26]

Governor Warmoth and his supporters knew what the news from North Carolina meant. Reconstruction might not last much longer unless they could convince the citizenry that a Republican government benefitted everyone—whites as well as blacks. Redoubling his efforts, Warmoth pressed forward with his plans for building railroads and factories, and, at the risk of alienating his own constituency, he appointed additional Democrats to plum patronage positions. Both Warmoth and Chief Badger also continued to hope that professional police work and an efficient and fair justice system could counter the Democrats' charge that the biracial government was inept and corrupt.[27]

Other Republicans pushed ahead with more radical plans, hoping to force real change while they had the chance. In December 1870, as Louisa Murray, Ellen Follin, and George Blass waited for their trial to begin, the Republican legislature ordered the integration of the New Orleans public schools. First the children of elite Afro-Creoles enrolled in the previously all-white schools, but soon the sons and daughters of former slaves entered as well. Five thousand white parents protested by enrolling their children in private academies. The Democratic press accused the Republicans of trying to "provoke a war between races" by destroying "the usefulness of the public schools." But no mass violence occurred, and by the end of December 1870 almost a third of the city's schools had desegregated and almost one thousand black and several thousand white children studied side by side. Republican newspapers across the country pointed to New Orleans as a model of progress. As the Digby case prepared to resume in Judge Abell's court, some observers saw a glimmer of hope that race relations in the city might improve.[28]

The trial of *The State of Louisiana v. Louisa Murray, Ellen Follin, and George Blass* opened on January 4, 1871, near Jackson Square in the oldest part of the French Quarter, where the First District Criminal Court was housed. Originally scheduled for December, it had been delayed because defense attorney A. A. Atocha was again experiencing the painful symptoms of Bright's disease. By January he was on the mend, and as the trial began New Orleanians were in a festive mood. The weather was mild and sunny. The week had seen crowds turning out on sixty-degree afternoons for horse racing at the fairgrounds, roller-skating at Turner's Hall, and the opportunity to view a touring "panorama of New York City" at the Lyceum. On the streets, the city "wore a gala look," with flags and brightly colored bunting adorning porches and balconies. Mardi Gras, the city's most social season, began that week with the elaborate twenty-one-float

parade of the Twelfth Night Revelers. Although Mardi Gras was often politi-
cized (in 1873 floats would depict President Grant as a tobacco grub, Governor
Warmoth as a snake, and Police Chief Badger as a dopey bloodhound) and all
Carnival krewe members were white, African Americans and white Republicans
joined the sidewalk multitudes marveling at the parades' torchlit floats, brass
bands, costumed riders, and rolling tableaux.[29]

Even as the season of parades and elaborate balls began, "the celebrated
Digby kidnapping case" commanded the attention of New Orleanians. The
public's fascination with the "Affaire Digby" (as the French language newspaper
L'Avenir dubbed it) remained intense. Noting that every citizen "felt in the trial a
personal sympathy," the Picayune predicted that "the public will watch with eager
interest each development in the case, and will await the final verdict with pro-
found concern." When bailiffs opened the courtroom doors on January 4, "a
throng of anxious spectators" jockeyed for the available seats. As in July, crowds
gathered outside to watch the key players arrive.[30]

Serving as the defense lawyers once again, Atocha and Theodore Hunt faced
a difficult task. Prosecutor Luzenberg was intent on conviction, and Judge Abell
was a law-and-order jurist who held African Americans in low regard. Born in
Kentucky, Abell was a former slaveholder who had once publicly vowed to "fight
every proposition that looks to the commingling of the colored with the white
race." In 1867, Union General Philip H. Sheridan had briefly removed Abell
from the bench, accusing him of issuing rulings that encouraged white violence
and allowed reactionary rioters to go unpunished. Abell had opposed black
voting rights because, he said, most African Americans had "no more ideas of
the principles of government than...children seven years old." As former slaves
moved into New Orleans after the war, Abell complained that the city had filled
with idlers and criminals who should be forced to work. "No city on this con-
tinent," he said, "possesses so many prostitutes, street-walkers, vagabonds and
thieves, in proportion to the population, as the city of New Orleans."[31]

In addition to facing a tough prosecutor and an unsympathetic judge, Atocha
and Hunt had the thorny task of finding impartial jurors. Everyone in New
Orleans, it seemed, had an opinion about the case, and for months the press
had assumed the guilt of their clients. The Picayune, for example, labeled the

proceedings "the regular trial of the child stealers." New Orleans juries were notorious for succumbing to prejudice in sensational cases. All too often, as Edward Livingston noted in his famous 1833 treatise on Louisiana law, public outrage created "a ferocious thirst for vengeance" that skewed jury verdicts. "When public zeal requires a victim, the innocent lamb is laid on the altar" and "suffers on the slightest presumption of guilt," Livingston had warned. Atocha and Hunt could have filed a change-of-venue petition, claiming that a fair trial was impossible in Orleans Parish, but given the judge's biases, the public's intense interest, and the state's desire for a swift verdict, such a motion stood little chance for success.[32]

Jury selection for the trial became a long slog. During the process of *voir dire*, Atocha, Hunt, and Luzenberg grilled prospective jurors about their backgrounds, biases, and knowledge of the case, and one potential juror after another disqualified himself. Some revealed strong racial animosities. Others had personal connections to the Digbys, the Follins, or other key figures. Atocha and Hunt quickly exhausted the twelve peremptory challenges allotted to the defense that allowed them to reject potential jurors for any reason at all. With a peremptory challenge, the defense could disqualify a venireman (as members of the jury pool were called) for an insolent look, a smirk, a snide reply, or anything that made the lawyers uncomfortable. But with all of those challenges expended, Atocha and Hunt resorted to challenging potential jurors "for cause," which required convincing Judge Abell that a prospective juror was unfit to serve or had already formed a "deliberate opinion as to the guilt or innocence of the accused." In a trial where virtually every venireman knew something about the case, the result was protracted wrangling between the lawyers and the judge. District Attorney Luzenberg challenged veniremen as well, and he, too, quickly burned through the six peremptory challenges allowed to the prosecution.[33]

On the trial's first day, it took eight hours to select eight jurors, and the process exhausted the original seventy-five-man jury pool with four seats still unfilled. Judge Abell, adjourning court until the next day, asked the sheriff to spend the night rounding up a new jury pool from any registered voters he could find on short notice. Abell also ordered that the eight jurors already selected be sequestered. He wanted them cut off from the public and from overheated newspaper coverage of the trial. The sheriff was to provide lodging and "proper refreshments," but also place the jurors under guard. They could not go home or read a paper until the trial concluded.[34]

That night, reporters learned of a bizarre coincidence. In June, the fire in the Digbys' neighborhood at Seligman's Photographic Studio had prompted Rosa Gorman to leave Mollie Digby in the care of the abductress. On the very day the kidnapping trial began, the same building caught fire once more. Calling it a "remarkable occurrence," the *Picayune* hinted that the conflagration was some sort of sinister omen: "Under the mystery that now envelopes the whole affair, a strange thrill of dread pervades the community."[35]

The trial's second day began with four more contentious hours of *voir dire*, and not until the afternoon had Atocha, Hunt, and Luzenberg found their four final jurors. With a twelve-member jury finally seated, testimony could begin. From the perspective of the defense, the jury had both strengths and weaknesses. A majority of the jurors were white and had children. A few were former Confederates potentially unsympathetic to African-American defendants. Louis Palms, a clerk, had fought in Robert E. Lee's Army of Northern Virginia. Felix Fleicher, a German immigrant who would be chosen as the jury's foreman, had served briefly in the Confederate Louisiana militia but now worked as a meat inspector for Warmoth's government. Atocha and Hunt could hope that two other jurors born outside the South—an Austrian immigrant and a twenty-eight-year-old lawyer from Massachusetts—would not let race poison their judgment, but Northerners and immigrants often held their own racial biases. The defense did manage to seat two Afro-Creoles: Dessoura Quessaire, a thirty-eight-year-old tailor in the French Quarter, and Placide Boutin, a twenty-three-year-old post office clerk. As was the case with the grand jury, the presence of black men in the jury box seemed to ensure that the defendants' fate would not be decided by their color alone. To gain the unanimous verdict required to convict in a criminal case, Luzenberg would have to convince two Afro-Creole men that fellow Afro-Creoles Murray, Follin, and Blass were guilty.[36]

With testimony set to begin, expectations were high that the trial would resolve the remaining mysteries surrounding the case. Luzenberg was now under particular pressure to prove a motive for the crime. He had promised the grand jury that he would. The press and the public expected answers as well. What new evidence had Badger's police and the District Attorney's Office uncovered since the Recorder's Court proceedings? Could the state prove Minnie Green hatched the plot, or was there now some other theory? "If Louisa Murray and Ellen Follin were the kidnappers, they had a motive. What is it?" the *Picayune* asked. "This trial should unravel this web of difficulty and intricate plot. The public should know...the reason and motive of this strange abduction." While Louisiana law did not require evidence of motive for a conviction, failure to offer one would hurt Luzenberg's case and damage the reputation of Badger's force. What good were detectives if they could not ferret out the motive for a kidnapping that had consumed so much time and manpower? To convict, Luzenberg had to prove the defendants' guilt beyond a reasonable doubt, and proving guilt without a motive would be difficult. As a legal treatise writer remarked at the time, "Crime is a response of the evil mind to some temptation. Without the temptation, that is, an impelling motive, it is never committed."[37]

Luzenberg also could not count on tripping up the defendants on the stand, since Murray, Follin, and Blass did not have to testify. Since early statehood, the Louisiana constitution had guaranteed a defendant's right against self-incrimination. With their freedom at stake, defendants were justifiably afraid of being tricked by a clever or badgering prosecutor into giving inaccurate testimony that might sway a jury against them. "It cannot be denied that an innocent man of very weak nerves may sometimes, in his confusion, give contradictory or false statements that may endanger his safety," Louisiana legal theorist Edward Livingston wrote. No one knew this better than Murray, Follin, and Blass. Prosecutors had thus far based much of the case against them on the contradictory answers Follin, her flustered family, and Minnie Green gave to the detectives who barged into Follin's home.[38]

When testimony finally began that afternoon, Luzenberg's first three witnesses—Police Chief Badger, Thomas Digby, and Bridgette Digby—provided no new information. To the disappointment of spectators and the press, all three gave testimony that was "exactly the same as before Recorder Houghton." Badger's performance was particularly confounding. He retold the story of the investigation and the conflicting accounts the residents of Follin's house had given him and his officers. But he said nothing of a motive or of other new evidence having been gathered by his detectives. The prosecution, it began to appear, had nothing fresh to offer. Judge Abell adjourned the court at 3 p.m. allowing time for everyone except the jurors—who would remain sequestered—to prepare for the evening's Mardi Gras festivities.[39]

That night the city turned out for the parade of the Twelfth Night Revelers, celebrating the Epiphany and the opening of the eight-week Carnival season. Lanterns illuminated the Pickwick and Boston Clubs as well as stores and homes along the parade route. Crowds packed sidewalks and filled bunting-draped balconies along Camp, Carondolet, and Canal Streets. Boys climbed lamp and awning posts, and "ladies, gentlemen, and children...occupied every place favorably situated for seeing into the street" as more than thirty mule-drawn floats depicting Mother Goose, Old King Cole, and other nursery rhyme characters rolled by. Atop one float rode a mysterious costumed figure—the mischievous Lord of Misrule—who made his first appearance on the streets of New Orleans that year and became an annual tradition thereafter. Marchers included a masker dressed as Santa Claus throwing trinkets to the crowd, torch-carrying *flambeaux*, and "a score of cornets, trombones, bassoons, and horns of every fashion." Cheers went up for the aged veterans of the War of 1812 who marched to honor the fifty-sixth anniversary of the Battle of New Orleans. While all citizens were welcome to view the spectacle, its organizers—elite white men opposed to Reconstruction—banned Republicans like Governor Warmoth from the elaborate costumed ball at the French Opera House after the parade. Most of the next day's papers included glowing accounts of the ball, the ornate costumes and decorations, and the festive cutting of a massive King Cake. The *Republican's* editor, however, had been blocked at the door. "We would have reported more than we did," he wrote, "but it happened that the persons who had control of the revel thought proper to withhold from the *Republican* the courtesy usually accorded to the press and...extended to other papers."[40]

The next morning the courtroom filled quickly. If the spectators suffered from lingering effects of the previous night's revelry, it was not apparent. Neither the festivities nor the trial's unsatisfying opening testimony had diminished interest in the case. The public's fascination with the trial was "as widespread and general as any time during the excitement consequent upon the abduction," the *Picayune* observed. From the opening gavel onward, reporters noted, the audience listened with "eager and absorbed attention." The day promised dramatic testimony: the prosecution planned to call to the stand Minnie Green, the woman around whom so many kidnapping plot rumors swirled.[41]

The prosecution's first three witnesses that morning—little Georgie Digby, Rosa Gorman, and August Singler—should have been central to the state's case. Each had identified Louisa Murray as the woman who had abducted Mollie Digby in June. Earlier, in the Recorder's Court, however, each had offered a problematic account, thereby undermining what should have been direct and compelling evidence of Murray's guilt. Both Rosa Gorman and Georgie Digby had admitted that when they were first asked to identify Louisa Murray as the abductress they could not do so and that it was only after Chief Badger employed a prop—having Murray don a seaside hat—that their identification of Murray became more certain. Singler's testimony had been even more nettlesome. Although he had said he was certain Murray was the culprit, Atocha exposed so many inaccuracies and inconsistencies during his cross-examination that it appeared likely that Singler was simply lying.

To Luzenberg's dismay, the testimony of his three eyewitnesses did not improve at the trial. First, Rosa Gorman, who was annoyed to have been subpoenaed again, announced that she had become even less certain than she was in August that Murray was the woman who had walked off with Mollie. In her Recorder's Court testimony, Gorman had said she could not be sure but she "thought" that Murray was the person. In front of the trial jury, she disclosed that she was never convinced that Murray was the abductress, even after Chief Badger had Murray put on a seaside hat. All Gorman would admit was that Murray "resembles that woman." August Singler's testimony also fell flat. In the Recorder's Court, Singler's recollections of what the kidnapper wore, said, and did on June 9 had contradicted both Rosa Gorman's and Georgie Digby's memory of the events. Singler had said that Murray wore a dark second mourning dress; Georgie had testified that her dress was white. Singler said he saw Murray try to give Mollie candy and the child push her away; Georgie had said he did not remember Mollie being offered candy, nor did he remember seeing Singler on that fateful day. Singler had also testified that he went for weeks without telling Mollie's father that he had witnessed the crime, even though he had helped him search for his child the evening she disappeared. Although Singler now adjusted details of his account, Atocha referred back to Singler's Recorder's Court testimony and was able to subject him "to the severest possible cross-examination." Singler stuck to his claim that "the woman who talked to the children...was Louisa Murray," but Atocha exposed him once more as an unreliable witness—and possible perjurer.[42]

Of the prosecution's three eyewitnesses, only ten-year-old Georgie Digby's testimony seemed strong, at least initially. Guided by Luzenberg, Georgie pointed directly at Louisa Murray and stated definitively that she was "the woman who carried Molly away." He recalled her speaking to him the night of the kidnapping, and "how she got him away from his sister by sending him after fruit." But on cross-examination, Atocha destabilized Georgie's story by asking him to remember the events of August 12 when Chief Badger brought Louisa Murray to the Digbys' house for Georgie and Rosa Gorman to identify. In the Recorder's Court, Georgie had testified that "my father asked me if that was the woman and I told him no, this was not the woman." Only after Murray put on the seaside hat had he identified her. "Then I said 'yes, that's the woman!'" he had testified. "I know'd it was the woman as soon as she put the hat on." Atocha now got Georgie to admit once more that his father and Chief Badger had pushed him to identify Murray and that it may have been the hat, not Murray, that he recognized. Was it not true, Atocha asked, that his father had told him the kidnapper was in their house even before he saw her?[43]

"When your father came out did he not tell you that the woman who stole Mollie was in the house?" Atocha inquired.

"Yes, sir," Georgie answered.

"Did you recognize her?" Atocha continued.

"No sir; not until she lifted her veil."

"When did you recognize her?"

"When she put on the hat like the one she wore when she stole Molly away."

"What did your father tell you?"

"He said that the reason I didn't know her at first was because she had a different hat on; as soon as she put the seaside hat on I knew her."

Luzenberg objected. Georgie had identified Murray as the kidnapper, and now Atocha was trying to bamboozle the child. But Atocha "disclaimed any intention to confuse the witness," and Judge Abell allowed the cross-examination to continue. By the time "the little fellow was permitted to leave the witness stand," the newspapers noted, Georgie had acknowledged that he "had been influenced and prompted by his father to identify Louisa Murray."[44]

Throughout the day's testimony, reporters and spectators once again studied the faces of Murray, Follin, and Blass for reactions that might hint at their guilt or innocence. "Every fleeting emotion, if visible for an instant only on the face[s] of the accused was watched with absorbing interest," one reporter noted. Ellen Follin seemed unfazed by anything that was said and "exhibited the stolid indifference" that "characterized her manners from the morning of her first arrest to the present time." "Nothing," the *Picayune* observed, "seems to be able to shake or disturb her quiet and placid nature." Although Murray's countenance bore an "air of uneasiness," she too revealed little. Consequently, reporters were left to their usual remarks on the defendants' complexions. Murray, the *Picayune* reminded readers, was "a tall, dark, slender mulatress" with "handsome" features, while Follin was "darker than her sister." George Blass, they added, was "a bright mulatto" whose "features are of the Italian type, his father, it is understood, being of that nationality."[45]

The prosecution next called the trial's most anticipated witness, Minnie Green. Ever since the police theories that Green had masterminded the kidnapping had reached the press, New Orleanians had debated whether Louisa Murray had abducted Mollie at Green's behest. The public was "anxious and expectant" that the "motive activating the party" would finally be revealed. In August, Green's advanced pregnancy had kept her from attending court, and Recorder Houghton and the lawyers had taken her testimony at Follin's house. Since then, she had given birth, gone home to Alabama, and, having been subpoenaed, returned to New Orleans to testify—this time in the courtroom. In August, prosecutor Hughes had focused his questions on the discrepancies between Green's account of when Mollie arrived at Follin's house and those offered by Follin and Murray. No one had suggested to her then that they believed she had commissioned the crime.[46]

Green took the stand amid the public's desire for revealing testimony. Luzenberg, however, quickly disappointed those who expected him to tie Green more closely to the plot. His examination was a simple repetition of the questions prosecutor Hughes had asked her in August: was Mollie there when she came to Follin's house? Why did she tell detectives a white child was there when she arrived? These questions were germane to the state's case against Follin, who had told police that a veiled white woman dropped Mollie off at her gate on August 3. If Mollie was at Follin's house on July 20 when Green checked in, Follin was lying. But these were not the questions people hoped to hear. Answering Luzenberg, Green kept to her story that the white child she saw on July 20 belonged to Mrs. Tracy, a white woman who had also boarded at Follin's house. Mollie, Green testified, did not arrive until August 3, and when she did, she "was treated like one of Ellen's own children" and "never concealed." Green explained that if she initially gave confused answers to the detectives, it was because of the "rough and brutal way in which the officers who searched the house had acted" and because she was "frightened by the police into admissions which were untrue."[47]

The prosecution's case had not evolved over the past five months. Despite all their efforts, Badger's detectives had failed to find documents or witnesses proving Minnie Green was involved in an alimony or inheritance dispute. No plot explaining the kidnapper's "mysterious and dark" motives would be exposed. Instead, Luzenberg would rely only on shaky eyewitness testimony, the fact that Mollie Digby was found at Ellen Follin's house, and the contradictory statements Follin, her family, and Minnie Green had initially made. The prosecution's final two witnesses—Detectives Malone and Pierson—simply "corroborated the evidence given by Chief of Police Badger," with Malone reiterating that Green had initially "informed him that she had found the child there already on her arrival from Mobile with Louisa Murray." The prosecution then rested, and Judge Abell adjourned the court until the next day.[48]

At nearly any other time in Louisiana's history, Luzenberg could have been fairly confident of securing a verdict of guilty, even without offering a motive. August Singler, a white man, had testified unequivocally that he saw Louisa Murray, a mulatto woman, abduct a white child, and that child had surfaced at

Murray's sister's house. All-white Louisiana juries had convicted black defendants on far less evidence. But Reconstruction changed the equation. The 1871 Digby jury contained two Afro-Creoles who would have to agree that the defendants were guilty beyond a reasonable doubt before a conviction could be secured. And at trial, unlike in the Recorder's Court and in grand jury proceedings, defense attorneys Atocha and Hunt would call witnesses of their own.

Saturday morning was "bright and balmy," and spectators eager to hear defense testimony arrived early on the trial's fourth day. After Abell gaveled the court into session, the defense called Detective John Baptiste Jourdain as its first witness. Jourdain had once seemed essential to Governor Warmoth's and Chief Badger's plan to use the Digby case for political purposes. They had hoped that having a black detective solve the crime would demonstrate the competency of their biracial police force. But even though Jourdain had played a crucial role in the investigation that led to the defendants' arrest, Luzenberg failed to call him as a trial witness. In the Recorder's Court, Jourdain's testimony had frustrated the prosecutors, and as a defense witness he once again described the deceptions he had employed to entrap Murray and his efforts to intimidate Follin and her family into confessions. If Murray, Follin, and Follin's family had told conflicting stories, Jourdain's testimony suggested that they may have done so as a result of the conduct of the police.[49]

After Jourdain, the defense called four of the Digbys' black neighbors who claimed to have witnessed the abduction on June 9. Jane Lewis, Eliza Lewis, Susan Moore, and Emma Williams each testified that they had been chatting on Howard Avenue the afternoon that they saw the women who walked off with Georgie and Mollie Digby, and that Louisa Murray and Ellen Follin were not the women they had seen. In June, they had given descriptions of the kidnappers to the police. In August, Chief Badger had brushed them off when they told him Louisa Murray was not the culprit. The first to testify, Jane Lewis, was a thirty-three-year-old, mixed-race housekeeper, married to a carriage driver, who lived two doors down from the Digbys. She had been in front of the Digbys' house in August when Chief Badger brought Louisa Murray there for Georgie and Rosa Gorman to identify, and when she approached Badger to tell him that Murray was not the woman she had seen—that the kidnapper was taller and had skin even lighter than Murray's—Badger responded by warning Lewis that if she were lying he "would arrest her." After that, the police had never spoken with her again. There was a long tradition in New Orleans of policemen discounting black eyewitnesses, particularly if they were female and illiterate like Lewis and the others. Although Lewis and her friends may have hoped for more respect from the Republicans' biracial force, Badger, it seemed, had ignored their exculpatory statements and relied instead on a white man's testimony—August Singler's identification of Murray.[50]

Atocha made clear to the jury that his witnesses were as certain that Louisa Murray was not the kidnapper as Singler was sure that she was.

"Are you positive the accused are not the women?" Atocha asked Jane Lewis.

"Yes sir, I am," Lewis replied.

"You cannot be mistaken?"

"No."[51]

Next Susan Moore and then Eliza Lewis took the stand, and they both corroborated Jane Lewis's account. Moore, a twenty-seven-year-old mixed-race laundress who was also married to a carriage driver, said the abductress was more "bright"—the term often used for light skin—than Murray. Eliza Lewis, a twenty-five-year-old housekeeper and wife of a laborer, testified that the abductress wore a poplin dress and seaside hat and "passed right by" her and the other women. She testified that she had told Badger in August that Murray was "not as bright and not as tall as the child stealer," but that Badger had been dismissive. He had said that "if he had Louisa Murray laced and fixed up, she might be the woman who stole the child after all." For dramatic effect, Atocha asked Louisa Murray to stand up, and then he asked Williams once more if Murray was the woman she saw steal Mollie Digby on June 9. "No, she is not," Lewis answered.[52]

Emma Williams, a twenty-year-old washerwoman and the last of the black women from the Digbys' neighborhood to testify, agreed with the others. She also said that the woman who took Mollie "did not resemble the accused."

"You are positive of this?" Atocha asked.

"Yes, Sir," Williams replied with an assured tone. "The woman who took the child was much lighter than Louisa."

"Did you ever say as much to anyone before?"

"Yes, sir; I told Chief of Police Badger so when he brought Louisa Murray to Mr. Digby's to be recognized."

"Did you have a good look at the woman who took the child?"

"Yes, she passed right by me."[53]

On cross-examination, prosecutor Luzenberg failed to investigate whether any of the women had a motive to lie. Were there tensions in the neighborhood? Two of the women's husbands were carriage drivers. Did they resent Irish cabbies like Thomas Digby who were pushing black men out of that business? Luzenberg did not ask, attempting instead to trip each woman up on small details. Where were they standing when they witnessed the crime? How could they see the kidnapper under her seaside hat? How could their memory be so clear months after the incident? Emma Williams told Luzenberg that she was certain of what she had observed, and although she saw the abductress only once, she "would recognize her again." When Luzenberg wondered why Eliza Lewis did not try to thwart the kidnapping at the time, she replied calmly that they did not know a crime was being committed and "heard of the kidnapping some two or three hours after."[54]

As the next witness, the defense recalled Minnie Green. Atocha wanted to make sure that the jury understood her version of events. Because her initial testimony had been repeatedly interrupted, Atocha feared that the jury may have been confused. Moreover, after Green spoke earlier in the trial, Detective Malone had subsequently testified that Green told him that Mollie was at Follin's house when she arrived on July 24 and that Murray had recognized the child and called her "Charley Camellia." If the jury believed Malone's account, it would be a major blow to the defense. Despite the risk of giving Luzenberg another chance to grill Green (this time on cross-examination), Atocha called her back to the stand so that she could explain why she may have initially given confused answers to Badger and his detectives. "She should be permitted to explain the circumstances of her conversations with the officers," Atocha told the court. "She was young and in bad health. These officers came there and tortured her with questions. It was reasonable that she would be confused."[55]

With Atocha prompting her, Green recounted once again her interrogation at the hands of Badger and Malone. She had been lying on her bed in Follin's house feeling ill effects from her pregnancy when Badger asked permission to enter her room. She had refused, telling him to go away, but the police officers entered her room anyway. They demanded to know when she had first seen a white child in the house. She told them a white child was there on July 24 "but it was Mrs. Tracy's child." Maybe the men misheard her, she theorized on the stand. "There was a good deal of confusion there that morning and some mis-understanding might have taken place," Green added. She reiterated that the first day she saw Mollie at Follin's was August 4.[56]

Luzenberg used his cross-examination to suggest that Green changed her story because she feared that if she did not, Follin and Murray would kill her or alert her family in Alabama to her illicit pregnancy. During Green's Record-er's Court testimony, Alexander Dalsheimer had asked her if she feared that someone might harm her if she did not tailor her story to fit Follin's version. In August, Green had answered, "There are no facts that I failed to disclose out of fear." Luzenberg raised the question again. Did she ever tell Chief Badger that "she was there in the power of these women?" Green denied having done so. She had never told Badger that she could not testify against Follin and Murray. She was "never afraid that if she did they would kill her." Luzenberg must have known it was unlikely that Green would suddenly change her story and thereby admit to having perjured herself twice, but perhaps he assumed that his ques-tions might resonate with the jury.[57]

After Green stepped down, the defense called William Cottrell, a young Afro-Creole who kept a cigar stand inside Tattersall's Saloon on St. Charles Avenue. August Singler, the prosecution's main eyewitness, frequented Tatter-sall's, and Cottrell had occasionally talked with him about the case. In August, "a few days after [he] had testified before the Recorder," Cottrell had asked Singler about his testimony. According to Cottrell, Singler, perhaps after a few drinks, had confided that "he didn't really know whether Louisa Murray was the woman who took the child or not." Months later, with the trial approach-ing, Cottrell and Singler had chatted at Tattersall's again. On Christmas Eve day, Singler had again told Cottrell "he was not sure about the woman taking the child." Why Singler would reveal so much to a cigar-stand employee was unclear. Perhaps unable to distinguish his race in a white man's saloon, Singler assumed

Cottrell was a white man who shared his desire to see Follin and Murray convicted by any means necessary. Maybe he thought Cottrell was harmless or powerless. Or Singler may simply have been a loose-lipped drunk. In any case, Cottrell's testimony, if believed by the jury, could entirely discredit the only eyewitness who had unequivocally identified Murray as the kidnapper.[58]

Luzenberg's cross-examination revealed, however, that Cottrell had not simply been following the case in the newspapers. He was a close friend of Follin and Murray.

"How long have you known Louisa Murray and Ellen Follin?" Luzenberg asked.

"All my life," Cottrell answered.

"Are you intimate with them?"

"Oh yes, I visit their homes very often. When I go to Mobile I go and see Murray, and I very often go to Ellen Follin's."

"When was the last time you were at Ellen Follin's house?"

"Christmas night."[59]

Although Cottrell's long friendship with the defendants did not necessarily mean he was lying about his conversations with Singler, it did reveal that he had an incentive to lie. So did Singler. One or the other was committing perjury to help his friends. Which would the jury believe?

Defense attorney Atocha next called Julia Yarrington, who offered an alibi for Louisa Murray. A twenty-nine-year-old Afro-Creole, Yarrington was a music teacher in Mobile ("and a colored one too!" the *Picayune* condescendingly remarked). Originally from New Orleans, Yarrington had lived in Alabama since 1868, when she married Mobile's assistant chief of police George Yarrington, a white Republican "carpetbagger" from Massachusetts who had served as lieutenant colonel of a black Union regiment during the Civil War. She recalled that on June 9, the day of the abduction, she had seen Murray in Mobile. Yarrington was putting together "tableaux by children"—as performances were called—on June 15, and she wanted to see if Murray's daughter, Emmetta, would sing in her production. She had sent Murray a note on June 7, and "Louisa had promised to send her an answer in a day or two, but did not do so." The note, which Atocha submitted to the court as evidence, described the dress in which

Yarrington wanted Murray's daughter to appear. With the event only six days off, Yarrington went to Murray's home on June 9 to ask her in person. Murray was at home, but she had "a sick white woman in her house and could not give me a positive answer." "This was the nature of the business I had with her," Yarrington summarized, "and is the reason I remember distinctly it was the 9th of June." Atocha then asked her if she knew "Louisa Murray's general reputation in Mobile?" "She was regarded as a respectable woman," Yarrington responded.[60]

On cross-examination, Luzenberg tried to confuse Yarrington in order to place her testimony in doubt. If the jurors believed Murray had an alibi, the state's case would be crushed. Luzenberg seized on the fact that Yarrington had testified that when she visited Murray's house, the only person there was the "sick white woman." Did she mean Minnie Green was there, but not Murray? If so, he suggested, Murray could have been in New Orleans abducting Mollie Digby.

"Did you not say distinctly that when you went to Louisa Murray's house on the 9th of June, you saw no one but a white women?" Luzenberg asked.

"Yes, sir," Yarrington replied.

"Then you didn't see Louisa Murray."

"Oh yes, sir. I saw her too."

"Then you can't be mistaken?"

"No, sir," Yarrington answered.[61]

Luzenberg did get Yarrington to make one important admission. Although Yarrington claimed that her acquaintance with Murray was limited and purely professional, Luzenberg asked with whom she had traveled to New Orleans for the trial. Yarrington acknowledged that she took the boat from Mobile with "Louisa Murray, Miss Green, and some others." The suggestion, of course, was that Yarrington was actually creating an alibi for a friend. Luzenberg implied that, like William Cottrell before her, Yarrington was part of a tightly knit Afro-Creole community that was rallying to the defendants' cause.[62]

Atocha's next witness, Benjamin Scott, a black carpenter from Ellen Follin's neighborhood, testified that he had seen a veiled white woman leave a baby at Follin's gate. Until Scott took the stand, no one outside Follin's immediate family had corroborated what seemed to be the weakest part of her story. The *Picayune* spoke for many when it noted that Follin's tale of the veiled white woman was "too ridiculous to deceive a child." But now the defense produced a witness who claimed to have watched it happen. Scott lived a block from Follin on Chestnut Street, near Bellecastle Street, and he knew Follin because she occasionally allowed him to draw water from her cistern. "Some time in August, about the 3rd I believe, I was standing on the corner…and saw a veiled white woman go up to Ellen Follin's house with a little child," he testified. The woman was coming from Soniat Street and seemed agitated, so he watched. "She said a few words to…Follin and then went away, leaving the child on the banquette. A few moments afterwards Follin's son came out and led the child into the house." Scott did not think much of it at the time. There had been other white women and children at Follin's house. He had no reason to think it might be Mollie Digby. He had heard that Mollie had been found in Baton Rouge. "Some days after that a man told me the child had been found in my neighborhood, and told me what Ellen said about it,…and I remembered the circumstance I have just related," Scott concluded.[63]

On cross-examination, Luzenberg suggested that Scott's testimony was too perfect and that he had been coached by the defense attorneys.

"What made you start off to tell how you became a witness before anybody asked you?" Luzenberg queried.

Scott seemed confused. "Because when I ask anybody a question I like to give the grounds," he said.

Luzenberg changed tacks. "How did you know the woman was white?"

"I saw her face."

"You said she had a veil over it?"

"Yes, but I saw through it."

Luzenberg asked if he was perhaps a close friend of Follin's. Scott said no, he was only an acquaintance. She was neighborly and allowed him to take water occasionally. That was all.[64]

As the proceedings moved into the afternoon, Judge Abell urged both sides to hurry the trial along. It was already Saturday. He did not want to have to continue on Monday and sequester the jury for two more nights, particularly during Mardi Gras. But the defense still had nine more witnesses ready to testify. Atocha and Hunt picked up the pace. Captain Broadwell and his wife,

Evelina, each took the stand and repeated the same story about how the baby came into their possession that they had told in the Recorder's Court. They both emphasized their conviction that Ellen Follin was no criminal. After the Broadwells, the defense called a string of witnesses who attested to Murray's and Follin's good character. Perhaps to balance the fact that so many of the key defense witnesses—Yarrington, Cottrell, Scott, Jourdain, the women from the Digbys' block—had been black, all of the character witnesses were white. They included Henry Dawes, the white engineer who had initially posted Follin's bond but then tried to back out of his obligation when public pressure became too great. He had evidently regained his courage and joined white friends and neighbors of Murray and Follin in testifying on their behalf.[65]

After four of seven character witnesses had testified, Atocha informed Judge Abell that in the interest of time he "did not deem it necessary to call them all." The defense rested. Atocha's co-counsel, Theodore Hunt, then addressed the court and made a surprising proposal that would also save time: he and Atocha would skip closing arguments if Luzenberg would as well. "May it please the court, as senior counsel, I propose to submit the case to the jury," Hunt said. "We believe that they will not be moved by prejudice, but will render a verdict according to the evidence and their oaths." It was a risky gambit, as it would deny the defense an opportunity to summarize its case and ask the jury to rise above public anger and bigotry. But it also meant that Luzenberg would not have a chance to appeal to the jurors' possible prejudices. When Luzenberg told Abell that he too was willing to forgo closing arguments, Abell announced that the case would to go to the jury forthwith, and he had Luzenberg once again read the state's kidnapping law, which provided penalties of up to twelve years in prison for kidnapping or for aiding, advising, or abetting a kidnapper.[66]

Judge Abell then gave his instructions to the jury. He impressed upon them "a sense of their high responsibility to the public, as well as to the accused." If a crime was committed against the state, it should be punished. But it was also essential that the state not punish an innocent person. To convict, they would have to be certain beyond a reasonable doubt that Murray, Follin, and Blass had committed the crimes with which they were charged. "Reasonable doubt," however, did not mean "no doubt." Jurors could believe there was a slight chance that Follin's story of the veiled white woman was true and still convict if they believed the evidence against the defendants was sufficient enough "that a prudent man would feel safe in acting upon it."[67]

To convict Follin and her son, George Blass, the jurors would also need to believe that Follin and Blass had intended to violate the law. Mere possession of the kidnapped child was not enough. As one legal treatise writer noted, "It is...no offence at common law to *have* in one's possession counterfeit coin, or forged paper, or bills of a non-existing bank." But if the state could show that a person knowingly acquired those items with the intent to pass them as authentic, it was a crime.[68]

As the jury retired for deliberations, the outcome was in doubt. The prosecution never had offered a motive for the abduction. The testimony of the state's key witnesses—Rosa Gorman, Georgie Digby, and August Singler—had been uneven. But Luzenberg's cross-examinations had revealed that key defense witnesses like William Cottrell and Julia Yarrington were friends of the accused who had possible motivations to lie. In the past, white testimony, no matter how problematic, could doom a black defendant in a criminal case, but in this case two Afro-Creole jurors might view white testimony with skepticism. No one could be sure how racial politics would affect a biracial jury deliberating in a sensationalized case at a time when the city was a racial tinderbox. Would the white jurors, as Chief Badger had, dismiss the testimony of the defense's black witnesses out of hand? How would they view Detective Jourdain's having testified for the defense? Was that another instance of an Afro-Creole siding with his own? White editors had predicted all along that black policemen and detectives would be lenient toward black criminals. Did the white jurors fear the criticism (or worse) that they might receive if they let the alleged kidnappers go free? If the jurors divided along racial lines, the possibility of a mistrial loomed.

To the great surprise of many observers, the verdict in *The State of Louisiana v. Louisa Murray, Ellen Follin, and George Blass* came with startling speed. The lawyers and spectators had barely left the courtroom when word arrived that the jury had reached a verdict after only eight minutes of deliberation. Audience members hurried back to their seats as Judge Abell called the court back into order. Court procedure required the clerk to call each juror's name and to ask each if he agreed with the verdict that had been reached. All the jurors—including Dessoura Quessaire and Placide Boutin, the jury's two Afro-Creole members—said yes. Judge Abell then asked Murray, Follin, and Blass to stand and hold up their right hands. He also asked jury foreman Felix Fleicher to stand. "Look upon the prisoners, you that are sworn," he said to Fleicher. "How say you, are they guilty of the felonies whereof they stand indicted, or not guilty?" Fleicher announced the jury's verdict: "Not guilty."[69]

Inexplicably, the newspapers and the court reporter failed to note the reaction to the verdict in the courtroom. A biracial jury had unanimously decided after only eight minutes of deliberation that the defendants in the celebrated Digby trial were not guilty of the crime. After a five-month ordeal, Follin, Murray, and Blass were free to go home.

Although no record appears to exist of what transpired during the jury's perfunctory deliberations, it is clear that the jurors had already reached their verdict before they entered the jury room. In just eight minutes there would have been time for little more than a tally of votes. Sequestered together each night throughout the trial, the jurors had probably violated protocol by discussing the evidence and sharing their concerns that the prosecution had not proved the defendants' culpability beyond a reasonable doubt. By returning a verdict so swiftly, they left the impression that the prosecution's case was so weak that it did not warrant thoughtful jury-room deliberation. It could be they hoped to signal their frustration that the prosecution had not offered a motive for the crime. Maybe they believed the testimony from witnesses like the black women from the Digbys' neighborhood who had previously been ignored by the police and the press. What role did the white and black Creoles on the jury play in the jury's discussions? Did they convince the others that elite Afro-Creoles like Follin and Murray could not be kidnappers? Did the sisters' dignified appearance, when combined with the long roster of white witnesses who testified to their sterling character, sway a jury made up of middle-class men? Would the result have been different if the accused kidnappers had been illiterate former slaves? During their unofficial deliberations each evening, the jurors would doubtless have discussed the race, class, and gender of the defendants and witnesses. But barring discovery of new letters, diaries, or other accounts, it is impossible

206 — MICHAEL A. ROSS

to know how those considerations shaped the jury's verdict. Reporters did not hound the jurors after the trial as they do today.

What is certain is that the Digby trial occurred at a propitious moment for Ellen Follin and Louisa Murray. Had the sisters been tried only a few years earlier, when ex-Confederates still controlled the justice system and white police, judges, and juries sought to control an emancipated black population, the outcome probably would have been different. At that moment of intense white insecurity, an alleged crime by black women against a white family probably would have been punished even if the defendants were Afro-Creoles. But in 1871, with black men serving as jurors, and expert lawyers employed by the defense, the Louisiana justice system lived up to the values the legal elite professed to believe in. "Among the principles of liberty which our immediate ancestors brought from the motherland to this," a famous treatise author wrote at the time, "there is no one more important for the protection of the citizen in times of civil commotion or of public passion and prejudice, than that which secures to men accused of crime an open trial by a jury of their peers." In the Digby case, the courts created an atmosphere that allowed ten white and two black jurors to overcome the race hatred and hysteria that newspapers had helped stoke in the wake of Mollie Digby's abduction, and to unanimously agree that the state's flawed case left reasonable doubt about the defendants' guilt.[70]

Had the trial occurred after 1877, when white supremacists "redeemed" Louisiana and all-white juries returned, Follin, Murray, and Blass would again have faced steep odds. Even the old ties between white and black Creoles would have been of little help as Louisiana increasingly embraced and enforced the racial mores of the rest of the Deep South. White Creoles succumbed to this strictly segregated world, distancing themselves from their mixed-race relatives and associates. In the 1890s, Follin and Murray might have even been lynched. In the post-Reconstruction South the threat of vigilante justice against blacks and immigrants loomed constantly, even after an acquittal. In one famous incident in New Orleans in 1891, a bloodthirsty mob stormed the parish prison, seized eleven Sicilians whom a jury had just acquitted of murdering the city's police chief, and shot and clubbed the men to death. Across the South, crowds seeking immediate retribution for crimes both real and imagined regularly lynched black men and women. But in 1871, the *Picayune* noted "no manifestation of violence."

The defendants were acquitted after "a fair and impartial trial." Follin, Murray, and Blass went free and went on with their lives unharmed. It would be almost a hundred years before black defendants in the South would be guaranteed the same due process Murray, Follin, and Blass received.[71]

Although New Orleanians found the decision shocking, the account sent out by the Associated Press on the national wire was matter-of-fact. "Telegraphic News—The Digby Kidnapping Case Was Concluded Saturday in New Orleans," read a typical out-of-state headline. "The prisoners Ellen Follin, Louisa Murray, and George Blass were acquitted." But in New Orleans, editors voiced their dissatisfaction that the trial had left so many questions unanswered. The French language newspaper *L'Avenir* spoke for many the next day: "Le jury dans cette affaire a rendu un verdict de non-culpabilité. Qui donc a enlavé l'enfant? Répondez messieurs les jurés" ("The jury has rendered a verdict of not guilty. Then who took this child? Tell me, men of the jury.")[72]

Governor Warmoth had hoped the Digby case would prove the effectiveness of his integrated Metropolitan Police, but the massive investigation and manhunt had failed to garner a conviction. The Democratic press blamed the verdict on shoddy police work, rather than on District Attorney Luzenberg, a Democrat and ex-Confederate. "The District Attorney...had but very little to base the case on, and has made much of the poor material delivered to him as he properly could," the *Times* maintained. Although Warmoth did not comment publicly on the verdict, the *Republican* newspaper gamely tried to portray the outcome as a victory for justice, as well as proof of the legal acumen of a leading Republican—A. A. Atocha. It had required all of Atocha's "energy and talent to convince a jury the parties were innocent, for there was the admitted fact that the child had been in Ellen Follin's care." "Firmly believing in the innocence of the accused," the paper said, Atocha worked "day and night to overthrow all the...circumstances which appeared sufficient to dishearten most men."[73]

Two weeks after the trial's conclusion, *The Louisianian*, a monthly paper edited by black Republicans, gave its succinct assessment of the verdict in the Digby case. "The prosecution of the Follins for the stealing of the 'Digby' child, failed to make out a case, and the jury rendered a verdict of acquittal. And so the mystery is yet unveiled."

Chapter Ten

THE CASE THAT "EXCITED ALL NEW ORLEANS"

F or seven months, the Great New Orleans Kidnapping Case had riveted the Crescent City. News of Mollie's disappearance, the unfolding investigation, and the trial itself had received unprecedented notice, even as new crimes filled the police blotter. Everyone, it seemed, rich and poor, black and white, had been enthralled, even after Mollie was safely returned to her parents. "The Digby Kidnapping Case created more excitement and interest than half a dozen murders in this community," the *Republican* remarked at the trial's conclusion. The case would be "long remembered" for exciting a wider interest in "all classes of the population" than "was perhaps ever felt in a similar case before," the *Picayune* added.[1]

When a town, city, or nation focuses intense interest on a particular courtroom drama, the event is often revealing of that society's hopes or fears. Trials can teach conventional morality, and sensational trials often expose a society's cultural, economic, political, and social fault lines. In New Orleans in 1870, the public's fascination with the Digby case reflected the anger, optimism, confusion, and anxiety felt by black and white residents of a metropolis turned upside down by the Civil War and Reconstruction.[2]

To those white New Orleanians who opposed emancipation, the Fourteenth and Fifteenth Amendments, and Republican rule, the Digby kidnapping was evidence of a world spinning out of control. With tens of thousands of former slaves having moved to the city and with black men holding office, sitting on juries, and serving as police, many whites feared that black criminals had become emboldened and their crimes would go unpunished. White newspaper editors and reporters deliberately fueled those fears. By spreading the rumor that Mollie had been abducted for use as a Voodoo sacrifice, the white press helped spur a moral panic—a panic that could be manipulated for political purposes. White reactionaries used the Digby kidnapping to discredit Governor Warmoth and foment dissatisfaction with his biracial government. The Digby case even provided the city's elite women with a rare opportunity to enter the public debate over Reconstruction and to publicly express their anger at Warmoth, his police force, and Louisiana's new racial and political order.[3]

When the investigation led to two Afro-Creole women the case became more complex. The heated racial politics of Reconstruction forced white Creoles to reassess their longstanding and deeply intertwined relationships with Creoles of African descent. Because Afro-Creoles held many prominent positions in Louisiana's controversial Reconstruction government, crimes committed by members of their class received extra scrutiny. As the press leveled charges of corruption and malfeasance against Afro-Creole legislators, it chipped away at the respect many elite whites held for this class. If even the Afro-Creoles could not be trusted, many whites concluded that the only solution was a return to an unalloyed white supremacy. Ellen Follin's and Louisa Murray's alleged crimes revealed these underlying anxieties. Newspaper accounts wavered, at times offering admiring descriptions of the defendants that implied they might be falsely accused women from a still-trusted class, and at times suggesting that the kidnapping was yet another crime by blacks against whites that indicated widespread social disorder.[4]

Follin's and Murray's beauty, fashionable dress, and dignified demeanor also fed into a national fascination with heinous crimes committed by outwardly respectable people. Because city dwellers in urbanizing nineteenth-century America relied on dress, etiquette, and manners to distinguish themselves from the sidewalk crowds, bourgeois citizens particularly feared swindlers, confidence men, and conniving women who used the trappings of respectability to dupe the unsuspecting. The rumors that Minnie Green, a white woman seemingly from a reputable family, was the plot's mastermind, or the conjectures that Captain Broadwell had orchestrated the affair, heightened such concerns.[5]

Black New Orleanians had also followed the Digby proceedings intently, and they had joined whites in the early morning crowds of those hoping to gain admission to Judge Houghton's and Judge Abell's courtrooms. In the past, many black citizens had held a fatalistic view of a justice system rigged in favor of whites and against black defendants. But with equal protection and due process now enshrined in both the state and federal constitutions, and with black men seated in the jury box, courtroom spectacles held a new appeal. As the *Picayune* noted, the intense interest "from the different classes in the community was new in criminal trials." To be sure, some black New Orleanians had conflicted feelings about the kidnapping investigation and prosecution. The John Brown Republican Club reflected this ambivalence when, early in the investigation, it issued its statement praising the efforts of the biracial police while suggesting that black women were being unduly harassed. Whether most black citizens thought Follin and Murray were innocent is unclear, but newspapers noted that everyone in the city seemed to have a strong opinion one way or the other.[6]

Afro-Creoles had particular reason to be engaged because Detective Jourdain, Ellen Follin, and Louisa Murray were all Creoles of color. Given the publicity the case received, Jourdain's performance assumed special significance. During Reconstruction, almost all of the black elected officials from New Orleans and almost all of the black officers on the Metropolitan Police came from the mixed-race Creole community. Although some Afro-Creoles sought social distance from former slaves, they knew that whites considered them representatives of the race as a whole and that their success or failure could affect the status of all black people in Louisiana. If they proved inept, it would bolster the opponents of biracial governance.[7]

The pressure on Detective Jourdain was particularly great. At a time when Northern police departments still had not hired black patrolmen, let alone detectives, Jourdain's actions in the Digby case were the first accounts in the national press of a black detective interrogating white and black witnesses and using disguise and empirical skill to help solve a sensational crime. Although, in the end, he did not singlehandedly crack the case, the newspaper accounts of his apprehension of Louisa Murray, his interrogations of Ellen Follin, and his other efforts would have been a revelation to readers outside the South. His trial testimony may have frustrated prosecutors, but it also demonstrated his rigorous intellect and deductive powers. Jourdain proved himself worthy of the title "detective" at the very moment when detectives were becoming the most glamorous and storied figures in law enforcement.[8]

The Digby case was also the first kidnapping trial in American history to become sensationalized national news. Dramatic accounts of kidnappings were nothing new, of course. In the Old Testament, Joseph is abducted by his brothers and sold into slavery. Colonial Americans read unsettling narratives of children taken captive by Indians. And newspapers had long listed kidnappings of children, slaves, and wrongfully seized free black people along with other crimes in their "City Intelligence" columns. But the Digby case ushered in an era when the press sensationalized these crimes. At a time when middle-class Americans increasingly sentimentalized childhood, editors realized that tales of abducted children, parental anguish, large rewards, and community outrage sold papers. If the story had a racial or ethnic subplot, so much the better. The Digby case was the first of dozens of kidnapping or child-stealing accounts that made headlines during the Gilded Age.[9]

Historians often claim that the 1874 abduction of Charley Ross in Philadelphia was the first kidnapping case to become a major media event, and, unlike the Digby case, it is the subject of numerous books and articles. Like so many incidents from the Reconstruction era, the Digby case was forgotten over time. Yet it occurred four years before the Ross kidnapping, and the striking similarities between the two abductions suggest the possibility that the Ross case was a "copycat" crime. Charley Ross, the four-year-old son of a wealthy Philadelphia merchant, was playing with his brother in the front yard of their family's home when two "swarthy" men in a horse-drawn carriage lured the boys on board with an offer of candy and fireworks. The men took the boys to a local store and gave Charley's brother 25 cents to go inside to buy firecrackers. When

Charley's brother emerged from the grocery, the carriage, the men and Charley were gone. After Charley's father offered a large reward for his son's return, an extensive manhunt began. Police raided gypsy campgrounds and burst into the homes of Italian immigrants who fit the descriptions of the kidnappers. The kidnapping became national news. Prominent Philadelphians enlisted the help of the famous Pinkerton detective agency, which circulated millions of flyers with Charley's likeness. Charley Ross was never found, but an ex-Philadelphia police officer was eventually accused, tried, but then acquitted of the crime.[10]

Northern readers of the *New York Times* and other newspapers would also have viewed the Great New Orleans Kidnapping Case through the lens of Reconstruction politics. In 1870, any story that involved a biracial police force in the South was inherently political. When it appeared that Mollie Digby might not be found, Northern Democrats, who opposed Radical Reconstruction, would have viewed the apparent failure of Warmoth's police force as further evidence that the experiments in interracial governance and policing were failing. At the same time, Northern Republicans, weary of reports from the South of Klan violence, corruption, and fraud, may have found solace in a true crime story from New Orleans featuring a dashing young Republican governor, his Massachusetts-born police chief, and an expert black detective—particularly after the child was returned.[11]

Placing the Digby case in historical perspective also helps demonstrate why Reconstruction was such a pivotal moment in the history of American politics and race relations. Historians have called the Reconstruction era an "unfinished revolution" because the federal government's effort to create a racially just society in the South collapsed so quickly. For Governor Warmoth, the failure to secure a conviction in the Digby case was just one of many disappointments that year. By 1871, his dreams for postwar Louisiana were collapsing. Commercially minded, moderate black and white men would never unite under the Republican Party banner. Despite the conciliatory gestures Warmoth had made, most white Louisianans continued to view him as a corrupt carpetbagger and the Republicans as an illegitimate political organization foisted on the state by federal bayonets and black votes. Many of his black supporters had turned against him as well, irritated by his overly generous overtures to white

Democrats and his half-hearted support for social equality. In an effort to lure more white men into the party, Warmoth had given patronage positions to Democrats, invited some former Confederates into the state militia, allowed ex-Confederate Luzenberg to remain as district attorney, and vetoed a civil rights bill that he feared would unnecessarily antagonize white voters. He counseled black leaders to be patient, telling them that building a viable Republican party was the first priority. Equal access to public accommodations could come later. Many black leaders found Warmoth's strategy demeaning, and few whites accepted his extended hand. Louisiana's Republican Party descended into factional infighting.[12]

During Warmoth's final months in power in 1872, his fellow Republicans actually impeached (but did not remove) him. Unable to secure reelection, he retreated to private life, purchased a plantation—"Magnolia," in Plaquemines Parish—and devoted his energies to bringing Northern efficiency to sugar production. From his plantation he watched glumly as Reconstruction ended in 1877. President Rutherford B. Hayes ordered federal troops to stand down while white supremacist Democrats retook control of Louisiana. After operating his plantation for a decade, Warmoth, unable to resist the lure of politics, made one more quixotic run for governor, even though by 1888 the days when nineteenth-century Louisiana voters would elect a Republican had passed. In 1890, his party loyalty paid off when Republican President Benjamin Harrison appointed Warmoth collector of customs for New Orleans. The federal position allowed him to give patronage appointments to some of his old Republican supporters, both black and white. He served in that position for four years before retiring to a house on Marengo Street in uptown New Orleans. At the end of his life, Warmoth wrote a memoir of the postwar years, *Stormy Days in Louisiana*, in which he challenged the pro-Southern, white-supremacist interpretation of Reconstruction that by the 1920s had found its way into popular American culture. Novels, plays, and movies such as *The Clansman* (1905) and *Birth of a Nation* (1915) depicted the Ku Klux Klan as a heroic organization. College and high-school history textbooks offered a one-sided view of Reconstruction. Both Southern and Northern students learned that it was a tragic era during which villainous carpetbaggers, elected with the votes of illiterate former slaves, ravaged the South for their own personal gain. Warmoth fought back in his memoir, defending himself and his fellow Republicans as men who "honestly strove to protect the loyal people of the South, both white and back, after the Civil War." He died in 1931 at age eighty-nine, undaunted in his belief that Reconstruction had been a noble effort.[13]

Warmoth's New Orleans police chief, Algernon Badger, hung on to his post for a few years after Warmoth's ouster. In September 1874, he was still in charge of the Metropolitan Police when the Crescent City White League, a reactionary paramilitary army, attempted to overthrow the state government and install white supremacy by force. White Leaguers fought a bloody battle on Canal Street against Badger, his men, and loyal units of the state's militia. Badger, who had been wounded in the Civil War, was shot once again. This time bullets shattered his hand, arm, and leg. When Badger fell, his men broke and ran, and the White League ruled the city and state for a few days until President Ulysses S. Grant sent federal troops to crush the rebellion. Badger survived, but surgeons amputated his leg, and for the rest of his life he walked awkwardly on a prosthetic limb. When Reconstruction ended, Democrats purged Badger and his fellow Republicans from the police force and the militia. After 1877, Badger, like Warmoth, found employment through the patronage of Republican presidents who hoped to sustain what was left of the Republican Party in the South by appointing loyal members to federal positions in the Post Office and the Customs House. Threats on Badger's life continued. In 1879, despite his prosthetic leg, Badger thwarted a potential assassin by knocking the gun from his assailant's hands and wrestling him to the ground. In the 1880s and 1890s he devoted much of his time to the Grand Army of the Republic, the main Union veterans' association. Serving as the commander of the organization's Department of the Gulf, Badger campaigned successfully to allow black veterans to join the formerly all-white department. He lived in his house at 3311 Coliseum Street in New Orleans until his death in 1905 at age sixty-five.[14]

After Badger was removed from his position in 1877, the New Orleans police force quickly reverted to its old ways. Democratic governors and mayors once again filled the force with their cronies and political henchmen, and they discarded Warmoth's physical fitness and literacy tests. A few police veterans like Detective Leonard Malone survived the mass firings, but Warmoth's vision of a modernized, professional force unraveled. In 1884, a *New York Times* reporter's account of the patrolmen he encountered in New Orleans reflected the decline of the Metropolitan Police. "They are mostly under-sized men, who go about with common stiff felt hats, blue coats, generally unbuttoned, and they slouch along, often smoking comfortably and chatting pleasantly with corner groups and doorway idlers," the reporter wrote. "They enter barrooms freely and stay at pleasure....They are the only visible embodiment of city authority and are said to represent very fairly its dignity, discipline, and efficiency under a combination of boss and hoodlum rule." By the 1890s, the rigorous training and strict rules of conduct of the Warmoth era were a distant memory.[15]

Detective Jourdain remained on the Metropolitan Police force for two years after his appearance in the Digby trial, but the press never again credited him with a significant role in an investigation. For the remainder of his career as a detective, his name appeared in the papers only once, when he helped solve the murder of a French visitor whose body was found dumped by a canal outside of town. In that case, the press gave the lion's share of the credit to a white sergeant. When murders or robberies made headlines, other detectives took the lead. Jourdain's refusal to tailor his testimony to fit the state's case against Ellen Follin and Louisa Murray could not have endeared him to his superiors. His fierce pride and independence made him an unpredictable witness on whom prosecutors could not rely.[16]

In 1873, Jourdain joined an extraordinary but short-lived political organization called the Louisiana Unification Movement. Although to outsiders it seemed that Louisiana politics had irrevocably divided into "two sullen, bitter camps of racial and political hatred," in New Orleans a movement of white Creoles, Afro-Creoles, Jewish leaders, and black and white businessmen made a final effort to form a political party led by Louisiana's moderates—educated, longtime residents of the state, who were willing to put commerce ahead of race. Elite Afro-Creoles like publisher Louis Roudanez and philanthropist Aristide Mary joined whites with deep Louisiana ties, including the state's greatest Confederate hero, Creole General Pierre Gustave Toutant Beauregard (of Fort Sumter and Manassas fame), on a committee chaired by Beauregard that drafted a platform that pledged to uphold integrated public schools, black voting rights, and equal access to public transportation and accommodations. Behind the scenes, black and Afro-Creole participants in the movement agreed to abandon the "carpetbaggers" and unite politically with pragmatic Louisiana whites. To do so, Afro-Creole leaders had to put aside their fears that the movement might be a cynical ploy to divide the Republican Party. Jourdain had earlier warned that white men like former sheriff Harry T. Hays—a professed supporter of the moderate movement—would "laugh and smile at you, and at the same time...put a knife in your back." But participation by hundreds of the city's most prominent white Creole gentlemen assuaged those fears and led Jourdain and others to publicly affirm their support.[17]

The movement quickly collapsed. Reactionary white Democrats across the country ferociously assailed the effort. "Unification on the basis of perfect equality of whites and blacks!" a typical editorial exclaimed. "We abhor it in every fiber of our being." Jourdain attended the organization's one public meeting at Exposition Hall in July 1873. It was a disaster. Key white leaders such as General Beauregard, having been attacked mercilessly in the press, failed to show up, and many white men who did attend grew infuriated when some black speakers used the podium to lecture whites about their previous misdeeds. The movement never recovered. Around the country, Democratic papers cheered the disintegration of the nascent alliance. "Our Louisiana friends," a Georgia editor commented, "have wooed the negroes in vain; and now let them regain their composure. Let the whites of America maintain their right to the government and control of the country won by their forefathers for their children and not negroes." The demise of the Unification Movement marked the final political break between white Creoles and Afro-Creoles. The next year, many white Unificationists supported the Crescent City White League in its armed attempt to overthrow the Republican government.[18]

In November 1874, Jourdain decided to run for the state legislature as part of a Republican slate pledged to moderation, racial conciliation, and reform. Refusing to be disillusioned by his experiences as a Union officer, police detective, and Unificationist, Jourdain sought yet another opportunity to build bridges between Louisiana's "best men." Although the Crescent City

White League's attempted coup d'état weeks earlier should have signaled to Republicans that most whites' interest in moderation or conciliation had died with the Unification Movement, the party's convention "steered clear of extremists [or] radicals in the common acceptance of the term" when picking their nominees for office. Republicans chose Jourdain and other candidates like him to prove that they were a party committed to good governance. In an election plagued by violence, threats, and white thugs ripping registration certificates from black voters' hands, Jourdain managed to win the seat representing the city's Seventh Ward.[19]

In the legislature, the Republicans made Jourdain a point man in the effort to root out corruption, placing the former detective on the Committee of Retrenchment and Reform and on special committees investigating the affairs of the Metropolitan Police and excessive legislative expenses. In those roles, Jourdain tried to rise above partisanship. Although he voted to expel from the legislature a white Democrat from Grant Parish who made violent threats against black representatives, he joined white Democrats in voting against the impeachment of a Democratic judge accused of obstructing federal officials.[20] But Jourdain's moderation proved impractical in a deadlocked statehouse (forty-four Democrats and forty-four Republicans) where knives and revolvers were regularly "drawn and displayed in a threatening manner." Rather than welcome Jourdain's conciliatory gestures, Democrats set out to destroy him. In January 1876, they put forward a resolution calling for an investigation into allegations that Jourdain and six other Republican leaders had accepted bribes from the Louisiana Levee Company. In an evenly split House, the Republicans could have blocked the resolution, but Jourdain voted to approve it, even thought its passage meant that he would lose his committee seats until the investigation was concluded. He wanted his name cleared.[21] The Democrats did not stop there. Armed with the approved resolution, they successfully pressured the state's attorney general, A. P. Field, to bring criminal charges against Jourdain and the other accused men. Claiming that they had "unlawfully, willfully, and corruptly prostituted" their positions, Field had them all arrested. He soon dropped the charges against Jourdain, but Jourdain's good name had been sullied and his final year in office squandered.[22]

After 1877 Jourdain saw his fortunes, and those of other Creoles of color, decline. Afro-Creoles, like other white and black Republicans, were driven out of state government positions. In 1879, white Democrats called a new state constitutional convention that eliminated the constitutional protections for equal access to public accommodations. Owners of steamboats, restaurants, taverns, theaters, and other businesses could once again discriminate with impunity on the basis of race. Barred from government employment, Jourdain suffered another setback when in 1875 an arsonist burned the black Episcopal church in his Tremé neighborhood and the flames consumed twenty other buildings, including property Jourdain rented to a blacksmith on St. Ann Street. Jourdain eventually found employment with his Afro-Creole friend Francis Dumas, who hired him as a furniture salesmen, but the pay was meager. He contracted malaria and was able to work only sporadically. His savings dwindled.[23]

As race relations hardened, white Creoles cut themselves off from their former Afro-Creole allies. Indeed, many of them became increasingly embarrassed about their history of economic and romantic intermingling with Afro-Creoles. The old mores that had allowed men like Jourdain's father to live openly with their partners of African descent fell away. Some white Creoles even began to claim that the term *Creole* had never included persons of mixed race. In 1886, they formed the Creole Association of Louisiana, an organization whose leaders denied that blacks could be Creoles and celebrated those white Creoles who had fought for the Confederacy and opposed Reconstruction. When push came to shove, white Creoles sided with the rigid white supremacists rather than the mixed-race men and women with whom they shared familial and cultural ties.[24]

By early April 1888, Jourdain had had enough. Twenty years earlier, the world had been full of promise; as a detective he had made national news. Now he occupied a world that day by day looked more like the "Black Codes" society that Andrew Johnson and his allies had tried to create after the Civil War. Jourdain, despite his intellect and polish, had been reduced to a part-time clerk in a furniture store. On April 4, he left his Tremé neighborhood home without speaking to his wife and set off for nearby St. Louis Cemetery #1. There he chatted pleasantly with the cemetery's sexton, saying he wanted to visit some of the graves. He walked through the rows of aboveground tombs until he reached the crypt far back in the cemetery where his white father, Afro-Creole mother, and other members of his family were interred. He sat down in front of the tomb, pulled a .38-caliber pistol from his coat, placed its muzzle to his ear, and pulled the trigger. The sexton, rushing to the sound of the gunshot, found Jourdain "lying on his back with his head resting in a pool of blood."[25]

Jourdain's suicide received only brief mention in the New Orleans papers. None of the accounts mentioned who he was or what he had achieved. On April 6, *L'abeille de la Nouvelle-Orleans*, the French-language newspaper read by the city's white Creoles, reported Jourdain's death. In the past, the story's tone might have been somber, given that Jourdain was a descendant of one of Louisiana's most prominent white Creole families. Instead, the article's sarcastic tenor exemplified the distance white Creoles now placed between themselves and Afro-Creoles. "Apparently, the heat wave's return is affecting some people's mentalities," it read (in French). "A certain mulatto named J. B. Jourdain, age 56, who deciding that he had lived long enough, made up his mind to exit this world. To that end, he went yesterday morning...and blew his brains out near the family tomb. Jourdain...presumably did it to put an end to his sorrows. An effective remedy, no doubt, but fortunately one most of us wouldn't take." That same day Jourdain's funeral was held and his body interred in the family's tomb in St. Louis Cemetery #1.[26]

By the time of his death Jourdain had been forgotten, and he remains little known today. Viewed from a historical distance, however, that 1888 scene— Jourdain lying dead from a self-inflicted wound in front of his family's tomb— seems freighted with symbolism. His suicide poignantly reflects the fate of Reconstruction in the South and the thwarted political and social aspirations of Afro-Creoles in the late nineteenth century.

Other Afro-Creoles fought on, struggling tooth and nail against the return of white supremacy. When the Louisiana legislature, two years after Jourdain's death, followed other Southern states in passing a Separate Car Act that required railroads to segregate their passengers on the basis of race, Aristide Mary, Rodolphe Desdunes, and other Afro-Creoles leaders formed the Comité des Citoyens—an organization committed to challenging the law and other "caste legislation" in court. In 1892, the Comité launched the ill-fated test-case litigation that culminated four years later in the U.S. Supreme Court's infamous *Plessy v. Ferguson* decision. The court's sanction in *Plessy* of "separate but equal" segregation helped usher in the era of Jim Crow. Aristide Mary, however, did not live to see that grim result. In 1893, he too committed suicide.[27]

Shortly after Jourdain's death, his wife, Josephine Celina, wrote to the Commissioner of Pensions in Washington, applying for a Civil War military pension in her husband's name. She implored the commissioner to "please sir answer my letter," for "I am in great adversity." The commissioner rejected her application. Because General Banks had driven Jourdain out of the Union army prior to serving his ninety days, he failed to qualify for a pension. How Josephine, a destitute widow, survived in her remaining years is unknown.[28]

After their acquittal, Ellen Follin, George Blass, and Louisa Murray spent the rest of their lives out of the spotlight. Follin's and Blass's names would not appear in the newspapers again until their short obituaries ran many decades later. Follin continued to live in her house at Bellecastle and Camp, but, perhaps to escape her notoriety from the trial, she assumed her deceased partner's surname—Blass. Her days running a lying-in hospital appear to have ended after her business, which depended on her ability to protect her boarders from public scrutiny, had been exposed. For the remainder of her life she worked as a seamstress, an occupation popular with Afro-Creole women who preferred working at home rather than under white supervision as servants, cooks, or nannies. Follin may not have entirely abandoned taking in lodgers as a means of supplementing her income: when the census-taker came to her door in 1900, he found a five-year-old black child named Louis Miller boarding there. By the time she died in 1906 at the age of seventy-five, few, it seemed, remembered her for her role in the famous Digby case. Her perfunctory obituary said only that she was the widow of Angelo Blass and a longtime resident of the city. It made no reference to the trial. Her death received no other public notice.[29]

Follin's son, George Blass, also lived quietly. He married soon after his acquittal in the Digby case, but he and his wife, Helena, had no children. Although he was smart and literate—reporters during the trials had remarked on his intelligence—he labored for most of his life as a waiter and then as a butler. His career reflected the shrinking opportunities mixed-race and Afro-Creole men in New Orleans faced at the turn of century. Black artisans lost ground to mechanization, white competition, and Jim Crow when white Creoles stopped patronizing black Creoles' businesses. Many of the economic niches Afro-Creoles had once filled disappeared. Though the stigma of Blass's association with the Digby case may also have hurt him for a time, his career nevertheless paralleled those of countless talented black men throughout the South in the late nineteenth century who found employment only in low-skilled jobs. Like others, he turned to the city's many black fraternal organizations for mutual support, joining the African American lodge of the Order of Odd Fellows and other clubs. After his mother died in 1906, Blass used his inheritance to buy a house at 818 Harmony Street. He and Helena took in his wayward brother Thomas, a carriage driver, who was homeless after a failed marriage. George died in 1916 at age sixty-one and was interred in uptown New Orleans in Lafayette Cemetery #1.[30]

The post-trial whereabouts of Louisa Murray, the third defendant in the Digby case, are mysterious. Murray, whose beauty, style, and deportment garnered so much attention during the trial, vanished from the historical record after her acquittal. She and her daughter, Emmetta, last appear in the 1870 U.S. census, living in Mobile. Even in the modern age of digitized genealogical and legal documents, Murray remains hidden. It could be that she changed her surname in an effort to return to anonymity, or perhaps she and Emmetta followed the path taken by two of Ellen Follin's offspring who deliberately detached themselves from their family's history.[31]

Ellen Follin's youngest child, Mary Belle, who was six years old when her mother's trial took place, eventually renounced her mixed-race heritage, moved North, and "passed" for white. As a young woman in New Orleans, she married a white, Vermont-born steamboat engineer named Julius Powers, with whom she had three children in the 1880s, Julius Jr., Joseph, and Culotta. Although under Louisiana law children like Mary Belle's, who had one grandparent of African ancestry, were considered "colored," Mary Belle and her husband identified their offspring as white on baptismal certificates and in municipal records. After Mary Belle's and Julius's marriage collapsed, she moved north with her daughter Culotta. They lived in New York, Chicago, and Detroit, and in each locale she told her new neighbors and census officials that both she and Culotta were white. Follin's youngest son, Eugene, took a similar path, marrying a white German immigrant and legally designating their daughter Ella as "white." In 1914, Ella, Ellen Follin's granddaughter, married an Italian immigrant named Joseph Saccaro and integrated herself into that family so successfully that even close relatives had no knowledge of her mixed-race heritage.[32]

The decision made by some of Ellen Follin's children and grandchildren to present themselves as white was hardly unique. They were just a few of the tens of thousands of light-skinned African Americans around the turn of the century who realized that life would be easier if they were considered white and who thus chose to recreate their identities. Throughout American history, people of African ancestry have crossed the color line in order to escape slavery or prejudice or to gain the privileges whiteness conferred. The years between 1880 and 1925 were, however, what one historian has called "the great age of passing." After Reconstruction collapsed and Southern states enacted draconian Jim Crow laws, Louisiana and the rest of the Deep South embraced the "one-drop" rule, by which any traceable African ancestry or reputation of color classified an individual as "colored." For many light-skinned people, passing became an economically rational choice. Ellen Follin's sons and grandson illustrate the point. In both the North and the South, being identified as black severely limited one's career opportunities. Ellen's sons George and Thomas remained in New Orleans their entire lives, where they were regarded as black men despite their light skin. George worked as a waiter and butler while Thomas drove a carriage, and both lived in a world of segregated theaters, streetcars, schools, and water fountains, a world in which black men had lost the right to vote, serve on juries, and hold state office. Ellen's grandson Julius, Jr., left New Orleans for New York as a young man, presented himself as white, and became a stockbroker and corporate manager.[33]

When Mary Belle, Julius, Ella, and Ellen Follin's other descendants became white, they lost touch with their extended family and their rich heritage. For better or worse, they also erased from their family's memory their connection to the Digby case. Unlike the descendants of Thomas and Bridgette Digby, for whom the 1870 kidnapping became a part of family lore, most of Ellen

Follin's living descendants have learned of the great kidnapping case—and of the African Americans in their family lineage—only in the twenty-first century, either as they undertook genealogical research or when they were contacted by the author of this book.[34]

For the Digbys, Mollie's kidnapping eventually became a colorful family legend, even though Thomas and Bridgette Digby initially hoped to put the traumatic events of 1870 behind them. At the end of the trial, Thomas announced that they would move from Howard Avenue because Bridgette could not "live in the same house where she had experienced so much suffering." Later that year they bought a new house on Gasquet Street (today's Cleveland Avenue), at the corner of Tonti. There their lives slowly returned to normal. Over the next decade, Bridgette and Thomas had five more children: Martin, John, Charles, Annie, and James. Two of their sons would later join their father in the carriage business, and another joined the police force. Their other children became merchants and salesmen or took office jobs. As the Digby offspring and other second- and third-generation Irish in New Orleans overcame the prejudice once faced by their immigrant forebears, new opportunities and higher-paying white-collar jobs opened to them. As an adult, George (Georgie Digby), the son whom the kidnappers had sent for bananas, worked in the office of an oil company. George's son Fred Digby became an influential sports writer and editor who led the effort to establish the Sugar Bowl college football game in New Orleans. George, Mollie, and their siblings had large families of their own, and today numerous Digby descendants live in New Orleans and across the country. By the time of their deaths in 1902 and 1911 respectively, Thomas and Bridgette were the patriarch and matriarch of a large, assimilated American family.[35]

The Digbys' elder daughter, Mollie, the kidnapped baby, married another child of Irish immigrants, Patrick Golden, and together they had four children of their own. Mollie stayed at home raising their family while Patrick found success, first as a clerk, then as assistant supervisor, then as manager for the Metropolitan Life Insurance Company. Well connected with the Choctaw Club—the Democratic political machine that controlled the city and state—Patrick secured a lucrative patronage position as deputy state tax collector. The Goldens moved into a new house in the neighborhood developers built at the far end of Canal

Street as the city expanded. They were a family rising both socially and economically when forty-six-year-old Patrick died unexpectedly in 1918. Without her
husband, Mollie's finances suffered. During the 1920s, she worked as a boardinghouse laundress, sold the family home, and moved with her daughter into one
side of a two-family abode at 137 North Solomon Street.[36]

Back in 1870, at the time of the kidnapping, the New York *Tribune* had
predicted that Mollie was as famous at age two as she would ever be. As an
adult, the paper prognosticated, Mollie would never be "the sensation" she was
as a child, "nor evoke half so much conversation by anything she may say as she
had before she was able to talk."[37] Six decades later, that prediction seemed to
have come true, as Mollie had led an inconspicuous life far from the public eye.

Then in 1932, in the wake of the kidnapping of the Lindbergh baby, the
Digby case once more made news in New Orleans. As the Great Depression
began, kidnappings for ransom became a national epidemic. Hundreds of abductions of children and adults occurred each year. The wealthy and famous were
particularly vulnerable as Prohibition-era mobsters began to view ransoms as
a lucrative source of revenue. Detectives thwarted a notorious plot to kidnap
film star Mary Pickford, but other schemes succeeded. Lloyd's of London began
selling ransom insurance to American customers. No kidnapping garnered more
attention than the abduction of Charles A. and Anne Morrow Lindbergh's two-
year-old boy. Charles Lindbergh's 1927 flight from New York to Paris in the
Spirit of St. Louis—the first solo nonstop transatlantic flight ever completed—had
made him the most celebrated man in America. In a kidnapping-plagued era,
fame brought danger, and his child accordingly had been "one of the most carefully guarded infants in the world." Yet on March 1, 1932, a kidnapper managed
to climb into the Lindberghs' rural New Jersey home, steal their son, and leave
a menacing ransom note. Outrage and fear swept the country, state legislatures
held emergency sessions to vote for tougher kidnapping penalties, and President
Herbert Hoover ordered the largest manhunt in the history of the United States.
In New Orleans, coverage of the kidnapping and the controversial trial of Bruno
Richard Hauptmann that followed dominated the headlines for months.[38]

The Lindbergh case sparked renewed interest in famous kidnappings of the
past, and in New Orleans reporters besieged "old residents" who remembered

anything about the abduction of Mollie Digby sixty-two years earlier. Recognizing that the case had "acquired new and macabre interest since news came of the kidnapping of the Lindbergh baby," the *Times-Picayune* ran a long story on March 3 recounting the facts of the Digby abduction. Assembled quickly, the article was full of factual errors. But Mollie Digby was once again on the front page.[39]

Three days after the article appeared, the *Times-Picayune* announced that it had tracked down *the* Mollie Digby. She was alive, still living in New Orleans, and, the paper reported, her tale had taken a modern turn. Mollie, now in her early sixties, was writing "the story of her own kidnapping for the movies." While she was willing to speak generally about the case, she declined to share recently taken photographs of herself, as she planned to send them to the movie companies and, she said, "the motion picture people might not like it" if the photos ran first in the newspaper.[40]

Mollie was indeed in the midst of preparing a detailed account of her kidnapping that she hoped she could sell to Hollywood. Throughout her life, she had heard tales told by her parents, her siblings, and family friends who could recall her abduction and the subsequent investigation and legal proceedings. In 1930, she began writing her own version of those events—first in longhand and then on a typewriter—making efforts to get the story right. She collected the original newspaper articles about her ordeal and even contacted former governor Henry Clay Warmoth, who was still alive, retired and living in his Marengo Street house. She sent Warmoth a draft of her manuscript and suggested he might want to collaborate with her on the project. In his late eighties and with only months to live, Warmoth begged off, saying he was too old and infirm to offer assistance. "I have read part of your manuscript, enough to have to say that I am not able to master it and do the work needed," he wrote to Mollie. "It needs a young and vigorous man, who has the eye sight and strength to take it up and go through it and put it in shape."[41]

Mollie's Hollywood dreams never materialized. But her unfinished manuscript, which has been passed down by her descendants, does offer a final plot twist to the Digby case. Back in 1871, New Orleanians had expressed frustration that the trial had left two major questions unanswered: who orchestrated

Mollie's kidnapping, and why was it done? After listening to stories and theories about the case for more than sixty years, and after doing her own archival research, Mollie delivered provocative answers which, if true, provide an epilogue to the Digby drama worthy of a detective novel.

According to Mollie, the mastermind of her kidnapping was James Broadwell, the captain of the *Eclipse*, the man who returned her to her parents, helped fund the legal defense of Ellen Follin, and tried unsuccessfully to claim the reward offered by Governor Warmoth. In Mollie's account, the events that led to her kidnapping began when Captain Broadwell fell in love with his future wife Evelina, who was then seventeen and living with her wealthy parents in New York. When Broadwell proposed marriage, her father objected. He felt Broadwell was far too old for his daughter. When "contrary to the wishes of the parents the couple eloped" and moved to New Orleans, the parents punished their daughter by changing their will, thus denying her an "inheritance that would have [been] hers had she obeyed and married some young New Yorker." But when the Broadwells then had a child, the parents' hearts softened and the father sent his daughter a letter saying the inheritance had been restored.[42]

The Broadwells' good fortune turned to tragedy, Mollie went on, when their baby sickened and died. The couple was grief-stricken. They had lost their child—and possibly the restored inheritance as well. The fear that they would be once again disinherited spawned the nefarious kidnapping plot that followed. The Broadwells, Mollie wrote, employed a nanny who had often strolled with their child at Lee Circle, where nurses "[took] their charges to enjoy the evening breeze."[43] There the Broadwells' nurse, a "colored" woman, had regularly walked with another "colored nurse employed by Mrs. Thomas Digby [who] also frequented Lee Circle with her little charge, Mollie Digby." The nurses noticed that the Broadwells' baby and Mollie "had the same size and had the same general features and coloring." At her nanny's urging, Mrs. Broadwell had even gone to see the two infants together for herself, and she too was struck by the babies' uncanny resemblance to one another. "When she returned she commented on it to her husband," Mollie wrote.[44]

With his wife's inheritance threatened, Captain Broadwell decided to kidnap the Digbys' baby to use as a replacement for his own, and he recruited Ellen

Follin and her sister Louisa to abduct the child. According to Mollie's account, Follin had been Captain Broadwell's mistress ever since the death of her husband Angelo, and she agreed to help her paramour with his scheme. Neither Follin nor Broadwell, however, anticipated the extraordinary publicity the case would receive. It even came to the attention of "the Queen of England of that time, Queen Victoria," Mollie claimed. The queen, Mollie wrote, contacted Governor Warmoth, "suggested that a liberal reward should be offered," and contributed $500 to the cause. When word of the monarch's concern reached the press, "the affection of the entire United States towards this famed sovereign was aroused, and her offer created especial comment and drew even more attention to the case." Broadwell and Follin, fearful of arrest and serious punishment, hid the child for sixty-one days until the police investigation closed in. That was when Broadwell appeared at the Digbys' door, announcing that he had their child.[45]

In addition to her efforts to write a screenplay, Mollie shared her manuscript with Dorothy Branson, a researcher for the Works Progress Administration (WPA), who hoped to turn the story into a book. Branson began writing her own account of the Digby abduction. A fifty-four-year-old widow from Ohio, Branson was one of the many women and men the WPA hired during the Great Depression as part of President Franklin D. Roosevelt's New Deal jobs programs. Researchers like Branson helped organize city archives, took oral histories from former slaves and other figures whose stories might be lost if not recorded, and assisted the writers then preparing the famous WPA guides to American cities.[46]

Using Mollie's manuscript as a guide, Branson prepared her own "raw outline of the true facts of this most noted case of kidnapping in the State of Louisiana." While her account did not mention the Broadwells by name, she too told a story of a New Orleans couple who needed to kidnap a baby in order to protect an inheritance and of the steamboat captain's "beautiful, expensive Octoroon" mistress who assisted in the plot.[47] As in Mollie's version, Branson claimed that Queen Victoria took an interest in the case and "offered the Governor one-half of the reward... for the return of the stolen baby." The kidnappers, meanwhile, kept the abducted child hidden by traveling "up and down the river in the original steamboat the *Robert E. Lee*" and back and forth between New Orleans and Mobile. As detectives chased the culprits "up and down bayous, and all through the Deep South...Indians, negroes of every type, tramps and bums of every description were involved in holding the child." Eventually, Branson wrote, the kidnappers "were rounded up—the child returned—and a big trial against the perpetrators of the crime, filled with interest and excitement" took place.[48]

What is to be made of these accounts? Did both Mollie Digby and a WPA researcher somehow discover the motive for the Digby kidnapping? Was Captain Broadwell the plot's mastermind? The archives in New Orleans provide only small bits of evidence. Although there is no evidence that Evelina Broadwell's father disinherited her or that her inheritance depended on her producing an heir, the Broadwells did have legal squabbles with Evelina's siblings over real estate Evelina inherited from her mother in 1871. After a long legal battle, a district court judge ordered Evelina to partition her property and distribute land to her brothers and sisters. The Broadwells, it also appears, were indeed in financial trouble. In 1872, they sold their elegant Chestnut Street home and spent the rest of their lives as renters moving around the city, first to Constance Street, then to St. Thomas and North Miro Streets, and then on to four other addresses. And Captain Broadwell grew increasingly cantankerous. In 1873, police arrested him for assaulting his neighbor, and five days later he had an entire family on his block arrested for "assaulting and abusing him."[49]

Broadwell's fiscal problems may have been enough to confirm the suspicions of the Digbys and others about his guilt. At the time of the trial, rumors circulated that Broadwell and Follin were lovers and that he knew more about the plot than he let on. The Broadwells' post-trial insolvency and inheritance squabbles may have turned suspicion to certainty, as they suggested a possible motive for the crime. Theory may also have become fact as the story of the kidnapping was told and retold at Digby family gatherings. By the time Mollie began writing her account in 1930, Broadwell's role as mastermind was central to the tale.

While it is possible that Digby family legend got it right and Captain Broadwell did plot the abduction, Mollie's and Dorothy Branson's "true" versions of events suffer from embellishments and errors that suggest a purposeful blending of fact and fiction to construct a cinematic tale. There is no record, for example, of the Broadwells ever having had a child. And while Captain Broadwell was indeed older than his wife by eighteen years, Evelina's parents were from Cuba and Louisiana, not New York.[50]

In her manuscript, Mollie also took real events from 1870 and altered them. Although she had in her possession the newspaper accounts of the raid by Detectives Jourdain and Pierson on Ellen Follin's home, in her version she replaced Jourdain and Pierson with two fictional white detectives "dressed as negroes, their faces blacked." And rather than rushing into Follin's house shouting, "Where is the stolen child?" as Jourdain and Pierson had done, Mollie claimed the white detectives, disguised in blackface, repeatedly visited Follin's house pretending to be romantically minded suitors of Follin and her sister. Soon, Mollie wrote, the detectives "had their dusky companions in their confidence," and Follin then divulged to them her role in the Digby kidnapping. Follin, Mollie added, finally caught on to the ruse one evening when "the two detectives [were] talking to their lady loves…on a dark porch" and "one of the other negroes about the home passed by and whispered" to Follin: "Them's white men!" "The effect was instantaneous," Mollie wrote. "Not a particle of additional information could be secured. But the two detectives had enough to go on."[51]

Mollie probably found the inspiration for this invented scene in the July 10, 1870, article in the *Daily Picayune* that described Detective Jourdain's efforts to use a disguise to fool the Digbys' black neighbor, Rosa Lee, into divulging what she knew about the kidnapping. Because people had stopped talking to the police, that article recounted, Jourdain and Detective Jordan Noble had dressed in soiled work clothes and pretended to be former slaves. While they were talking to Lee, a friend of hers walked up and whispered to her that the men were disguised officers, and "her whole manner changed."[52]

In her manuscript, Mollie transformed the news account of Jourdain's undercover efforts into a yarn about detectives the in blackface bamboozling Ellen Follin. Maybe Mollie feared no one in the 1930s would believe there was ever a time in New Orleans when black men were detectives, but clearly she was also twisting the facts for comic effect. Throughout her lifetime, America's popular culture had included minstrel shows, vaudeville acts, and, later, radio programs like *Amos and Andy* that sought laughs by portraying African Americans as gullible buffoons. Mollie was a woman of her era. At another point in her manuscript she described steamboats on the levee with "hordes of picanninies and lazy black workmen...crowded about them." Mollie likely included the detectives in blackface as an amusing vignette that might appeal to Hollywood producers.[53]

At another point in her manuscript, Mollie noted that in 1870, "Voodoo rites were still practiced in the superstitious Crescent City and dozens of offers to find Mollie Digby were based on the belief that she was being held captive by women practicing the strange ceremonies." In the manuscript's margin next to that sentence, written in pencil in Mollie's hand, is a note saying "get descriptions here...have girl see them." Had Mollie's manuscript become a screenplay and film, it could have included scenes of her as a terrified child witnessing a Voodoo ritual.[54]

Mollie's most fantastic claim, that Queen Victoria wrote to Governor Warmoth offering to supplement the advertised reward, also was either invented or based solely on family legend. The newspapers of 1870 and 1871 in New Orleans and around the country made no mention of Queen Victoria's participation, nor did newspapers in London. There are also no references in Governor Warmoth's letters or memoirs to his having been contacted by the queen.[55]

Dorothy Branson's "outline of true facts" about the case repeated many of Mollie's exaggerations. Branson's 1939 version, moreover, included additional flourishes that cannot be found in the trial transcripts, newspapers, or other materials from 1870. There is no evidence that Mollie's abductors took her on the *Robert E. Lee* or that she was hidden for a time by Indians or "tramps and bums of every description." Where Mollie claimed that Queen Victoria offered a reward of $500, Branson increased the amount to $50,000. And Branson's supposedly "true" account closed with the patently false statement that the accused kidnappers "were sentenced for twenty years to the Penitentiary!"[56]

Why would a federal researcher join Mollie in presenting so many fictions as fact? Part of the answer may lie in the goals of the WPA and the Federal Writers Project for which Branson worked. The WPA encouraged its staff to collect folklore and colorful stories along with more traditional historical material as they assembled the WPA city guides and other works. Fueled by the New Deal populism of the 1930s, WPA staffers took seriously the musical, culinary, folk art, and folklore traditions of poor Cajuns, African Americans, and other marginalized groups. In Louisiana, WPA writers published numerous books that often blurred fact and fiction in tales of Voodoo, ghosts, pirates, and swamp creatures. In preparing her "outline of true facts," Branson seems to have replicated the style of the WPA writers with whom she worked, supplementing Mollie's manuscript with other legends she had heard. Still, Branson thought she was presenting a work of nonfiction. Unlike Mollie, who dreamed of being the subject of a Hollywood film, Branson hoped to collaborate on a book with a professional writer. She included her outline in a proposal to one such author, asking "Can you use it?" and adding, "Should you desire, I am in a position to do any research on the story for you."[57]

When Mollie Digby died of a heart attack on October 12, 1944, the New Orleans newspapers took note, and the articles announcing her death once again treated Digby family lore as fact. In an edition brimming with war news from Europe and the Pacific, the *Item* paused to memorialize the woman "whose kidnapping seventy years ago rocked New Orleans and the nation, and even caused a Queen of England to offer a reward for her safety." The *Times-Picayune* reported that Mollie's abduction in 1870 had "excited all New Orleans" and that it was believed "that the child was stolen to replace an heir to an estate who had died shortly before." The *Item* included Mollie's theory that she had been kidnapped to substitute for Captain Broadwell's baby. Contrary to facts detailed on its own pages seventy-three years earlier, the *Times-Picayune* concluded by noting that "two Negro women were later convicted of the kidnapping" and sent to prison. Perhaps no one in Jim Crow New Orleans in 1944, including the reporter, could imagine black defendants being acquitted of such a sensational crime.[58]

Mourners attended Mollie's funeral at Our Lady of the Holy Rosary Church near Bayou St. John before her burial in St. Patrick's #1, the sprawling cemetery established before the Civil War for Irish immigrants who died in yellow fever epidemics, digging the city's New Basin Canal, or at end of hard lives as draymen, stevedores, and laundresses.

Who abducted Mollie Digby and why? Unless revealing letters or diaries surface in an attic or archive, we will probably never know with certainty. For some readers, there may even be lingering doubt about whether the baby Ellen Follin turned over to Captain Broadwell was indeed Mollie Digby. Thomas Digby, after all, had initially been unable to recognize the recovered child as his own. Would two boils on a child's face be sufficient to make her unrecognizable to her father after only two months' absence? Thomas had recoiled when Evelina Broadwell first attempted to hand the toddler to him. "Is that my Molly?" he had asked in disbelief. To be sure, Bridgette Digby's immediate identification of the child is compelling evidence she was Mollie. "I would know it anywhere," Bridgette had exclaimed. "A mother cannot be deceived." But barring tests matching the DNA of Mollie's direct descendants with those of the Digbys' other children, there remains the possibility that Bridgette, desperate and traumatized, claimed the child as her own despite any doubts she may have held.[59]

For some readers, Ellen Follin's account of the veiled white woman leaving Mollie Digby at her gate may seem implausible, just as it did to the Democratic press in 1870. Skeptical reporters had compared Follin's story to a lie a child might concoct to avoid punishment. But other readers might accept Follin at her word. Maybe the real kidnappers, in an effort to extricate themselves from their plot, chose to leave Mollie at Follin's house precisely because Follin's race and profession made it unlikely that she would rush to the police once she suspected she had the Digby baby in her care. The operator of a lying-in hospital might also know how to discreetly place an unwanted child in an orphanage or new home. Given the public fervor surrounding the case, Follin's initial prevarications during police questioning are understandable. She had good reason to claim that the Digby baby had been in her house for only a short time. She feared correctly that she would be accused.

What we do know is that in the January 1871 trial, a biracial jury reached a verdict that runs counter to tales of biased trials in the Deep South before the civil rights movement. The wrongheaded juries that convicted the Scottsboro Boys in Alabama in the 1930s and that acquitted the murderers of Emmett Till in Mississippi in 1955 remain emblematic of an era when jury trials served as tools of racial oppression. But the verdict in the Great New Orleans Kidnapping Case tells an unexpected story.

In 1870 and 1871, no one knew for sure whether Reconstruction and biracial government in Louisiana would last. For many New Orleanians, white and black, the Digby case and the fate of Republican rule were intertwined. For Governor Warmoth and the Republicans, the jury's verdict was at once a victory and a defeat. His biracial Metropolitan Police had failed to secure a conviction in a case Warmoth hoped would prove the competence of his force. But the verdict also suggested that racial hardliners had not yet won, that in 1870 and 1871 there were still white men in the South's most important city who wished, at least within the context of law, to see black people treated fairly.

If it is true, as some legal writers argue, that in jury trials "it is almost impossible to secure a verdict which runs counter to the settled convictions of the community," then the outcome in the Digby case suggests that despite the best efforts of white supremacist editors, politicians, and thugs, the convictions of white New Orleanians had not yet hardened into the solid white South of later years. Despite the newspapers' sensational, race-baiting coverage of the kidnapping, Follin, Murray, and Blass received due process. The jury, it seems clear, gave credence to the testimony of black witnesses, discounted that of unreliable whites like August Singler, and demanded that the state make a compelling case. The lingering respect some whites held for elite Afro-Creoles may have influenced the proceedings. But the outcome nevertheless suggests that in 1870 in New Orleans, Reconstruction remained a moment of possibility; that the rigid and often rigged justice of the Jim Crow era was not inevitable, and that the minds of many white New Orleanians had not yet closed to the idea of legal justice for all.[60]

There were glimmers of hope in other Southern states as well. Even after most federal support for Reconstruction ended in 1877, populist political leaders in Virginia, North Carolina, Alabama, and Tennessee found success, albeit short-lived, by fostering political cooperation across the color line. There were still moderate whites who could have been won over. If only the economy had boomed under Republican leadership rather than collapsed, or the violence of the Ku Klux Klan and other racist paramilitary groups had been curbed more effectively, or the Republicans had not descended into bitter infighting, the result could have been different. Counterfactual history is problematic, but so is reading Southern history backward from *Plessy v. Ferguson.* The surprising outcome of the Great New Orleans Kidnapping Case cautions us against doing so.[61]

Unlike famous courtroom dramas that remain fixed in the nation's memory, the Digby case was largely forgotten over time. The pathbreaking Detective Jourdain and all twelve jurors returned to historical anonymity. Ellen Follin's children purposely hid their past from view. Louisa Murray disappeared. Although Digby family lore kept parts of the story alive, essential details of the trial and verdict were lost in the telling. But for seven months in 1870 and 1871, the Great New Orleans Kidnapping Case turned its participants into consequential figures in the story of Reconstruction's rise and fall and in the continuing drama of race, law, and justice in America.

AFTERWORD AND
ACKNOWLEDGMENTS

Every historian has had a moment like it. You are immersed in old letters, newspapers, or other archival material when a story different from the one you are researching catches your eye. In the documents you find an account of something no one has written about before, an untold story begging to be told. Usually when this happens, you pause, shake your head, think "wow, that would be great to tackle someday," and then return to the task at hand. *The Great New Orleans Kidnapping Case* is an example, for better or worse, of what happens when you actually take the bait and decide that the event you stumbled across is too rich, too full of historical implications, to pass up. When I first found the Digby case, I was researching John Archibald Campbell's legal campaign to obstruct Reconstruction and reading all of the 1870 New Orleans newspapers in search of references to cases Campbell was litigating in the state and local courts. When I reached the June 1870 editions, the story of an alleged Voodoo abduction demanded a quick read. That can't possibly have happened, I thought. The press had to be exaggerating. The New Orleans papers, after all, also reported ghost sightings. But to my amazement, each day's paper contained new articles about the Digby kidnapping—including reports of the police arresting and interrogating Voodoo practitioners. By the time it was clear that the human sacrifice rumors were false, the story had taken other compelling turns. I was hooked, and, just like the readers in 1870, I looked to each day's newspapers for the latest revelations in the Digby investigation.

I also checked to see if anyone had written about the case before. I had never heard of the Digby case, but surely someone had already authored an article or book about it. I was surprised to find that the story was almost untouched by historians. The only reference I could locate to it were a few sentences in Martha Ward's biography of the Voodoo priestess Marie Laveau. Without mentioning Mollie Digby by name, Ward used the human sacrifice rumors that followed her kidnapping as evidence of white people treating Voodoos as "the 'Other.'" No historian had ever recreated the investigation or the dramatic legal proceedings that followed, even though both had made national headlines in 1870. No one, it seemed, knew of Ellen Follin or John Baptiste Jourdain or the role the case played in the story of Reconstruction. I dived in. The Digby kidnapping case was the perfect subject for a micro-history.[1]

Had I realized at the time how hard micro-history is to write, I might have had second thoughts. Authors of micro-history often have the benefit of writing about vivid events. Even as they focus on the lives of hitherto obscure people, micro-historians can count on the drama of the New York Slave Conspiracy of 1741, or the burning of the Charlestown Convent in 1834, or, in my case, the search for Mollie Digby and the trial of her alleged abductors to pull the narrative and analysis along.[2] What I did not know, however, was how challenging a task it is to reconstruct the lives of individuals like Ellen Follin or Bridgette Digby, who left a limited historical footprint. My first book was a biography of a Supreme Court justice during the Civil War era, and I was accustomed to having troves of letters, diaries, judicial opinions, and other biographical material to draw on. Piecing together the life of an August Singler or Gardner Houghton or Louisa Murray was something different altogether. I gained a deep respect for social historians and family genealogists who have undertaken similar efforts. Even in the age of online genealogical records, bringing obscure individuals back to life is a painstaking (but ultimately satisfying) task. It is sometimes said that writing a biography about a deceased person is like trying to interview someone who has gone down the hall and around the corner. When writing micro-history, it often seems as if your subjects have gone down the hall, around the corner, and out the door.

But then there are moments when the events and the people you are writing about seem very close at hand. When I first found the Digby case, I was teaching in New Orleans at Loyola University, and my wife, Ashley, and I lived uptown in a house at 5229 Camp Street on the northeast corner of Camp and Bellecastle streets. As I dug into the story, mapping out what took place and where, I realized that Ellen Follin's house was located on the northeast corner of Camp and Bellecastle. We were living on the exact site where Follin had run her lying-in hospital and significant moments in the story took place! Our house was one of two built on the lot after Follin's house was torn down in the 1920s. In the preface to his book *Entertaining Satan: Witchcraft and the Culture of Early New England*, John Demos recounts having had similar experiences. During his research he discovered that he had a genealogical link to the Putnams of Salem witch trials fame, and that Elizabeth Knapp, an accused witch central to his story, had grown up in the house next door to his Connecticut home. "I suspect that many writers, at one stage or another, feel joined by fate to their particular topics and projects," Demos wrote of those coincidences. "But when the topic is witchcraft, such feeling grows unusually—albeit 'superstitiously'—strong."[3] Well, my book wasn't about witchcraft (even the allegations of Voodoo turned out to be spurious), but as I looked out from my study at the same houses, all still standing, that Ellen Follin would have seen from her front window, it did seem a little uncanny that I had stumbled across the Digby case and decided to write about it.

There were other moments when past and present merged. While working on this book, I received a grant from the Louisiana Endowment for the Humanities that included funds to hire New Orleans photographer Harold Baquet to take pictures of the Jourdain tomb and other locations in the Digby story. Before he and I went out on our photo shoot, an email arrived from a woman named Isabel Baquet, who lives in Atlanta. She had been doing genealogical research and discovered that her husband Edward is a descendant of J. B. V. Jourdain, the father of Detective Jourdain in the Digby case. She had seen online that I had delivered a conference paper about the Jourdains and was curious as to its content. Isabel and I became fast friends, sharing our knowledge of J. B. V., his wives Aimee and Marie, and their children. It turned out that Isabel's husband Edward and Harold, the photographer, are cousins, and that Harold too is a Jourdain descendant. When we agreed to work together, neither Harold nor I knew he was linked by blood to the story and that his photographs for me would also document an evocative part of his own family's history.

Harold Baquet in St. Louis Cemetery #1, January 2014. Photo: Michael Ross.

Isabel and Harold led me to other Jourdain descendants, including her brother-in-law Wayne Baquet, owner with his wife, Janet, of the renowned Creole restaurant Lil Dizzy's on Esplanade Avenue in New Orleans. Wayne and Janet are part of a storied branch of the Baquet clan. Wayne's father and mother were also famous New Orleans restaurateurs. Wayne's brother is the Pulitzer Prize–winning journalist and *New York Times* Executive Editor Dean Baquet. It is a complicated story, but both Wayne *and* Janet are Jourdain descendants, and they hold the title to the family tomb in St. Louis Cemetery #1 where Detective Jourdain took his own life in 1888. Their restaurant is filled with memorabilia that commemorates the achievements of their family and other members of the city's Afro-Creole community. On the center of the back wall is an enlarged copy of the petition the Afro-Creoles of New Orleans presented to President Lincoln during the Civil War, urging him to grant black men the right to vote. At the bottom, amongst the petition's signatories, are John Baptiste Jourdain and his father J. B. V.

In 2010, I was contacted by Sandra Guenther-Clark, another descendant of a key character in the Digby story. Like Isabel Baquet, Sandra and her parents, Jerry and Marilyn Guenther, discovered through genealogical research that they had ancestors in New Orleans—Angelo Blass and Ellen Follin. Sandra and Marilyn were descendants of Ellen Follin's daughter Mary Belle Blass, who had moved north, married a white man, and passed as white. Mary Belle was Marilyn's great-grandmother and Sandra's great-great-grandmother. Mary Belle, it seems, successfully hid her mixed-race background even from her children and grandchildren. It was only through their research that the Guenthers learned they had Afro-Creole forebears. The Guenthers' family research also led them to Ellen Follin's role in the Digby case. Sandra's father, Jerry, became as fascinated by the story as I did. He collected newspaper accounts of the kidnapping and found the trial transcripts in the archives of the New Orleans Public Library. And, like Isabel Baquet, Sandra and Jerry contacted me when they saw online that I too was examining the case. I took the train to New York to interview them, and our meeting was one of those moments that make historical research so much fun. Sandra was then working on Wall Street and we met in her stylish apartment overlooking Union Square, but for a few hours we were all transported back to the summer of 1870. I had once thought that I might be the only person alive who knew the whole Digby story, but Sandra and Jerry knew it well too and spoke of Ellen Follin and Louisa Murray as if they were friends and as if the events of Reconstruction had happened only yesterday. The Guenthers' efforts to reclaim their family's lost history also provide a poignant postscript to the Blass-Follin family saga and to the increasingly distant time when people believed that their access to the American Dream hinged on hiding their heritage. When Sandra, Jerry, and Marilyn revealed to their relatives that they had black ancestors, all but one older member of their family found the news intriguing and were eager to learn more about Ellen Follin and her New Orleans travails.

I also found, and was found by, descendants of the Digbys. Because Thomas and Bridgette had seven children and many of their children then had large families as well, there are numerous Digby descendants in Louisiana and throughout the country. Hoping to find that the family had kept the story alive, I opened the telephone directory and began calling people whose surnames suggested a link to the Digbys of Howard Street and the events of 1870. I quickly hit pay dirt, reaching several descendants of Thomas and Bridgette who indeed had a vague knowledge of the story and who steered me to Susan Golden Perkins, who, along with her cousin Gayle Golden, are known as the "keepers of the family history." Both Sandra and Gayle are direct descendants of Mollie Digby and her husband, Patrick Golden. Another of Mollie's great-grandchildren surfaced when I received an email from Gary Golden and his wife, Anne, who, although they had lost touch with the larger Digby clan, had discovered the kidnapping story (much as did the Baquets and Guenthers) while doing genealogical research. To my and their surprise, Susan Golden Perkins and Gary Golden, cousins who had never met, lived a short distance from one another in Cary, North Carolina, and I drove there to interview their families in April 2012.

It was during the meeting with the Goldens that Susan Golden produced the family "archives," a box of materials about the case that her relatives had collected over the years. Inside were tantalizing documents—Mollie's own handwritten and typed accounts of the 1870 events, the version of the kidnapping authored by Dorothy Branson of the WPA, and the letter in which Governor Warmoth gently declined Mollie's suggestion that they collaborate in writing the story of her abduction. For a moment I thought I had in my hands documents that could solve the remaining mysteries surrounding the case. It was clear from Mollie's letter to Warmoth and from other materials that Mollie had made an effort to research the facts, and a quick reading of her manuscript revealed that she concluded that Captain Broadwell had orchestrated the plot. But I was disappointed when it became clear Mollie's account could not be fully trusted, that she had invented composite characters and dialogue. I think the Goldens were a bit miffed too, as I debunked cherished family legends including Mollie's claim that Queen Victoria offered a reward for her return. Trust me, as an author I wish it were true, but the claim does not hold up to historical scrutiny.

Susan kindly allowed me to make copies of her originals, and when I reread them later I realized that some of Mollie's factual errors—including the claim that the jury convicted Ellen Follin and Louisa Murray—had their own historical significance. Mollie was writing about her kidnapping sixty years after the event. During the intervening decades, memories inevitably faded. Meanwhile, negative depictions of Reconstruction filled schoolbooks in both the North and South. Jim Crow arrived. It seems only natural that, as the kidnapping story was told and retold over the years, the story might be embellished, and that facts that would have made some listeners uneasy—the collaboration between Thomas Digby and a black detective or the unexpected acquittal—were dropped from the tale. It is not surprising that Mollie told a story that fit the zeitgeist of her times, or that it was her version of the events that appeared in the articles written about her life when she died in 1944. The history of her kidnapping had been filtered and rewritten by history itself.

As I met with the Guenthers, Goldens, and Baquets, I was reminded of the famous quote from William Faulkner's *Requiem for a Nun*: "The past is never dead. It's not even past." Faulkner's character Gavin Stevens utters these words while discussing the volatile history of a complex family in Faulkner's fictional Yoknapatawpha County. But they are words that seem equally apt for New Orleans, a city where people regularly honor and invoke their ancestors and traditions. Since the late nineteenth century, politicians and urban planners have tried to turn New Orleans into a "New South" city. Yet it remains a place where people look to the past for meaning, and, as the genealogical sleuthing by the Baquets, Guenthers, and Goldens revealed, the past in New Orleans is still full of surprising revelations. I want to thank all three families for sharing their findings, memories, and histories with me. They added depth and nuance to the Digby story and to this book.

To recreate the Great New Orleans Kidnapping Case I had to do lots of digging in docket books, notarial and baptismal records, Sanborn fire-insurance maps, and other materials with which I was initially unfamiliar. My efforts were aided immensely by the librarians and archivists at the Archives of the Archdioceses of Mobile and New Orleans, the Hill Memorial Library at Louisiana State University, the Louisiana Collection in the Earl K. Long Library at the University of New Orleans, the History Museum of Mobile, the Library of Congress, the Louisiana State Museum, Loyola University New Orleans Special Collections, the National Archives of the United States, the Notarial Archives of New Orleans, and the Southern Historical Collection at the University of North Carolina. Particular thanks are due to Georgia Chadwick at the Law Library of Louisiana, Charlotte Chamberlain at the Mobile Public Library, Richard Chestang at the Archdiocese of Mobile, Mary Lou Eichorn at the Historic New Orleans Collection, and Leon Miller and Ken Owen at the Louisiana Research Collection at Tulane University. I also owe an irredeemable debt to a legendary trio at the Louisiana Division of the New Orleans Public Library: Wayne Everard, Gregory Osborn, and Irene Wainwright. There is a reason why everyone who writes about New Orleans thanks Wayne, Greg, and Irene. Their knowledge of the nooks and crannies of the city archives is unsurpassed, and all three are fine historians. Wayne has recently retired after a long career. Greg and Irene are still on duty and are indefatigably helpful despite budget cuts, hurricanes, and other obstacles.

Numerous friends and colleagues read draft chapters and offered advice that improved this book immensely. These include Richard Bell, Ira Berlin, Stacy Braukman, Michael Crutcher, Arthur Eckstein, Laura Edwards, Michael Fitzgerald, Julie Greene, Judith Hunt, Emily Landau, Lawrence Powell, Leslie Rowland, David Sartorius, Robert Tinkler, Ella Yeargin, and the anonymous readers for Oxford University Press. At key moments I turned for research advice to Bruce "Sunpie" Barnes, Peter Coclanis, Melissa Daggett, Mark Fernandez, Paul Finkelman, Scott Marler, David Moore, Justin Nystrom, Adam Rothman, Judith Schafer, Rebecca Scott, David Sicilia, Pamela Tyler, Charles Vincent, and James

Wilson. Comments from Kathy Peiss, John Rodrigue, and Christopher Waldrep on conference papers I presented about the Digby case proved invaluable as well. Richard Campanella, Michael Crutcher, and Gary Van Zante provided their expertise about New Orleans maps and geography, and Gary kindly allowed photos from his beautiful book *New Orleans 1867* to be reproduced. After Ashley and I moved to Maryland, our New Orleans friends Christine and Steve Greenebaum, Elizabeth and Elliott Hammer, Justin Gricus and Kate Orvold, and Laura and Emma Ricks kindly housed me during my research trips to the Crescent City. I am also grateful for the generous research support provided by an American Historical Association Littleton-Griswold Grant, a Louisiana Board of Regents ATLAS Grant, a Louisiana Endowment for the Humanities Publishing Initiative Grant, a Loyola University Marquette Faculty Fellowship, and a University of Maryland RASA Award.

Sylvia Frank Rodrigue and Leslie Rowland deserve special thanks for reading multiple drafts with their laser-like eyes for detail. My agent, Albert LaFarge, used his charm, knowledge, and savvy to find this book the perfect home at Oxford University Press. Susan Ferber, my editor at Oxford, is a storied figure in the field who has edited some of this era's most important monographs. I was touched by her unfailing support for this project. Susan knows how a good book is constructed and how a good story is told, and her editorial acumen has made this one far better than it otherwise would have been. I also owe a debt of gratitude to my friends and family, too numerous to mention, in Asheville, Atlanta, Chapel Hill, Charlotte, Huntington, Nashville, New Orleans, Omaha, Philadelphia, Santa Fe, and other locales who have listened to me talk about the Digby case far too often and for far too long. You know who you are. Regular encouragement from my father, Spencer Ross, helped bring this book to fruition. His immense pride in his children's accomplishments is perhaps the greatest reward for completing a project like this one. I hope to be as good a father to my new son, Andrew, as he has been to me. This book is dedicated to my wife, Ashley Murchison Ross. Ashley's love, support, and humor make my life worth living.

Michael Ross

College Park, Maryland 2014

NOTES

—⟋⟍—

Introduction

1. For accounts of real trials that fit the pattern, see Dan T. Carter, *Scottsboro: An American Tragedy* (New York: Oxford University Press, 1969); Mamie Till-Mobley and Christopher Benson, *Death of Innocence: The Story of the Hate Crime That Changed America* (New York: Ballantine Books, 2004); Maryanne Vollers, *The Murder of Medgar Evers: The Trials of Byron De La Beckwith, and the Haunting of the New South* (New York: Back Bay Books, 1995); Howard Ball, *Murder in Mississippi: United States v. Price and the Struggle for Civil Rights* (Lawrence: University Press of Kansas, 2004).

2. Harper Lee, *To Kill a Mockingbird* (New York: J. B. Lippincott, 1960).

3. For the efforts of the white-controlled press to use the Digby kidnapping and trial for political purposes, see Chapter 1.

4. For a discussion of the legal changes wrought by Reconstruction and the historical literature on the topic, see Chapters 1 and 2.

5. For a discussion of the extensive literature about the Afro-Creole community in New Orleans and the impact of Reconstruction on that community, see Chapters 2, 4, and 10.

6. See Chapters 2, 4, and 10.

7. The opening line of William Blake's poem "Auguries of Innocence," "To see a World in a Grain of Sand" is often quoted by authors of micro-histories as an evocative metaphor for using the study of a single event, object, or behavior to explore larger historical patterns. See Tonio Andrade, "A Chinese Farmer, Two African Boys, and a Warlord: Toward a Global Microhistory," *Journal of World History* 21 (December 2010): 573. For a good discussion of the field of micro-history, see Jill Lepore, "Historians Who Love Too Much: Reflections on Microhistory and Biography," *Journal of American History* 88 (June 2011): 129–44.

8. The historical literature on the reasons for the failure of Reconstruction is discussed in detail in the notes to Chapters 5 and 10. For the best single-volume discussion of Reconstruction, see Eric Foner, *Reconstruction: America's Unfinished Revolution, 1863–1877* (New York: Harper & Row, 1988). For a provocative example of the argument that Radical Reconstruction was doomed to failure, see Adam Fairclough, "Was the Grant of Black Suffrage a Political Error? Reconsidering the Views of John W. Burgess, William A. Dunning, and Eric Foner on Congressional Reconstruction," *Journal of the Historical Society* 12 (June 2012): 155–88. For discussions of the type of moderate white businessmen in New Orleans and the South that Republicans hoped to woo, see Jonathan Daniel Wells, *The Origins of the Southern Middle Class 1800–1861* (Chapel Hill: University of North Carolina Press, 2004), 5–6, 14, 21, 67–68, 140, 151–62, 192–200, 215–29; William C. Chenault and Robert C. Reinders, "The Northern-born Community of New Orleans in the 1850s," *Journal of American History* 51 (September 1964): 232–47.

Chapter One: A Kidnapping in the Back of Town

1. The Digbys lived on the old Howard Street, between Poydras and Lafayette Streets, which is today the portion of Lasalle Street that is next to the Superdome. Howard Street became Lasalle Street in 1924. The street that today is Howard Avenue was called Triton's Walk in 1870. For occupations of residents in the Digbys' neighborhood, see *Graham and Madden's City Directory* (1870), which lists as residents on the Digbys' block twelve laborers, one shoemaker, one wheelwright, one chair bottomer, one laundress, one carriage driver (Digby), and a baker. For a description of the neighborhood known as the "back of town," see Richard and Marina Campanella, *New Orleans Then and Now* (Gretna, LA: Pelican Publishing, 1999), 282, 299, 316; Coleman Warner, "Freret's Century: Growth, Identity, and Loss in a New Orleans Neighborhood" (M.A. thesis, University of New Orleans, 1999), 5–7. For Irish immigration to New Orleans, see Earl F. Niehaus, *The Irish in New Orleans, 1800–1860* (Baton Rouge: Louisiana State University Press, 1965), 23, 24–26.

2. This account of the events of June 9 has been assembled from newspaper articles and Recorder's Court trial transcripts. See *New Orleans Daily Picayune*, June 10, 11, 14, 1870, August 10 ("straight features," "low heavy set"), 25, 1870; *New Orleans Bee*, June 10, 1870; *New Orleans Commercial Bulletin*, June 10, 1870; *New Orleans Republican*, June 11, 12, 1870. See also *State of Louisiana vs. Louisa Murray, Ellen Follin, and George Blass* (Docket No. 2370), 1st District Court of the Parish of Orleans, Louisiana Division, City Archives, New Orleans Public Library. Although the Digbys spelled their daughter's name Mollie, the New Orleans newspapers often spelled it Molly. That difference is reflected hereinafter in quotations from newspaper accounts.

3. *Daily Picayune*, August 10, 1870 ("Hold Molly"); testimony of George Digby, Recorder's Court Testimony, 1st Recorders Court, Docket #49, August 23, 1870, Louisiana Division, City Archives, New Orleans Public Library, p. 16 ("No, bubby").

4. Testimony of George Digby, August 23, 1870.

5. *Daily Picayune*, June 10, 1870; *New Orleans Republican*, June 10, 1870; *New Orleans Times*, June 10, 11, 1870; *Commercial Bulletin*, June 10, 1870.

6. *Daily Picayune*, June 10, 1870; *New Orleans Times*, June 10, 1870. Also see *New Orleans Republican*, July 10, 1870, discussing the fact that most people thought the child would be quickly found.

7. *New Orleans Times*, June 25, 1870 ("terrible anxiety"). For rewards offered by Thomas Digby, see *New Orleans Republican*, June 11, 1870, and *New Orleans Bee*, July 31, 1870.

8. Article 13 of the Louisiana Constitution of 1868 ("patronage of all persons") in *Digest of the Statutes of the State of Louisiana in Two Volumes*, vol. I (New Orleans: Republican Printing Office, 1870), 114. Liva Baker, *The Second Battle of New Orleans: The Hundred-Year Struggle to Integrate the Schools* (New York: Harper Collins, 1996), 19–22; Louis R. Harlan, "Desegregation in New Orleans Public Schools during Reconstruction," *American Historical Review* 67 (April 1962): 663–75; Roger A. Fischer, *The Segregation Struggle in Louisiana 1862–1877* (Urbana: University of Illinois Press, 1974), 20–45, 110–13. For descriptions of African Americans demanding service, see *New Orleans Times*, June 7, 1870; *Daily Picayune*, June 17, 19, 1870; *New Orleans Bee*, June 17, 1870. The black population of New Orleans doubled in size during Reconstruction, growing from 24,000 in 1860 to 50,000 in 1870. See David C. Rankin, "The Origins of Black Leadership in New Orleans during Reconstruction," *Journal of Southern History* 40 (August 1974): 417–40. For white people's reactions to the influx of former slaves into the city, see Ted Tunnell, *Crucible of Reconstruction: War, Radicalism, and Race in Louisiana, 1862–1877* (Baton Rouge: Louisiana State University Press, 1984), 6, 153–54, 159, 175; Joe Gray Taylor, *Louisiana Reconstructed 1863–1877* (Baton Rouge: Louisiana State University Press, 1974), 162–63, 170, 174.

9. Michael A. Ross, "The Commemoration of Robert E. Lee's Death and the Obstruction of Reconstruction in New Orleans," *Civil War History* 51 (June 2005): 135–50.

10. For accounts of the Louisiana Legion drilling, see *Commercial Bulletin*, June 13, 20, 1870; *New Orleans Times*, June 26, 1870; *Louisiana State Register*, July 2, 1870 ("keeping the negroes straight"). For the role Campbell played in undermining Reconstruction in Louisiana, see Michael A. Ross, "Obstructing Reconstruction: John Archibald Campbell and the Legal Campaign against Louisiana's Republican Government, 1868–1873," *Civil War History* 49 (September 2003): 235–53 (quotation on 241–42).

11. Otis Singletary, *Negro Militia and Reconstruction* (Austin: University of Texas Press, 1957; reprint Westport, CT: Greenwood, 1984), 4, 13–14, 23, 67.

12. *Daily Picayune*, August 10, 1870.

13. For an introduction to recent sociological work on moral panics, see Bryan E. Denham, "Folk Devils, News Icons, and the Construction of Moral Panics," *Journalism Studies*, 9 (December 2008): 945–61; Sian Nicholas and Tom O'Malley, *Moral Panics, Social Fears, and the Media: Historical Perspectives* (New York: Routledge, 2013); Stanley Cohen, *Folk Devils and Moral Panics*, 2nd ed. (New York: Routledge, 2003); Eruch Goode and Nachman Ben-Yehuda, *Moral Panics: The Social Construction of Deviance* (Malden, MA:

Wiley-Blackwell, 1994). For the newspaper campaign to malign the legislature and foment discontent, see Michael A. Ross, "Justice Miller's Reconstruction: The *Slaughter-House Cases*, Health Codes, and Civil Rights in New Orleans, 1861–1873," *Journal of Southern History* 64 (November 1998): 649–76; Michael A. Ross, "Resisting the New South: Commercial Crisis and Decline in New Orleans, 1865–1885," *American Nineteenth-Century History* 4 (Spring 2003): 59–76.

14. See, for example, *Daily Picayune,* July 1, 6 ("Can it be possible…?"), 1870; *Louisiana Democrat,* July 6, 1870 ("corrupt, depraved--or worse"); *Commercial Bulletin,* July 11, 30, 1870; *New Orleans Times,* June 25, July 10, 14 ("sorriest spectacle"), August 6 ("all shades"), 11, 1870; *New Orleans Bee,* June 25, 1870; *Charleston Daily Courier,* July 26, 1870.

15. *New Orleans Commercial Bulletin,* July 8, 1870; *Mobile Register* July 24, 1870.

16. Martha Ward, *Voodoo Queen: The Spirited Lives of Marie Laveau* (Jackson: University of Mississippi Press, 2004), ix–xv; 4–17, 23–44, 99, 113, 120–40; Carolyn Morrow Long, *A New Orleans Voudou Priestess: The Legend and Reality of Marie Laveau* (Gainesville: University Press of Florida, 2006). For first-hand accounts of Voodoo practices in New Orleans in 1870, see Joseph Hartzell to Sister Pearson, June 30, 1870, Joseph C. Hartzell Papers, Box 1, Folder 6, Louisiana and Lower Mississippi Valley Collection, Hill Memorial Library, Louisiana State University, Baton Rouge; *New Orleans Times,* June 8, 15, 28, 1870; *Daily Picayune,* June 22, 1870. Voodoo was often also spelled Voudou in the newspapers of the time. That difference is reflected hereafter in quotations from newspaper accounts.

17. For critical descriptions of Voodoo practices at the time, see *New Orleans Bee,* June 25, 1870 ("ignorance and fanaticism"), June 25, 1870; *New Orleans Times,* June 8, 15, 23, 25, 1870; *Daily Picayune,* June 22, 1870; Comments from the New Orleans Correspondent in the *Nashville Union and American,* July 29, 1870 ("white civilization," "savage superstition").

18. For coverage of Voodoo altars and rituals, see *Daily Picayune,* June 10, 1869; *New Orleans Times,* June 8, 15, 23, 28, December 9, 1870 ("Next to the bowl"); *New Orleans Commercial Bulletin,* December 9, 1870 ("Officer E. Planchard"); *New Orleans Bee,* June 25, 1870; correspondent on voodoo in New Orleans in Charleston *Daily Courier,* June 26, 1870.

19. Account of a child sacrifice at a New Orleans Voodoo ceremony provided by a correspondent to *Charleston Daily News,* reprinted in *Mobile Register,* July 24, 1870.

20. *Mobile Register,* July 24, 1870.

21. *New Orleans Republican,* June 18, 1870 (description of women preparing to leave for summer), July 14, 1870 (Thomas Digby's thank you to "the ladies of New Orleans").

22. For a description of the women's demands in the Digby Case see *Daily Picayune,* July 6, 1870. The husbands of the women who signed the petition to Governor Warmoth included at least twelve former Confederate officers (including Valerin Allain, Charles Leverich, and C. H. Slocomb, who were members of the elite Washington Artillery), the president of the New Orleans Gas Light Company (George Duncan), the Commissioner of Water Works (Eugene Waggaman), the owner of the Orleans Cotton Press (Sawyer Hayward), four commission merchants, several cotton factors, a number of well-known

Creole gentlemen, and prominent attorneys and bankers. Although some Crescent City women would become more involved in reform movements later in the nineteenth century, in 1870 an overtly political act like petitioning the governor was rare. See the discussion of women's activism in New Orleans in Pamela Tyler, *Silk Stockings and Ballot Boxes: Women and Politics in New Orleans, 1920–1963* (Athens: University of Georgia Press, 1996); Antonette M. Tardo, "An Earlier Dawn: The 'Southern Lady' Enters Public Life in New Orleans, 1876–1898" (M. A. thesis, University of New Orleans, 2001). Neither study mentions the Digby case, but both suggest that such activism by elite women in New Orleans was uncommon before the late 1870s. An important turning point for women's public political involvement came in 1876 when Eliza Poitevent Nicholson, upon the death of her husband, took over the editorship of the *Daily Picayune*. See Jonathan Daniel Wells, *Women Writers and Journalists in the Nineteenth-Century South* (New York: Cambridge, 2011), 13–14, 191–99.

23. *Daily Picayune*, July 9, 1870 (quotation).

24. For rewards offered by Governor Warmoth and others, see *Daily Picayune*, July 2, 6, 10, August 10, 1870 ("on watch"), 1870; *New Orleans Times*, July 10, 12, 21, 1870; *Opelousas Journal*, July 16, 1870; *New Orleans Bee*, July 31, 1870; *New Orleans Republican*, July 12, 14, 1870.

25. Ross, "Obstructing Reconstruction," 239; Henry Clay Warmoth, *War, Politics, and Reconstruction: Stormy Days in Louisiana* (1930; reprint, University of South Carolina Press, 2006), 79–81, 88; Joe Gray Taylor, *Louisiana Reconstructed, 1863–1877* (Baton Rouge: Louisiana State University Press, 1974), 187; Tunnell, *Crucible of Reconstruction*, 151–52; Ella Lonn, *Reconstruction in Louisiana* (New York: G. P. Putnam, 1918), 7; Michael Les Benedict, *The Fruits of Victory: Alternatives in Restoring the Union, 1865–1877*, rev. ed. (Lanham, MD: University Press of America, 1986), 44; New Orleans *Republican*, May 11, 1870 (Warmoth turns twenty-eight). For a critical view of Warmoth, see Caryn Cossé Bell, *Revolution, Romanticism, and the Afro-Creole Protest Tradition in Louisiana* (Baton Rouge: Louisiana State University Press, 1997), 255–73. For the antebellum origins and ideology of the class of New Orleans businessmen Warmoth courted politically, see Jonathan Daniel Wells, *The Origins of the Southern Middle Class 1800–1861* (Chapel Hill: University of North Carolina Press, 2004), 5–6, 14, 21, 67–8, 140, 151–62, 192–200, 215–29; William C. Chenault and Robert C. Reinders, "The Northern-born Community of New Orleans in the 1850s," *Journal of American History* 51 (September 1964): 232–47.

26. Dennis Rousey, *Policing the Southern City: New Orleans, 1805–1899* (Baton Rouge: Louisiana State University Press, 1997), 68–90, 115–22, 126–29; Tunnell, *Crucible of Reconstruction*, 102–7; James G. Hollandsworth, Jr., *An Absolute Massacre: The New Orleans Race Riot of July 30, 1866* (Baton Rouge: Louisiana State University Press, 2001), 64, 72; Judith Kelleher Schafer, *Brothels, Depravity, and Abandoned Women: Illegal Sex in Antebellum New Orleans* (Baton Rouge: Louisiana State University Press, 2009), 5–13; *New Orleans Times*, June 19, 1870; *New Orleans Republican*, May 11, August 16, 1870.

27. Rousey, *Policing the Southern City*, 126–48; *New Orleans Bee*, June 4, 1870; *Digest of the Statutes of the State of Louisiana*, Vol. II (New Orleans: Republican Office, 1870), 172–73; Gilles Vandal, "The Nineteenth-Century Municipal Responses to the Problem of Poverty: New Orleans' Free Lodgers, 1850–1880, as a Case Study," *Journal of Urban History* 19 (November 1992): 30–59; Hollandsworth, *An Absolute Massacre*, 75; Justin A. Nystrom, *New Orleans after the Civil War: Race, Politics, and a New Birth of Freedom* (Baltimore: Johns Hopkins University Press, 2010), 88.

28. For a long list of vices the Metropolitan Police were responsible for eradicating, see *Digest of the Statutes of the State of Louisiana*, vol. 2 (New Orleans: Republican Office, 1870), 169, 171.

29. For New Orleans's reputation as a crime-filled city and for jails filled with Irish thieves see: Judith Kelleher Schafer, "Slaves and Crime: New Orleans, 1846–1862," in *Local Matters: Race, Crime, and Justice in the Nineteenth Century South*, eds. Christopher Waldrep and Donald Nieman (Athens: University of Georgia Press, 2001), 53–91; Judith Kelleher Schafer, *Brothels, Depravity, and Abandoned Women: Illegal Sex in Antebellum New Orleans* (Baton Rouge: Louisiana State University Press, 2009), 5–13; Rousey, *Policing The Southern City*, 80–81 ("dueling capital of the South"), 89; John Bailey, *The Lost German Slave Girl* (New York: Atlantic Monthly Press, 2003), 48–67.

30. *New Orleans Republican*, May 8, 1870.

31. Dennis C. Rousey, "Black Policemen in New Orleans During Reconstruction," *Historian* 49 (February 1987): 223–43.

32. For Cain's resignation, see *Daily Picayune*, May 5, 1870. Cain, who described his period as police chief as "little else but vexation and toil," was particularly angered by outrageous instances of jury nullification. For descriptions of Badger and his career, see "Algernon Badger," *The National Cyclopædia of American Biography* (New York: James T. White, 1900), vol. 10, p. 488; *Daily Picayune*, May 5, 6, 1870; Rousey, *Policing the Southern City*, 144–47; "Badger Obituary," *Daily Picayune*, May 10, 1905; Nystrom, *New Orleans after the Civil War*, 35–38. For Badger at the 1866 New Orleans Riot, see his testimony to the House Select Committee on the New Orleans Riot in "Message of the President Transmitting all Papers on the New Orleans Riot," Ex. Doc.—House of Representatives, 39th Congress, 2nd Session; no. 68 (Washington: Government Printing Office, 1867), 164–65.

33. See sources cited in note 32, supra.

34. *Daily Picayune*, May 6 ("His appointment"), 10, 1905; *New Orleans Republican*, May 8, 1870 ("much is expected").

35. *New Orleans Times*, July 10, 1870; *New Orleans Republican*, July 9, 1870; *Commercial Bulletin*, July 9, 11, 1870.

36. *New Orleans Times*, July 10, 1870 (quotes); *Picayune*, July 10, 1870.

37. "Constitution and By-Laws of the John Brown Pioneer Radical Republican Club and Protective Association, Third Ward, City of New Orleans, Louisiana (May 1870),

Library of Congress, Special Collections, Rare Book Reading Room; New Orleans *Republican*, July 13, 1870 (proclamation); New Orleans *Times*, July 14, 1870 (criticism quotations). The state constitution and 1870 Louisiana code provided that inns, hotels, restaurants, and saloons could not discriminate on account of race and that persons denied service could sue for damages. See sections 456–59 of the Louisiana code reprinted in *Digest of the Statutes of the State of Louisiana in Two Volumes*, vol. I (New Orleans: Republican Printing Office, 1870), pp. 287–88.

38. New Orleans *Times*, July 8, 1870. On vigilance committees, see David Grimsted, *American Mobbing 1828–1861: Toward Civil War* (New York: Oxford, 2003).

39. New Orleans *Republican*, July 8, 10, 1870; *Commercial Bulletin*, July 8, 1870; New Orleans *Times*, July 9, 1870. For a description of the Louisiana Retreat, see *Daily Picayune*, October 28, 1866.

40. New Orleans *Times*, July 12 ("time immemorial"), 20, 1870; *Daily Picayune*, July 21, 1870 (Badger quotation).

41. New Orleans *Times*, July 21, 1870.

42. *Daily Picayune*, July 2, 1870, July 6, 9, 10, 1870; New Orleans *Times*, July 9, 10, 12, 21, 1870; *Opelousas Journal*, July 16, 1870; New Orleans *Bee*, July 31, 1870; New Orleans *Republican*, July 12, 14, 1870.

43. New Orleans *Republican*, August 13, 1870 ("sent his dispatches"). For accounts of Thomas Digby's trip to Canton, see *Republican*, July 19, 21, 1870; *New Orleans Times*, July 19, 1870; *Commercial Bulletin*, July 19 ("sadly disappointed"), 20, 1870; *Daily Picayune*, July 21, 1870.

44. For examples of coverage of the Digby case in the regional and national press, see *Baton Rouge Courier*, July 30, 1870; *Bossier Banner* (Bellevue, La.), August 13, 1870; *Charleston Daily Courier*, July 26, 1870; *Chicago Tribune*, August 16, 1870; *Cincinnati Enquirer*, August 13, 1870; *Louisiana Democrat* (Alexandria), July 27, August 17, 1870; *Mobile Register*, July 24, August 12, 14, 16, 23, 1870; *Nashville Union and American*, July 29, 1870; New Orleans *Times*, July 21, 1870 (reprinting story from *New York Times*); *New York Times*, August 15, 18, 1870; *Richmond Daily Dispatch*, August 17, 1870.

45. For accounts of the leads pouring in from around the state, region, and country, see New Orleans *Times*, July 13, 14, 15, 16, 22, August 2, 1870; New Orleans *Republican*, July 19, 20, 25, 30, 31, August 17, 1870; *Commercial Bulletin*, July 19, August 4, 1870; *Daily Picayune*, July 21, 24, 1870; New Orleans *Bee*, August 4, 1870; *Opelousas Journal*, July 16, 1870; *Louisiana Democrat* (Alexandria), July 6, 1870. For events on the *Wild Wagoner*, see New Orleans *Republican*, July 20, 1870; *Daily Picayune*, July 21, 1870.

Chapter Two: Detective John Baptiste Jourdain and His World

1. Karen Halttunen, *Murder Most Foul: The Killer and the Gothic Imagination* (Cambridge, MA: Harvard University Press, 1998), 91–134; Richard F. Hamm, *Murder, Honor, and Law: Four Virginia Homicides from Reconstruction to the Great Depression* (Charlottesville: University

of Virginia Press, 2003), 5, 13; Hazel Dicken-Garcia, *Journalistic Standards in Nineteenth-Century America* (Madison: University of Wisconsin Press, 1989), 123–29; David Ray Papke, *Framing the Criminal: Crime, Cultural Work, and the Loss of Critical Perspective 1830–1900* (Hamden, CT: Archon Books, 1987), 33–164; Michael Trotti, *The Body in the Reservoir: Murder and Sensationalism in the South* (Chapel Hill: University of North Carolina Press, 2008). For excellent case studies of early sensationalized crimes, see Patricia Cline Cohen, *The Murder of Helen Jewett: The Life and Death of a Prostitute in Nineteenth-Century New York* (New York: Knopf, 1998); Amy Gilman Srebnick, *The Mysterious Death of Mary Rogers* (New York: Oxford University Press, 1995); Andie Tucher, *Froth and Scum: Truth, Beauty, Goodness, and the Ax Murder in America's First Mass Medium* (Chapel Hill: University of North Carolina Press, 1994). For Victorian views of child abduction, see Paula Fass, *Kidnapped: Child Abduction in America* (New York: Oxford University Press, 1997), 1–56.

2. Halttunen, *Murder Most Foul*, 109–10; Hamm, *Murder, Honor, Law*, 13; Papke, *Framing the Criminal*, 33–53, 99; Lawrence Friedman, *Crime and Punishment in America* (New York: Basic Books, 1993), 203–8; Dan Schiller, *Objectivity and the News: The Public and the Rise of Commercial Journalism* (Philadelphia: University of Pennsylvania Press, 1981).

3. W. Marvin Dulaney, *Black Police in America* (Bloomington: Indiana University Press, 1996), 12, 116, 117.

4. David C. Rankin, "The Origins of Black Leadership in New Orleans during Reconstruction," *Journal of Southern History* 40 (August 1974): 427; New Orleans *Daily Picayune*, March 26, 1856 ("Ethiopian blood"); *Adelle v. Beauregard* (1810) quoted in David C. Rankin, "The Impact of the Civil War on the Free Colored Community of New Orleans," *Perspectives in American History* 11 (1977–78): 381–82, 405 ("intelligent and well-educated"); testimony by Jourdain, December 27, 1866, in *Report of the Select Committee on the New Orleans Riots* (Washington: Government Printing Office, 1867), 204 ("slightly colored"); *The Louisianian*, February 13, 1875 ("African lineage"). For a clear and succinct discussion of racial terminology in New Orleans, see Carol Wilson, *The Two Lives of Sally Miller: A Case of Mistaken Racial Identity in Antebellum New Orleans* (New Brunswick, NJ: Rutgers University Press, 2007), 65–66.

5. See Emily Clark, *The Strange History of the American Quadroon: Free Women of Color in the Revolutionary Atlantic World* (Chapel Hill: University of North Carolina Press, 2013), 46–70, 88, 97, 101–102; Caryn Cossé Bell, *Revolution, Romanticism, and the Afro-Creole Protest Tradition in Louisiana* (Baton Rouge: Louisiana State University Press, 1997), 75–78, 112–13; Monique Guillory, "Some Enchanted Evening on the Auction Block: The Cultural Legacy of the New Orleans Quadroon Balls" (PhD dissertation, New York University, 1999), x, 12, 15, 21, 31–32, 42–45 51, 65–67; Paul F. LaChance, "The Formation of a Three-Caste Society," *Social Science History* 18 (1994): 211–42; Eric Foner, *Freedom's Lawmakers: A Directory of Black Officeholders during Reconstruction* (Baton Rouge: Louisiana State University Press, 1993), 124. Before the Civil War, the term often used for "race mixing" by critics of interracial sex was "amalgamation." After 1864, the term "miscegenation"

became more common. See Peggy Pascoe, *What Comes Naturally: Miscegenation Law and the Making of Race in America* (New York: Oxford University Press, 2009), 1; Peter Wallenstein, *Tell the Court I Love My Wife: Race, Marriage, and Law: An American History* (New York: Palgrave Macmillan, 2002), 50.

6. One of John's white aunts, Isabelle Jourdain, married Jean Ursin de la Villebeuvre, III, one of the most prominent citizens of Louisiana, and the couple entertained the Marquis de Lafayette and General Zachary Taylor at their plantation upriver from New Orleans. Jourdain's lineage has been reconstructed using *New Orleans Louisiana Birth and Death Records Index, 1790–1899*, vol. 6, p. 170–71, vol. 41, p. 776, vol.11, p. 1079; obituary of his father J. B. V. Jourdain, in *Daily Picayune*, February 18, 1868; Stanley Clisby Arthur, *Old Families of Louisiana* (New Orleans: Hermanson Publishers, 1931), 274–75; Orleans Parish Recorder of Wills Will Book, vol. 8, p. 397, no. 1676; Louisiana Court of Probates (Orleans Parish), Parish Suit Record, VCP 290 1818, 1564, #1613; Saint Louis Cathedral Baptismal Records, Record # 01-4-42-018-0116, vol. B42, p. 18, Act. 116, New Orleans Archdiocese Archives; *St. Louis Cathedral New Orleans [s/fpc]*, Record number 01-4-42-018-0116, Published vol. 19, Church Code SLC, vol. B42, p. 18, Act 116. Information about Jourdain's godfather found in *New Orleans Birth Records 1790–1899*, vol. 4, p. 180 (Fabre had a "colored" child with Josephine Gossurun on June 6, 1834, named Jean Joseph Pierre Fabre), vol. 4, p.181 (and he had a second "colored" child with Josephine Gossurun on July 9, 1836, named Victor Augustin Fabre). Fabre was also owner of a twenty seven-year-old mulatto slave, listed in the 1860 federal census, who may be his son Jean. See Shirley Elizabeth Thompson, *Exiles at Home: The Struggle to Become American in Creole New Orleans* (Cambridge, MA: Harvard University Press, 2009), 9–10; Loren Schweninger, *Black Property Owners in the South, 1790–1915* (Urbana: University of Illinois Press, 1990), 99. For interracial sex being somewhat permissible in the Spanish colonial period in New Orleans, see Kimberly S. Hanger, *Bounded Lives, Bounded Places: Free Black Society in Colonial New Orleans, 1769–1803* (Durham, NC: Duke University Press, 1997), 89–108; Jack D. L. Holmes, "Do It! Don't Do It!: Spanish Laws on Sex and Marriage," in *Louisiana's Legal Heritage*, ed. Edward F. Haas, (Pensacola, FL.: Perdido Bay Press, 1983). For antebellum Louisiana views on "open and notorious concubinage," see Judith Kelleher Schafer, *Slavery, the Civil Law, and the Supreme Court of Louisiana* (Baton Rouge: Louisiana State University Press, 1994), 180–200; Loren Schweninger, "Socioeconomic Dynamics among the Gulf Creole Populations: The Antebellum and Civil War Years," in James H. Dorman, ed., *Creoles of Color of the Gulf South* (Knoxville: University of Tennessee, 1996), 53–62.

7. Clark, *Strange History of the American Quadroon*, 101–2, 120–21; Thompson, *Exiles at Home*, 9–15, 167; Virginia R. Domíguez, *White by Definition: Social Classification in Creole Louisiana* (New Brunswick, NJ: Rutgers University Press, 1986), chap. 3, pp. 62–79; Bernie D. Jones, *Fathers of Conscience: Mixed-Race Inheritance in the Antebellum South* (Athens: University of Georgia Press, 2009), 64–66; *Badillo v. Tio*, 6 La. Ann. 129 (1851) at 138 ("had been so lost"); *Pigeau v. Duvernay*, 4 Mart. (O.S.) 265 (La. 1816); *Jung v. Doriocourt*, 4 La. 175

(1831); Rankin, "The Impact of the Civil War," 380; Schweninger, "Socioeconomic Dynamics among the Gulf Creole Populations," 57.

8. Testimony of John Baptiste Jourdain, December 27, 1866, *Select Committee on the New Orleans Riot*, 209 ("I am a colored man").

9. For the definition of the term "Creole" used here, see Joseph G. Tregle, Jr., "Creoles and Americans," in *Creole New Orleans: Race and Americanization*, eds. Arnold Hirsch and Joseph Logsdon (Baton Rouge: Louisiana State University Press, 1992), 137. For discussions of Creoles of color during Reconstruction, see Caryn Cossé Bell and Joseph Logsdon, "The Americanization of Black New Orleans, 1850–1900," in *Creole New Orleans*, eds. Hirsch and Logsdon, 201–61; John Blassingame, *Black New Orleans, 1860–1880* (Chicago: University of Chicago Press, 1973); Louis Fischer, *The Segregation Struggle in Louisiana* (Urbana: University of Illinois Press, 1974); Paul Lachance, "The Limits of Privilege: Where Free Persons of Color Stood in the Hierarchy of Wealth in Antebellum New Orleans," *Slavery and Abolition* 17 (1996): 65–83; Rankin, "Origins of Black Leadership," 420–21, 436–40; Charles Vincent, "Black Louisianians During the Civil War and Reconstruction: Aspects of Their Struggles and Achievements" in *Louisiana's Black Heritage*, eds. Robert Macdonald, John Kemp, and Edward Haas (New Orleans: Louisiana State Museum, 1979), 85–106; Charles Vincent, *Black Legislators in Louisiana* (Baton Rouge: Louisiana State University Press, 1976). For the cultural and professional sophistication of New Orleans Afro-Creoles, see Blassingame, *Black New Orleans*, xvi, 10, 21; Charles Edwards O'Neill, "Fine Arts and Literature; Nineteenth-Century Louisiana Black Artists and Authors," in *Louisiana's Black Heritage*, eds. Macdonald, Kemp, Hass, 63–84; Rankin, "The Origins of Black Leadership," 420–38; Schweninger, *Black Property Owners in the South*, 71, 129; Loren Schweninger, "Antebellum Free Persons of Color in Postbellum Louisiana," *Louisiana History* 30 (1989): 345–64; Thompson, *Exiles at Home*, 112–15; Shirley Elizabeth Thompson, "*Ah Toucoutou, ye conin vous*": History and Memory in Creole New Orleans," *American Quarterly* 53 (June 2001): 232–66.

10. For Jourdain marriage, see Orleans Parish (La.), Third Justice of the Peace, Marriage Licenses, *v.4* (VED 678 p.425). What Rodolphe Desdunes said of Creole poet Armand Lanusse could also have applied to Jourdain and many of his cohort: "His pride in being Creole was more dear to him than his being a Louisianan, or than anything else pertaining to his origin. All his preferences and resentments stemmed from this." See Rodolphe Desdunes, *Our People and Our History*, trans. Sister Dorothea Olga McCants (Baton Rouge: Louisiana State University Press, 1973), 21. For Afro-Creoles' Francophone identity and legal standing, see Ira Berlin, *Slaves without Masters: The Free Negro in the Antebellum South* (New York: Pantheon Books, 1975), 369–80; Virginia Meachem Gould, "The Free Creoles of Color of the Antebellum Gulf Ports of Mobile and Pensacola: A Struggle for the Middle Ground," in *Creoles of Color of the Gulf South*, ed. James H. Dorman (Knoxville: University of Tennessee, 1996); David C. Rankin, "The Impact of the Civil War," 385; Judith Kelleher Schafer, *Becoming Free, Remaining Free:*

Manumission and Enslavement in New Orleans, 1846–1862 (Baton Rouge: Louisiana State University Press, 2003), 76; Judith Kelleher Schaefer, "Forever Free From the Bonds of Slavery," in *A Law Unto Itself?: Essays in the New Louisiana Legal History*, eds. Warren Billings and Mark Fernandez (Baton Rouge: Louisiana State University Press, 2001), 158–59; Schweninger, "Antebellum Free Persons of Color in Postbellum Louisiana," 345–64; Schweninger, *Black Property Owners in the South*, 87–90, 126–27, 131, 133, 136; Thompson, *Exiles at Home*, 9–10, 35, 138.

11. Louisiana Legislative Council, "An Act Prescribing the Rules and Conduct to Be Observed with Respect to Negroes and other Slaves of this Territory," L. Moreau Lislet, *A General Digest of the acts of the legislature of Louisiana: passed from the year 1804 to 1827 inclusive, and in force at this last period*, vol. I (New Orleans: Benjamin Levy, 1828), 121–28; Albert Voorhies, *A Treatise on the Criminal Jurisprudence of Louisiana* (New Orleans: Bloomfield and Steel, 1860), 148. Important legal precedents also recognized the unique status of Louisiana's Afro-Creoles. As the Louisiana Supreme Court noted in 1850 in a case upholding the validity of legal testimony by free persons of color, "Our legislation and jurisprudence upon this subject differ materially from those of the slave States generally…. This difference of public policy has no doubt arisen from the different condition of that class of persons in this State. At the date of our earliest legislation as a territory, as well as at the present day, free persons of color constituted a numerous class. In some districts they are respectable from their intelligence, industry and habits of good order. Many of them are enlightened by education, and the instances are by no means rare in which they are large property holders. So far from being in that degraded state which renders them unworthy of belief, they are such persons as courts and juries would not hesitate to believe under oath. Moreover, this numerous class is entitled to the protection of our laws; but that protection would in many instances be illusory, and the gravest offences against their persons and property might be committed with impunity, by white persons, if the rule of exclusion contended for were recognized." *State v. Levy*, 5 La. Ann. 64 (1850).

12. Liva Baker, *The Second Battle of New Orleans: The Hundred-Year Struggle to Integrate the Schools* (New York: Harper Collins, 1996), 16; Bell, *Revolution, Romanticism, and the Afro-Creole Protest Tradition in Louisiana*, 74–79, 136; Rankin, "Origins of Black Leadership," 422; Richard Tansey, "Out-of-State Free Blacks in Late Antebellum New Orleans," *Louisiana History* 22 (Fall 1981): 369–86.

13. Bell, *Revolution, Romanticism, and the Afro-Creole Protest Tradition in Louisiana*, 74–79, 84, 136; *The Louisianian*, February 13, 1875; Justin A. Nystrom, *New Orleans after the Civil War* (Baltimore: Johns Hopkins University Press, 2010), 19; Ellen Holmes Pearson, "Imperfect Equality: The Legal Status of Free People of Color in New Orleans, 1803–1860," in *A Law Unto Itself?*, eds. Billings and Fernandez, 191–210; Baker, *The Second Battle of New Orleans*, 14; Rankin, "Origins of Black Leadership in New Orleans During Reconstruction," 422; Rebecca J. Scott, *Degrees of Freedom: Louisiana and Cuba*

after Slavery (Cambridge, MA: Harvard University Press, 2005), 14–16, 26–27; Judith
Kelleher Schafer, "Slaves and Crime: New Orleans, 1846–1862," in *Local Matters: Race,
Crime, and Justice in the Nineteenth-Century South*, eds. Christopher Waldrep and Donald
G. Nieman (Athens: University of Georgia Press, 2001) 53–91; Tansey, "Out-of-
State Free Blacks in Late Antebellum New Orleans," 369–86; Schafer, *Becoming Free,
Remaining Free*, 150; Ted Tunnell, *Crucible of Reconstruction: War, Radicalism, and Race in
Louisiana, 1862–1877* (Baton Rouge: Louisiana State University Press, 1984), 67–68;
Voorhies, *A Treatise on the Criminal Jurisprudence of Louisiana*, 583, 614.

14. New Orleans *Daily Picayune*, March 26, 1856 ("without any antecedent formality")
quoted in Judith Kelleher Schafer, *Brothels, Depravity, and Abandoned Women: Illegal Sex in
Antebellum New Orleans* (Baton Rouge: Louisiana State University Press, 2009), 32.

15. Jourdain's New Orleans Riot Testimony, 209 ("I am not a rebel"). The reasons some
Creoles of color tried to join the Confederacy have been much debated. Some said
they hoped it would bring equality for free persons of color. Others maintained that
they volunteered for the state militia in order to defend their property in the city and
would have balked at service in the regular Confederate army. Some historians suggest
that whites pressured free blacks to enlist, fearing that otherwise they would lead slave
revolts. See Blassingame, *Black New Orleans*, 33–35; Donald Everett, "Ben Butler and the
Louisiana Native Guards, 1861–1862," *Journal of Southern History*, 24 (May 1958): 202–
17; James G. Hollandsworth, Jr., *The Louisiana Native Guards: The Black Military Experience
during the Civil War* (Baton Rouge: Louisiana State University Press, 1995), 7, 10–11;
Roland C. McConnell, "Louisiana's Black Military History, 1729–1865," in Robert
Louisiana's Black Heritage, eds. Macdonald, John Kemp, Edward Haas (New Orleans:
Louisiana State Museum, 1979), 35, 44–45, 47, 48, 49; Nystrom, *New Orleans after the
Civil War*, 21; Thompson, *Exiles at Home*, 211; Tunnell, *Crucible of Reconstruction*, 69–70;
Howard C. Westwood, "Benjamin Butler's Enlistment of Black Troops in New Orleans
in 1862," *Louisiana History* 26 (Winter 1985): 5–22.

16. It is important to note that many of the original Louisiana Native Guards officers
who had volunteered to defend Louisiana's Confederate government declined to join
the Union army; whether their position was shaped by loyalty to the Confederacy,
slavery, or other reasons is difficult to determine. Benjamin F. Butler to Edwin M.
Stanton, May 25, 1862, in U.S. War Department, *The War of the Rebellion: A Compilation of
the Official Records of the Union and Confederate Armies*, 128 vols. (Washington: Government
Printing Office, 1880–1901), ser. I, vol. 15, p. 442 (quotation); Blassingame, *Black
New Orleans*, 33–35; Everett, "Ben Butler and the Louisiana Native Guards," 202–17;
Hollandsworth, *The Louisiana Native Guards*, 7, 10–11; Thompson, *Exiles at Home*, 211;
Tunnell, *Crucible of Reconstruction*, 69–70; Westwood, "Benjamin Butler's Enlistment of
Black Troops in New Orleans in 1862," 5–22.

17. Jean B. Jourdain Service Record, Compiled Military Service Records of Volunteer
Union Soldiers Who Served With the United States Colored Troops, 7th Louisiana

Infantry, Microfilm: M1820, Roll: 86, National Archives and Records Administration, Washington, DC; Index to Compiled Military Service Records, Official Army Register of the Volunteer Force 1861–1865, U.S. Civil War Soldier Records and Profiles [Ancestry.com]; Everett, "Ben Butler and the Louisiana Native Guards, 1861–1862," 205 (quotation from orders), 206–10; Eric Foner, *Freedom's Lawmakers*, 124; Rankin, "The Origins of Black Leadership," 434, 438; *House Reports*, 39 Cong., 2 Sess., No. 16 (Serial. 1304), p. 209; Thompson, *Exiles at Home*, 212; Donald R. Shaffer, *After the Glory: The Struggles of Black Civil War Veterans* (Lawrence: University of Kansas Press, 2004), 12–16. Although many of the men in his regiment were former slaves who had fled to Union lines, Jourdain and the other line officers were Afro-Creoles. Some were sons of former Governors, senators, and other members of the white elite. All hoped their efforts would lead to enhanced rights. Jourdain's friend Francis Dumas made the point clearly: "No matter where I fight, I only wish to spend what I have, and fight as long as I can, if only my boy may stand in the street equal to a white boy when the war is over." Hollandsworth, *Louisiana Native Guards*, 24–56, 40 (Dumas quotation); McConnell, "Louisiana's Black Military History, 1729–1865," 48–49, 110–11.

18. McConnell, "Louisiana's Black Military History," 48–49; Fred Harvey Harrington, *Fighting Politician: Major General N.P. Banks* (Philadelphia: University of Pennsylvania Press, 1948) ("humiliation", Banks's "annoyance and embarrassment"); *New Orleans Tribune*, May 14, 1865 ("shoulder the musket"); Hollandsworth, *Louisiana Native Guards*, 42–44; Thompson, *Exiles at Home*, 212–13; Ira Berlin, Joseph P. Reidy, and Leslie S. Rowland, eds, *The Black Military Experience: Freedom, a Documentary History of Emancipation, 1861–1877*, ser. 2 (New York: Cambridge University Press, 1982), 321–28; Shaffer, *After the Glory*, 15; Mary Ellison, "African American Music and Muskets in Civil War New Orleans," *Louisiana History* 35 (Summer 1994): 285–319; Manoj K. Joshi and Joseph P. Reidy, "'To Come Forward and Aid in Putting Down This Unholy Rebellion,': The Officers of Louisiana's Free Black Native Guard during the Civil War Era," *Southern Studies*, 21 (Fall 1982): 326–42; Christian G. Samito, *Becoming American under Fire: Irish Americans, African Americans, and the Politics of Citizenship During the Civil War Era* (Ithaca, NY: Cornell University Press, 2009), 24, 64, 66; Jourdain's New Orleans Riot Testimony, 208.

19. John C. Rodrigue, *Lincoln and Reconstruction* (Carbondale: Southern Illinois University Press, 2013), 79–83 (quotations); Hollandsworth, *Louisiana Native Guards*, 94–96.

20. These state laws and local ordinances recreated the antebellum pass system, forced freedmen to work on plantations or be charged with vagrancy, created apprenticeship laws, banned black meetings after sunset, and prohibited black people from carrying firearms.

21. W. R. Brock, *An American Crisis: Congress and Reconstruction, 1865–1867* (New York: Harper & Row, 1966), 36–37; Dan Carter, *When the War Was Over: The Failure of Self-Reconstruction in the South, 1865–1867* (Baton Rouge: Louisiana State University Press, 1986), 148–50, 177, 217–27 (quotations); Joseph G. Dawson, III, *Army Generals and*

Reconstruction: Louisiana, 1862–1877 (Baton Rouge: Louisiana State University Press, 1982), 31, 43, 67; Eric Foner, *Reconstruction: America's Unfinished Revolution* (New York: Harper & Row, 1988), 199–202; James G. Hollandsworth, Jr., *An Absolute Massacre: The New Orleans Race Riot of July 30, 1866* (Baton Rouge: Louisiana State University Press, 2001), 74, 119; Harold Hyman and William Wiecek, *Equal Justice under Law: Constitutional Developments, 1835–1875* (New York: Harper Collins, 1982), 319–20; Michael A. Ross, *Justice of Shattered Dreams: Samuel Freeman Miller and the Supreme Court during the Civil War Era* (Baton Rouge: Louisiana State University Press, 2003), 114; Tunnell, *Crucible of Reconstruction*, 96, 101, 117; Joe Gray Taylor, *Louisiana Reconstructed 1863–1877* (Baton Rouge: Louisiana State University Press, 1974), 99–103, 106, 11; Christopher Waldrep, "Substituting the Law for the Lash: Emancipation and Legal Formalism in a Mississippi County Court," *Journal of American History* 82 (March 1996): 1425–51; Theodore Brantner Wilson, *The Black Codes of the South* (Tuscaloosa: University of Alabama Press, 1965), 77–80.

22. Jourdain's New Orleans Riot Testimony, 208.

23. Foner, *Reconstruction*, 204–5; Howard N. Rabinowitz, "The Conflict between Blacks and the Police in the Urban South, 1865–1900," *Historian*, 39 (November 1976): 63–64; George C. Rable, *But There Was No Peace: The Role of Violence in the Politics of Reconstruction* (Athens: University of Georgia Press, 1984), 21–28; Edward L. Ayers, *Vengeance and Justice: Crime and Punishment in the Nineteenth-Century American South* (New York: Oxford University Press, 1985); Hyman and Wiecek, *Equal Justice Under Law*, 317, 322–25.

24. Jourdain's New Orleans Riot Testimony, 204–9; Hollandsworth, *An Absolute Massacre*, I ("absolute massacre"), 28–35, 37, 40, 64, 99, 118.

25. Jourdain's New Orleans Riot Testimony, 205, 206 ("the low class of citizens," "a few loyal men"), Hollandsworth, *An Absolute Massacre*, 37, 40, 64, 99, 118.

26. Jourdain's New Orleans Riot Testimony, 206.

27. Michael A. Ross, "Justice Miller's Reconstruction: The *Slaughter-House Cases*, Health Codes, and Civil Rights in New Orleans, 1861–1863," *Journal of Southern History* 64 (November 1998): 649, 661; Jourdain's New Orleans Riot Testimony, 207–8 (quotations).

28. *Digest of the Statutes of the State of Louisiana in Two Volumes*, vol. I (New Orleans: Republican Printing Office, 1870), 114; *Digest of the Statutes of the State of Louisiana*, vol. 2 (New Orleans: Republican Office, 1870), 2843; Rebecca Scott and Jean Hébrard, *Freedom Papers: An Atlantic Odyssey of Emancipation* (Cambridge, MA: Harvard University Press, 2012), 127–34; Ross, *Justice of Shattered Dreams*, 195–96; Joseph G. Dawson III, *Army Generals and Reconstruction*, 46–93; Taylor, *Louisiana Reconstructed*, 152; Tunnell, *Crucible of Reconstruction*, 117–18; *New Orleans Tribune*, May 5, 24, 30 ("perfect equality," "Republican principles"), 31 (Jourdain's Republican party service and radicalism), 1867; *New Orleans Bee*, January 24, 1869.

29. Richard Tansey, "Out-of-State Free Blacks in Late Antebellum New Orleans," 369–86; Rankin, "The Origins of Black Leadership," 422; Bell, *Revolution, Romanticism, and the*

Afro-Creole Protest Tradition in Louisiana, 74–79, 84, 136; Schafer, *Becoming Free, Remaining Free*, 150; *The Louisianian*, February 13, 1875.

30. For discussions of the Victorian ideal of manliness as self-restraint, see Gail Bederman, *Manliness and Civilization: A Cultural History of Gender and Race in the United States, 1880–1917* (Chicago: University of Chicago Press, 1996), 12–18, 30–36, 45–49, 52, 66, 72–3, 79–83, 86–95, 205, 218; John F. Kasson, *Rudeness and Civility: Manners in Nineteenth-century Urban American* (New York: Hill & Wang, 1990), 112–81; Amy S. Greenberg, *Manifest Manhood and the Antebellum American Empire* (New York: Cambridge University Press, 2005), 10–11, 135–69; Michael T. Smith, "P. B. S. Pinchback, Masculinity, and Race during Reconstruction," paper delivered at the 2010 meeting of the Louisiana Historical Association (Lafayette, LA, March 26, 2010). For Metropolitan Police regulations, see *Manual of the Metropolitan Police Force of the State of Louisiana* (New Orleans: Republican Printing Office, 1871), 25, 35, 39. For attacks on black policemen, see Nystrom, *New Orleans after the Civil War*, 77–78.

31. Rankin, "Origins of Black Leadership," 420–21, 436–40; Dennis C. Rousey, "Black Policemen in New Orleans During Reconstruction," *Historian*, 49 (1987): 223–43; New Orleans *Picayune*, July 6, 1870 ("lasting shame"). For examples of Jourdain's earlier investigations, see *Daily Picayune*, September 16, 1869, June 16, 1870.

32. For Northern newspaper readers and Northern perceptions of Radical Reconstruction, see Heather Cox Richardson, *The Death of Reconstruction: Race, Labor, and Politics in the Post-Civil War North, 1865–1901* (Cambridge, MA: Harvard University Press, 2001), xv, 41–139; Papke, *Framing the Criminal*, 56; Mark Wahlgren Summers, *The Press Gang: Newspapers and Politics, 1865–1878* (Chapel Hill: University of North Carolina Press, 1994), 206–22; Carl R. Osthaus, *Partisans of the Southern Press: Editorial Spokesmen of the Nineteenth Century* (Lexington: University of Kentucky Press, 1994), 128–29. For an excellent case study of another postbellum crime that became entangled with Southern politics, see Suzanne Lebsock, *A Murder in Virginia: Southern Justice on Trial* (New York: W.W. Norton, 2004).

Chapter Three: A Trace of the Missing Child?

1. Samuel Edwards, *The Vidocq Dossier: The Story of the World's First Detective* (New York: Houghton Mifflin, 1977); Émile Gaboriau, *Monsieur Lecoq* (Paris: E. Dentu, 1869). Edgar Allan Poe made his fictional detective, the Chevalier C. August Dupin, famous in his short stories "The Purloined Letter," "The Murders in the Rue Morgue," and "The Mystery of Marie Rogêt." See Peter Thomas, "Poe's Dupin and the Power of Detection," in *The Cambridge Companion to Edgar Allan Poe*, ed. Kevin Hayes (New York: Cambridge University Press, 2002), 133–34. For calls for French detectives, see *Daily Picayune*, July 6, 8 (quotations), 1870.

2. See Jordan Noble's obituaries in *Daily Picayune*, June 21, 1890, and New Orleans *Times-Democrat*, June 21, 1890. See also Dennis Rousey, *Policing the Southern City: New Orleans, 1805–1899* (Baton Rouge: Louisiana State University Press, 1997), 142.

3. *Daily Picayune*, July 10, 1870.

4. Ruth Brandon, *The Spiritualists: The Passion for the Occult in the Nineteenth and Twentieth Centuries* (New York: Knopf, 1983), 2–8, 42–52; Ann Braude, *Radical Spirits: Spiritualism and Women's Rights in Nineteenth-Century America* (Boston: Beacon Press, 1989), 2–10, 27–30; Bret E. Carroll, *Spiritualism in Antebellum America* (Bloomington: Indiana University Press, 1997), 4, 8, 30.

5. See the sources cited in note 4, supra.

6. For a typical report of a haunted occurrence, see *Daily Picayune*, May 29, 1870 (reporting a luminous ghost then appearing regularly at midnight at the corner of Washington and Prytania Streets). For New Orleans as a stronghold of spiritualism, see Braude, *Radical Spirits*, 29–30; Caryn Cossé Bell, *Revolution, Romanticism, and the Afro-Creole Protest Tradition in Louisiana* (Baton Rouge: Louisiana State University Press, 1997), 187–218; *Buchanan's Journal of Man* (Cincinnati), November 1851. The estimate of the number of believers in New Orleans found in Uriah Clark, ed., *Fourth Annual Spiritual Register, with a Calendar and Speakers' Almanac, for 1860; Facts, Philosophy, Statistics of Spiritualism.* (Auburn, NY: Spiritual Clarion Office, 1860). For transcripts and other records of the séances in Henry Louis Rey's home, see René Grandjean Collection (MSS 85), Series IX, Spiritualism Records Subseries IX.1, Séance Registers 85–31, 85–32, Subseries IX.2: Translations nos. 85–66, Earl K. Long Library, University of New Orleans.

7. New Orleans *Republican*, July 9, 1870.

8. *Commercial Bulletin*, July 12, 1870, New Orleans *Times*, July 10, 1870.

9. New Orleans *Times*, July 10, 12, 1870; New Orleans *Republican*, July 12, 1870 (quotation).

10. *Commercial Bulletin*, July 26, 1870 (quotation); *Daily Picayune*, July 26, 27 (story of Mollie en route), 1870; New Orleans *Republican*, July 26, 1870; *Charleston Daily Courier*, July 26, 1870; *Baton Rouge Courier*, July 30, 1870.

11. *Daily Picayune*, July 30, 1870, *New Orleans Bee*, August 5, 1870.

12. *New Orleans Times*, August 7, 1870; New Orleans *Bee*, August 9, 1870; *Commercial Bulletin*, August 9, 1870; *Daily Picayune*, August 7 ("colored man"), 19, 1870.

13. See sources cited in note 12, supra.

14. Account from *Cincinnati Commercial*, August 14, 1870, reprinted in *Daily Picayune*, August 19, 1870.

15. *Cincinnati Commercial*, August 14, reprinted in *Daily Picayune*, August 19, 1870, supra note 14.

16. *Daily Picayune*, August 19, 1870.

17. *Daily Picayune*, August 10, 1870.

18. New Orleans *Times*, August 2, 1870; *Commercial Bulletin*, August 4, 1870; New Orleans *Bee*, August 4, 1870.

19. *Daily Picayune*, June 8 ("martyrs," "equal rights," "petty malignity"), 9 ("dictatorial"), 1870; *Daily Picayune*, November 17, 1895 (George obituary). Rule 167 of the Metropolitan Police Regulations allowed members of the force to claim rewards. See *Manual of the*

Metropolitan Police Force of the State of Louisiana (New Orleans: Republican Printing Office, 1871), 38.

20. For cows still roaming free in the Sixth District (formerly Jefferson City), see *Daily Picayune*, October 11, 1870. For architecture and development of the district, see Dorothy Schlesinger, Robert Cangelosi, and Sally Reeves, eds., *New Orleans Architecture: Jefferson City* (Gretna, LA: Pelican Publishing, 1989), 31. For the description of house on the northeast corner of Bellecastle and Camp streets, see *Daily Picayune*, August 10, 1870 ("well-to-do").

21. Article 9 of the Louisiana State Constitution of 1868, *Digest of the Statutes of the State of Louisiana in Two Volumes*, vol. I (New Orleans: Republican Printing Office, 1870), 114, 454.

22. The events of August 7 have been recreated from court testimony reprinted in various newspapers. See New Orleans *Times*, August 23, 1870 ("he had gone out"); New Orleans *Bee*, August 23, 1870; *Daily Picayune*, August 10 (rosewood furniture) ("Very well then"), 23, 24, 25 ("hallooing and screaming"), 1870.

23. Testimonies of John Baptiste Jourdain and J. J. Pierson, *Daily Picayune*, August 23, 24, 1870.

24. New Orleans *Republican*, August 21, 1870.

25. In his famous narrative of his life as a slave, Solomon Northup, a free black man kidnapped by slave traders and sold into bondage near Cheneyville in the 1840s, noted the large number of slaves planter Peter Compton purchased to labor in his fields. For Northup's reference to Peter Compton buying seventeen slaves at the same auction at which Northup was sold, see Solomon Northup, *Twelve Years A Slave* (Auburn, NY: Derby and Miller, 1853), 104–5. For the evolution of labor relations in the Louisiana sugar parishes after the Civil War, see John C. Rodrigue, *Reconstruction in the Cane Fields: From Slavery to Free Labor in Louisiana's Sugar Parishes 1862–1880* (Baton Rouge: Louisiana State University, 2001), 1–8, 58–77. For the size of the Compton Estate on the eve of the Civil War see "Rapides Parish History—Section II—The Antebellum Period 1804–1861," http://www.rootsweb.com/~larapide/history/eakin/eakin2.htm.

26. New Orleans *Republican*, August 21, 1870.

27. New Orleans *Republican*, August 21, 1870.

28. New Orleans *Republican*, August 21, 1870 (quotations).

29. New Orleans *Republican*, August 21, 1870 (quotations). For the activities of the Knights of the White Camellia in Louisiana, see Charles Lane, *The Day Freedom Died: The Colfax Massacre, the Supreme Court, and the Betrayal of Reconstruction* (New York: Henry Holt and Company, 2008), 38–46.

30. New Orleans *Republican*, August 17, 1870 (quotations), August 21, 1870.

Chapter Four: A Knock at the Digbys' Door

1. For descriptions of New Orleans during the summer, see Jo Ann Carrigan, *The Saffron Scourge: A History of Yellow Fever in Louisiana, 1796–1905* (Lafayette: Center for Louisiana

Studies, Lafayette, LA, 1994), 59, 60, 87; *New Orleans Republican*, July 15, 1870 (discussing gutters "reeking with foul and offensive matter").

2. For the annual summer exodus from the city, see *New Orleans Republican*, June 28, 1870; *Daily Picayune*, June 29, 30, 1870. For other discussions of summer in the city, see New Orleans *Times*, July 6, 1870 (article on how to keep cool); *Daily Picayune*, May 29, 1870 (white suits and panama hats), July 7 ("can't get aways"), 29 ("ice cream"), 1870; New Orleans *Republican*, June 16 (summer fruits), 28, 1870; *Commercial Bulletin*, August 16 (summer fruits and vegetables), 20 (reports of sunstroke victims and heat exhaustion), 1870; New Orleans *Bee*, August 20, 1870. For hurricanes and yellow fever, see Alcée Fortier, *Louisiana: Comprising Sketches of Parishes, Towns, Events, Institutions, and Persons Arranged in Cyclopedic Form* (Madison, WI: Century Historical Association, 1914), vol. I, p. 519 (last major hurricane); Margaret Humphreys, *Yellow Fever and the South* (New Brunswick, NJ: Rutgers University Press, 1992), 2, 5, 6.

3. *Daily Picayune*, August 10, 1870.

4. New Orleans *Republican*, August 13, 1870 (quotations). For mid–nineteenth century views of manhood, see E. Anthony Rotundo, *American Manhood: Transformations in Masculinity from the Revolution to the Modern Era* (New York: Basic Books, 1993), 132–38, 144, 176, 178–79; Patricia Kelleher, "Class and Catholic Irish Masculinity in Antebellum America: Young Men on the Make in Chicago," *Journal of American Ethnic History*, 28 (Summer 2010), 7–42; David Anthony, "Banking on Emotion: Financial Panic and the Logic of Male Submission in Jacksonian Gothic," *American Literature* 76 (December 2004): 719–47.

5. New Orleans *Times*, July 6, 1870 ("higher circles"). Thomas arrived in New Orleans on December 27, 1851. Bridgette's route to America is less clear. She may have been the "Bridget Gibbons" (Gibbons was her maiden name) who arrived on the *IKL* on March 22, 1851. See New Orleans Passenger Lists, 1820–1845, National Archives and Records Administration, Microfilm: M259_34, M259_35. See also Edward Laxton, *The Famine Ships: The Irish Exodus to America* (New York: Henry Holt, 1998), 28, 112, 154, 175–77, 209.

6. For the world of Irish immigrants in New Orleans, see Laura Kelley, "Erin's Enterprise: Immigration by Appropriation, The Irish in Antebellum New Orleans," (PhD diss., Tulane University, 2004), pp. 1–166; Frederick Marcel Spletstoser, "Back Door to the Land of Plenty: New Orleans as an Immigrant Port, 1820–1960" (PhD diss., Louisiana State University, 1978), 291, 380; P. Frazer Simons, *Tenants No More: Voices from an Irish Townland, 1811–1901 & The Great Migration to Australia and America* (Richmond, Australia: Prowling Tiger Press, 1996); Earl F. Niehaus, *The Irish in New Orleans, 1800–1860* (Baton Rouge: Louisiana State University Press, 1965); Dennis C. Rousey, "Hibernian Leatherheads: Irish Cops in New Orleans, 1830–1880," *Journal of Urban History* 10 (November 1983): 61–84; Patrick Brennan, "Fever and Fists: Forging an Irish Legacy in New Orleans," (PhD diss., University of Missouri-Columbia, 2003), pp. 13–14; David T. Gleeson, *The Irish in the South, 1805–1877* (Chapel Hill: University of North Carolina Press, 2001); Richard Campanella, *Bienville's Dilemma: A Historical Geography of New Orleans* (Lafayette: Center for Louisiana Studies, 2008), 170–75.

7. *Daily Picayune*, August 10, 1870 (hottest days of the season). Street scenes from "How The City Wakes Up," *Daily Picayune*, November 23, 1873.

8. Testimony of Bridgette Digby, Thomas Digby, and James Broadwell (quotations) reprinted in the *Daily Picayune*, August 21, 24, 25, 1870. See also New Orleans *Times*, August 10, 1870.

9. See sources cited in note 8, supra.

10. Frederick Way, Jr., *Way's Packet Directory 1848–1983: Passenger Steamboats of the Mississippi River System since the Advent of Photography in Mid-Continent America* (Athens, OH: Ohio University Press, 1983), 138; clipping from *Tell City News* (Indiana), September 23, 1960, in the Joseph M. Jones Steamboat Collection, Manuscripts Department, Tulane University, New Orleans, LA. For descriptions of the famous race between the *Natchez* and the *Robert E. Lee*, see Alcée Fortier, *Louisiana: Comprising Sketches of Parishes, Towns, Events, Institutions, and Persons Arranged in Cyclopedic Form* (Madison, WI: Century Historical Association, 1914), vol. 2, p. 510; *Daily Picayune*, July 1, 2, and 6, 1870. For representative advertisements and articles touting Broadwell as captain, see *Daily Picayune*, November 14, 1837; *New Orleans Daily Creole*, September 22, 1856; *Daily Picayune*, January 28, 1857; *New Orleans Times*, December 6, 1865. For an advertisement featuring Broadwell's Mexican War efforts and for advertisements using his endorsement to sell painkillers, see *The Tri-Weekly Ohio Statesmen* (Columbus), June 10, 1846; *Daily Picayune*, July 25, 1849.

11. Testimony of Thomas Digby ("elegant one") and James Broadwell both in the *Daily Picayune*, August 21, 24, 25, 1870. For a description of Broadwell's neighborhood, see Richard and Marina Campanella, *New Orleans Then and Now* (Gretna, LA: Pelican Publishing, 1999), 306, 320. For the occupations of those who lived in Broadwell's neighborhood, see: *Graham & Madden's Crescent City Directory* (New Orleans: Graham & Madden, 1870) under "Chestnut Street Between St. Mary and St. Andrew."

12. Testimony of Evelina Broadwell (quotations) and James Broadwell in the *Daily Picayune*, August 23, 24, 1870.

13. Testimony of James Broadwell reprinted in the *Daily Picayune*, August 24, 1870.

14. Testimony of Bridgette Digby, reprinted in the *Daily Picayune*, August 25, 1870 ("I would know it," "mammy!"); *Commercial Bulletin*, August 10, 1870 ("quickness of wind"); *Daily Picayune*, August 10, 1870 ("narrow streets," "white and black," "little one tenderly,"); New Orleans *Times*, August 10, 1870.

15. Testimony of James Broadwell in *Daily Picayune*, August 24, 1870.

16. Testimony of Thomas Digby and John Baptiste Jourdain, in *Daily Picayune*, August 21, 23, 24, 1870.

17. *Daily Picayune*, August 10, 1870; New Orleans *Times*, August 10, 1870.

18. New Orleans *Times*, August 10, 1870; *Daily Picayune*, August 10, 1870 ("catch a peep").

19. Testimony of Evelina Broadwell, reprinted in the *Daily Picayune*, August 23, 1870 (quotations).

20. Testimony of Evelina Broadwell, in *Daily Picayune*, August 23, 1870 ("the matter," "no questions," "you must tell," "appearing before a court"); *Daily Picayune*, August 10, 1870 ("a crime has been committed").

21. Testimony of Evelina Broadwell, in the *Daily Picayune*, August 23, 1870 (quotations).

22. *New Orleans Bee*, August 10, 1870 ("confident the woman"); *Daily Picayune*, August 10, 1870 ("though colored").

23. Testimony of Evelina Broadwell, in *Daily Picayune*, August 23, 1870 (quotations).

Chapter Five: The Arrest of the Alleged Accessories

1. *Daily Picayune*, August 7, 1870, July 14, 1898; *Daily States*, October 29, 1896; Dennis Rousey, *Policing the Southern City: News Orleans, 1805–1889* (Baton Rouge: Louisiana State University Press, 1997), 6, 144; Dennis C. Rousey, "Hibernian Leatherheads: Irish Cops in New Orleans, 1830–1880," *Journal of Urban History* 10 (November 1983): 61–84; Patrick Brennan, "Fever and Fists: Forging an Irish Legacy in New Orleans," (PhD diss., University of Missouri-Columbia, 2003), 114, 311–28.

2. See sources cited in note 1, supra. For a description of Pierre Bertin and Jean Capdeville as "New Orleans' most celebrated home-grown burglars," see Herbert Asbury, *The French Quarter: An Informal History of the New Orleans Underworld* (New York: Hippocrene Books, 1989), 324.

3. For accounts of events at Ellen Follin's house that afternoon, see testimony of John Baptiste Jourdain reprinted in *Daily Picayune*, August 23, 24, 1870 ("asked me," "directed him"); testimony of Algernon Badger reprinted in *Daily Picayune*, August 21, 1870 ("dissipated in appearance"); testimony of Leonard Malone reprinted in *Daily Picayune*, August 21, 1870; testimony of George Blass reprinted in *Daily Picayune*, August 25, 1870; testimony of Minnie Green reprinted in *Daily Picayune*, August 11 ("hurried and agitated manner"), 25, 1870.

4. See sources cited in note 3, supra.

5. Testimony of Leonard Malone reprinted in *Daily Picayune*, August 21, 1870; testimony of George Blass reprinted in *Daily Picayune*, August 25, 1870; *Commercial Bulletin*, August 10, 1870 ("cross and crying"); *New Orleans Times*, August 10, 1870.

6. *Daily Picayune*, August 8, 1870; *New Orleans Times*, August 10, 1870.

7. *New Orleans Bee*, August 10 ("largely *enceinte*"), 11 ("not been with," "very near her accouchement"), 1870.

8. *New Orleans Times*, August 10, 1870 ("conceal their shame," "handsomely furnished"); *Daily Picayune*, August 10, 1870 ("want for money"). For antebellum relationships between free women of color and white women, see Lois Virginia Meacham Gould, "'In Full Enjoyment of Their Liberty': The Free Women of Color of the Gulf Ports of New Orleans, Mobile, and Pensacola, 1769–1860" (PhD diss., Emory University, 1991), 137, 153–53, 149–50. For views of pregnancy, see Richard Wertz and Dorothy Wertz, *Lying-In: A History of Childbirth in America* (New York: The Free Press, 1977),

79 ("confinement"). For the shame associated with an illegitimate birth, see V. Lynn Kennedy, *Born Southern: Childbirth, Motherhood, and Social Networks in the Old South* (Baltimore: Johns Hopkins University Press, 2010), 5, 6, 7, 10–11, 19–30.

9. New Orleans *Republican*, August 10, 1870 ("House of Secret Obstetrics"); Natasha L. McPherson, "'There Was a Tradition among the Women': New Orleans's Colored Creole Women and the Making of a Community in the Tremé and Seventh Ward, 1791–1930" (PhD diss., Emory University, 2011), 100–19; David Rankin, "The Impact of the Civil War on the Free Colored Community of New Orleans," *Perspectives in American History*, 11 (1977–1978) 379–416; Loren Schweninger, "Antebellum Free Persons of Color in Postbellum Louisiana," *Louisiana History* 30 (Fall 1989): 345–64; Arthé A. Anthony, "The Negro Creole Community in New Orleans, 1880–1920," (PhD diss., University of California, Irvine, 1978); Joseph G. Tregle, Jr., "Creoles and Americans," and Joseph G. Tregle, Jr. and Caryn Cossé Bell, "The Americanization of Black New Orleans, 1850–1900," in *Creole New Orleans: Race and Americanization*, eds. Arnold Hirsch and Joseph Logsdon (Baton Rouge: Louisiana State University Press, 1992), 131–85 and 201–61; Jacqueline Jones, *Labor of Love, Labor of Sorrow: Black, Women, Work, and the Family from Slavery to the Present*, revised and updated ed. (New York: Basic Books, 2010), 72–73.

10. For the property owned by Ellen Follin, see Tax Assessment Records, 6th Municipal District, 14th Assessment District, square 252, SO 1875, Roll No. 694, CJ 436. For the occupations of free women of color, see Gould, "'In Full Enjoyment of Their Liberty,'" 275, 276, 284; Loren Schweninger, *Black Property Owners in the South, 1790–1915* (Urbana, IL: University of Illinois Press, 1990), 85–86, 132.

11. Albert Voorhies, *A Treatise on the Criminal Jurisprudence of Louisiana* (New Orleans: Bloomfield and Steel, 1860), 164; Wertz and Wertz, *Lying-In*, 25, 46, 47, 55, 65, 70. See also Sally McMillen, *Motherhood in the Old South: Pregnancy, Childbirth, and Infant Rearing* (Baton Rouge: Louisiana State University Press, 1990).

12. *New Orleans Bee*, August 11, 1870 ("has not been with," "to be more secure").

13. Louisa Murray was twenty-six years old in 1870. In the 1870 census she is listed as Louisa Follin, a "mulatto," with a seven-year-old daughter, Emmetta. See United States 9th Census 1870, Mobile County, Mobile City Alabama, Mobile Ward 7, microfilm M593, Roll 31; p. 271B; image 547.

14. *Daily Picayune*, August 10, 1870 ("being a stranger"); *New Orleans Times*, August 10, 1870; testimony of Algernon Badger reprinted in *Daily Picayune*, August 21, 1870.

15. Testimony of Algernon Badger, supra note 3.

16. *New Orleans Bee*, August 11, 1870 ("probably the planner," "culture and refinement," "no reason to doubt"); *Commercial Bulletin*, August 11, 1870 ("was a party," "her manners and conversation").

17. *Daily Picayune*, August 10, 1870 ("accessories"); testimony of Algernon Badger reprinted in *Daily Picayune*, August 21, 1870 ("all equally guilty," "have to lock up").

18. *Daily Picayune*, August 10 ("take her place"), 1870; Testimony of James Broadwell reprinted in the *Daily Picayune*, August 23 ("a lady alone"), 1870; *New Orleans Times*, August 23 ("unwarrantable and unjustifiable"), 1870.

19. *Commercial Bulletin*, August 10, 1870 ("to make capital"); Testimony of James Broadwell reprinted in the *Daily Picayune*, August 24, 1870 ("circumstances were").

20. Testimony of James Broadwell, reprinted in the *Daily Picayune*, August 24, 1870 ("derogatory," "if it was not corrected"); *New Orleans Bee*, August 10, 1870 ("the relations"); *Commercial Bulletin*, August 10, 1870.

21. *Commercial Bulletin*, August 10, 11, 1870.

22. *Daily Picayune*, August 10, 1870.

Chapter Six: The Woman in the Seaside Hat

1. *Daily Picayune*, August 11, 1870; *New Orleans Republican*, August 13, 1870. Events also recreated using Detective Jourdain's testimony in *The State of Louisiana v. Louisa Murray alias Follin*, First District Recorders Court, Docket no. 49, August 20, 22, 23, 24, 1870, New Orleans City Archives, Louisiana Division, New Orleans Public Library. Although the term "extradition" rather than "rendition" was used widely in the popular press to describe the interstate rendition of fugitives from justice, it was not legally accurate. Extradition applied only to international law. See John Bassett Moore, *A Treatise on Extradition and Interstate Rendition*, vol. 2 (Boston: Boston Book Company, 1891), 819, 840.

2. 1 *Statutes at Large* 302 (1793), "An Act respecting fugitives from justice, and persons escaping from the service of their masters."

3. *Kentucky v. Dennison*, 65 U.S. 66 (1861); Moore, *Treatise on Extradition and Interstate Rendition*, vol. 2, 825–28. For northern resistance to the Fugitive Slave Act of 1850, see Paul Finkelman, *An Imperfect Union: Slavery, Federalism, and Comity* (Chapel Hill: University of North Carolina Press, 1981); Earl M. Maltz, *Fugitive Slave On Trial: The Anthony Burns Case and Abolitionist Outrage* (Lawrence, KS: University Press of Kansas, 2010).

4. Testimony of John Baptiste Jourdain reprinted in the *Daily Picayune*, August 24, 1870 ("a little plan,").

5. Testimony of John Baptiste Jourdain, reprinted in the *Daily Picayune*, August 24, 1870.

6. Michael W. Fitzgerald, *Urban Emancipation: Popular Politics in Reconstruction Mobile, 1860–1890* (Baton Rouge: Louisiana State University Press, 2002), 5, 11–13, 101–8; Lois Virginia Meacham Gould, "'In Full Enjoyment of Their Liberty': The Free Women of Color of the Gulf Ports of New Orleans, Mobile, and Pensacola, 1769–1860'" (PhD diss., Emory University, 1991), 273. Although the Confederate government in Richmond turned down Mobile's Afro-Creole volunteers, a few members of Mobile's "Native Guard" did serve briefly on the city's fortifications. See Fitzgerald, *Urban Emancipation*, 17–18. Before the Civil War, Alabama law, unlike that of Louisiana, allowed interracial marriages. See Peter Wallerstein, *Tell the Court I Love My Wife: Race, Marriage, and Law—An American History* (New York: Palgrave Macmillan, 2002), 48–49, 70–71.

7. Kent Gardien, "The Domingan Kettle: Philadelphian-Emigre Planters in Alabama," *National Genealogical Society Quarterly*, 76 (September 1988): 177–87; Lois Virginia Meacham Gould, "'In Full Enjoyment of Their Liberty,'" 273, 218. For genealogical and property ownership information for Ellen Follin and Louisa Follin Murray, see U.S. Census Office, 9th Census, Mobile City, Alabama, microfilm 593, roll 31, p. 271B; Tax Assessment Records, 6th Municipal District, 14th Assessment District, New Orleans, Louisiana, square 252, SO 1875, roll 694, CJ 436, 1873–1878, Louisiana Division, New Orleans Public Library; New Orleans, Louisiana, Death Records Index, 1804–1949 (Ellen Follin), vol. 138, p. 23; *Daily Picayune*, May 7, 1906, p. 6, c. 5.

8. *Mobile Register*, August 12, 1870 ("quadroon"); *New Orleans Republican*, August 13, 1870; Testimony of John Baptiste Jourdain, reprinted in *Daily Picayune* August 2, 1870. For a profile of Chief Turner, who later left Mobile and became wealthy as a western mine owner, see George Ward Burton, *Men of Achievement in the Great Southwest* (Los Angeles: Los Angeles Times, 1904), 121–22. No newspaper account or court testimony describes Louisa Murray's house which no longer exists. The 1870 Census indicates Louisa (listed with the surname Follin, rather than Murray) owned $800 in real estate. U.S. Census Office, 9th Census (1870), Mobile County, Mobile City Alabama, p. 271.

9. *Commercial Bulletin*, August 13, 1870 ("good and graceful"); *New Orleans Republican*, August 13, 1870; *Nashville Union and American*, August 16, 1870 ("oh no sir," "because it was white," "your little niece," "transient flash," "child is mistaken"); *New Orleans Republican*, August 13, 1870 ("seemed to know"); Testimony of John Baptiste Jourdain, reported in *Daily Picayune*, August 24, 1870.

10. *New Orleans Republican*, August 13, 1870.

11. Testimony of John Baptiste Jourdain reprinted in the *Daily Picayune*, August 24, 1870 ("there would be," "wherever you wish"); *Mobile Register*, August 12, 1870 ("no surprise").

12. *Mobile Register*, August 12, 1870 ("interpose any delay," "pack her trunk,"); Testimony of John Baptiste Jourdain reprinted in *Daily Picayune*, August 24, 1870 ("I did not request," "Certainly, sir," "She came with me," "she inspired me"). It is not clear what Louisa did with her seven-year-old daughter Emmetta while she accompanied Jourdain to New Orleans. It is possible she stayed behind with a cook who, according to the census, also resided in Murray's house. U.S. Census Office, 9th Census (1870), Mobile County, Mobile City Alabama, p. 271.

13. The reporter wrote that he gained access to the prisoners "through the courtesy of police officers." See *Daily Picayune*, August 11, 1870.

14. *Digest of the State of Louisiana in Two Volumes*, vol. I (New Orleans: Republican Office, 1870), 457 (right to counsel).

15. *Daily Picayune*, August 11, 1870.

16. *Daily Picayune*, August 11, 1870.

17. Hunt's brothers, Randell, Thomas, and William, were similarly accomplished. Thomas founded Louisiana's medical college, William served as the state's attorney general and

later as U.S. secretary of the Navy, and Randell litigated some of the city's most famous cases while also serving as president of the University of Louisiana. See Alcée Fortier, *Louisiana: Comprising Sketches of Parishes, Towns, Events, Institutions, and Persons Arranged in Cyclopedic Form* (Madison, WI: Century Historical Association, 1914), vol. I, p. 518; New Orleans *Times-Democrat*, March 23, 1892 (Randell Hunt obituary); James Renshaw, "The Hunt Family: A Sketch of Men of Great Attainment," *Louisiana Historical Quarterly* 5 (1922): 339–51.

18. *Daily Picayune*, November 11, 1893 ("electrified"); Terry L. Jones, *Lee's Tigers: The Louisiana Infantry in the Army of Northern Virginia* (Baton Rouge: Louisiana State University Press, 1987), 237; Renshaw, "The Hunt Family," 339–51. For unionism among New Orleans businessmen, see William C. Chenault and Robert Reinders, "The Northern-Born Community in New Orleans in the 1850s," *Journal of American History* 51 (September 1964): 232–47; Peyton McCrary, *Abraham Lincoln and Reconstruction: The Louisiana Experiment* (Princeton, NJ: Princeton University Press, 1978), 96–97; Ted Tunnell, *Crucible of Reconstruction: War, Radicalism, and Race in Louisiana 1862–1877* (Baton Rouge: Louisiana State University Press, 1984), 10–20, 127.

19. T. G. Hunt, Confederate, Louisiana, Adjutant General, microfilm M378, roll 14, National Park Service, *U.S. Civil War Soldiers, 1861–1865* ; T. G. Hunt, Col., Co. F, and S., 5th La Inf.. May 10, 1861, Deep Creek, VA. Rolls from Nov., 1861, to Feb., 1862, Present. Roll for July and August., 1862, Resigned July 31, 1862, 5th Louisiana Infantry, 5th Regiment, Colonel in, Colonel Out, microfilm M378, roll 14, National Park Service, *U.S. Civil War Soldiers, 1861–1865*; Jones, *Lee's Tigers*, 93, 105, 106, 108, 237 ("considerable opinion of his influence").

20. See sources cited in note 19, supra.

21. Orleans Parish, Louisiana 2nd District Court Successions, 1846–1880 (No. 40, 672) (1867), T. G. Hunt, esq., appointed attorney for Follin and heirs.

22. Sections 805 and 806 of Louisiana code reprinted in *Digest of the Statutes of the State of Louisiana in Two Volumes*, vol. I (New Orleans: Republican Printing Office, 1870), 387–88.

23. *Commercial Bulletin*, August 11, 1870 ("the offense imputed," "to weigh all," "delay and vexation"); *Constitution Adopted by the State Constitutional Convention of the State of Louisiana, March 7, 1868* (New Orleans: Republican Printing Office, 1868), Title I—Bill of Rights, Article 7 ("shall be bailable"), Article 8 ("excessive bail"); Albert Voorhies, *A Treatise on the Criminal Jurisprudence of Louisiana* (New Orleans: Bloomfield and Steel, 1860), 335–52.

24. For information on Houghton, see United States Census Office, Ninth Census (1870), Louisiana, Orleans Parish, City of New Orleans, Ward 3, p.709; Obituary, *Daily Picayune*, January 12, 1879; Civil War Record of Gardner P. Houghton, Union, Louisiana, 1st Louisiana Cavalry, Lieutenant, microfilm M387, roll 2, National Park Service, *U.S. Civil War Soldiers, 1861–1865*. Houghton was commissioned as 1st Lieutenant on October 1, 1863.

25. *Commercial Bulletin*, August 11, 1870 (quotations). For information on Dawes, see his obituary in the *Daily Picayune*, July 16, 1889; 1860 Eighth Census of the United States, New Orleans Ward 3, microfilm M653, roll 417. For value of Follin's property, see Tax Assessment Records, 6th Municipal district, 14th Assessment District, square 252, 1875, SO 1875, Board of Assessors, Real Estate Tax Assessment, Roll No. 694, CJ 436, 1873–1878, Square 252 Camp & Bellecastle, Louisiana Division, New Orleans Public Library; and the *New Orleans Republican* of August 11, 1870, which said Dawes owned four houses. For the constitutional prohibition against "excessive bail," see *Constitution Adopted by the State Constitutional Convention of the State of Louisiana* (New Orleans: Republican Printing Office, 1868), 3.

26. *New Orleans Republican*, August 12, 13, 1870; *New Orleans Times*, August 13, 1870; testimony of John Baptiste Jourdain reprinted in the *Daily Picayune*, August 23, 24, 1870; testimony of Leonard Malone reprinted in the *Daily Picayune*, August 21, 1870.

27. *Commercial Bulletin*, August 13, 1870 ("a remarkable woman"); *New Orleans Republican*, August 13, 1870 ("gaudy").

28. One famous example of this lingering respect was the ill-fated Louisiana Unification Movement of 1873, in which elite whites and leading merchants attempted to form a political alliance with Afro-Creoles like Louis Roudanez and C. C. Antoine. The movement quickly collapsed amid mutual recriminations and suspicions, but the fact that it was attempted at all speaks to the esteem some whites still had for some Afro-Creoles. See T. Harry Williams, "The Louisiana Unification Movement of 1873," *Journal of Southern History* 11 (August 1945): 349–69.

29. See John F. Kasson, *Rudeness & Civility: Manners in Nineteenth Century America* (New York: Hill & Wang, 1990), chaps 1, 2; Karen Halttunen, *Confidence Men and Painted Women: A Study of Middle-Class Culture in America, 1830–1870* (New Haven, CT: Yale University Press, 1982), 34–43, 59–79, 92–123, 153–69, 186–97. For sensationalized crimes involving seemingly respectable defendants, see Benjamin Feldman, *Butchery on Bond Street: Sexual Politics and The Burdell-Cunningham Case in Ante-bellum New York* (New York: The New York Wanderer Press, 2007); Patricia Cline Cohen, *The Murder of Helen Jewett: The Life and Death of a Prostitute in Nineteenth-Century New York* (New York: Knopf, 1991); Simon Schama, *Dead Certainties: Unwarranted Speculations* (New York: Knopf, 1992); A. Cheree Carlson, *The Crimes of Womanhood: Defining Femininity in a Court of Law* (Urbana: University of Illinois Press, 2009).

30. Kasson, *Rudeness & Civility*, 108–109 (quoting Farley); Philip Farley, *Criminals of America; or Tales of the Lives of Thieves* (New York: Philip Farley, 1876), 142–45, 206; *New Orleans Times*, August 13, 1870 ("waiting maid"); *New Orleans Republican*, August 13, 1870.

31. *New Orleans Times*, August 13, 1870; *New Orleans Republican*, August 13, 1870.

32. *New Orleans Times*, August 13, 1870 ("Contrary to"). For relationships between the Irish and African Americans in New Orleans, and the Irish and Creoles, see Eric

Arnesen, *Waterfront Workers of New Orleans: Race, Class, and Politics, 1863–1923* (Urbana: University of Illinois Press, 1994), 5–7; Patrick Brennan, "Fever and Fists: Forging an Irish Legacy in New Orleans" (PhD diss., University of Missouri-Columbia, 2003), 104–106, 124, 177; Michael Doorley, "Irish Catholics and French Creoles: Ethnic Struggles within the Catholic Church in New Orleans, 1835–1920," *Catholic Historical Review* 87 (January 2001): 34–54; David T. Gleeson, *The Irish in the South, 1815–1877* (Chapel Hill: University of North Carolina Press, 2001), 173–94; G. Howard Hunter, "The Politics of Resentment: Unionist Regiments and the New Orleans Immigrant Community, 1862–1864," *Louisiana History* 44 (Spring 2003): 187, 204–205; Laura Kelley, "Erin's Enterprise: Immigration by Appropriation: The Irish in Antebellum New Orleans" (PhD diss., Tulane University, 2004), 41–42, 101, 106–107, 110, 113–14, 122, 132–33, 146, 150–51, 222, 226; Robert C. Reinders, "The Louisiana American Party and the Catholic Church," *Mid-America*, 29 (October 1959): 222.

33. *New Orleans Republican*, August 13, 1870.

34. *New Orleans Times*, August 13, 1870 ("put to too much trouble"). For hard feelings between Rosa Gorman and Bridgette Digby, see *New Orleans Times*, July 10, 1870.

35. *New Orleans Republican*, August 13, 1870; *New Orleans Times*, August 13, 1870 ("confused," "moment of inspiration," "and directed").

36. *New Orleans Times*, August 13, 1870 ("That's the lady," "I'm pretty well"); *New Orleans Republican*, August 13, 1870 ("go into the theater," "iron nerves"); *Commercial Bulletin*, August 13, 1870 ("more assured").

37. *New Orleans Republican*, August 13, 1870.

38. *New Orleans Times*, August 13, 1870.

39. *New Orleans Republican*, August 13, 1870.

40. New Orleans *Republican*, August 10, 1870 ("indefatigable"); *Daily Picayune*, August 12, 1870 ("commendable").

41. *New Orleans Republican*, August 13, 1870; *New Orleans Times*, August 14, 1870 (quotations).

42. Louisiana State Register, August 13, 1870.

43. *New Orleans Republican*, August 13, 1870.

44. *Commercial Bulletin*, August 15, 1870.

45. *Daily Picayune*, August 12, 1870 (all quotes), *New Orleans Times*, August 13, 1870.

46. For examples of national coverage of the arrest of the Follin sisters, see *New York Times*, August 15 (quotation), 18, 1870; *Chicago Tribune*, August 16, 1870; *Cincinnati Enquirer*, August 13 (quotation), 16, 1870; *Nashville Union and American*, August 16, 1870; *Public Ledger* (Memphis), August 12, 1870; *Richmond Daily Dispatch*, August 17, 1870; *Baltimore Sun*, August 18, 1870 For coverage in the black press, see *The Cambria Freeman* (Edensburg, PA), August 18, 1870. For regional coverage, see *Mobile Register*, August 12, 14, 16, 18, 1870; *Bossier Banner* (Bellevue, LA), August 13, 1870; *Louisiana Democrat* (Alexandria, LA), August 17, 1870.

Chapter Seven: The Recorder's Court

1. *Daily Picayune*, August 20, 1870 ("fair and impartial,"), August 21, 1870 ("strength and severity"); New Orleans *Republican*, August 10, 1870 ("the great matter"). For the penalty for kidnapping, see *Revised Statutes of the State of Louisiana* (1870), Section 806: "Whoever shall take, with or without his consent, any child under the age of 14 years, or any female under the age of twelve years, from the custody of his or her parents, tutor, or guardian, without authority of law, and all persons aiding, advising, and abetting therein, on conviction, shall be imprisoned at hard labor, or otherwise, for a period not exceeding twelve years." Albert Voorhies, comp. and ed., *Revised Laws of Louisiana, Approved March 14, 1870, with copious references to the acts of the legislature from 1870 to 1882* (New Orleans: F. F. Hansell, 1884), Sections 805, 806, p. 134.

2. *Commercial Bulletin*, June 22, 1870.

3. For allegations of bias, seethe New Orleans *Republican*'s criticism of Luzenberg and Conservative 1st District Court Judge Edmund Abell, a Conservative, for letting violent white suspects go free. *New Orleans Republican*, May 12, 1870. For the loyalty provisions of the 1868 state constitution and its provisions creating the parish district attorneys' offices, see Articles 92 and 99 of *Constitution Adopted by the State Constitutional Convention of the State of Louisiana, March 7, 1868* (New Orleans: Republican Printing Office, 1868), 13–15.

4. *New Orleans Times*, August 11, 1870.

5. Tom Smith, *The Crescent City Lynchings: The Murder of Chief Hennessy, the New Orleans "Mafia" Trials, and the Parish Prison Mob* (New York: Lyons Press, 2007), 68, 122; William Howard Russell, *My Diary North and South* (London: Bradbury and Evans, 1863), chapter 31 ("dreadful," "sickness and loathing"); Gary A. Van Zante, *New Orleans 1867* (New York: Merrell, 2008), 109–10 ("disgrace to civilization").

6. *New Orleans Times*, August 14, 1870; *New Orleans Republican*, August 14, 25, 1870; Judith Kelleher Schafer, *Becoming Free, Remaining Free: Manumission and Enslavement in New Orleans, 1846–1862* (Baton Rouge: Louisiana State University Press, 2003), 116. For heat and related deaths in August 1870, see *Commercial Bulletin*, August 20, 1870, which reported that "several sudden deaths have occurred in the city during the last week or ten days, owing... chiefly to the oppressive heat."

7. Although Afro-Creoles like the Follins fared better in antebellum Louisiana courts than slaves, state laws and state courts helped preserve the South's rigid racial hierarchy. In the 1850s, the Louisiana Supreme Court ruled that members of the "African race are strangers to our Constitution, and are subjects of special and exceptional legislation." Even the richest free black person could be arrested for the crime of "insulting a white person" or hauled into court by any policemen or white citizen and forced to prove his or her freedom. See Judith Kelleher Schafer, *Slavery, the Civil Law, and the Supreme Court of Louisiana* (Baton Rouge: Louisiana State University Press, 1994), 6 n. 9, 20–21, 64, 85; Schafer, *Becoming Free, Remaining Free*, 97–114, 146; *Bore v. Bush*, 6 Mart. 1 (La. 1827). For

discussions of justice for black defendants in antebellum courts in other parts of the South, see Ariela Gross, "The Law and the Culture of Slavery: Natchez, Mississippi," and Timothy Huebner, "The Roots of Fairness: State v. Caeser and Slave Justice in Antebellum North Carolina," in *Local Matters: Race, Crime, and Justice in the Nineteenth-Century South*, eds. Donald Nieman and Christopher Waldrep (Athens: University of Georgia Press, 2011), 29–52, 92–124; Martha Hodes, *White Women, Black Men: Illicit Sex in the Nineteenth Century South* (New Haven, CT: Yale University Press, 1997); Diane Miller Somerville, *Rape and Race in the Nineteenth-Century South* (Chapel Hill: University of North Carolina Press, 2004); Kimberly Welch, "People at Law: Subordinate Southerners, Popular Governance, and Local Legal Culture in Antebellum Mississippi and Louisiana," (PhD diss., University of Maryland, 2012).

8. Dan Carter, *When the War Was Over: The Failure of Self-Reconstruction in the South, 1865–1867* (Baton Rouge: Louisiana State University Press, 1986), 148–50, 177, 217–27; Eric Foner, *Reconstruction: America's Unfinished Revolution* (New York: Harper & Row, 1988), 199–202; Eric Foner, *Nothing But Freedom: Emancipation and Its Legacy* (Baton Rouge: Louisiana State University Press, 2007); Donald Nieman, *To Set the Law in Motion: The Freedmen's Bureau and the Legal Rights of Blacks, 1865–1868* (New York: KTO Press, 1979); Harold Hyman and William Wiecek, *Equal Justice Under Law: Constitutional Developments, 1835–1875* (New York: Harper Collins, 1982), 319–25; Howard N. Rabinowitz, "The Conflict Between Blacks and the Police in the Urban South, 1865–1900," *Historian* 39 (November 1976): 63–64; George C. Rable, *But There Was No Peace: The Role of Violence in the Politics of Reconstruction* (Athens: University of Georgia Press, 1984), 21–28; Ted Tunnell, *Crucible of Reconstruction: War, Radicalism, and Race in Louisiana 1862–1877* (Baton Rouge: Louisiana State University Press, 1984), 96, 101, 117; Joe Gray Taylor, *Louisiana Reconstructed 1863–1877* (Baton Rouge: Louisiana State University Press, 1974), 99–103, 106, 11; Christopher Waldrep, "Substituting the Law for the Lash: Emancipation and Legal Formalism in a Mississippi County Court," *Journal of American History* 82 (March 1996): 1425–51; Theodore Brantner Wilson, *The Black Codes of the South* (Tuscaloosa: University of Alabama Press, 1965), 77–80.

9. *Daily Picayune*, August 20, 1870.

10. *New Orleans Republican*, April 7, 1870 (Recorder's Court judges appointed by city council), May 7, 1870 (large proportion of prisoners sent to workhouse); Albert Voorhies, *A Treatise on the Criminal Jurisprudence of Louisiana* (New Orleans: Bloomfield and Steel, 1860), 328–29 ("probable cause," "wholly groundless"); *Digest of the State of Louisiana in Two Volumes*, vol. 1 (New Orleans: Republican Office, 1870), 459–63; *Digest of the Statutes of the State of Louisiana*, vol. 2 (New Orleans: Republican Office, 1870), 105–6; Judith Kelleher Schafer, "Slaves and Crime: New Orleans, 1846–1862," in *Local Matters*, 53–91; *New Orleans Bee*, June 30, 1870; *New Orleans Times*, August 27, 1870 ("probable cause"). For Houghton's military service at 1st Lieutenant in 1st Louisiana Cavalry (U.S.A), see Carded records Showing Military Service of Soldiers Who Fought in Volunteer Organizations During the American Civil War, compiled 1890–1912,

documenting the period 1861–1866, Records of the Adjutant General's Office, record group 94, microfilm rolls 5 and 47, NARA.

11. *New Orleans Republican*, July 6, 1870 ("worse than"), *New Orleans Times*, August 19 ("densely crowded"), 20, 1870.

12. *New Orleans Times*, August 19 ("mixed crowd"), 20, 1870; *Daily Picayune*, August 21, 1870, *New Orleans Republican*, August 21, 1870 ("The crowd of loafers").

13. Joel Prentiss Bishop, *Commentaries on the Law of Criminal Procedure*, vol. 1, 2 nd ed. (Boston: Little, Brown and Company, 1872), 588–89.

14. *Daily Picayune*, August 21, 1870 ; *New Orleans Times*, August 21, 1870 (description of Follin's attire). A third lawyer, Thomas S. McKay, also participated in the defense. McKay had served as a district attorney before the war and was an active member of the Democratic Party. Because he played only a limited role in the Digby trial, he is not introduced formally in this account. For articles and references to McKay's legal career, see *Daily True Delta*, May 13, 1858 (fights duel against another lawyer), *Daily Picayune* July 6, 1865 (advertisement announcing return to practice after war), October 25, 1866 (prosecution on behalf of the state), August 4, 1867 (role in "the Royal Street Homicide" case), January 19, 1870 (representing the City of Jefferson), November 4, 1870 (marching in torch-lit Democratic party parade).

15. *Daily Picayune*, August 21, 1870.

16. *Daily Picayune*, August 21, 1870 ("strikingly alike," "Both are tall," "nerve and address"); *New Orleans Times*, August 21, 1870 ("dark spotted," "a dress of," "Handsome quadroon," "small features").

17. *Daily Picayune*, August 21, 1870 ("A thrill").

18. For newspaper accounts of Atocha's rulings as provost judge, see *Daily Picayune*, September 24, 1863, October 1, 7, 10, 11, 1863, January 13, 1864, February 13, 1864; *New Orleans Times*, October 4, 5, 8, 14, 1863. See also Thomas H. Helis, "Of Generals and Jurists: The Judicial System of New Orleans under Union Occupation, May 1862–April 1865," *Louisiana History* 29 (Spring 1988): 143–62; Dennis Rousey, *Policing the Southern City: New Orleans, 1805–1889* (Baton Rouge: Louisiana State University Press, 1997), 112–13; Peyton McCrary, *Abraham Lincoln and Reconstruction: The Louisiana Experiment* (Princeton, NJ: Princeton University Press, 1978), 4, 6–8, 14, 126, 185–93, 208, 234, 242, 348; John C. Rodrigue, *Lincoln and Reconstruction* (Carbondale: Southern Illinois University Press, 2013), 51–53, 66–74.

19. *Harper's Weekly*, July 9, 1864; *The Era*, February 14, 1864; *Daily True Delta*, February 14, 1864, August 30, 1864; *Daily Picayune*, August 21, 1870; *New Orleans Republican*, September 9, 1870 (Crescent City Republican Club); *Daily Memphis Avalanche*, December 11, 1866 (duel).

20. *Daily Picayune*, August 4, 1869, August 21, 1870, September 10, 1870, October 18, 1870. For a description of Bright's Disease, see Wikipedia: http://www.fact-index.com/b/br/bright_s_disease.html.

21. *New Orleans Republican*, March 21, 23, 24, 1870, April 10, 1873; Rousey, *Policing the Southern City*, 112–13; Rosemarie Davis Plasses, "Tools of the Profession: New Orleans Attorneys and Their Law Libraries from Statehood to Secession (1813–1861)," (MA thesis, University of New Orleans, 1996).

22. *New Orleans Times*, August 19, 1870. For Hughes's war record, see Andrew Booth, *Records of Louisiana Confederate Soldiers and Confederate Commands*. volume 1–3. New Orleans: LA, n.p., 1920); Sergeant, 22nd Louisiana Infantry, microfilm 378, Roll 14, National Park Service, U.S. Civil War Soldiers, 1861–1865, 2ndLieutenant, Miles' Legion, Louisiana; *New York Times*, June 13, 14, 1863 (accounts of the prisoner rebellion on the *Maple Leaf*).

23. Simon Wolf, *The American Jew as Patriot, Soldier, and Citizen* (New York: Brentano's, 1895), 190–94; *Daily Picayune*, December 9, 1849 (Leopold Dalsheimer runs ad for runaway slave); Elliot Ashkenazi, ed, *The Civil War Diary of Clara Solomon: Growing Up in New Orleans 1861–62* (Baton Rouge: Louisiana State University Press, 1995), 43–440; Eli Evans, *Judah P. Benjamin: The Jewish Confederate* (New York: Free Press, 1989); Robert Douthat Meade, *Judah P. Benjamin: Confederate Statesmen* (Baton Rouge: Louisiana State University Press, 2001).

24. Alexander Dalsheimer Obituary, *Daily Picayune*, October 22, 1878; Obituary, *New Orleans Times*, October 23, 1878; Ashkenazi, ed., *Civil War Diary of Clara Solomon*, 43–440. For Dalsheimer's military record, see Andrew B. Booth, *Records of Louisiana Confederate Soldiers & Confederate Commands. Vol. I–III*. New Orleans, LA: n.p., 1920. Also National Park Service, U.S. Civil War Soldiers, 1861–1865 http://www.civilwar.nps.gov/cwss/soldiers.cfm, microfilm number: M378, Roll 7 (last name is misspelled in records as Dalshamer). Dalsheimer was first a private in the 3rd Louisiana Infantry; he was then taken prisoner in on October 4, 1862 at the Battle of Corinth. He was paroled on October 13, 1862, and then captured and paroled once more after the confederate surrender at Vicksburg, July 4, 1863. For Alice Dalsheimer's career as poet and essayist, see James Wilson, ed., *Appleton's Cyclopaedia of American Biography* (New York: Appleton, 1898), vol.2, p. 60. The New Orleans city directory for 1871 listed Dalsheimer as an "Attorney for the Metropolitan Police." *Edward's Annual Directory to the Inhabitants, Institutions, Incorporated Companies, Manufacturing Establishments, Business, Business Firms, Etc, Etc. in the City of New Orleans* (New Orleans: Southern Publishing Company, 1871). For Dalsheimer's defense of a black policeman accused of rape, see *New Orleans Times*, June 10, 17, 1870.

25. Houghton and the lawyers also agreed to try all three defendants at once rather than separately, "as it would save time." *New Orleans Republican*, August 21, 1870 (quotation); *New Orleans Times*, August 21, 1870. For the right of the defense to call witnesses in a preliminary hearing, see Albert Voorhies, *A Treatise on the Criminal Jurisprudence of Louisiana*, volume 2 (New Orleans: Bloomfield & Steel, 1860), 327–29.

26. See the sources cited in note 25, supra.

27. *New Orleans Republican*, August 21, 1870 (quotations), *New Orleans Times*, August 21, 1870.

28. *New Orleans Republican,* August 21, 1870; *New Orleans Times,* August 21, 1870; *New Orleans Bee,* August 21, 1970 ("prevent collusion"). Prosecuting George Blass as an accomplice presented difficulties because as under the common law, children could not be convicted as accomplices to crimes committed by their parents. Hughes might have been able to argue that at age seventeen, George was no longer a child, was capable of making his own decisions, and therefore fell outside the common-law rule. *New Orleans Times,* August 21, 1870. For application of common law rule on accomplices in criminal cases in Louisiana, see Edward Livingston, *The Complete Works of Edward Livingston on Criminal Jurisprudence consisting of Systems of Penal Law for the State of Louisiana, vol. 2* (New York: National Prison Association, 1873), chapter 5, articles 59, 65, 68, 71.

29. *New Orleans Times,* August 21, 1870 (includes weather); testimony by Algernon Badger, *The State of Louisiana v. Louisa Murray alias Follin,* First District Recorders Court, Case no. 49, August 20 (Badger testimony), 22, 23, 24, 1870, New Orleans City Archives, Louisiana Division, New Orleans Public Library.

30. *New Orleans Republican,* August 21, 1870 ("dissipated in appearance"); *New Orleans Times,* August 21, 1870; *Daily Picayune,* August 21, 1870; *New Orleans Bee,* August 21, 1970.

31. See sources cited in note 30, supra.

32. *Daily Picayune,* August 21, 1870 ("breathless silence"); *New Orleans Times,* August 21, 1870 ("disdainfully"); *New Orleans Bee,* August 21, 1970.

33. Testimony by Badger, in *The State of Louisiana v. Louisa Murray alias Follin,* August 20 ("crumpled up"), 1870; *New Orleans Republican,* August 21, 1870 ("when he learned"); *New Orleans Times,* August 21, 1870 ("pertained to nothing"); *Daily Picayune,* August 21, 1870 ("took something"); *New Orleans Bee,* August 21, 1970 ("muttered").

34. *New Orleans Times,* August 21, 1870 ("considerable agitation"); *Daily Picayune,* August 21, 1870 ("entirely voluntarily made").

35. *New Orleans Times,* August 21, 1870 (quotations); *Daily Picayune,* August 21, 1870; *New Orleans Bee,* August 21, 1970. See also Thomas Digby's Testimony, *The State of Louisiana v. Louisa Murray alias Follin,* August 20, 1870.

36. *Daily Picayune,* August 21, 1870; *New Orleans Times,* August 21, 1871 ("he thought," "thankful to him").

37. *Daily Picayune,* August 21, 1870 ("I recognized"); *New Orleans Times,* August 21, 1871 (all other quotations); *New Orleans Republican,* August 21, 1870; *New Orleans Bee,* August 21, 1970.

38. *Daily Picayune,* August 21, 1870 ("Did you not"); *New Orleans Times,* August 21, 1871 ("Do not answer," "The question is," "I will not press"); *New Orleans Republican,* August 21, 1870 ("Digby is only a witness," "vox populi"); *New Orleans Bee,* August 21, 1970 ("second visit to Captain Broadwell's").

39. *Daily Picayune,* August 21, 1870 ("covered in boils"); *New Orleans Times,* August 21, 1871; *New Orleans Republican,* August 21, 1870.

40. *Daily Picayune,* August 21, 1870 ("call it familiarly"); *New Orleans Times,* August 21, 1870 ("greatly excited," "nothing to do," "more than you think").

41. *Daily Picayune*, August 21, 1870 ("Do you ever," "Did you ever," "character is"); *New Orleans Times*, August 21, 1870 ("cannot be attacked").

42. Albert Voorhies, *A Treatise on the Criminal Jurisprudence of Louisiana*, vol. 2 (New Orleans: Bloomfield and Steel, 1860), 614; *New Orleans Times*, August 21, 1870 (quotation).

43. *Commercial Bulletin*, July 11, 1870 (quotations).

44. *New Orleans Times*, August 22, 1870 ("when asked the grounds"), *Commercial Bulletin*, August 18, 1870 ("to receive all rewards").

45. *New Orleans Times*, August 21, 1870 ("If we do not work faster"); *Daily Picayune*, August 21, 1870.

46. *New Orleans Republican*, August 21, 1870 ("pressure of public opinion"); Albert Voorhies, *A Treatise on the Criminal Jurisprudence of Louisiana, vol. 2* (New Orleans: Bloomfield & Steel, 1860), 356 ("at any time before"). For discussions of "scalawags" and their role in Reconstruction, see James Alex Baggett, *The Scalawags: Southern Dissenters in the Civil War and Reconstruction* (Baton Rouge: Louisiana State University Press, 2004); Foner, *Reconstruction*, 294–99, 322, 439; William Piston, *Lee's Tarnished Lieutenant: James Longstreet and His Place in Southern History* (Athens: University of Georgia Press, 1990), 104–17; Tunnell, *Crucible of Reconstruction*, 136–50; Jeffrey Wert, *General James Longstreet: The Confederacy's Most Controversial Soldier* (New York: Simon & Schuster, 1994), 413.

47. *New Orleans Republican*, August 21, 1870 (quotations); *New Orleans Times*, August 21, 1870; *New Orleans Bee*, August 21, 1870; *Daily Picayune*, August 21, 1870.

48. *New Orleans Picayune*, July 27, 1865 (Green's minimal literacy and coffee stand); *New Orleans Times*, August 21, 1870; *New Orleans Republican*, August 21, 1870; *Edward's Annual Directory to the Inhabitants, Institutions, Incorporated Companies, Manufacturing Establishments, Business, Business Firms, Etc., Etc. in the City of New Orleans* (New Orleans: Southern Publishing Company, 1871).

49. *Daily Picayune*, August 21, 1870 (quotations).

Chapter Eight: A Highly Unusual Proceeding

1. *Daily Picayune*, August 23 ("As to their guilt or innocence"), 24 ("It is talked of," "Each person"), 25 ("it is not surprising"), 1870.

2. *Daily Picayune*, August 23, 1870 (quotation).

3. *Daily Picayune*, August 23, 1870 ("whisperings"); *New Orleans Times*, August 23, 1870 ("far up town," "in court shortly").

4. *Daily Picayune*, August 23, 1870 (quotation).

5. Jourdain was the second witness to take the stand that day. The first, J. J. Pierson, the black detective who had accompanied Jourdain to Follin's house on August 7, offered an account of those events that differed little from what had been reported in the newspapers. See *New Orleans Republican*, August 24, 1870.

6. *Daily Picayune*, August 23, 1870 ("I asked Mrs. Follin," "he told me," "she replied"); *New Orleans Bee*, August 23, 1870 ("she denied it"); *New Orleans Times*, August 23, 1870 ("damn little rascal"); *Commercial Bulletin*, August 23, 1870.

7. *Daily Picayune*, August 23, 1870; *New Orleans Bee*, August 23, 1870; *New Orleans Times*, August 23, 1870 ("books of the boat"); *Commercial Bulletin*, August 23, 1870.

8. *Daily Picayune*, August 23, 1870 (quotations); *New Orleans Bee*, August 23, 1870; *New Orleans Times*, August 23, 1870.

9. *Daily Picayune*, August 23, 1870 (quotations); *New Orleans Bee*, August 23, 1870; *New Orleans Times*, August 23, 1870.

10. *Daily Picayune*, August 23, 1870 (quotations); *New Orleans Bee*, August 23, 1870; *New Orleans Times*, August 23, 1870.

11. *New Orleans Times*, August 23, 1870 (quotations); *Daily Picayune*, August 23, 1870; *New Orleans Bee*, August 23, 1870.

12. *Daily Picayune*, August 23, 1870 (quotations); *New Orleans Bee*, August 23, 1870; *New Orleans Times*, August 23, 1870. For the defunct rule regarding a lawyer discrediting his own witness, see Edward Livingston, *A System of Penal Law for the State of Louisiana* (Philadelphia: James Kay, Jun, & Brother, 1833), 651.

13. *Daily Picayune*, August 23, 1870 (quotations); *New Orleans Bee*, August 23, 1870; *New Orleans Times*, August 23, 1870.

14. *Daily Picayune*, August 23, 1870 (quotations); *New Orleans Bee*, August 23, 1870; *New Orleans Times*, August 23, 1870.

15. *Daily Picayune*, August 23, 1870 (quotations); *New Orleans Bee*, August 23, 1870; *New Orleans Times*, August 23, 1870.

16. *New Orleans Times*, August 23, 1870 ("not afraid," "doing the right thing"); *Daily Picayune*, August 23, 1870 (all other quotations), *New Orleans Bee*, August 23, 1870.

17. For information on the life of Angelo Blass, see his obituary, *Daily Picayune*, March 21, 1867; New Orleans, Louisiana, Death Records Index, 1804–1949, vol. 40, p. 38 (where Blass is identified as "white"); 1860 United States Federal Census, Orleans Parish, Louisiana, Ward 10, Microfilm M653_416, p. 0, (where Blass is identified as "mulatto"); Second District Court Successions, Orleans Parish, Louisiana 1846–1880 (No. 40, 672), Louisiana Division, New Orleans Public Library; *New Orleans Times*, August 23, 1870. For the Reconstruction-era law legitimizing pre-1868 interracial marriages, see *Digest of the Statutes of the State of Louisiana*, vol. 2 (New Orleans: Republican Office, 1870), 148–49. On laws prohibiting interracial marriage in the South, see Peggy Pascoe, *What Comes Naturally: Miscegenation Law and the Making of Race in America* (New York: Oxford University Press, 2010), 1–130; Charles F. Robinson II, *Dangerous Liaisons: Sex and Love in the Segregated South* (Fayetteville: University of Arkansas Press, 2003), 29, 30, 129; Peter Wallenstein, *Tell the Court I Love My Wife: Race, Marriage, and Law—An American History* (New York: Palgrave Macmillan, 2002), 1–122; Joel Williamson, *New People: Miscegenation and Mulattoes in the United States* (New York: Free Press, 1980). Broadwell quoted in *The State of Louisiana v. Louisa Murray alias Follin*, First District Recorders Court, Docket no. 49, August 20, 22, 23, 24, 1870, New Orleans City Archives, Louisiana Division, New Orleans Public Library, 14–16.

18. *New Orleans Times*, August 21, 1870. For antebellum relationships between free women of color and white men on the Gulf Coast, see Lois Virginia Meacham Gould, "'In Full Enjoyment of Their Liberty': The Free Women of Color of the Gulf Ports of New Orleans, Mobile, and Pensacola, 1769–1860" (PhD diss., Emory University, 1991), 140 (Dunn quotation), 189–90, 209–11, 218, 329–35, 339 ("exploitative"); Martha Ward, *Voodoo Queen: The Spirited Lives of Marie Laveau* (Oxford: University of Mississippi Press, 2004), xv, 44.

19. Robinson, *Dangerous Liaisons*, 29, 30, 129; New Orleans, Louisiana, Death Records Index, 1804–1949, vol. 40, p. 38.

20. *New Orleans Times*, August 23, 1870 ("I wish the defense"); *Daily Picayune*, August 23, 1870 (all other quotations); *New Orleans Bee*, August 23, 1870, *Commercial Bulletin*, August 25, 1870.

21. *New Orleans Times*, August 23, 1870 ("stock and trade," "settle outside"); *New Orleans Bee*, August 23, 1870; *Commercial Bulletin*, August 25, 1870 ("well-behaved industrious woman"); *Daily Picayune*, August 23, 1870 (all other quotations).

22. *New Orleans Bee*, August 23, 1870 ("expects to force"); *New Orleans Times*, August 23, 1870 ("I am not the king"); *Daily Picayune*, August 23, 1870 (all other quotations).

23. *New Orleans Times*, August 23, 1870 ("always decent"); *New Orleans Bee*, August 23, 1870; *Daily Picayune*, August 23, 1870 (all other quotations).

24. *Daily Picayune*, August 23, 1870.

25. *New Orleans Times*, August 23, 1870 ("was not signed"); *Daily Picayune*, August 23, 1870 (all other quotations); *New Orleans Bee*, August 23, 1870.

26. *Daily Picayune*, August 23, 1870 (all quotations); *New Orleans Times*, August 23, 1870; *New Orleans Bee*, August 23, 1870.

27. *Daily Picayune*, August 23, 1870 (all quotations); *New Orleans Times*, August 23, 1870; *New Orleans Bee*, August 23, 1870.

28. *New Orleans Times*, August 23, 1870, ("he could have gone out"); *Daily Picayune*, August 23, 1870 (all other quotations); *New Orleans Bee*, August 23, 1870.

29. *New Orleans Times*, August 23, 1870.

30. *New Orleans Times*, August 23, 1870; entry for residence of Louisa Follin, Mobile Alabama, Ward 7, Ninth Census of the United States, 1870, record group 29, microfilm M593, National Archives and Records Administration, Washington DC. For perjury penalties, see *Digest of the Statutes of the State of Louisiana in Two Volumes*, vol. 1 (New Orleans: Republican Printing Office, 1870), 400.

31. *New Orleans Times*, August 23, 1870.

32. *New Orleans Times*, August 23, 1870.

33. *New Orleans Times*, August 23, 1870.

34. *Daily Picayune*, August 24, 1870.

35. *Daily Picayune*, August 24, 1870; *New Orleans Republican*, August 24, 1870.

36. *Daily Picayune*, August 24, 1870 (quotations); *New Orleans Times*, August 24, 1870; *New Orleans Bee*, August 24, 1870.

37. *Daily Picayune*, August 24, 1870; *New Orleans Times*, August 24, 1870 ("if they do not present," "covered with mud," "no objection").

38. *Daily Picayune*, August 24, 1870 ("I am aware an offense"); *New Orleans Times*, August 24, 1870 ("He talked to them," "They were compelled," "This is only one," "I will simply remind").

39. *New Orleans Times*, August 13, 1870 ("put to too much trouble"). For the punishment for failing to comply with a subpoena, see *Digest of the Statutes of the State of Louisiana*, vol. I p. 414.

40. *Daily Picayune*, August 24, 1870.

41. *Daily Picayune*, August 24, 1870 (quotations); *New Orleans Times*, August 24, 1970.

42. *Daily Picayune*, August 24, 1870 ("on the banquette," "I cannot say"); *New Orleans Times*, August 24, 1870.

43. *Daily Picayune*, August 24, 1870 (all quotations); *New Orleans Times*, August 24, 1870.

44. *New Orleans Times*, August 24, 1870 ("She was dressed,"); *Daily Picayune*, August 24, 1870 (all other quotations).

45. *Commercial Bulletin*, August 13, 1870 ("more assured"); *Daily Picayune*, August 24, 1870 (all other quotations), *New Orleans Times*, August 24, 1870; *Mobile Register*, August 26, 1870.

46. *Daily Picayune*, August 24, 1870 (quotations), *New Orleans Times*, August 24, 1870.

47. *New Orleans Times*, August 13, 1870.

48. *New Orleans Republican*, August 13, 1870 (all quotations). See also testimony of August Singler, August 23, 1870, *The State of Louisiana v. Louisa Murray alias Follin*.

49. *Daily Picayune*, August 24, 1870.

50. *Daily Picayune*, August 24, 1870.

51. Livingston, *System of Penal Law*, p. 648.

52. *Daily Picayune*, August 24, 1870 (quotations); *New Orleans Times*, August 24, 1870; *New Orleans Bee*, August 24, 1870; *New Orleans Republican*, August 24, 1870.

53. Testimony of Georgie Digby, August 23, 1870, *The State of Louisiana v. Louisa Murray alias Follin*, ("yellow woman"); *Daily Picayune*, August 24, 1870 (all other quotations); *New Orleans Times*, August 24, 1870; *New Orleans Bee*, August 24, 1870; *New Orleans Republican*, August 24, 1870.

54. *New Orleans Times*, August 24, 1870 ("recollect as well as you can"); *Daily Picayune*, August 24, 1870 (all other quotations); *New Orleans Bee*, August 24, 1870; *New Orleans Republican*, August 24, 1870. For the punishment for perjury being "no less than five years," see Section 857 of the Louisiana Code reprinted in *Digest of the Statutes of the State of Louisiana in Two Volumes*, Vol. I (New Orleans: Republican Printing Office, 1870), p. 400; Livingston, *A System of Penal Law*, p. 393.

55. *New Orleans Times*, August 24, 1870.

56. *New Orleans Times*, August 24, 1870 (weather); *Daily Picayune*, August 21, 1870 (quotation).

57. *Daily Picayune*, August 25, 1870 (quotations); *New Orleans Times*, August 25, 1870; *New Orleans Bee*, August 25, 1870.

58. *Daily Picayune*, August 25, 1870 ("wrangling"); *New Orleans Times*, August 25, 1870; *New Orleans Bee*, August 25, 1870; *Commercial Bulletin*, August 25, 1870; *New Orleans Republican*, August 25, 1870.

59. *Daily Picayune*, August 25, 1870 ("woman had not come back to reclaim it"); testimony of Minnie Green, August 24, 1870, *The State of Louisiana v. Louisa Murray alias Follin*, ("retired and quiet"); *New Orleans Bee*, August 25, 1870 ("They did not ask"); *New Orleans Times*, August 25, 1870 (all other testimony); *Commercial Bulletin*, August 25, 1870; *New Orleans Republican*, August 25, 1870, *Mobile Register*, August 25, 1870.

60. *Daily Picayune*, August 25, 1870; *New Orleans Times*, August 25, 1870 (testimony); *New Orleans Bee*, August 25, 1870; *Commercial Bulletin*, August 25, 1870; *New Orleans Republican*, August 25, 1870.

61. *Daily Picayune*, August 25, 1870; *New Orleans Times*, August 25, 1870 (quotation); *New Orleans Bee*, August 25, 1870; *Commercial Bulletin*, August 25, 1870; *New Orleans Republican*, August 25, 1870.

62. *Daily Picayune*, August 25, 1870 (quotations); *New Orleans Times*, August 25, 1870; *New Orleans Bee*, August 25, 1870; *Commercial Bulletin*, August 25, 1870; *New Orleans Republican*, August 25, 1870. For the right of a witness to refuse to testify, see Livingston, *A System of Penal Law*, 651.

63. *Daily Picayune*, August 25, 1870 (quotations); *New Orleans Times*, August 25, 1870; *New Orleans Bee*, August 25, 1870; *Commercial Bulletin*, August 25, 1870; *New Orleans Republican*, August 25, 1870.

64. Livingston, *System of Penal Law*, p. 216.

65. *Mobile Register*, August 27, 1870 (Houghton's pronouncements); *Daily Picayune*, August 25, 1870; *New Orleans Times*, August 25, 1870 ("bravo"); *New Orleans Bee*, August 25, 1870; *Commercial Bulletin*, August 25, 1870; *New Orleans Republican*, August 25, 1870.

66. *Daily Picayune*, August 26, 1870 (quotations); *New Orleans Times*, August 25, 1870; *New Orleans Bee*, August 25, 1870; *Commercial Bulletin*, August 25, 1870; *New Orleans Republican*, August 25, 1870.

67. *New Orleans Times*, August 27, 1870; *Commercial Bulletin*, August 23 (quotation), 25, 1870; *New Orleans Republican*, August 25, 1870.

68. *Daily Picayune*, August 25, 1870 ("what inducements were offered?"); *New Orleans Times*, August 25, 1870 ("woeful lack," "*outré* in the extreme," "regular process of law," "seaside hat,"); *New Orleans Bee*, August 25, 1870; *Commercial Bulletin*, August 25, 1870.

69. *Daily Picayune*, August 25, 1870; *New Orleans Times*, August 25, 1870 (quotations); *New Orleans Bee*, August 25, 1870; *Commercial Bulletin*, August 25, 1870.

70. *New Orleans Republican*, August 25, 1870 (quotation); *New Orleans Times*, August 25, 1870.

Chapter Nine: Unveiling the Mystery

1. On yellow fever in New Orleans and the nineteenth-century South, see Margaret Humphreys, *Yellow Fever and the South* (New Brunswick, NJ: Rutgers University Press,

1992), 1–11 ("strangers disease"); Jo Ann Carrigan, *The Saffron Scourge: A History of Yellow Fever in Louisiana, 1796–1905* (Lafayette: Center for Louisiana Studies, 1994), 1–49, 103; John Duffy, *The Sword of Pestilence: The New Orleans Yellow Fever Epidemic of 1853* (Baton Rouge: Louisiana State University Press, 1966); Patrick Brennan, "Fever and Fists: Forging an Irish Legacy in New Orleans" (PhD diss., University of Missouri-Columbia, 2003), 133–65.

2. *Daily Picayune*, August 31, 1870 ("unnecessary alarm"), October 28, 1870; *Carrollton Times*, July 9, 1870 ("three persons"), September 24, 1870 ("the season of business,"); *New Orleans Bee*, September 9, 1870; *Commercial Bulletin*, September 9, 15, 1870, November 24, 1870; Humphreys, *Yellow Fever and the South*, 3, 9; Carrigan, *Saffron Scourge*, 103; Letter from businessman L.A. Thompson to Henry J. Leavy, October 3, 1870, Henry J. Leavy Papers, MSS 487, folder 13, Historic New Orleans Collection.

3. *New Orleans Republican*, June 14, 1870 ("ghost on the highway"), September 20, 1870 ("noxious exhalations"); *Daily Picayune*, October 8, 1870 (list of nostrums), October 25, 1870 ("putrescence"). For physicians' understanding of the disease, see Humphreys, *Yellow Fever and the South*, 18–19; Carrigan, *Saffron Scourge*, 103 ("evil reputation"), 207–8; Brennan, "Fever and Fists," 155–56. For reports of dozens dying every day, see *Republican*, September 22, 30, 1870; *Commercial Bulletin*, September 27, 1870, October 1, 4, 6, 8, 10, 11, 13, 15, 1870.

4. New Orleans *Times*, September 20 (black crepe, hearses), October 14, 1870 ("winds heavy with disease").

5. Joel Prentiss Bishop, *Commentaries on the Law of Criminal Procedure*, vol. 1, 2nd ed. (Boston: Little, Brown and Company, 1872), 527–28; Edward Livingston, *A System of Penal Law for the State of Louisiana* (Philadelphia: James Kay, Jun., & Brother, 1833), 514–15; Albert Voorhies, *A Treatise on the Criminal Jurisprudence of Louisiana* (New Orleans: Bloomfield and Steel, 1860), 378–79, 394, 438; *Digest of the Statutes of the State of Louisiana in Two Volumes*, vol. 1 (New Orleans: Republican Printing Office, 1870), 313.

6. To this day Louisiana law includes concepts such as "forced heirship," "usufruct," and "lesion beyond moiety" that are foreign to the common law. See Mark F. Fernandez, *From Chaos to Continuity: The Evolution of Louisiana's Judicial System, 1712–1862* (Baton Rouge: Louisiana State University Press, 2011), 16–39; Lawrence M. Friedman, *A History of American Law* (New York: Simon & Schuster, 1973), 151–56; George Dargo, *Jefferson's Louisiana: Politics and the Clash of Legal Traditions* (Cambridge, MA: Harvard University Press, 1975), 25–28, 47–50, 173; Judith Kelleher Schafer, *Slavery, the Civil Law, and the Supreme Court of Louisiana* (Baton Rouge: Louisiana State University Press, 1994), 16–19; Richard Holcomb Kilbourne, Jr., *A History of the Louisiana Civil Code: The Formative Years, 1803–1839* (Baton Rouge: Louisiana State University Press, 1987); Edward Haas, "Louisiana's Legal Heritage: An Introduction," in Edward Haas, ed., *Louisiana's Legal Heritage* (Pensacola, FL: Perdido Bay Press, 1983), 1–3; Warren Billings, "A Course of Legal Studies: Books That Shaped Louisiana Law," in Warren Billings and Mark Fernandez, eds., *A Law Unto Itself?:*

Essays in the New Louisiana Legal History (Baton Rouge: Louisiana State University Press, 2001), 25–39; Mark Fernandez, "Local Justice in the Territory of Orleans: W. C. C. Claiborne's Courts, Judges, and Justices of the Peace," in Billings and Fernandez, eds., *A Law Unto Itself?*, 79–98.

7. Warren M. Billings, "Origins of Criminal Law in Louisiana," *Louisiana History* 32 (Winter 1991): 63–76; Fernandez, "Local Justice in the Territory of Orleans," 90–92; *Acts Passed at the First Session of the Legislative Council of the Territory of Orleans* (New Orleans: James Bradford 1805), 416–64; *Acts Passed by the Legislature of the State of Louisiana* (New Orleans 1855), 130–50; Joel Prentiss Bishop, *Commentaries on the Law of Criminal Procedure*, 516; *Digest of the Statutes of the State of Louisiana in Two Volumes*, vol. 1 (New Orleans: Republican Office, 1870), 455. Sections 18 and 19 of the Louisiana State Constitution of 1812 read as follows: "Sect. 18th. In all criminal prosecutions, the accused have the right of being heard by himself or counsel, of demanding the nature and cause of the accusation against him, of meeting the witnesses face to face, of having compulsory process for obtaining witnesses in his favour, and prosecutions by indictment or information, a speedy public trial by an impartial jury of the vicinage, nor shall he be compelled to give evidence against himself," "Sect. 19th. All prisoners shall be bailable by sufficient securities, unless for capital offences, where the proof is evident or presumption great, and the privilege of the writ of Habeas Corpus shall not be suspended unless when in cases of rebellion or invasion the public safety may require it."

8. Livingston, *A System of Penal Law* 514–15, 525; Voorhies, *Treatise on the Criminal Jurisprudence of Louisiana*, 378–79, 394, 422, 438, 424–25; *Digest of the Statutes of the State of Louisiana*, vol. 1, p. 129, 130, 313; *Digest of the Statutes of the State of Louisiana*, *Digest of the Statutes of the State of Louisiana in Two Volumes*, vol. 2 (New Orleans: Republican Office, 1870) 102, 121–25.

9. Tom Smith, *The Crescent City Lynchings: The Murder of Chief Hennessy, the New Orleans "Mafia" Trials, and the Parish Prison Mob* (Guilford, CT: Lyons Press, 2007), 136.

10. *Proceedings of the Physico Medical Society of New Orleans in Relation to the Trail and Expulsion of Charles A. Luzenberg* (New Orleans: Physico Medical Society of New Orleans, 1838), 1 ("immoral"), 25 ("Abrupt in speech"); Samuel D. Gross, ed., *Lives of Eminent American Physicians and Surgeons of the 19th Century* (Philadelphia: Lindsay & Blakiston, 1861), 557; John Duffy, "Medical Practice in the Antebellum South," *Journal of Southern History* 25 (February 1959): 53–72; A. E. Fossier, "Charles Aloysius Luzenberg, 1805–1848: A History of Medicine in New Orleans during the years 1830 to 1848," *Louisiana Historical Quarterly*, 26 (1943): 49–137 at 88 ("strong friendships"); John Duffy, *The Rudolph Matas History of Medicine in Louisiana* (Baton Rouge: Louisiana State University Press, 1962).

11. *Daily Picayune*, August 7, 1897 ("quiet, unostentatious," "coolly and without"); Nathaniel Cheairs Hughes, Jr., *Yale's Confederates: A Biographical Dictionary* (Knoxville: University of Tennessee Press, 2008), 128; *Daily True Delta*, December 19, 1860 (supporting "Friends of United Southern Action").

12. New Orleans Birth Index 1790–1899, vol. 75, p.416 (Charles), vol. 51, p. 132 (Charles, Jr.), vol. 51, p. 133 (Chandler and William), vol. 53, p. 14 (John); New Orleans Louisiana Death Records, vol. 46, p. 385; New Orleans *Times*, May 6, 1866 (speech supporting President Johnson).

13. Livingston, *A System of Penal Law*, 517–19; Voorhies, *A Treatise on the Criminal Jurisprudence of Louisiana*, 440. The race and occupations of the grand jurors was determined by cross-checking the published list of jurors' names with the New Orleans city directories and the 1870 U.S. manuscript census. For four of the men it was impossible to determine both race and occupation. For the published list of the grand jury's members (who served for a three-month period), see *Commercial Bulletin*, July 6, 1870; New Orleans *Republican*, July 7, 1870. For the city directories, see *Edward's Annual Directory to the Inhabitants, Institutions, Incorporated Companies, Manufacturing Establishments, Business, Business Firms, Etc, Etc. in the City of New Orleans* (New Orleans: Southern Publishing Company, 1870 and 1871).

14. *New Orleans Times*, August 25, 1870 ("remarkable coincidence"); Livingston, *A System of Penal Law*, 516 (grand jury's subpoena powers).

15. *New Orleans Republican*, September 17, 1870 (all quotations).

16. *New Orleans Republican*, September 17, 29 ("true bills"), 1870; *Commercial Bulletin*, September 17, 1870 ("a crime had been charged"); *New Orleans Times*, September 17, 1870; *New Orleans Bee*, September 17, 1870.

17. New Orleans *Republican*, September 17, 1870 (all quotations); New Orleans *Bee*, September 17, 1870; New Orleans *Times*, September 17, 1870; *Commercial Bulletin*, September 17, 1870. For Wilson's political roles, see *Daily Picayune*, September 11, 1867, March 11, 1870, April 16, 1872.

18. *New Orleans Times*, August 26, 1870; *Mobile Register*, August 27, 1870 (quotations).

19. New Orleans *Republican*, August 25, 1870.

20. *Mobile Register*, August 27, 1870 ("would any woman," "eventually be traced"); *New Orleans Times*, August 26, 1870 ("deceive the law"); *New York Tribune*, August 18, 1870 ("last place in the world").

21. New Orleans *Republican*, September 17 (quotations), 25 1870.

22. John Ray, comp., *Digest of the Statutes of the State of Louisiana*, vol. 2 (New Orleans: Republican Office, 1870), 56; New Orleans *Bee*, September 17, 1870; New Orleans *Times*, September 17, 1870; *Commercial Bulletin*, September 17, 1870; *Daily Picayune*, October 1, 1870. Orleans Parish had seven district courts. The First District Court had exclusive jurisdiction in all criminal cases.

23. *Daily Picayune*, August 30, 1870; *Commercial Bulletin*, August 31, 1871 ("should he obtain").

24. *New Orleans Republican*, September 21, 1870; *New Orleans Times*, September 20, 1870 ("negress").

25. Carrigan, *Saffron Scourge*, 103 (number of yellow fever deaths); New Orleans *Republican*, October 1, 1870; *Commercial Bulletin*, November 4, 7 (quotations), 8, 11, 12, 16, 21, 1870; New Orleans *Times*, November 5, 1870; *Daily Picayune*, November 4, 1870.

26. New Orleans *Times*, August 14, 1870.

27. For Warmoth's centrist strategy, which included appointing Democrats, see Lawrence N. Powell, "Centralization and its Discontents in Reconstruction Louisiana," *Studies in American Political Development* 20 (December 2006): 105–31.

28. Louis Harlan, "Desegregation in New Orleans Public Schools During Reconstruction," *American Historical Review* 67 (April 1962): 663–75; Liva Baker, *The Second Battle of New Orleans: The Hundred-Year Struggle to Integrate the Schools* (New York: Harper Collins, 1996), 19–22; Roger A. Fischer, *The Segregation Struggle in Louisiana, 1862–1877* (Urbana: University of Illinois Press, 1974), 110–16; *Commercial Bulletin*, November 11, 1870 ("destroy the usefulness"); *Carrollton Times*, January 11, 1870 ("war between races"); New Orleans *Bee*, January 1, 1871 (announcing that "the mixing of the public schools has been finally accomplished").

29. New Orleans *Times*, January 3 ("gala look"), 4 (roller skating, Lyceum), 7, 1871; *Commercial Bulletin*, January 7, 1871; James Gill, *Lords of Misrule: Mardi Gras and the Politics of Race in New Orleans* (Jackson: University of Mississippi Press, 1997), 77–108; Arthur Burton La Cour, *New Orleans Masquerade: Chronicles of Carnival* (New Orleans: Pelican Publishing, 1952), 31.

30. *L'Avenir*, January 8, 1870; New Orleans *Times*, January 5, 1871 ("celebrated"); New Orleans *Republican*, December 22, 1870; New Orleans *Bee*, December 22, 1870; *Commercial Bulletin*, December 22, 1870; *Daily Picayune*, January 5 ("the public"), 6 ("felt in the trial," "a throng"), 1871.

31. Alcée Fortier, *Louisiana: Comprising Sketches of Parishes, Towns, Events, Institutions and Persons Arranged in Cyclopedic Form* (Madison, WI: Century Historical Association, 1914), vol. I, 17; "Testimony of Edmond Abell," in the *Report of the Select Committee on the New Orleans Riots* (Washington, DC: Government Printing Office, 1867), 269 (quotations); *New Orleans Times*, November 19, 1870 ("No city"); James G. Hollandsworth, *An Absolute Massacre: The New Orleans Race Riot of July 30, 1866* (Baton Rouge: Louisiana State University Press, 2001), 21, 37, 40; Fischer, *The Segregation Struggle in Louisiana*, 25; Joseph G. Dawson, III, *Army Generals and Reconstruction: Louisiana, 1862–1877* (Baton Rouge: Louisiana State University Press, 1982), 47; Gilles Vandal, "The Origins of the New Orleans Riot of 1866, Revisited," *Louisiana History*, 22 (Spring 1981): 135–65; Roger W. Shugg, *Origins of Class Struggle in Louisiana: A Social History of White Farmers and Laborers during Slavery and After, 1840–1875* (Baton Rouge: Louisiana State University Press, 1939), 204.

32. *Daily Picayune*, January 7, 1871 ("trial of the child stealers"); Livingston, *A System of Penal Law for the State of Louisiana*, 21, 36; Voorhies, *A Treatise on the Criminal Jurisprudence of Louisiana*, 425–28, 441, 449–52; *Digest of the Statutes of the State of Louisiana*, vol. II, 79.

33. *Digest of the Statutes of the State of Louisiana in Two Volumes*, vol. I, 457; *Digest of the Statutes of the State of Louisiana*, vol. II, 126; *Daily Picayune*, January 6, 1871; Charles Lane, *The Day*

Freedom Died: The Colfax Massacre, the Supreme Court, and the Betrayal of Reconstruction (New York: Henry Holt, 2008), 164–65.

34. *Daily Picayune*, January 6, 1871; *The State of Louisiana vs. Louisa Murray, Ellen Follin, and George Blass* (Docket No. 2370), 1st District Court of the Parish of Orleans Minute Book, Louisiana Division, City Archives, New Orleans Public Library ("proper refreshments"). Under Louisiana law, if the regular panel was exhausted, jurors *de talibus* could drawn during the trial. Jurors *de talibus* were summoned from among such persons as might be casually present who had the qualifications of jurors, but if it was obvious that the jury could not be completed with bystanders, recourse could be had to talesmen— that is persons not within the immediate presence of the court. Livingston, *A System of Penal Law for the State of Louisiana*, 528–31; Voorhies, *A Treatise on the Criminal Jurisprudence of Louisiana*, 425–28, 441, 449–52, 462–63, 467; *Digest of the Statutes of the State of Louisiana*, vol. 1, 457; *Digest of the Statutes of the State of Louisiana*, vol. 2, 126.

35. *Daily Picayune*, January 6 ("remarkable"), 8 ("dread"), 1871.

36. Four of the jurors (E. Victor, Joseph Martin, J.A. Taylor, M. Warwick) had names so common that it is impossible to tell which of the men of that name in the historical record they were. In 1870, for example, there were at least eight Joseph Martins in New Orleans (some were black and some white). Of the jurors who could be reliably identified, one Prosper Saillot was a twenty-five-year-old white Creole, also from the French Quarter. One was an Austrian immigrant laborer, another a young white carpenter from Louisiana, and another a twenty-eight-year-old "carpetbagger" lawyer from Massachusetts named H. G. Morgan. For the other jurors' occupations, addresses, and race, see *Edward's Annual Directory to the Inhabitants, 1871*; 1870 United States Census, 10th Ward (Microfilm: M593 Roll 524, P. 236A) (Fred Kern), Ward 5 (Microfilm M593, Roll 521, P. 72B) (Dessoura Quessaire), Ward 6 (Microfilm M593, Roll 522, P. 311B) (Placide Boutin), Ward 8 (Microfilm 593, Roll 523, P. 699A) (Louis Teoso), Ward 1 (Microfilm M593, Roll 519, P. 23B) (H.G. Morgan). Also U.S. Civil War Soldiers 1861–1865, online database, National Park Service, (Louis Palms); New Orleans, Louisiana, Death Records Index, Louisiana Secretary of State, Division of Archives, Vitale Records Indices, Baton Rouge, LA (Prosper Saillot).

37. *Daily Picayune*, January 8, 1871 ("hatched the plot"). For the role of motive, see Bishop, *Commentaries on the Law of Criminal Procedure*, vol. 1, 648–55 ("crime is a response"), 672.

38. *Digest of the Statutes of the State of Louisiana in Two Volumes*, vol. 1, 58, 80, 114; Livingston, *A System of Penal Law for the State of Louisiana*, 215 (quotation).

39. *Daily Picayune*, January 6, 1871; New Orleans *Times*, January 6, 1871 ("exactly the same").

40. New Orleans *Republican*, January 7, 1871 ("ladies, gentlemen"), January 8, 1871 ("persons who had control"); New Orleans *Times*, January 7, 1871 ("score of cornets");

Commercial Bulletin, January 7, 1871; Arthur Burton Lacour, *New Orleans Masquerade: Chronicles of Carnival* (New Orleans: Pelican Publishing, 1952), 31.

41. *Daily Picayune,* January 6 ("wide spread and general"), 7, 1871 ("eager and absorbed").

42. *Daily Picayune,* August 24, 1870 ("thought"), January 7, 1871 ("resembles," "severest possible" New Orleans *Times,* August 24, 1870, January 7, 1871; *Commercial Bulletin,* January 7, 1871.

43. *Daily Picayune,* August 24, 1870 (quotations); New Orleans *Times,* August 24, 1870; *New Orleans Bee,* August 24, 1870; New Orleans *Republican,* August 24, 1870.

44. *New Orleans Times,* January 7, 1871 ("influenced and prompted"); *Daily Picayune,* January 7, 1871 (all other quotations).

45. *Daily Picayune,* January 6, 1871.

46. *Daily Picayune,* January 8, 1871.

47. New Orleans *Republican,* August 25, 1870; New Orleans *Times,* January 7, 1871 ("rough and brutal way," "own children," "never concealed"); *Daily Picayune,* January 7 ("frightened by the police").

48. *Daily Picayune,* January 7, 1871 ("corroborated"), 8 ("mysterious and dark"), 1871; New Orleans *Times,* January 7, 1871 ("informed him that").

49. *Daily Picayune,* August 23, 1870 (quotations); New Orleans *Bee,* August 23, 1870; New Orleans *Times,* August 23, 1870.

50. In August, the *Republican* did report that two black women from the neighborhood ("Aunt Jane" and "Sukey") had tried to tell Badger that they had witnessed the kidnapping and that Murray was not the abductress. *New Orleans Republican,* August 13, 1870; New Orleans *Times,* January 8, 1871 ("would arrest her"). Lewis lived at 185 Howard Street. The addresses of the defense witnesses appear in the list of subpoenas issued by Judge Abell when the case was fixed for December. *The State of Louisiana v. Louisa Murray alias Follin,* First District Recorders Court, Case No. 49, August 20, 22, 23, 24, 1870, New Orleans City Archives, Louisiana Division, New Orleans Public Library. For Lewis's literacy status and the occupations of Lewis and her husband, see *1870 United States Census,* New Orleans, 3rd Ward, Microfilm: M593, Roll 520, p. 558B, Image 318 (Note that the court records spell the last name of Jane and Eliza as Lewis, while the census lists it as Louis).

51. *Daily Picayune,* January 8, 1871.

52. New Orleans *Times,* January 8, 1871.

53. *Daily Picayune,* January 8, 1871.

54. *Daily Picayune,* January 8, 1871 ("I would recognize"); New Orleans *Times,* January 8, 1871 ("two or three hours after").

55. *Daily Picayune,* January 8, 1871 (Atocha quotations).

56. *Daily Picayune,* January 8, 1871 (quotations).

57. *Daily Picayune,* January 8, 1871 (quotations); New Orleans *Republican,* January 8, 1871. For Green's August testimony, see *Daily Picayune,* August 25, 1870 ("disclose out of

fear"); New Orleans *Times*, August 25, 1870; testimony of Minnie Green, August 24, 1870, *The State of Louisiana v. Louisa Murray alias Follin.*

58. *Daily Picayune*, January 8, 1871 ("whether Louisa Murray"); New Orleans *Republican*, January 8, 1871.

59. *Daily Picayune*, January 8, 1871.

60. New Orleans *Republican*, January 8, 1871 ("sick white women"); *Daily Picayune*, January 8, 1871 ("a colored one too!" "nature of the business," "general reputation," "respectable woman"); New Orleans *Times*, January 8, 1871 ("tableaux," "Louisa promised"); 1870 U.S. Census, Mobile, Alabama, Ward 7, Microfilm 593, Roll31, p. 244A. George Yarrington was Lt. Colonel of the 86th United States Colored Infantry Regiment. *The War of the Rebellion: A Compilation of the Official Records of the Union and Confederate Armies*, series I, vol. 48, part I (Washington, DC: Government Printing Office, 1896), 1023.

61. *Daily Picayune*, January 8, 1871.

62. New Orleans *Times*, January 8, 1871; *Daily Picayune*, January 1, 1870 (quotation).

63. *Daily Picayune*, January 8, 1871 (quotations); New Orleans *Republican*, January 8, 1871; New Orleans *Times*, January 8, 1871.

64. *Daily Picayune*, January 8, 1871.

65. New Orleans *Times*, January 8, 1871.

66. New Orleans *Times*, January 8, 1871.

67. New Orleans *Times*, January 8, 1871; Bishop, *Commentaries on the Law of Criminal Procedure*, vol. I, 650–52; Voorhies, *A Treatise on the Criminal Jurisprudence of Louisiana*, 467–68 ("prudent man"); Livingston, *A System of Penal Law for the State of Louisiana*, 532.

68. Bishop, *Commentaries on the Law of Criminal Procedure*, vol.I, 210–11, 216 ("no offence"), 219–20, 246; Robert H. Marr, *The Criminal Jurisprudence of Louisiana* (New Orleans: F. F. Hansell & Brother, 1906), i, iv; Albert Voorhies, *A Treatise on the Criminal Jurisprudence of Louisiana*, 79–80.

69. New Orleans *Republican*, January 8, 1871; New Orleans *Times*, January 8, 1871; *Daily Picayune*, January 8, 1871. For Fleicher's reading of the jury verdict, see *The State of Louisiana v. Louisa Murray, Ellen Follin, and George Blass* (Docket No. 2370), 1st District Court of the Parish of Orleans Minute Book, Louisiana Division, City Archives, New Orleans Public Library. For courtroom procedure, see Bishop, *Commentaries on the Law of Criminal Procedure*, vol.I, 2nd ed., 618–19.

70. *Daily Picayune*, August 21, 23, 1870; Bishop, *Commentaries on the Law of Criminal Procedure*, vol. I, 2nd ed., 541.

71. Michael J. Pfeifer, "Lynching and Criminal Justice in South Louisiana, 1878–1930," *Louisiana History* 40 (Spring 1999): 155–77; Suzanne Lebsock, *A Murder in Virginia: Southern Justice on Trial* (New York: W. W. Norton, 2003), 63; Stewart E. Tolnay and E. M. Beck, *A Festival of Violence: An Analysis of Southern Lynching, 1882–1930* (Urbana: University of Illinois, 1995); Crystal Feimster, *Southern Horrors: Women and the Politics of Rape and Lynching* (Cambridge, MA: Harvard University Press, 2011); W. Fitzhugh

Brundage, *Lynching in the New South: Georgia and Virginia, 1880–1930* (Urbana: University of Illinois Press, 1993). For the lynching of the Sicilians, see Smith, *The Crescent City Lynchings*; George C. Rable, *But There Was No Peace: The Role of Violence in the Politics of Reconstruction* (Athens: University of Georgia Press, 1984), 21–28; Edward L. Ayers, *Vengeance and Justice: Crime and Punishment in the Nineteenth-Century American South* (New York: Oxford University Press, 1985).

72. *Hartford Courant*, January 9, 1871 ("Telegraphic News"). The *L'Avenir* editorial in the text is a corrected version of the actual grammatically incorrect editorial which read "Affaire Digby-Le Juri dens cette affiare a renda un verdict de non culpante. Que one a enlevé l'enfant? Respondez messieurs les juris?" *L'Avenir*, January 8, 1870.

73. New Orleans *Times*, January 8, 1871 (defense of Luzenberg); New Orleans *Republican*, January 9 (quotations about Atocha). Ever sensitive to slights, Theodore Hunt, a Democrat, took offense to the *Republican* giving all of the credit to his co-counsel Atocha and demanded an apology. The paper subsequently published a statement crediting Hunt for a "searching and rigid" cross-examination of Chief Badger, and for being the one to propose to Luzenberg that the case be submitted to the jury without closing arguments. "We believe in doing Justice to all, and therefore this explanation," the *Republican's* editor said. New Orleans *Republican*, 10 (apology to Hunt), 1871.

Chapter Ten: The Case That "Excited All New Orleans"

1. New Orleans *Republican*, January 8, 1871; *Daily Picayune*, January 5, 6, 1871.

2. Robert Ferguson, *The Trial in American Life* (Chicago: University of Chicago Press, 2007), 1–74; Lawrence Friedman, *Crime and Punishment in American History* (New York: Basic Books, 1993), 11; Richard F. Hamm, *Murder, Honor, and Law: Four Virginia Homicides from Reconstruction to the Great Depression* (Charlottesville: University of Virginia Press, 2003), 3.

3. For the literature on moral panics, see Chapter 1, note 13. For the larger newspaper campaign to malign the legislature and foment discontent, see Michael A. Ross, "Justice Miller's Reconstruction: The *Slaughter-House Cases*, Health Codes, and Civil Rights in New Orleans, 1861–1873," *Journal of Southern History* 64 (November 1998), 649–76; Michael A. Ross, "Resisting the New South: Commercial Crisis and Decline in New Orleans, 1865–1885," *American Nineteenth-Century History* 4 (Spring 2003): 59–76.

4. For fraying relationships between elite whites and Afro-Creoles, see Justin A. Nystrom, *New Orleans after the Civil War* (Baltimore: Johns Hopkins University Press, 2010), 142–43.

5. John F. Kasson, *Rudeness and Civility: Manners in Nineteenth Century America* (New York: Hill & Wang, 1990), chaps 1–2; Karen Halttunen, *Confidence Men and Painted Women: A Study of Middle-Class Culture in America, 1830–1870* (New Haven, CT: Yale University Press, 1982), 34–43, 59–79, 92–123, 153–69, 186–97. For sensationalized crimes involving seemingly respectable defendants, see Benjamin Feldman, *Butchery on Bond Street: Sexual Politics and The Burdell-Cunningham Case in Ante-bellum New York* (New York: The New York Wanderer Press, 2007); Patricia Cline Cohen, *The Murder of Helen Jewett* (New

York: Knopf, 1991); Simon Schama, *Dead Certainties: Unwarranted Speculations* (New York: Knopf, 1992); A. Cheree Carlson, *The Crimes of Womanhood: Defining Femininity in a Court of Law* (Urbana: University of Illinois, 2009); Philip Farley, *Criminals of America; or Tales of the Lives of Thieves* (New York: Philip Farley, 1876), 142–45, 206.

6. *Daily Picayune,* August 23, 1870.

7. David C. Rankin, "The Origins of Black Leadership in New Orleans during Reconstruction," *Journal of Southern History* 40 (August 1974): 420–21, 436–40; Dennis C. Rousey, "Black Policemen in New Orleans during Reconstruction," *Historian,* 49 (February 1987): 223–43; New Orleans *Picayune,* July 6, 1870.

8. Karen Halttunen, *Murder Most Foul: The Killer and the Gothic Imagination* (Cambridge: Harvard University Press, 1998), 109–10; Hamm, *Murder, Honor, and Law,* 13; David Ray Papke, *Framing the Criminal: Crime, Cultural Work, and the Loss of Critical Perspective 1830–1900* (Hamden, CT: Archon Books, 1987), 33–53, 99; Lawrence Friedman, *Crime and Punishment,* 203–8; Dan Schiller, *Objectivity and the News: The Public and the Rise of Commercial Journalism* (Philadelphia: University of Pennsylvania Press, 1981); W. Marvin Dulaney, *Black Police in America* (Bloomington, IN: Indiana University Press, 1996), 12, 116, 117.

9. Paula Fass, *Kidnapped: Child Abduction in America* (New York: Oxford University Press, 1997), 7, 8, 17–18, 21–55, 56. For captivity narratives, see John Demos, *The Unredeemed Captive: A Family Story from Early America* (New York: Knopf, 1994); June Namias, *White Captives: Gender and Ethnicity on the American Frontier* (Chapel Hill: University of North Carolina Press, 1993).

10. Carrie Hagen, *We Is Got Him: The Kidnapping That Changed America* (New York: Overlook Press, 2011); Papke, *Framing the Criminal,* 61; Norman Zierold, *Little Charley Ross: America's First Kidnapping for Ransom* (Boston: Little, Brown, & Company, 1967).

11. Eric Foner, *Reconstruction: America's Unfinished Revolution, 1863–1877* (New York: Harper & Row, 1988), 346–511; Heather Cox Richardson, *The Death of Reconstruction: Race, Labor, and Politics in the Post–Civil War North, 1865–1901* (Cambridge, MA: Harvard University Press, 2001), xv, 41–139; Papke, *Framing the Criminal,* 56; Mark Wahlgren Summers, *The Press Gang: Newspapers and Politics, 1865–1878* (Chapel Hill: University of North Carolina Press, 1994), 206–22; Carl R. Osthaus, *Partisans of the Southern Press: Editorial Spokesmen of the Nineteenth Century* (Lexington: The University Press of Kentucky, 1994), 128–29. For an excellent case study of another postbellum crime that became entangled with Southern politics, see Suzanne Lebsock, *A Murder in Virginia: Southern Justice on Trial* (New York: W. W. Norton, 2004).

12. John C. Rodrigue, "Introduction" to reprint edition of Henry Clay Warmoth, *War, Politics, and Reconstruction: Stormy Days in Louisiana* (Columbia: University of South Carolina Press, 2006), xi. See also Lawrence N. Powell, "Centralization and Its Discontents in Reconstruction Louisiana," *Studies in American Political Development* 20 (October 2006): 105–31; Nystrom, *New Orleans After the Civil War,* 87–114, 132–33, 214, 228–29.

13. See the sources cited in note 12, supra.

14. *Daily Picayune*, May 10, 1865, New Orleans *Times-Picayune*, September 10, 1939, Rousey, *Policing the Southern City*, 144–47; Nystrom, *New Orleans after the Civil War*, 162–76, 201–4; James K. Hogue, *Uncivil War: Five New Orleans Street Battles and the Rise and Fall of Radical Reconstruction* (Baton Rouge: Louisiana State University Press, 2006), 116–43; Rebecca J. Scott, *Degrees of Freedom: Louisiana and Cuba after Slavery* (Cambridge, MA: Harvard University Press, 2005), 58–60.

15. *New York Times*, December 29, 1884.

16. For the murder case, see *New Orleans Times-Picayune*, July 22, 1873.

17. T. Harry Williams, "The Louisiana Unification Movement of 1873," *Journal of Southern History*, 11 (August 1945): 349–69 ("two sullen," "perfect equality"); testimony of John Baptiste Jourdain, December 27, 1866, *Report of the Select Committee on the New Orleans Riots*, 207–8 ("knife in the back"); T. Harry Williams, *P.G.T. Beauregard: Napoleon in Grey* (Baton Rouge: Louisiana State University Press, 1955), 270–71; Nystrom, *New Orleans after the Civil War*, 149–53. While serving as sheriff, Harry T. Hays had helped orchestrate the New Orleans Riot of 1866. For Jourdain's participation in the 1873 movement, see the signed public appeal and announcement of mass meeting in *Daily Picayune*, July 11, 1873.

18. Monroe *Ouachita Telegraph*, June 21, 1873 ("We abhor"); *Macon Weekly Telegraph*, July 29, 1873 ("Our Louisiana friends"). For an account of the disastrous mass meeting, see Williams, "The Louisiana Unification Movement of 1873," 364–67. For an excellent discussion of the role of white Creole businessmen in the Unification Movement, see Scott Marler, *The Merchants' Capital: New Orleans and the Political Economy of the Nineteenth-Century South*, 198–99 (New York: Cambridge University Press, 2013), 198–99, 203–5.

19. New Orleans *Republican*, October 9, 11, 1874; October 16, 1874 ("steered clear"). See also David C. Rankin, "The Impact of the Civil War on the Free Colored Community of New Orleans," *Perspectives in American History* 11 (1977–78): 394; Scott, *Degrees of Freedom*, 61–62.

20. Jourdain's efforts as a legislator to improve conditions at the New Orleans Charity Hospital through a tax on auctioneers, theaters, and balls earned him praise from the black press, as did his resolution to increase the pay for the porters who cleaned the statehouse. *Official Journal of the Proceedings of the House of Representatives of the State of Louisiana at the Session Begun and Held in New Orleans January 4, 1875* (New Orleans: Republican Office, 1875), 15, 19, 27, 34, 36, 40, 87, 127, 128; *The Louisianian*, February 13, 1875 (praise for Jourdain).

21. *Official Journal of the Proceedings of the House of Representatives of the State of Louisiana at the Session begun and held in New Orleans January 4, 1875*, 15 ("knives and revolvers"); 24; New Orleans *Republican*, January 5, 1876.

22. For the bribery case brought by Attorney General Field, see *State of Louisiana v. Milton Jones, J. C. Parker, and J. B. Jourdain*, Docket #835, Filed December 20, 1875, Records of

Superior Criminal Court, Louisiana Division, New Orleans Public Library. The case was *Nolle Prosequi* as to J. B. Jourdain on January 4, 1876. See also *New Orleans Times*, January 5, 1876.

23. Loren Schweninger, *Black Property Owners in the South, 1790–1915* (Urbana, IL: University of Illinois Press, 1990), 166–67, 190–94, 217–18; *Constitution of the State of Louisiana Adopted in Convention at the City of New Orleans the Twenty-Third Day of July, A.D. 1879* (New Orleans: Jas. H. Cosgrove, Convention Printer, 1879); Rebecca J. Scott, "The Atlantic World and the Road to *Plessy v. Ferguson*," *Journal of American History* 94 (December 2007): 730. For the fire that destroyed Jourdain's St. Ann Street property, see *Daily Picayune*, September 7, 1875.

24. Schweninger, *Black Property Owners in the South*, 194. For the origins of the word "Creole" and white Creoles' claims to racial purity, see Joseph G. Tregle, Jr., "Creoles and Americans," in *Creole New Orleans*, eds. Arnold R. Hirsch and Joseph Logsdon (Baton Rouge: Louisiana State University Press, 1992), 131–85; Lawrence Powell, *The Accidental City: Improvising New Orleans* (Cambridge, MA: Harvard University Press, 2012), 108–109; Virginia Dominguez, *White by Definition: Social Classification in Creole Louisiana* (New Brunswick, NJ: Rutgers University Press 1994), 133–42; Scott, *Degrees of Freedom*, 70–75; Nystrom, *New Orleans after the Civil War*, 148–49, 155.

25. *The Daily States*, April 5, 1888; *New Orleans Times-Democrat*, April 6, 1888. Some of the newspaper accounts incorrectly identified the site of Jourdain's suicide as St. Louis Cemetery #2. His suicide took place in front of the Jourdain family tomb in which he would be buried two days later in St. Louis Cemetery #1.

26. *L'abeille de la Nouvelle-Orleans*, April 6, 1888. Jourdain is buried in St. Louis Cemetery #1, in the Jourdain Family tomb, lower vault. St. Louis # 1, Interment Books, vol. 3 (February 17, 1886–October 20, 1892), Louisiana Division, New Orleans Public Library.

27. *Plessy v. Ferguson* 163 U.S. 537 (1896). For discussions of *Plessy* and the role Aristide Mary and the Comité des Citoyens played in the litigation, see Keith Weldon Medley, *We As Freemen: Plessy v. Ferguson* (New Orleans: Pelican Publishing, 2003), 169–71; Williamjames Hull Hoffer, *Plessy v. Ferguson: Race and Inequality in Jim Crow America* (Lawrence: University of Kansas Press, 2012), 60 (Desdunes quotation); Charles A. Lofgren, *The Plessy Case: A Legal-Historical Interpretation* (New York: Oxford University Press, 1987), 28–43; Mark Elliott, *Color-Blind Justice: Albion Tourgée and the Quest for Racial Equality from the Civil War to* Plessy v. Ferguson (New York: Oxford University Press, 2006), 249–61; Scott, *Degrees of Freedom*, 88–93.

28. Civil War Pension Index, General Index to Pension Files, 1861–1934, National Archives and Records Administration, Application #495, 521, September 26, 1890, Microfilm T288.

29. Natasha L. McPherson, "'There Was a Tradition Among the Women': New Orleans's Colored Creole Women and the Making of a Community in the Tremé and Seventh Ward, 1791–1930," (PhD Diss., Emory University 2011), 100–119; *Daily Picayune*,

May 7, 1906 (Follin obituary); 1900 Federal Census, New Orleans, Ward 11, Roll 474, p. 10A, Enumeration District 109; *Edward's Annual Directory for the City of New Orleans* (New Orleans: Southern Publishing Co., 1871) (the first directory to list Follin as Ellen Blass and to describe her as a colored seamstress).

30. *Times-Picayune*, November 12, 1916 (Blass obituary); 1880 Federal Census, New Orleans, Ward 11, Roll 464, p. 309C, Enumeration District 085; *1900 Federal Census*, New Orleans Ward 11, Roll 574, Page 19A, Enumeration District 109. For the increasingly constricted job opportunities available to mixed-race and Afro-Creole men, see McPherson, "'There Was a Tradition among the Women,'" 100–119; Rankin, "Impact of the Civil War on the Free Colored Community of New Orleans," 379–416; Loren Schweninger, "Antebellum Free Persons of Color in Postbellum Louisiana," *Louisiana History* 30 (Fall 1989): 345–64; Arthé A. Anthony, "The Negro Creole Community in New Orleans, 1880–1920" (PhD diss., University of California, Irvine (1978); Tregle, "Creoles and Americans," 131–85; Caryn Cossé Bell and Joseph Logsdon, "The Americanization of Black New Orleans, 1850–1900," in *Creole New Orleans*, eds. Arnold Hirsch and Joseph Logsdon, 201–61.

31. Alabama records list a woman named Louisa Murray who died there in 1911, but the details are sparse and inconsistent. See State of Alabama, Index of Vital Records for Alabama Deaths, 1908–59, Mobile, vol. 17, certificate 373, Roll 1; 1870 United States Federal Census, Mobile Ward 7, Mobile, Alabama, microfilm: M593, Roll 31, p. 271B image 547.

32. For the birth of Julius Eugene Powers in 1883, New Orleans, Louisiana Birth Records Index 1790–1899, vol. 88, p. 1037; baptismal certificate of Julius Eugene Powers, Archdiocese of New Orleans Archives, Baptisms BK. 9 (1880–1884), p. 660, act no. 198. For the birth of Joseph Elmer Powers, see New Orleans, Louisiana, Birth Records Index 1790–1899, vol. 88, p. 1038. For the birth of Ella Blass, see New Orleans, Louisiana Birth Records 1790–1899, vol. 106, p. 639. Death Certificate for Mary Belle Powers, City of Detroit, April 8, 1947 (Courtesy of Gerry Guenther). For birth of Joseph Elmer Powers in 1885, see *New Orleans, Louisiana Birth Records 1790–1899*, vol. 88, p. 1038. For Culotta and Mary Belle in Chicago, see 1940 United States Federal Census, Chicago, Cook County, Illinois, microfilm T627, Roll 955; p.6B, Enumeration District: 1103–1120. Phone interview with Salvador Sacarro (Monroe, LA), August 7, 2012.

33. For Julius Jr. as a stockbroker (and his wife Loretta as the daughter of an Irish immigrant), see 1920 United States Federal Census, Manhattan Assembly District 12, New York, NY, microfilm T625, roll1207, Enumeration District 891. For discussions of "passing," see Daniel Sharfstein, *The Invisible Line: Three American Families and the Secret Journey From Black to White* (New York: Penguin Press, 2011), 3; Joel Williamson, *New People: Miscegenation and Mulattoes in the United States* (Baton Rouge: Louisiana State University Press, 1995), 103 ("great age of passing"); Dominguez, *White by Definition*, 23–55, 200–204;

Nystrom, *New Orleans after the Civil War*, 143, 155–56; Elliott, *Color-Blind Justice*, 288 ("colored").

34. Interview with Jerry Geunther and Sandra Geunther-Clark, April 2, 2010 (New York, NY); phone interview with Marilyn Geunther, August 6, 2012; phone interview with Salvador Sacarro, August 7, 2012. For difficulties associated with passing, see Williamson, *New People*, 100–106.

35. New Orleans *Republican*, August 13, 1870 (quotation); *Edward's Annual Directory for the City of New Orleans* (New Orleans: Southern Publishing Co., 1871); 1880 United States Federal Census, Ward 3, Orleans Parish, La., Roll 459, p. 5670, Enumeration District 024; 1900 United States Federal Census, Ward 3, Orleans Parish, La., Roll 571, p. 4B, Enumeration District 27; 1920 United States Federal Census, Ward 14, Orleans Parish, La., microfilm 625, Roll 624, p. 2B, Enumeration District 238 (Martin as merchant with six children of his own); 1910 United States Federal Census, Ward 3, Orleans Parish, La., microfilm T624, Roll 520, p.5A, Enumeration District 0037 (George as oil company clerk with four children of his own); 1910 United States Federal Census, Ward 3, Orleans Parish, La., microfilm T624, Roll 520, p.15B, Enumeration District 0048 (John as cab driver with two children of his own); 1940 United States Federal Census, Orleans Parish, La., microfilm T627, Roll 1420, p. 5B, Enumeration District 36–90 (James as policemen with four children of his own); Leonard V. Huber, *New Orleans: A Pictorial History* (New York: Crown Publishers, 1971), 259; David T. Gleeson, *The Irish in the South, 1815–1877* (Chapel Hill: University of North Carolina Press, 2001), 185; *Daily Picayune*, June 15, 1902 (Thomas Digby obituary); *Daily Picayune*, December 14, 1911 (Bridgette Digby obituary).

36. 1910 United States Federal Census, Ward 3, Orleans Parish, La., microfilm T624, Roll 520, page 2A, Enumeration District 0059 (Mollie and Patrick married with four children); New Orleans Louisiana Marriage Index, 1831–1920, Louisiana Vital Records, vol. 17, p. 363; *Times-Picayune*, September 3, 1918 (Patrick Golden obituary); *New Orleans States*, September 3, 1918 (Golden Obituary); *Soards' New Orleans City Directory for 1920* (New Orleans: Soards Publishing, 1920); *Soards' New Orleans City Directory for 1929* (New Orleans: Soards Publishing, 1929).

37. *New York Tribune*, August 18, 1870.

38. *New Orleans Times-Picayune*, March 2, 1932 ("carefully guarded"); A. Scott Berg, *Lindbergh* (New York: G. P. Putnam's Sons, 1998), 5–9, 113–77, 220, 246–306; Lloyd C. Gardner, *The Case That Never Dies: The Lindbergh Kidnapping* (New Brunswick, NJ: Rutgers University Press, 2004), 5–10.

39. *New Orleans Times-Picayune*, March 3, 1932.

40. *New Orleans Times-Picayune*, March 3, 1932.

41. Copy of Mollie's handwritten and typed manuscript (hereafter the "Digby Manuscript"), and letter from Henry Clay Warmoth to Mary Laura Digby Golden, September 16, 1930, copies of both in possession of the author (courtesy of Susan Golden Perkins, Cary, NC).

42. Digby Manuscript, handwritten portion ("eloped") p. 2, typewritten portion pp. 3–4.

43. Digby Manuscript, handwritten portion, p. 2.

44. Digby Manuscript, typewritten portion, p. 6.

45. Digby Manuscript, handwritten portion, p. 12 ("even the Queen"); typed portion, p. 2 ("the affection"). Interviews with Gary Golden, Shirley Motreuil Golden, Anne Marie Newhouse Golden, and Susan Golden Perkins, all on May 5, 2012, Cary, NC.

46. For Dorothy Branson's age and background, see 1940 United States Federal Census, New Orleans, Orleans Parish, LA, microfilm T627, Roll 1428, p. 62A, Enumeration District: 36–275; 1930 United States Federal Census, Chicago, Cook County, IL., Roll 494, page 11B, Enumeration District: 1894.

47. Dorothy Branson, "A Story of the Deep South" (A proposal submitted on May 30, 1939 to an unknown publisher) (Copy in possession of author courtesy of Gary Golden, Cary, NC).

48. Branson, "A Story of the Deep South."

49. *John B. Schmitt & Others v. Mrs. Evelina Broadwell,* Civil District Court Record no. 26, 981, New Orleans Suit Records (successions, divorces, and related matters), 1880–1925, Louisiana Division, New Orleans Public Library; *Daily Picayune,* August 1, 1873; August 6, 1873. Broadwell's subsequent addresses found in the city directories for each year.

50. For national origins of Evelina Broadwell's parents, see 1880 United States Federal Census, New Orleans, Orleans Parish, La., Roll 458, p. 73A, Enumeration District: 003.

51. Digby Manuscript, typed portion, p. 17.

52. *Daily Picayune,* July 10, 1870.

53. Digby Manuscript, typed version, p. 3. For detailed discussions of racism, minstrel show humor, and *Amos and Andy,* see Eric Lott, *Love and Thefts: Blackface Minstrelsy and the American Working Class* (New York: Oxford University Press, 1995); Melvin Patrick Ely, *The Adventures of Amos and Andy: A Social History of an American Phenomenon* (Charlottesville: University Press of Virginia, 2001).

54. Digby Manuscript, typed version, p. 9.

55. Digby Manuscript, typed portion, p. 2. Conclusion based on the author's reading of every day of every newspaper published in New Orleans from June 1870 to January 1871, as well as search of the national newspapers that covered the Digby case, three 1870 English newspapers, and the Henry Clay Warmoth Papers Southern Historical Collection, Manuscripts Department, University of North Carolina at Chapel Hill.

56. Branson, "A Story of the Deep South."

57. Branson note to publisher (attached to "A Story of the Deep South"), May 30, 1939 (quotation). For the WPA Research Projects in New Orleans, see Lawrence Powell, "Lyle Saxon and the WPA Guide to New Orleans," *Southern Spaces,* July 29, 2009, www.southernspaces.org/2009/lyle-saxon-and-wpa-guide-new-orleans; Federal Writers'

Project of the Works Progress Administration, *New Orleans City Guide, 1938*; reprint (New Orleans: Garrett County Press, 2009).

58. *New Orleans Item*, October 13, 1944 ("rocked New Orleans"); New Orleans *Times-Picayune*, October 14, 1944 ("excited all New Orleans").

59. Testimony of Evelina Broadwell ("My Molly") and James Broadwell reprinted in the *Daily Picayune*, August 23, 24, 1870; testimony of Bridgette Digby, reprinted in the *Daily Picayune*, August 25, 1870 ("I would know it").

60. For the difficulty in securing a jury verdict that runs counter to the settled convictions of the community, see George Louis Joughin and Edmund M. Morgan, *The Legacy of Sacco and Vanzetti* (New York: Harcourt, Brace and Company, 1948), 196 (quotation). See also Ferguson, *Trial in American Life*, 10.

61. For the brief success of biracial political coalitions in other Southern states, see Jane Dailey, *Before Jim Crow: The Politics of Race in Postemancipation Virginia* (Chapel Hill: University of North Carolina Press, 2000); C. Vann Woodward, *Origins of the New South 1877–1913* (Baton Rouge: Louisiana State University Press, 1951), chapter 4; Helen G. Edmonds, *The Negro and Fusion Politics in North Carolina, 1894–1901* (Chapel Hill: University of North Carolina Press, 1951). For an excellent argument against reading legal history backward from Jim Crow, see Pamela Brandwein, *Rethinking the Judicial Settlement of Reconstruction* (New York: Cambridge University Press, 2011). Almost all historians agree that a combination of political, economic, and social factors caused the relatively swift collapse of the Reconstruction regimes, but some historians place a greater emphasis on the factionalism; patronage squabbles; internal fiscal policy disagreements; and regional, racial, and class differences that undermined Southern Republicans' ability to govern effectively and eroded their support in the North. While historians who favor such interpretation do not discount the impact of violent resistance by reactionary white Southerners on the Republican regimes, they suggest that the violence simply sped the demise of governments with fatal internal flaws. Other scholars, however, have given greater emphasis to the debilitating effects of the violent acts of white paramilitary groups such as the Ku Klux Klan and the Crescent City White League had on the Republican governments and their supporters. For historians who highlight the internal weaknesses of the Republican governments, see Michael Les Benedict, *A Compromise of Principle: Congressional Republicans and Reconstruction, 1863–1869* (New York: Norton, 1974); Carl H. Moneyhon, *Republicanism in Reconstruction Texas* (Austin: University of Texas Press, 1980); Michael W. Fitzgerald, "Radical Republicanism and the White Yeomanry during Alabama Reconstruction," *Journal of Southern History* 54 (November 1988): 565–96; J. Mills Thornton, III, "Fiscal Policy and the Failure of Radical Reconstruction in the Lower South," in *Region, Race, and Reconstruction: Essays in Honor of C. Vann Woodward*, ed. J. Morgan Kousser and James McPherson (New York: Oxford University Press, 1982), 349–94; Sarah Woolfork Wiggins, *The Scalawag in Alabama Politics, 1865–1888* (Tuscaloosa: University of Alabama Press, 1977), 125. For examples of historians who emphasize

the debilitating effects of reactionary violence, see John Hope Franklin, *Reconstruction after the Civil War* (Chicago: University of Chicago Press, 1961), 153, 156, 176; Allen W. Trelease, *White Terror: The Ku Klux Klan Conspiracy and Southern Reconstruction* (New York: Harper and Row, 1971); Eric Foner, *Reconstruction: America's Unfinished Revolution 1863–1877* (New York: Harper and Row, 1988), 603; Michael Perman, *The Road to Redemption: Southern Politics, 1869–1879* (Chapel Hill: University of North Carolina Press, 1984); Michael Perman, "Counter Reconstruction: The Role of Violence in Southern Redemption," in *The Facts of Reconstruction: Essays in Honor of John Hope Franklin,* ed. Eric Anderson and Alfred A. Moss, Jr. (Baton Rouge: Louisiana State University Press, 1991), 121–40; Scott R. Nelson, *Iron Confederacies: Southern Railways, Klan Violence, and Reconstruction* (Chapel Hill: University of North Carolina Press, 1999), 125–38; George C. Rable, *But There Was No Peace: The Role of Violence in the Politics of Reconstruction* (Athens: University of Georgia Press, 1984), 102–3.

Afterword and Acknowledgments

1. Martha Ward, *Voodoo Queen: The Spirited Lives of Marie Laveau* (Oxford: University of Mississippi Press, 2004), 149.

2. See Jill Lepore, *New York Burning: Liberty, Slavery, and Conspiracy in Eighteenth-Century Manhattan* (New York: Random House, 2005); Nancy Lusignan Schultz, *Fire and Roses: The Burning of the Charlestown Convent, 1834* (New York: Free Press, 2000).

3. John Demos, *Entertaining Satan: Witchcraft and the Culture of Early New England* (New York: Oxford University Press, 1982), x.

INDEX

—✠—